THE COMPLETE CAMPUS COMPANION

EDITED BY ROBERT M. KACHUR

THE SURVIVAL GUIDE EVERY CHRISTIAN STUDENT NEEDS

Illustrated by
David Zentner
& Rob Suggs

INTERVARSITY PRESS
DOWNERS GROVE, ILLINOIS 60515

101991

InterVarsity Press is the book-publishing division of InterVarsity Christian Fellowship, a student movement active on campus at hundreds of universities, colleges and schools of nursing. For information about local and regional activities, write Public Relations Dept., InterVarsity Christian Fellowship, 6400 Schroeder Rd., P.O. Box 7895, Madison, WI 53707-7895.

Distributed in Canada through InterVarsity Press, 860 Denison St., Unit 3, Markham, Ontario L3R 4H1, Canada.

All Scripture quotations, unless otherwise indicated are from the Holy Bible, New International Version. Copyright © 1973, 1978, International Bible Society. Used by permission of Zondervan Bible Publishers.

A section of the chapter "Managing Your Time" is taken from How to Get Control of Your Time and Your Life by Alan Lakein. Copyright © 1973 by Alan Lakein. Reprinted by permission of David McKay Co., a Division of Random House, Inc.

The chapter "Winning the Financial Aid Game" first appeared in Campus Life magazine. © 1985 Campus Life magazine, Christianity Today, Inc. Used by permission.

The chapter "Tuning In: The Truth about Rock 'n' Roll" is adapted from Rock of This Age by Steve Lawhead. © 1987 by Steve Lawhead and used by permission of InterVarsity Press, Downers Grove, IL 60515.

The chapter "Winning the Dating Game" is excerpted from Equal Dating by Jean Stapleton and Richard Bright. Copyright © 1979 by Abingdon Press. Used by permission.

The chapter "Translating Your Faith into Social Action" is taken from Ideas for Social Action by Anthony Campolo. Copyright © 1983 by Youth Specialties. Used by permission of Zondervan Publishing House.

Cover illustration: David Zentner

ISBN 0-8308-1212-1

Printed in the United States of America

Library of Congress Cataloging in Publication Data

The Complete campus companion.

   1. College students—Religious life.   2. College students—Conduct of life.   I. Kachur, Robert M., 1961-
BV4531.2.C577   1987   248.8'34   87-29877
ISBN 0-8308-1212-1

17	16	15	14	13	12	11	10	9	8	7	6	5	4	3	2	1
99	98	97	96	95	94	93	92	91	90	89	88					

*To all my fun-loving
campus companions
at the University of Virginia
—especially my wife, Susan,
the best companion of all.*

PREFACE

I held the rope tight as my father adjusted the boxes on top of our car. In them were most of my worldly belongings—at least as many as I thought I could cram into my dorm room at college.

"I guess that's it, son," Dad said, mopping the sweat off his face with a handkerchief.

"Better be," I said, standing back to survey the tightly packed car.

"Think you need all this stuff?"

I shrugged. I couldn't believe that all the planning for and wondering about college was almost over. Tomorrow my parents and I would leave for Virginia. And I wasn't coming home with them.

I went back to my bedroom to see if I'd forgotten anything. It looked so empty. Maybe Dad was right—maybe I was taking too much stuff with me. Maybe I wouldn't even touch my high-school yearbooks or downhill skis. Maybe I wouldn't have room for all my posters and family photos. Anyway, would bringing these familiar things to school really help me feel at home there?

My mind wandered to the other questions I had. What if my roommate and I don't get along? Will my high-school study habits cut it—or will I have to change my ways? What will I major in? Will I rush a fraternity? Date? Find my dream woman? Meet other Christians on campus?

As the first few months of school passed by, I realized I wasn't the only one asking these questions. Most people had been wondering the same things. And no sooner had we found answers to some of those questions than new questions arose: How can I prepare for my French mid-term, write a ten-page paper comparing Thoreau and Emerson and lead the weekly Bible study I've committed myself to—tonight? Where's the money going to come from when they raise tuition seven per cent next year? Why is my religion professor saying all those nasty things about Christianity—and what should I do about my doubts? Would I be happier if I transferred to another school? What kind of career does God want me to pursue after graduation? How do I tell my parents I'm in love with someone they barely even know?

Answering these questions is what *The Complete Campus Companion* is all about. It contains practical, straightforward advice from experts, as well as real-life stories of students who have wrestled with these questions and lived to tell about it.

As you grow as a student and a Christian, your concerns will change. Think of this guide as a handbook—not something you'll sit down and read cover to cover in one sitting, but something you'll refer to again and again when different questions arise, on anything from broaching a touchy subject with your parents to dating to helping a younger Christian grow.

Long after you've unpacked your high-school yearbooks and waved good-bye to Mom and Dad, we trust that your faithful *Companion* will still be tagging along—not only providing answers from college-wise Christians, but encouraging you to rely on God, who alone can ultimately sustain you through the challenges of adult life.

Robert M. Kachur

ORIENTATION

Orientation might not prepare you for all the surprises and choices college life brings, but perhaps it will get you through the first week. Here are some suggestions for making the most— or the least—of the days and years ahead.

Surviving the First Week

Andy Le Peau

High School Graduation: The glory, the pomp, the achievement, the great expectations. The secure senior, lord of all you see. On to new conquests. Confidently strutting into the Field House to pick up class cards, you consider your goal at college: to grasp the vast reaches of knowledge, creativity and technical expertise developed throughout Western Civilization. Carefully perusing the catalog, you decide on Ancient Greek History 180, The Tragedies of Shakespeare 150, The Thought of Carlos Castaneda 222 and Physical Anthropology 110.

Eleven hours later you emerge, limbs shaking, eyes blurred and fixed on an unknown point, clutching class cards for Archery 11.1, Trombone Performance 17.1, Introduction to Grammar 41 and Library Resources 73. Happily you had stood in line for an hour and a half. "Sorry, you need your adviser's signature." Back for her signature and then in line again. By then your class was filled. Pick a new one. Adviser's signature. This time you get the card, but the guy behind you in line points out that you have a time conflict with another class. He gets kind of embarrassed when you drape your arms over him and weep convulsively.

Staggering back to your dorm, you meet your roommate for the first time. He's standing on his head reading Captain Fantastic comics with Motley Crue blaring from his stereo. "It's the way I relax," he says.

Sheer exhaustion gives you an uninterrupted night's sleep despite the wild party across the hall.

The next day you try to buy your texts. After waiting three hours in the rain, you squeeze your way into the turn-of-the-century, plaster-cracked University Bookstore, which is continually under renovation ("Sorry for the temporary inconvenience"). All your texts are out except for the $49.95, 900-page *Basic Library Tools and Research*. You cry yourself to sleep that night while your roommate "relaxes."

The first day of classes has its own special surprises. The archery instructor is an 80-year-old former "movie star" (she says) who dresses like she was 17. You get lost trying to find your grammar class. Your trombone instructor was a flute virtuoso who thinks trombonists are genetically inferior.

Knowledge? Creativity? Technical expertise? You are now a miserable blob parked in front of your adviser's desk. You tell him you feel like ending it all. He is concerned about your desire to commit suicide and, presumably to encourage you that you're not alone, tells you stories of other students of his who chose this same route.

Support Your Local Christian

Your first lesson: Survival is not to be taken for granted in college. Obviously you need support—and not necessarily the kind that your adviser offers.

When I was an idealistic high-school senior, an older and wiser friend said, "Andy, when you get to campus, you've got to find some Christians who can relate to your struggles—other students in a local church, InterVarsity Christian Fellowship, Campus Crusade, The Navigators, anybody! Somebody's got to be there. Look in the student activities office. Just look. You can't survive if you don't find them." Being naive, I did what he said. I never regretted it.

The apostle Paul wrote to the Corinthians that Christians need each other to support each other, to care for each other (and to help each other get through the four-year blitz to greater knowledge, truth and beauty). He used an analogy of the body in 1 Corinthians 12 to show how each part is important and needed by all the other parts. I needed other members of the body of Christ to help get my spiritual feet on the ground and to help orient me to the practical ins and outs of college life.

Once I had found some Christians through the student activities office, I accidentally started praying with them regularly, and with one friend in particular. Throughout college it uplifted me to pray honestly several times a week for about a half-hour with one other person who was trying to survive too. We could talk and pray about studies, dating, doubts, parents—whatever was on our minds.

Other Survival Tactics

One time my prayer partner encouraged me to start having "quiet times" with God. Now that sounded pretty religious (though I got used to that kind of talk as time went on). Bravely I asked what it was. "Oh, I try to spend time each day studying Scripture, praying, maybe reading some book about God. It's a time to be alone with Christ each day." I decided to give it a try. For me it became an essential time to slow down, to rest and recharge by turning myself to Christ in the midst of the harried university world.

These were the kinds of things that helped me survive during my tour of duty with Plato, Newton, Shakespeare and the gang. Luckily I discovered that there was life after my first week on campus.

TEN SURE-FIRE WAYS TO HAVE A LOUSY TIME IN COLLEGE

Greg Spencer

Carrying out a collegiate disaster is not as simple as it looks. Try as they might to louse things up, some people end up having a good time in college. You would think that people would be able to stay at least as miserable as they were in high school. But, no, some of these bimboes actually move out of the demoralizing world of zits and geekiness and into (shudder) productive Christian living. Never fear: that can be avoided. How? Follow my advice.

SORRY, CAN'T— GOT A FRISBEE FINAL TOMORROW

1. Don't Get Involved.

Be a recluse as much as possible. Don't simply go home occasionally; go home every weekend. Use any excuse you can muster: "I have to visit my boyfriend." "I have to check for gloves in the glove compartment of my parents' car." "I need to wax the basement floor for the neighborhood shuffleboard association." Why take the chance of making deep friendships? Of your seventy-odd years of existence on this planet, college accounts for a piddling four.

Hole yourself up. When a disturbingly assertive fellow tries to get you involved in his life, answer with an enigmatic saying. For example, if a Rhetoric 101 student asks you to join a study group, say, "The moon is so far away, yet we are so close."

In addition to working on your reputation as a hermit, restrict your risk-taking. Evangelizing in your dorm, for example, could be disastrously rewarding. Every time you feel obliged to defend the faith, tell yourself that "it would be much better to witness with my life." And, conversely, whenever you desire to demonstrate your faith, tell yourself that "it would be much better to witness with words . . . some other time." Why cause others to be uncomfortable?

2. Avoid Interaction with Professors.

Don't be deceived by those who say that meetings with professors are terrible—unfortunately, they can be learning experiences. If they prove fruitful, there goes your rotten time right out the window.

Besides, not getting to know your instructors will add to your misery later. When it comes time to seek professors' recommendations for graduate school or employment, you will have nowhere to turn and can thus enter into a delightful depression.

3. When Interaction Is Inevitable, Don't Squander the Opportunity: Be as Rude as You Can.

If you must speak in class, perform some subtle disrespect toward your professor such as: "Excuse me, pagan-face, but do you realize that, in this one lecture, you have managed to blaspheme the Creator of the Universe thirty-two times?" Another ploy for purposeful rudeness is to staple especially obnoxious evangelistic tracts to one's research papers. I like the one that looks like Drano and asks, "Need to clean up your life?"

Among your peers, the possibilities for offensiveness are only limited by your creativity. How about taping bumper stickers to your clothes? "In case of rapture, you can keep the Calvin Kleins." "Praise God, I'm saved; you're not—ha, ha, ha." "Pat my back if you love Jesus!" Another idea is to, upon meeting someone for the first time, say your name and then ask if they have received the baptism of the Holy Spirit.

4. Develop Elaborate Expectations.

Some people think that unhappiness results from being realistic. Nothing could be further from the truth. Illusion is much more profitable. Try on these unrealistic expectations for size:

"My roommate and I will be as tight as cellophane." "College will be just like high school, only more fun." "Partying frat boys are well-adjusted and always have a good time." "None of the Christians I meet will disappoint me." "Studying in the dorm will be simple and gratifying."

Such expectations will practically ensure psyche-shattering moments of anxious doubt and brooding introspection.

5. Divide Your Life Into Neat Spiritual and Secular Components.

Confine spirituality to only those things which are distinctly and measurably Christian—praying, reading your Bible, snoozing in church. Consider everything else, from taking out the garbage to voting about including contraceptives in the school lunch program, part of your secular life.

Since your spiritual life is more important than your secular life, you can justify all sorts of situations. Should you study for tomorrow's history exam or listen to the latest Amy Grant album? Relax and reach for the headphones—who

can argue with spiritual growth? If you fail the exam, you can always blame God for not giving you the answers. Shouldn't he reward you for your commitment?

6. Believe Everything You Hear.

As the great twentieth-century philosopher Marilyn Monroe once said, "I believe in everything, a little bit."

All you need to do is what most independent thinking undergraduates do: follow the crowd. There are certain nearly universal beliefs which, though mutually contradictory, have been bravely defended by most collegians. For instance, have you memorized this college creed?

We, the college community, hold these truths to be self-evident: Everything is okay as long as we don't hurt anybody else, except when not hurting someone keeps us from doing what feels good. We will tolerate all views except those which conflict with our own. The more absurd the idea, the more attractive and tolerable it will become. If we can't face the music, we will lose ourselves in rock 'n' roll. We believe in the Great Me, sex before commitment (but only with those with whom we are in love), the pursuit of happiness, and anything else which we can stuff into the knapsack of our minds. Amen.

Let me warn you—this is not an easy faith. It requires perseverance and courage, especially in light of rationality. But with diligence, your mind can become a muddled mess of mediocre morality.

7. Shop for a Christian Fellowship as Long as You Can.

Why ruin a positively rotten situation with commitment? If you jump into a fellowship early on, you might make friends, deal with doubts or grow in your faith. Bad news.

If somehow, dragged and screaming, you are backed into a group, be sure to refuse all requests for leadership or service. What appears innocent on the surface may become a slippery slope descending to dependence on God. In your march toward fruitlessness, do not neglect to cultivate the wonderful quality of complacency.

8. Do Every "Christian" Thing Possible before Actually Reading the Bible.

When, for whatever reason, you decide to give the appearance of Christian living, be sure to read books about Christianity, or study views which synthesize Christianity and some other major school of thought (feminism, Marxism, capitalism, Americanism), or examine public figures who claim to be Christian (the easier to criticize, the better), or peruse books with a Christian point of view (providing they do not entice you to read the Original Source), or even look at books about the Bible itself. Whatever you do, don't actually open those crinkly pages. The results can be disgustingly constructive.

9. Make the Busyness of College Life Your Highest Priority.

Be consumed with busyness. Filling up your day with "things to do," no matter how inconsequential, is a good way not only to justify your existence, but also to provide an instant excuse when others try to engage you in the more important things of life. "Frightfully sorry, old pal, but my Anthropologists-for-a-Culturally-Free-Future meeting is tonight."

Avoid situations such as a walk in the park where you might clear your mind. Don't be still and know that he is God; get moving and see if he's God-enough to keep up with you.

Also, be consumed with grades. One handy idea is to wear a button on your lapel that identifies your grade point average. Make the difference between a 3.47 and a 3.51 an obsession.

10. Just Get Through.
Show no interest in learning, only in completing assignments. Choose safe, dull, unmemorable, agonizing-to-work-on topics for papers, and take the easiest courses from the easiest teachers. I once made the mistake of taking a course from an exceptionally challenging educator who expected me to think.

Finally, ignore any suggestion that you ought to work on your study habits. Everybody knows that study skills are genetically determined. You can no more improve your study habits than you can grow another ear. Besides, why are you in college anyway? To goof off. By ignoring your studies, you'll be priming yourself for exquisite bouts with procrastination, cramming, caffeine fits and incompletes. And when it's all over, you, too, will be able to say, "Hallelujah—what a waste!"

THE CLASSROOM

You'll spend anywhere from twelve to twenty hours a week in class. In this section you'll find out how to make the most of them by building an academic strategy. You'll learn how to approach your studies with a Christian world view, even when your professor and text seem to contradict your faith. We'll help you hammer out a healthy attitude toward grades, success and failure—and offer practical ways you can improve your study habits.

MAKING THE GRADE: HOW IMPORTANT IS IT?

Paul Tokunaga

Sam and Dave are freshman roommates at Stanford. On Sam's desk sparkles one of those philosophical little wooden plaques:

> The Bottom Line
> The best GPA = the best job = the biggest bucks.
> Go for it.

On Dave's desk lay the campus events page of the *Stanford Daily* and Spiderman #714.

Sam graduates summa cum laude. A colored tassel and a hungry grin garnish his face.

Dave? Dave transfers to Cal Poly (thought it was Cal Tech), squeezing out a diploma between Spidey #'s 722 and 798 and membership in eight real fun campus clubs.

Sam begins management training with TRW. Three years later, Sam is still obsessed with the same ol' bottom line. After reworking a few numbers, he embezzled ol' TRW. "Two years in the slammer for you, bud," says the judge.

"Squeeze by, ease by," Dave would always say. Hey, it works. But then, oops, he missed a few squeezes: lost his job, wife and kids, even Spidey #1 to get out of hock. Finally, he's off to the coop for negligence.

Sam and Dave. Suite 1024 at the Men's Correctional Institute. Roomies again.

God, Grades or a Good Time?

What are your bottom-line reasons for going to college? Are they more like Sam's or Dave's? Is your bottom line good grades, big money, fancy titles and a slick little BMW? Or perhaps you have no bottom line. Maybe you haven't even found the starting line. You're not sure why you're in school.

Chances are you won't get tossed in jail—at least not a physical jail—for patterns and attitudes you develop in college. But how you approach your four years of college is important. The patterns you learn now will profoundly affect your career and home life later on. You will reap what you sow.

The Sam Syndrome

To be honest, many students choose the Sam Syndrome—an overpreoccupation with GPAs, academic performance and getting the "right" degree from the "right" school in order to assure a lifetime of yuppieness. In a national poll of 200,000 freshmen at 372 institutions, 75% said "being very well-off financially" was "very important" or "essential." Nearly one-fourth—an all-time high—plan to major in business. As one sophomore put it, "Sure I want an interesting job, but money is the key. Money is nice. Poor is not nice."

The Sam Syndrome makes some sense. For many, the future resembles a sinking Titanic. If tomorrow is questionable, then why not go down first class?

But is *summa cum laude* all it's cracked up to be? Does it really guarantee a ticket to The Fulfilled Life?

Working Woman magazine carries a column called "Career Advice." A twenty-six-year-old woman with B.S. and M.S. degrees wrote in complaining of burnout. In her letter she told of only working half-time and wanting to take a year off to travel and loaf. Betty Lehan Harragan, a business consultant, responded,

One thing that may be holding you back is a belated recognition that you wasted the best part of your undergraduate years. Your priorities were all wrong and now you regret it. From the tone of your letter, you seemed to believe that high marks, studious concentration on book learning plus self-absorbed research through your computer work-study job were the ultimate aims of your college education. Not so.

Those requirements are important but only in perspective. An adequate performance on scholastic endeavors is necessary to maintain your financial aid and accumulate credits to graduate. But what will count in future years is what you learn in extracurricular activities. The campus clubs or groups you participate in, the sports teams you play on, the parties you go to, the causes you take up, the political offices you run for, even the romances you get entangled with—all these lay the groundwork for dealing with people in structured organizations. *(Working Woman,* April 1985)

The Dave Dilemma

If Sam and his cohorts ignore the social whirl, Dave lives for it. Extra is everything. For him, the classroom is simply a necessary must-do to support his extracurricular habits. Clock in the minimum time and effort; clock out for the interesting, meaningful stuff: friendships, work, clubs, sports.

As an undergraduate, I rarely ventured into Summa Cum Laude Land. I majored in Extra-Curriculars. My college years were a wonderful time for self-discovery and service. Academics were a slice of my life, but never the whole pie.

In the name of Good Causes, I often skipped classes, and then relentlessly crammed for exams the twenty-four hours before. Somehow I managed to maintain decent grades, but I retained little classroom knowledge. By senior year I could say I was leading eight different organizations or projects and working two part-time jobs. But I also had to plead with a professor for a final grade I really didn't deserve. (He didn't give in.)

In retrospect, I'm glad I erred in the direction of extracurricular activities instead of living in a library cubicle for four years. The variety of challenges and experiences shaped my character and honed my leadership skills in ways the classroom could not. Most of my nonacademic energies were invested in talking about Jesus with students, faculty and administrators and helping believers grow in Christ. Our fellowship group left a deep imprint on the entire campus.

Unfortunately, I took my extracurriculars to an extreme. I didn't say no to enough things, and often felt as if I had spread myself a mile wide and an inch deep.

All things considered, whose approach is preferable, Sam's or Dave's? Actually, neither. Both extremes will either backfire quickly or, like rust, will corrode slowly over time.

A Better Way

The Scriptures propose a third bottom line, an approach to balancing out grades and extracurricular activities. The God of the Bible is preoccupied with our salvation. At its core, salvation means being delivered from anything that's not ultimately good for us. God is bent on restoring our wholeness.

Jesus best expressed our responsibility in the process when he said, " 'Love the Lord your God with all your heart, and with all your soul and with all your mind.' This is the first and greatest commandment. And the second is like it: 'Love your neighbor as yourself' " (Mt 22:37-39).

The "four loves" mandated here—heart, soul, mind, neighbor—are big orders to fill. They will take a lifetime (and then some!) to fulfill. In the doing of such love, however, come joy and peace and the other fruits of the Spirit that bring wholeness.

Following Jesus' agenda for wholeness demands a new approach to college life. Unlike Sam, we can no longer consider the bottom line to be the highest grades regardless of the cost to us spiritually, emotionally and physically; God cares too much about our well-being. And unlike Dave, we can no longer write off academics as secondary. Academics take on new meaning; no longer are they just a medium for tedium but an avenue for becoming more like Jesus.

Instead of asking questions such as "How can I make the most money?" or

"How can I have the most fun?" the new bottom line under Jesus' agenda becomes, "How can I use my college years—in and out of the classroom—to make them an expression of love, to bring Christlikeness or wholeness to my life?"

The best way to answer that question is to identify key areas of your life you can work on now—while you're in college—that you probably won't be in a position to work on later. Let me suggest a few, some of which I learned while in college, and some I wish I had learned there.

The Top Five Priorities

☐ *Spiritual disciplines.* That's fancy talk for your relationship with God. Do you spend regular, meaningful time with him? If you don't now, it only gets harder with increased demands later. No one in the marketplace will encourage you to have a regular time of Bible study, prayer and reflection, or to take time for spiritual retreats. Are your pursuits for a high GPA and other goals crowding God out?

☐ *Personal discipline.* Can you plan out a weekly schedule and stick to it? Do you meet deadlines? Are you on time for class and appointments? Do you keep your car or bike in good shape? Do you write Mom and Dad as you promised? Do you maintain good eating habits? Don't expect these areas to come together after graduation. Work hard now to develop patterns that will serve you well when you're thirty-five and really under pressure.

☐ *Lifestyle.* How do you "love your neighbor as yourself"? Many have properly criticized the North American church because its members seem just as greedy and consumer-oriented as their pagan neighbors. We feel it is our right to have as many comforts as we can. Friedrich Nietzsche, the German philosopher who coined the term "God is dead," shoots many of us between the eyes when he says, "Before I am saved, Christians will have to look more saved."

In college, we can choose to live as consumptively as possible, or to live within our means and sacrifice for the sake of others. Those who can't resist the latest nine-dollar album now will have difficulty saying no to the latest nine-hundred-dollar stereo system later. And those who willingly forgo a meal now to help send a friend to a weekend retreat will find it easier to support missionaries later.

☐ *Mind development.* In a recent report on college students, *Time* magazine said, "Today's students are taught how to give answers, rather than how to make a good argument. . . . [Students] are not ready for mature, critical thinking." Other studies show an alarming lack of ability in writing and reading.

Challenge yourself: For every hour of television you watch, match it with an hour's reading of a good, mind-stimulating book. (Sorry, Dave, Spiderman doesn't quite count.)

Write more letters, and make fewer long-distance phone calls.

When you receive syllabi at the start of each school term, set learning goals rather than grade point goals.

Buy a good dictionary. Whenever you run across a word you don't understand or can't confidently spell, look it up.

Make friends with one or two people who stretch and challenge you with their intellect. Don't be intimidated; soak up their insights and knowledge. It might be a grad student, a professor, maybe even a freshman. Once graduated, most of us will never again be in a place as intellectually stimulating as a college campus. Strike now!

☐ *Your choice of a major.* Some questions are more helpful than others in getting at God's will for your future. Here are two that are best placed on the back burner: "How many easy A's can I rack up in this subject?" and "How much money do people in this particular field make?"

I have a friend who refuses to ask about salary until after he has interviewed and has decided that the position is good for him. He knows how quickly a $50,000 job can become "God's will" over a $15,000 position.

Several questions worth asking:

What are my particular gifts and aptitudes? How can these gifts fit into God's plan of redemption for the world?

How can my life be best used to serve God and others?

What really "burns in my gut"? What do I feel so compelled to do that if I don't I will be shortchanging myself?

What chronic weaknesses do I have that might keep me out of certain vocations?

Stop for a moment and daydream: You're thirty-five years old. What do you want to be like? What are you doing to get there? The choices you make now as a student will matter later. You don't have to bunk with either Sam or Dave.

When to Drop a Class

Almost every term a certain friend of mine used to drop a class—whichever one he had the lowest grade in at the time. Every semester or quarter you too may be tempted to drop a class, to save your GPA or for other reasons. But before you do, make sure you ask yourself these key questions:

☐ What are my priorities at this time? School? Work? Family? Social life?

☐ Why do I want to drop this class? Too difficult? Incompetent professor? Boring? Irrelevant to my field of study or interests?

☐ Am I willing to pay the consequences of dropping a class—such as losing nonrefundable tuition, facing conflict with my parents or my instructor, delaying completion of school, or taking a heavier study load later on?

☐ Have I looked at all my alternatives? Have I talked to the professor about why I want to drop the class? Do I need additional tutoring?

☐ Will my dropping a class appear on my transcript? Will that affect the way future employers or graduate schools evaluate my application?

☐ Do I repeatedly have a difficult time finishing what I've started? If so, am I copping out again? Or do I have the opposite problem of constantly pushing myself beyond my limits? If so, are there any reasons why it wouldn't be healthy for me to drop the class?

—*Joan Wallner*

EASING THE PAIN OF STUDYING

Jeanne Doering Zornes

Despite my dismal SAT scores and the fact that good grades had never come particularly easy to me, I learned a lot in college—and even graduated magna cum laude. By implementing the right study habits, you can succeed in the classroom too.

I'm not talking about worshiping the Almighty A. The academic system en-courages grade idolatry, and as Christians we're to put what God wants above our drive for a 4.0. But Jesus calls us to use our time and resources at college wisely. In Matthew 25:14-30 he tells a story about a man who gave his servants money to invest while he was away on a long trip. The master simply asked them to work with what they had. The guy who missed the mark was the one who dug a hole and buried his resources rather than take the effort to make them work for him; and the severe punishment he received clues us in on what a serious matter investing our time and talents rightly, on campus and after graduation, is to God.

Freshman year I had my share of all-nighters and late papers snuck under professors' doors. But the stress wasn't worth it—and neither were the results. I wasn't using my time or abilities well.

Learning smart ways to study changed my day-to-day life at college. The following thirteen techniques I learned aren't all that profound. They boil down to making the most of your study time in light of the semester that lay ahead. But implementing them can definitely make a difference in how well you survive the ivy jungle.

1. Set Up a Set-up

That means a regular study area with a desk, some sort of bulletin board and a good lamp. (If the lighting isn't adequate on the page you are reading, your eye functions more slowly and you actually absorb less information.) Even though I often studied in the library, my room desk was my "dock," and everything I needed was right there.

To minimize distractions I faced the desk toward a wall and cleared the top of everything except a scratch pad and two mugs (one for drinks, the other for pens, pencils and scissors). Since the desk was large enough, I eventually added a two-tier plastic tray. The top level held typing paper; the bottom, correspondence and miscellaneous. I arranged my desk near a bookcase so I could reach my dictionary and thesaurus without getting up.

In a shoe box in one drawer I kept basic office supplies: stapler, ruler, tape, paper punch, paper clips, pencil sharpener, eraser, glue, gummed reinforcements, three-by-five cards, rubber bands, typewriter correction tabs and a calculator. This kept me from wasting time searching for, begging for or running out to buy the stuff I used most often. (The shoe box not only kept everything together, but was handy at moving time.) In the same drawer I stored letter- and legal-size envelopes and some stationery. Another drawer held file folders of class notes and research.

2. Become a Three-ringer

I gave up on keeping notes in pocket folders or spiral-bound notebooks. Papers fell out of the pockets. Handouts never fit in the spirals. Besides, quizzes written on pages ripped out of a spiral notebook looked tacky.

A simple, three-ring notebook with looseleaf paper and plastic-tabbed dividers served me well. At the beginning of each semester I just changed the divider labels and filled the sections with fresh paper. I placed the class syllabus at the beginning of each section.

3. Calendarize Your Future

I kept two calendars. A big one which the Student Activities office provided hung on the bulletin board by my desk. At the beginning of each semester, armed with class syllabi, I wrote in dates of major assignments and tests. With my "semester-at-a-glance" I could plan ahead more easily. (I also noted important birthdays and social events here.)

I kept a second calendar in the front of my three-ring notebook. Often I made this one myself by marking off a month of squares on a piece of typing paper. Each square was big enough for me to note not only papers, tests and reading assignments (including the ones a professor announced outside the syllabus), but any details on these shared in class. That calendar also became my appointment book.

4. Prioritize Your Assignments

As I got more and more familiar with professors' styles and expectations, I knew better which required reading, if any, was irrelevant and which optional assignments were a must. If, for example, a professor's lectures overlapped 99% with the text, and I felt I didn't need the reinforcement of reading the text to understand the material, I'd make those reading assignments low priority. If, on the other hand, an optional assignment shed light on major themes or principles I'd never understood, I'd make those a high priority.

5. Carefully Choose *Where* You Will Study

Conversations, radios and laughter usually seem more intriguing than the book you're trying to study. You will probably accomplish more in an hour's study at a quiet library or study lounge (not the one where guys go to meet girls and vice versa) than three hours in your dorm room.

6. Put Variety in Your Class Schedule

One semester a friend of mine took all history and literature classes—and continually freaked out over the volumes of reading he was behind no matter how hard he studied. When you plan your schedule, balance courses that require a lot of reading and papers (such as history and literature) with classes that require a lot of memorization (such as foreign languages) and classes that revolve around labs and problem sets (such as math and physics). This change of pace throughout the week can help keep your workload more manageable and your courseload more interesting.

7. Patch Up Time Leaks

Each quarter I took a piece of graph paper and drew up a personal schedule that accounted for every hour of the week. If nothing else, that schedule—tacked right above my desk—was an effective prod to keep me from frittering away study hours I had after sleep, classes and work. (Not that every hour of my week was set aside for studying, of course. I'd block out hours and even days just for rest, goofing off and getting to know people better.)

I kept my eye open for blocks of available time during the day. Often I got a lot done during the forty-five minutes between classes if I located an empty classroom or headed for the library. If I really wanted to concentrate, I avoided the more public areas of the library—such as tables, reading rooms or desks near busy windows or halls—and found obscure study carrels—such as those located in the reference books section.

I also hunted for ways to save time. When several of us got tired of waiting in lines at the overcrowded dining halls, we asked the cashier what times were least busy. By coming then we could sometimes save half an hour of waiting.

8. Keep Alert

Some how-to-study books suggest assigning certain hours of each day to studying certain subjects. That works for some, but I let the urgency of an assignment and my alertness be my guide.

My mind works faster in the morning; so that's when I'd tackle my tough assignments. In the afternoons, when I slowed down mentally, I'd set those aside, if possible, and type or plunge into research.

If I got drowsy while I was studying at the library, I'd get up and walk over to a water fountain or walk briskly up and down a flight of stairs. If I still felt like I was going nowhere fast, I'd pack up and go somewhere else. A change of scenery can help clear your mind and give you a fresh start when you're frustrated. Then there were times when I absolutely needed to catnap; I set my alarm for a half-hour, and usually woke up feeling refreshed.

Though a lot of my friends survived on coffee and Diet Pepsi, I found drinking ice water kept me going just as well when I was struggling to keep alert. And if I found a certain class boring, I'd make a point of sitting in one of the first few rows. I took better notes, under-stood more and felt more involved. This may sound wacky, but sitting in the front also made it easier for professors to see my "helplessly confused" look when they weren't making sense. More than one responded to my incredulous gaze by backing up to clarify.

9. Get the Big Picture

Author, speaker and Talbot Seminary President Jim Conway claims that your *mindset* is about 90% of your success in studying: "Before you start, pray for a moment and ask God to clear everything else from your mind so that you can concentrate only on the subject at hand. If you are looking at a book for the first time, a careful reading of the preface, table of contents and jacket will tell you a lot about it and will orient you to the material before you start to read. That will help you read the book more quickly.

"In all of your classes, keep thinking in terms of the overview. What are the main ideas that are being communicated? How do they all fit together? Take good notes. Don't slough off, thinking you can catch up later. Your notes will be a powerful tool for review at the end of the semester."

10. Anticipate Finals Early

Finals became less painful when I started studying with them in mind right from the beginning. I used extra minutes before a class began to glance over previous class notes. If a professors's lecture style included an introductory review, I'd underline and asterisk appropriately.

About three weeks before finals I'd go through my notes and mark them with key words on opposite pages (I restricted my class note-taking to one side of the page). Material that had to be memorized I transferred to three-by-five cards which I carried in my knapsack to review in spare moments. Last-minute bull-session reviews for finals can help; but generally I found they wasted time going over material I'd already mastered through regular reviewing throughout the semester.

Doing my best on other assignments also kept finals from looming so threateningly. One semester I really struggled through a class in Victorian literature. My weekly work was decent, but the final was a corker, and I was sick the day I took it. I walked out of it wondering if I'd flunked. When I later picked up my graded final I had bad news and good news. Yes, I'd done poorly on the exam. But the professor had added a note: He felt the final was not representative of my efforts that quarter and decided to weigh my assignments more heavily to give me a higher grade.

11. Learn To Type
I think typing ought to be a college entrance requirement. Typing skills saved me time by banging out papers faster and money by not having to hire someone else to type for me. Typing rough drafts gave me something in print which I could more easily decipher and refine than my scribblings. Word processors, which allow you to rewrite and make corrections on disk before you print your paper out, are even better.

Typing well also helped me comply with standard research-paper style so my papers looked professional. Whether they admit it or not, professors tend to look more favorably on papers that come in double-spaced with normal margins on ordinary typing paper. (That special erasable paper sticks to sweaty palms and smudges easily.) I know that when I helped grade student papers later on, the neat ones seemed to get higher marks.

12. Meet Your Professors
I aimed for at least one personal contact per semester with my professors, especially those in the same field as my major. Usually I met with them to discuss a paper topic or concept raised in class. Not only did I profit from their insights, but they were more able to put a face with my name.

In fact, one of these personal contacts led to my first job. Just before graduation, I popped in to see one of my journalism professors. He knew I'd been job-hunting because I'd asked him for leads on where to send résumés earlier in the semester. He'd been trying to reach me because a certain editor was on campus that afternoon looking for prospective newspaper interns. I quickly signed up for an appointment and ran home to change clothes and grab a few résumés. A week later I was hired for a "temporary" newspaper job that lasted for five years.

13. Share Your Struggles
Sometimes as school pressures dragged me down I'd feel like chanting Ecclesi-

astes 12:12: "Much study wearies the body." College can drain you physically, mentally, emotionally and spiritually.

When studies start overwhelming me and I felt like God was indifferent to my struggles, other Christians in the same situation helped a lot. Some were long distance—people I could call to hash over my feelings and ask for prayer. One friend lived 2400 miles away. But I knew she was praying for requests such as "re-moval of the block that keeps Jeanne from understanding her psychology readings" or "physical stamina to type her thesis." Other friends, such as a group of five women with whom I met weekly for Bible study and group prayer, were right on campus. Their encouragement and prayers kept me going—in a way that all the best study techniques in the world could not.

Reference Books You Can't Live Without

Here are a few basic reference tools to help you get through all the reports, term papers and take-home tests you'll be facing this year.

I strongly recommend a good full-sized dictionary. Consider the best-selling *Webster's Ninth New College Dictionary* ($15.95), *Webster's New World Dictionary* ($14.95; paper, $3.95), *Random House College Dictionary* ($15.95; paper, $3.50) and *Oxford American Dictionary* ($6.95).

My own all-time favorite is *The American Heritage Dictionary: Second College Edition* ($15.95). It not only has illustrations and photos (so that's what Béla Bartók looked like!) but also more than 800 usage notes. What's the difference between *between* and *among?* Which features compose the distinctions among *compose, comprise* and *constitute?* Must I go any further to understand *further* and *farther?* The *American Heritage's* usage notes will lead you through these and many other questions. There is a paperback edition available at $4.95, but it omits all the usage notes.

Hopeless spellers may be relieved to know that they can actually purchase a book called *The Bad Spellers' Dictionary* ($2.95).

The Research Search

Have you ever been happily reading a magazine or a textbook, and a statement jumps out and makes you feel like a dummy? "Of course this all hinged on the findings of François Quesnay and the Physiocrats" (a new wave band?). "The conference was organized by the same group that operates Arecibo Ionospheric Observatory" (the Green Bay Packers?).

What you need is *The Concise Columbia Encyclopedia* ($29.95; paper, $14.95). It is one of the best one-volume reference books around, loaded with all kinds of descriptions and minibiographies of known and not-so-known people, places, events and concepts.

If you're doing in-depth research for a term paper, get familiar with your school library's reference section. The *Readers' Guide to Periodical Literature* is probably the most used resource there. It lists recent magazine articles from about 180 periodicals by subject and writer. If you would like to use Christian magazines that don't appear in *Reader's Guide* as sources, try the *Christian Periodical Index* (published by the Association of Christian Librarians), which also lists articles by subject and author.

One often overlooked source is the *Subject Guide to Books in Print.* A current listing of "in print" books is presented by subject. The Title and Author volumes are also helpful in case you want to find more works by a certain author, or if you have the title of a book and need to find an author. (If the Subject volumes aren't available in your library, try a bookstore.)

If you're looking for the perfect quotation to start a term paper (or you can't for the life of you remember if it was Patrick Henry or Billy Martin who first said, "Give me liberty or give me death"), you need *Bartlett's Familiar Quotations* ($29.95) or *The New International Dictionary of Quotations* ($19.95).

Still other resources to look for in your library are government pamphlets, atlases, newspapers, bibliographies and telephone books. And don't forget the librarians. Take your list of sources to them and ask for any other suggestions they may have on your particular topic.

Writers' Helpers
The classic in this category is the skinny little

paperback, *The Elements of Style* by Strunk and White ($3.50). Also, check out Theodore Bernstein's *The Careful Writer* ($10.95), *Watch Your Language* ($7.95) and the *Students' Guide for Writing College Papers* ($3.95) by Kate L. Turabian. *A Dictionary of Modern English Usage* ($15.95; paper, $8.95) by H. W. Fowler will help guide your grammar and language, including idioms and slang.

A thesaurus can help you find the right word, but it's best used along with a dictionary. Two stand-outs are *Roget's Pocket Thesaurus* ($3.95) and *Roget's College Thesaurus in Dictionary Form* ($3.50).

Finally, if you're totally lost and don't know where to look, consult *The New York Times Guide to Reference Materials* ($3.95). Then make a little room on your desk or bookshelf. And enjoy the world of words.
—*Betsy Rossen Elliot and Shirley Kostka*

Six Ways to Weasel Out of an Exam

Rob Suggs

I've been working feverishly on this giant sculpture of you for art class and haven't had time left to study.

I'll be running radioactive experiments on myself in the physics lab that day, but if you still want me to come in . . .

I have strange, unexplainable telekinetic powers that cause objects to fly across the room when I become tense or nervous.

This is my friend Bruno. I *tried* to tell him I had an exam, but he's just really stubborn about taking me to his crocodile-wrestling match. Could you explain it to him?

I have this monstrous headache.

Have you heard that "60 Minutes" wants to interview me for a report on academic cruelty they're filming here on campus?

Taking Your Faith to Class

Brian Walsh

L eon Trotsky once observed that Russia's problem wasn't a lack of good writers, but a lack of good "communist" writers. In other words, few writers were so steeped in the communist world view that their literature naturally and integrally breathed communism.

We could say the same thing about the body of Christ today. It is not that the church lacks students, lawyers, doctors, politicians, farmers, scientists, business people and psychologists, but that so few could be termed "Christian" students, lawyers, doctors, politicians, farmers, scientists, business people and psychologists. Most of us don't know how to relate our daily tasks to our faith.

We confess that all truth is in Jesus Christ (Jn 1:14; 14:6). As college students, shouldn't this confession have far-reaching implications for our studies?

What happens when we combine a Christian student and a secular university? We end up with at least four possible results.

Four Formulas

1. Christian + University = Christian + University. This could be called the isolationist approach. These Christian students see no clear connection between their studies and their faith in Christ. Their Christian influence on campus is limited to participation at fellowship meetings, personal Bible study and perhaps some evangelism. They may find opportunities to share their faith with a non-Christian classmate, but they write their papers on Hopi Indians and take their engineering exams without hammering out a Christian approach to anthropology or technology.

2. *Christian + University = A Bit of Both.* This could be called the accomodating approach. As college studies cause these students to rethink their faith, they begin to modify their beliefs.

Although this can be a healthy experience (we *all* carry around misconceptions, no matter how long we've been Christians), it can also be dangerous. Some Christians end up accommodating their faith *whenever* it is challenged by their studies. For example, studying psychology leads some to view conversion as a merely psychological event in which God has little impact. Studying commerce leads others to spiritualize Jesus' concrete teachings in the Sermon on the Mount, which fly in the face of economic practices rooted in self-centered greed (Mt 6:19-34). And studying comparative religions leads still others to water down Jesus' claim to be the way, the truth and the life.

3. *Christian + University = Non-Christian.* Sometimes Christian students respond to the challenges of college life by giving up their faith. They read Freud's *The Future of an Illusion,* become persuaded that religion is an infantile projection, and decide to leave childish things behind. Or they study how the organized church has historically supported unjust and oppressive economic situations, and so they reject Christ and embrace Marx.

4. *Christian + University = Christian University Student.* Perhaps fewer students would abandon their faith if they understood this last option. Unwilling to isolate, accommodate or abandon their faith, these students *integrate* their faith with their studies. They strive to think Christianly.

Students who think Christianly understand Jesus Christ's claim over all aspects of life: "For by him all things were created: things in heaven and on earth, visible and invisible, whether thrones or powers or rulers or authorities; all things were created by him and for him. He is before all things, and in him all things hold together. . . . For God was pleased to have all his fullness dwell in him, and through him to reconcile to himself all things, whether things on earth or things in heaven, by making peace by his blood, shed on the cross" (Col 1:16-17, 19-20).

Do you notice how many times the words "all things" recur throughout these verses? Jesus is the Creator of all things, he is before all things, and all things are reconciled to him. Nothing lies outside his jurisdiction.

If everything is subject to Jesus Christ, then our studies must be too. But what does it mean to subject our studies to him? As rational people, shouldn't Christians and non-Christians study and think in much the same manner?

No. Christians should think differently.

The Bible portrays men and women as inherently religious creatures; we seek an orientation, a higher goal, an ultimate end, a god. If we do not reflect our Creator, we will mirror something else, an idol. Paul puts it this way: "Al-

though they claimed to be wise, they became fools and exchanged the glory of the immortal God for images made to
look like mortal man and birds and animals and rep-
tiles. . . . They exchanged the truth of God for a lie, and
worshiped and served created things rather than the Creator" (Rom 1:22-23, 25).

The pattern is inevitable: either we serve the Creator, or
we idolize and serve something he created. Every life is a
profession of faith; everyone places confidence in someone or something. In this sense, everyone is religious.
Whether we consciously define it or unconsciously express
it, we all interpret the events of life within some framework
that makes sense of our existence. Our decisions and
choices flow out of this vision of life.

What's Your World View?

In other words, everyone on your campus has a view of
the world, or world view, that affects the way they think
and approach their studies. A world view is a kind of road
map. It tells us the "lay of the land" and how to get from
one place to another. But we operate according to different
maps which portray reality differently and suggest different
routes through life. The question for us as Christians is not
whether we or someone else have a road map, but whether
that map is accurate or not.

A professor walks into the lecture hall at nine o'clock on
Monday morning. When she begins to lecture on electrical
engineering, the literary criticism of a play or the molecular
structure of a cell, is she simply giving us the bare facts? Is
her lecture totally divorced from who she is as a person
and her fundamental beliefs? No. She brings to her lecture
all of the baggage that comes with her world view. Her presuppositions are usually hidden from the class, and sometimes even she is not aware of them.

As Christian students, we must ask questions about our
professors' and textbooks' underlying presuppositions. The
Bible clearly warns us not to be conformed to the world
(Rom 12:2) or to swallow idolatrous philosophy (Col 2:8).

As an exercise to get you thinking along these lines, try answering the following questions: Why is economics generally reduced to a quantitative science? What is at stake in the synthesis of music and technology in much contemporary music? What fundamental assumptions about being human are at the root of conflicting schools of thought in psychology (behaviorism, Freudian psychoanalysis, transactional analysis, bioenergetics)? Why does science play the most formative role in the health professions? Why does the engineering department view technology as the route to social well-being? How does the social-work department define social well-being?

All of these questions get to the world-view roots of various fields of study. Students who do not ask questions such as these may buy into a non-Christian world view without realizing it.

If a false world view distorts our studies, imagine what positive results a Christian world view should have when we tackle English, history, chemistry or anything else.

Clearing Your Head

To begin integrating our faith with our studies, we must be thoroughly grounded in the biblical vision of life. That's why in-depth Bible study and the support of other Christians on campus is so important. We can only tell what's false if we understand what God has revealed to us to be true.

What Jesus taught about money, justice and the poor, for example, will affect our thinking about economics, business and political theory. What the Bible teaches about healing and the notion of *shalom* or blessing will affect our approach to health care and social work. The biblical view of human nature will shed light on psychological theories. And so on.

Responding to the academic world Christianly is not something you have to do alone. One of the purposes of InterVarsity Christian Fellowship and other campus fellowship groups is to help students integrate the biblical world

view into their studies and social lives. We should band together with other Christian students, seek out Christian
professors, study Christian authorities in our fields and develop a Christian perspective—together.

Jesus offers us no alternative. If we want to honor him,
we will pursue our studies under his guidance. After all, all
truth is from him.

A Reading List for Thinking Christians

Harry Blamires. *The Christian Mind* (Servant).

——— . *Recovering the Christian Mind*
(IVP).

F. F. Bruce. *The New Testament Documents:
Are They Reliable?* (IVP).

Arthur Holmes. *All Truth Is God's Truth*
(IVP).

——— . *Contours of a Christian World View*
(Eerdmans).

Charles Hummel. *The Galileo Connection:
Resolving Conflicts between Science and the
Bible* (IVP).

C. S. Lewis. *The Abolition of Man* (Macmillan).

——— . *Mere Christianity* (Macmillan).

Charles Habib Malik. *A Christian Critique of
the University* (IVP).

Francis Schaeffer. *The God Who Is There*
(IVP).

James W. Sire. *The Universe Next Door: A
Basic World View Catalog* (IVP).

John R. W. Stott. *Basic Christianity* (IVP).

——— . *Your Mind Matters* (IVP).

L. Duane Thurman. *How to Think About Evo-
lution and Other Bible-Science Controver-
sies* (IVP).

Mary Stewart Van Leeuwen. *The Person in
Psychology* (Eerdmans).

Brian J. Walsh and J. Richard Middleton. *The
Transforming Vision: Shaping a Christian
World View* (IVP).

Nicholas Wolterstorff. *Reason within the
Bounds of Religion* (Eerdmans).

——— . *Until Justice & Peace Embrace* (Eerdmans).

MAKING THE MOST OF RELIGION COURSES

John Duff

"What if Paul didn't actually write the letter to the Ephesians?" Mark asked. He was upset. "And what if the early church *did* make up the Gospel stories about Jesus?"

Mark, a guy I met to pray with regularly during my freshman year, was taking a course called Introduction to the New Testament. In it many of his beliefs about Jesus and the Bible were being questioned by highly trained scholars. Together we examined what he was learning, thought through our doubts and deepest convictions, and prayed. As a result of that course, we came to know God better and understand the Bible more fully.

Unfortunately, not all students who take religion courses come out with their faith strengthened—or even intact. Though college religion courses can be tremendous learning experiences, unprepared students may encounter pitfalls.

Pitfalls

Some students, for example, base their whole faith on a single doctrine that they've never carefully thought through—say, a certain view of the inspiration of Scripture. Such a student may be devastated when a professor argues that modern scholarship has made her "primitive notions" obsolete. With her single foundational belief gone, her whole understanding of Christianity may collapse. Three months later, when Christian friends begin to wonder why she doesn't come to fellowship meetings anymore, she's already put Christianity behind her.

Other students make religion courses heresy trials for their professors. Unfortunately, the guy who makes rebuttals and other zealous attempts to defend

And God said...

the gospel during lectures will only communicate to the professor and fellow students that he's narrow-minded and anti-intellectual.

Some Christian students avoid these pitfalls by avoiding religion courses altogether. But they rob themselves of the growth which comes through facing challenges, and they rob others of their insights into Scripture and faith.

Benefits

Religion courses can actually help you wrestle with false notions you have about the Bible. As Christians we know the Bible is our authority in questions of faith and practice. But do we know what the Bible says? Though we quote the Bible frequently, cultural factors (such as our economic status or ethnic heritage) can influence our doctrine as strongly as God's revelation does.

Even the apostle Peter found it hard to distinguish between biblical doctrine and cultural traditions. Peter's Scriptures often mentioned God's desire to bring blessing to the Gentiles. Yet this truth was hidden from him by mistaken assumptions inherited from his Jewish culture. It took a dramatic vision from God to open his eyes (see Acts 10).

Seeing biblical truths that have been hidden from us is not an easy experience. We buck against letting go of cherished ideas; and, in religion courses, we do face the danger of exchanging our own biases for those of the professor. But challenges to our beliefs can help us seek God's truth more clearly and begin to live it more fully.

By participating in religion courses, you can also become a more persuasive representative of orthodox Christianity. At one college, the deep suspicion between the campus fellowship group and the religion department faculty changed when a few students stopped waging theological warfare and began engaging in friendly dialogue. They learned to articulate their beliefs in a scholarly and informed manner. The faculty saw them honestly wrestling with tough issues and grew to respect their convictions.

Your personal faith and spiritual vitality may even encourage your professors in their faith. Professor Thomas Oden, long an innovative liberal theologian and spokesman, wrote a book defending the classical Christian tradition. Why? He writes in *Agenda for Theology*, "I have been astonished to discover that some of our best students, those who have grasped most deeply the hopes of modernity . . . those keenest, most perceptive students are the ones most insistent on letting the ancient tradition speak for itself. . . . Finally my students got through to me. They do not want to hear a watered-down modern reinterpretation. They want nothing less than the substance of the faith of the apostles and the martyrs."

Getting Ready

So how can you equip yourself for taking Survey of Biblical Literature or Introduction to the New Testament? Here are some practical suggestions on how to approach your courses:

1. Look for faulty presuppositions. At times your professor may seem to dismiss something you believe. But he will not always be right. Just because he says that Paul didn't write Ephesians or that Jesus didn't rise from the dead, that doesn't mean it is so. (On the other hand, don't assume that what every pastor or Christian leader says is always 100% accurate either.) Your professor may be mistaken, in spite of his intelligence and education, because he begins with a faulty presupposition that influences his conclusions.

For example, one common assumption today is that God does not actively control the course of nature or history. Because of this assumption, some scholars assert that divine intervention has no place in legitimate historical interpretations and that miracles are myth. It follows that they deny Jesus' resurrection and believe that the resurrection traditions developed over time as the early believers experienced a dynamic (but only human) new faith.

If, on the other hand, you start with the presupposition that God does take an active role in human affairs, it's reasonable to conclude that miracles do take place from time to time—and that a miraculous resurrection produced the

disciples' faith, rather than that their faith brought about the story of the resurrection.

2. Learn to use biblical criticism constructively. Biblical criticism is not the monster it is sometimes thought to be. "Criticism" is derived from a Greek word that simply means "a judgment." So a biblical "critic" in the broadest sense, as George Ladd writes in *The New Testament and Criticism,* is one "who makes intelligent judgments or decisions about questions associated with the books of the Bible."

Some biblical critics have done harm by approaching the Bible with the presupposition that God does not take the initiative to reveal truth to us—that is, that the entire Bible is man's word reaching out to God, rather than the other way around. Yet used with the right presuppositions, biblical criticism can help you better understand what the Bible is saying. You may be reading things into the Bible based on the unexamined impressions you've picked up from others; if so, the methods of biblical criticism you learn in class can help free you up to let the Bible speak for itself.

3. Be ready to learn new things. When religion courses challenge your faith, a closed mind is not a good defense. If the professor who is lecturing or the scholar who has written your text are wrong on some points, you can still learn from them. You should be ready to hear them out, even if it means sorting out truth from error.

My senior year I studied contemporary Third World theology with an African church leader and theologian. We strongly disagreed on certain issues. Yet God used that course to open up aspects of the Bible I had never seen before. In the process I gained real appreciation for the professor's own Christian commitment. I still believe he was overlooking some vital parts of the gospel, but he helped me see that I had been ignoring some too. I now have a much bigger picture of God and his purposes for creation.

4. Meet with God outside of class. Religion courses can't substitute for prayer and personal Bible study. In fact, studying God in a clinical classroom setting sometimes makes him seem more distant. When a friend of mine was studying theology at Cambridge University, he often didn't feel like praying in the evening with his wife. He was simply tired of thinking about God all day. You may sometimes feel the same way. To resist the danger of growing distant from God, commit yourself to spend time in fellowship with Christ as your own Lord and friend.

You might want to change the style of your personal devotions. If you look at Jesus critically in class, a rigorous inductive Bible study may be the last thing you need when you meet with God alone. Try finding things to do that will lead you into deep worship and enjoyment of God's presence. Sing songs of praise. Meditate on the psalms and what they mean to you personally so you can focus on the Father's relationship with you. Read Christian classics such as C. S. Lewis's *Chronicles of Narnia* to hear familiar truths in a fresh way.

You may also need to wrestle with God about the questions your course raises. If your studies cast doubt on some of your beliefs, don't run and hide from God while you figure it all out. Run to God with your questions instead. Yell at him for being so confusing. Confess your doubts. He can take it. And you'll discover security in his arms as your mind is being stretched.

5. Remain active in Christian community. Students who tackle religion courses have a special need to remember the exhortation of Hebrews 10:24-25: "Let us consider how we may spur one another on toward love and good deeds. Let us not give up the habit of meeting together, as some are in the habit of doing, but let us encourage one another—and all the more as you see the Day approaching."

You may be tempted to do just the opposite. If you find yourself questioning some of the beliefs shared by your church or campus fellowship group, you may want to withdraw because you feel hypocritical and fear that others would be shocked if they knew what you were thinking.

But isolating yourself is a huge mistake. God can seem very dead if you only meet him in the classroom. Instead, share your questions with faithful and understanding members of your church or fellowship. Have them pray for you and support you as you seek truth. And as you participate in the ministry of a Christian community, watch how God powerfully works through you and in the lives of other people. That experience of God's activity is an important counterbalance to the intellectual exercises of your religion courses.

6. Seek other resources that can help you sort through the issues. Don't expect to come up with satisfactory answers all by yourself. You are no match for a professor who has studied these matters for many years. You need help from Christians who can offer thoughtful, alternative perspectives.

Christian students and faculty on your own campus may have studied the questions before. Ask if they can meet with you to help you interpret the course material. For example, by the time I took Introduction to the New Testament myself two years later, Mark had become quite well informed. He was able to organize an informal study group for Christian students in the course.

There are also many books by evangelical scholars. Ask your pastor or another teacher for their recommendations. *The New Testament and Criticism* by George E. Ladd (Eerdmans) and *History, Criticism and Faith* edited by Colin Brown (IVP) are two of the best sources for understanding how to use the tools of modern scholarship constructively. As you are exposed to the claims of other world religions, you may want to read *The Universe Next Door* by James W. Sire (IVP) and *Christianity and World Religions* by Norman Anderson (IVP). Other helpful books include *"Fundamentalism" and the Word of God* by J. I. Packer (Eerdmans) and *The New Testament Documents: Are They Reliable?* by F. F. Bruce (IVP).

7. Be willing to leave some questions unanswered. Even the apostle Paul knew that some things were simply beyond his understanding. He struggled for three chapters in Romans with a question that troubled him deeply (the rejection by Israel of Jesus as the Messiah). Yet he concluded by reminding himself that God's truth is not always accessible to human investigation: "Oh, the depth of the riches of the wisdom and knowledge of God! How unsearchable his judgments, and his paths beyond tracing out! 'Who has known the mind of the Lord? Or who has been his counselor?' " (Romans 11:33-34).

Many times I have finished a course in biblical studies with questions unanswered. My former understanding of Scripture proved inadequate on some points; yet I wasn't convinced by the professor's interpretation either. When that happened, I reminded myself that I am seeking truth—not merely trying to prove a point or build an invulnerable fortress of theology. If God has not chosen to reveal himself fully on an issue, I can be content with incomplete knowledge.

I found Paul's perspective on the Christian life very helpful: "Brothers, I do not consider myself yet to have taken hold of it. But one thing I do: Forgetting what is behind and straining toward what is ahead, I press on toward the goal to win the prize for which God has called me heavenward in Christ Jesus. . . . Only let us live up to what we have already attained" (Phil 3:13-14, 16). Paul knew that he had not yet arrived—either in his knowledge or in his life. So he pressed on while remaining faithful to the truth he already knew.

The religion courses you take can be

the means God uses to teach you about himself. When questions raised in class make you feel uncertain about faith issues, remember that in Jesus Christ you have beheld God's glory. Remember that you have become his child and been given the power to share the joy of doing his work in the world. Hold on to these basic truths even as you strive to know more fully what they mean.

Campus Living

Going to college means learning, making friends, asserting your independence—and taking on new responsibilities. Sometimes keeping up with all the nitty-gritty details—managing your time, budgeting your money, securing financial aid for the coming year, finding the right place to live—can take up more energy than studying. In the following section you'll find practical help on how to tie up these loose ends. Learning such "life management skills" now will help you survive not only the next few years, but life on your own after graduation.

MANAGING YOUR TIME

Everyone wants a chunk of your time—professors, family, friends, campus fellowship, church, clubs. In the following pages Alice Fryling talks about the importance of setting priorities; Alan Lakein explains time-planning strategies; and Merrill and Donna Douglass share their secrets on how to use a calendar.

Setting Priorities (by Alice Fryling)
Success had crowned our freshman picnic—more than sixty new students had expressed interest in the campus fellowship. This excited everyone but me. As I drove back to the dorm with my staff worker, I burst into tears. "That's sixty more students to look up, make friends with and who-knows-how-many to meet with. Half of them will fade away anyway!"

My pessimism betrayed my disease—I felt responsible for every activity our campus fellowship endorsed. Reminders to look up students peppered the mirror above my dresser. I crafted my days to squeeze the most out of every hour. I "relaxed" by eating butterscotch sundaes while I studied.

Beating Burnout
Pressure mounts within us to respond to ever-increasing opportunities to serve, learn, give and enjoy. For Christians, this takes on spiritual overtones as we struggle with whether these are actually God's will for us. For many, saying no may be a more difficult act of obedience than saying yes.

I usually got caught in the bless-this-mess cycle: I saw a need or I had an idea, or someone tapped me for a project. Without carefully evaluating the request for my time, I would say yes because I liked to help people. Then when the going got tough, I'd ask God to bless me anyhow. "Please help me make it," went my prayer, "and take care of my health, my studies and my spiritual life so that I can make it through this crisis."

Frequently my crisis arose because I failed to acknowledge that in saying yes to one activity, I was saying no to another. I simply could not do two things at once.

This may sound like simple mathematics. But consider the following example. When I said yes to leading a Bible study, I found out that the study would take an hour to prepare and an hour to present. And if I wanted to develop friendships with people in the study, it would take another two or three hours a week. Finally, the emotional and spiritual drain would require an hour or two of rest. So saying yes to an hour-long Bible study once a week actually meant committing myself to at least six hours.

I slowly learned that when I did say yes to leading a Bible study, I would have to say no to other things such as planning a social event, taking a part-time job or adding an extra class. Some semesters I decided not to lead a study so that I could give my time to something else. Eventually I realized that when I had to decide whether to say yes to an opportunity, the primary issue was not whether I "should" do something or even whether I was gifted to do it, but whether it was the best thing for me to do at that time.

Sometimes this led me to some painful decisions. For instance, after a particularly chaotic and draining set of circumstances I had to let go of the high value I placed on being completely available to friends. I found that when I tried to befriend too many people at once I ended up physically and emotionally exhausted and unable to support them adequately.

It became very important to me not to expend my energies on things that God had not called me to do. So much has been written about how to know what the will of God is. Perhaps more should be said about how to know what the will of God is *not*. I found that the most effective way to know whether to say yes or no was to spend daily time with God. Because I tend to take on too much, I desperately need for God to confront my agenda through Scripture and prayer. And in those quiet moments before him, when my eyes are off me, I can ask if my life exhibits the warning signs that I'm in over my head:

☐ Is my inner life seldom joyful, peaceful or ordered?

☐ Are those close to me frequently lonely, discouraged or disappointed because I'm not available?

☐ Do I feel overwhelmed emotionally or experience signs of stress (stomach tightening, extreme fatigue, headaches) when I consider a new activity?

☐ Am I too busy to pray about an activity?

☐ Is my schedule so tight that I can't handle an occasional interruption or emergency?

If I can answer yes to any of these questions, I ask God if he is using my emotional and physical fatigue to redirect my life and goals. He may not only want to free my weary spirit and body from the plague of doing too much, but to have me evaluate my priorities and how they are affecting my schedule.

What Is Most Important to Me?

I used to wonder how some students seemed to manage their time so well. Eventually I realized that all of us have different ideas of what is worth spending time on, and that we consciously or subconsciously base our time management choices on these ideas or values.

To manage our time more effectively, we need to identify these values—the values we actually live by, that is—and then decide whether we want to continue living by them or whether we want to change them.

Try this exercise that helped me: On a piece of paper list the values that affect your lifestyle the most. Your list might include excelling in school, being liked by others, finding a spouse, being with family, having a well-paying job, serving others, getting involved in church or in your campus fellowship group, keeping your body in shape or whatever.

Remember that not all values will be healthy. If you're honest with yourself, you may discover, for instance, that you avoid taking risks because you're afraid of making a mistake. Or that you devote nearly all your time to helping others and virtually no time to caring for your own needs. Include these values on your list as well.

After listing your values, choose your top ten in order of importance and ask yourself the following questions about each:

☐ Where did this value come from? Par-

ents, friends, professors, books, church, television?

☐ Do I like this value?

☐ Do I actually live as if this value were true? Does it have an effect on my everyday living patterns? Why or why not?

☐ Do I really believe in this value, or do I merely feel that I'm *supposed* to believe it? Does it truly fit with my understanding of the world and of God's will for me?

☐ Do I believe in this value strongly enough to adopt it as a guiding force in my life?

Once you ask these questions, narrow your list down to five or six top values. Now, as you make decisions about how to spend your time—studies, extracurricular activities, friends, social life, whatever—consult your list. My list has often helped me keep priorities in perspective.

Making Plans (by Alan Lakein)

For some students, however, a handy-dandy values list alone doesn't solve anything. This list, posted above a desk or mirror, serves only as a convenient guilt trip. "If only I *could* do what I really *want* to do. If only I were in control!"

Control starts with planning—bringing the future into the present so that you can do something about it now. So after we have discovered our priorities and values, we need to learn the art of planning.

Everyone makes plans: what movie to see tomorrow night, which friends to visit next weekend, where to vacation next summer. But most people plan rather haphazardly—and only when they feel forced to. Perhaps you feel overwhelmed by the work you have to do and this forces you to plan your day. Or you have a large vacation break and you want to use it in a satisfying way. This kind of occasional, special-purpose planning is a valuable tool, but if you *only* plan this way you run the risk of not planning day-to-day, when you need to the most.

Planning and making choices are often hard work. They involve careful thinking and force you to recognize what criteria you use in setting priorities.

In all planning, you need to (1) make a list of your activities, and (2) prioritize these activities. All the items on a list are not of equal value. Once you have made a list, set priorities based on the values you have determined are important to you. No list is complete until it shows priorities.

To prioritize these activities, use the ABC Priority System: Write a capital letter "A" to the left of those items on the list that have a high value; a "B" for those with medium value; and a "C" for those with low value. You will get the most out of your time by doing the A's first, and saving the B's and C's for later.

As you rate your activities, you know that to some extent you're guessing. You're not sure you'll be right on the value. But comparing the items to one another will help you come up with the ABC priority choices for every entry on the list.

Your rating should also affect the amount of time you decide to invest in a project or activity. For example, you could probably satisfy your professor

with about two hours' work on the report she assigned (you give it "C" priority), impress her with about four hours (now it's a "B"), and get a top grade if you did extra research and devoted ten hours to the paper (you've made it an "A"). Only you can decide whether this paper is of a high enough value (relative to your other time demands) to spend a great deal of effort on it.

Finally, remember that ABC's are relative, depending on your point of view. As you and your circumstances change, so will your priorities. For example, a task might be an A-priority while you're thinking of all the rewards that come when it is done. But halfway through, when the going gets rough and the time it takes to accomplish that priority is higher than you feel able to pay, you may put it aside.

Today's A becomes tomorrow's B, while today's C becomes tomorrow's A. You need to set priorities continually, considering the best use of your time right now.

Using a Calendar (by Merrill and Donna Douglass*)

Mapping out your activities (with their appropriate ABC's!) is crucial to making sure they happen. Don't underestimate the importance of keeping a detailed calendar.

Buy a pocket calendar with enough space for you to write out your obligations for each day. At the start of each semester or quarter, enter the dates of your tests, papers, conferences, major meetings and so on. Then back up and plan the steps along the way—when to begin studying for a midterm, when to have a final outline. Set deadlines for yourself. Every night review the schedule for the next day and add routine tasks in specific time slots.

Make minor decisions quickly, but guard against unprofitable routines or activities that might crowd into your schedule. Periodically ask yourself: Does this calendar reflect the priorities I've set?

Tracking Your Time
Along with a calendar of what you plan to do, you might try keeping a daily time log of what you actually get done. Even logging a week's activities can help you discover inconsistencies.

Treat your time log like an abbreviated diary and record what you do, when you do it and how long it takes. Begin your record in the morning and carry it with you all day. Rather than trying to record every little thing, concentrate on the most important activities. Resist the tendency to generalize or make yourself look good.

At the end of each day, look over the log and ask yourself:
☐ What went right today? Why?
☐ What went wrong today? Why?
☐ What time did I start on my top-priority task? Why? Could I have started earlier?

☐ What patterns and habits are apparent from my time log?
☐ What were the most and least productive parts of my day? Why?
☐ Who or what accounted for most of my interruptions? How can these interruptions be controlled, reduced or eliminated?
☐ What did I do today that I wished I hadn't?
☐ What took longer than it should have? What can I do about it?
☐ What activities needed more time today?
☐ Beginning tomorrow, what will I do to make better use of my time?

After you have kept track of your time for a week or two, you may feel that you know enough to more accurately plan your time. But you may also find that it is a valuable exercise that you want to continue. If asking all these hard questions about how you manage your time reveals something about *you*—your desires, strengths and weaknesses—then you're on your way to getting control of your schedule. After all, our problem is never really managing our time, but managing ourselves.

*This section was adapted from *Manage Your Time, Manage Your Work, Manage Yourself* by Merrill E. Douglass and Donna N. Douglass (New York: AMACOM, 1980), pp. 58-61.

SETTING CHRISTIAN PRIORITIES

Rich Lamb

When I came to college I joined the marching band. I had enjoyed playing trumpet in my high-school band and wanted to continue playing. Unfortunately, there were few Christians in the band, which had a national reputation for demonstrating on TV its commitment to "Sex, Drugs and Rock 'n' Roll." While I could have approached the band as a mission field, I did not. I had neither the social skills nor the desire to make friends for the sake of the gospel. My involvement simply kept me from going to Christian fellowship meetings and some important conferences which could have helped me be a witness in the band. At the end of the first quarter I ended my musical career.

Two years later I had a different kind of experience with an extracurricular activity. I was given an opportunity to become a teaching assistant for a computer programming course. I discussed with my campus fellowship staff worker how being a teaching assistant would take time out of my schedule, making me less available. I eventually accepted the position, but decided to decrease my course load and stay active in Christian fellowship. During the following year I had many opportunities to serve students by being available late at night for help on their assignments. Students often asked about my involvement in the campus fellowship or about my plans to go on InterVarsity staff. I could talk quite naturally about the importance of following Jesus.

Well-Rounded or Fanatical?

People come to college with a wide variety of goals because the college environment offers a mind-boggling variety of pursuits. Academic, social, athletic, spiritual, pre-professional and romantic opportunities are all woven into the fabric of university life. Many universities and colleges state as one of their goals that their students become "well-rounded" individuals.

Jesus, however, was not a well-rounded individual. He was a radical. He was single-focused, narrow—a fanatic. And he called his disciples to be like him: "For whoever wants to save his life will lose it, but whoever loses his life for me and for the gospel will save it" (Mk 8:35). Jesus taught his disciples for three years—a college training which included inductive teaching, parables, meals together in intimate gatherings and huge crowds, miraculous healings and fieldwork. Jesus exposed his students to many different experiences, but not to produce well-rounded individuals. He spoke about and modeled a life which was sold out to one pursuit: giving up life for the sake of the gospel.

When Jesus asks us to give him our life, there's nothing left over to give to anything else. It is impossible to follow Jesus the way he talks about it and live what many call a "balanced" life. Following Jesus costs our life—all of our time, energy, money, future dreams and pride.

Living with Priorities

Every pursuit promises a reward. Academic achievement promises success. A romantic relationship promises intimacy and security. Activities, societies, fraternities and sororities promise friendship and belonging. All of these promise a slice of life. Jesus doesn't ask us to give up our lives for the sake of losing them. Rather he promises that if we lose our lives for his sake, we will gain life itself.

My experience as a band member and my experience as a teaching assistant were completely different. When I joined the band, I had not aligned my-self with other Christians on campus. I wasn't able to attend fellowship meetings because of band practice. Even if I had made friends in the band, I had nothing to invite them to which would have introduced them to Jesus and his people. I also lacked the social skills to befriend and serve people. By the time I was a teaching assistant, I had totally thrown myself into my fellowship group, and my life and schedule reflected that. I had learned social skills and enough about a servant attitude to see my extracurricular activity as a minis-try.

The principle here is not that extracurricular activities apart from those centered around Christian fellowship are bad, *but that bad priorities can draw us into trivial pursuits.*

At school I realized I needed to identify with the body of Christ. When I accepted the fact that during my freshman year I was too busy to meet with other Christians several hours a week for prayer and Bible study, I knew I had to eliminate some of the trivial pursuits from my schedule.

But I did not eliminate all extracurricular activities. I knew Jesus calls us to minister to and to serve others. Thus outside activities became a means of not only having fun but of having significant interactions and relationships with non-Christians.

God may lead you out of some activities only to lead you back to them later with a new vision. My brother, Dave, came to Stanford with his best friend from high school, Eric. They spent much time together freshman year and rushed the same fraternity that spring. After discussions with other Christians, Dave decided not to join. He realized it would be too difficult to be a committed member of both the fellowship and the fraternity. Eric, who wasn't a Christian, joined the fraternity.

At the end of Dave's sophomore year, he sought counsel from mature Christians about joining that fraternity and decided to rush again. He was accepted. Dave told the brothers that though he wanted to be an involved member of the fraternity, the fellowship group was his first priority. For example, he told them that he would have to miss "work week" to get the house in shape before school began in the fall because of the fellowship's conference schedule. The brothers understood. Dave wanted to be a friend to Eric and a witness in the fraternity, but he had identified himself first as a follower of Jesus, not as a Phi Delta Theta. Waiting a year before joining had given him tools that helped him serve the brothers without compromising.

The Consequences of Priorities

Setting aside time to meet with Christians and to care about those around you may cost a lot. If you're striving for A's, you might have to settle for a B. If you're shy, you may have to learn how to socialize in order to establish new relationships. If your focus is the social scene, perhaps you'll have to go to fewer parties or go on fewer dates.

Following Jesus may also cost money, especially when summer rolls around. Giving to other students going on missions projects or going yourself and setting aside a chance for summer income or work experience may be a cost of following Jesus. During the school year, cutting hours from your part-time job might make more time for seeking God and serving others; on the other hand, following Jesus might involve taking on a part-time job so you'll have your own money to give away.

Paul, like Jesus, was not a well-rounded person. As he talks about his own ministry, he tells the people of Corinth: "Do you not know that in a race all the runners run, but only one gets the prize? Run in such a way as to get the prize. Everyone who competes in the games goes into strict training. They do it to get a crown that will not last; but we do it to get a crown that will last forever" (1 Cor 9:24-25).

We run the race to receive the imperishable wreath, to gain eternal life. But we can forget we are running a race at all when there's so much activity on the sidelines. We must, with Paul, press on toward the goal. The only rule is that we lose our lives for Christ's sake. No other cause is worth our life. As martyr Jim Elliot wrote before his death: "He is no fool who gives what he cannot keep to gain what he cannot lose." Freed from the pursuit of trivialities, we can run the straight course for the true crown.

Sunday: This Day's for You

What does Scripture have to say about your busy college schedule? Basically this: You need a day of rest.

God—who created time, after all—knows that taking time off is good time management. If eighteen semester hours, leading a Bible study, holding a part-time job and getting involved in student government have left you feeling hassled, harried and less than productive, setting Sunday aside can revolutionize your schedule.

The fourth commandment urges us to cease all work on the Sabbath. And even though Christ fulfills the Sabbath (Col 2:17), the idea of a day of rest is never rejected in the New Testament. Jesus observed it, although not legalistically like the Pharisees. Common sense confirms that the Bible is right. Not having regular time off is exhausting.

Unfortunately, as a college student, you're going to face pressure to work all the time. I recently urged a student group not to study on Sunday so they could have a day of rest. One student told me that would be impossible because she was "committed to academic excellence." Our culture values success above all other things, but the price of success is high. As a Christian, you need to ask, "Will I do what Scripture says or what my culture says?"

If that sounds too black-and-white to you, remember that this pattern of regular worship and rest is not a legal requirement. God doesn't want his people gritting their teeth, going to church and spending the rest of Sunday moping in their rooms, anxious about all the homework they have to do. That misses the whole point: God wants you to have a good time! He wants you to take a special day out weekly to enjoy him and his creation.

Having the Time of Your Life

Another issue involved in God's commandment to rest is the sacredness of your time. Every moment of life is holy, set apart for God. Time is God's gift, given so his creatures may glorify him (see 1 Cor 10:31). Work, play and study can all be spiritual activities, given over to praising the Lord. When Christians commit themselves this way, their lives take on the quality of holiness.

But just as the 4.0 pre-med student shows by his lifestyle that he has consecrated himself to his grades and his career, Christians also show their commitments by the way they live.

On campus you have the opportunity to consecrate yourself to God by establishing a rhythm of worship in your life that you can carry with you after graduation. Many Christian students take time to meet with God daily, even though the Bible never says, "Thou shalt have Bible reading and prayer every morning for thirty minutes." They simply want to commit themselves to God on a daily basis. If you've tried it, you know that it strengthens you and gives a sense of wholeness to your day.

Consider this: the way you spend your time on campus influences your thinking as much or more than anything else. The rhythm of a life rules a life.

Getting Started

Sunday can be a day of light that illumines the entire week. As I've wrestled with taking the time I need for God and myself, I've come up with a few suggestions for Sundays that helped me steady my life rhythm. Maybe they'll help you too.

Don't crack the books. Perhaps the most effective thing you can do is to arrange not to study on Sunday. That doesn't mean you need to take a blood oath never to study on Sunday again. It just means planning so that normal circumstances do not necessitate it. It may mean studying on Saturday instead of putting everything off until Sunday.

I practiced this habit while in seminary. There were only two occasions in three years when I failed to follow through—both times because of final exams which demanded extra attention. It feels fantastic to wake up Sunday morning and say, "It's the Lord's Day—I don't have to study today!"

Hang out at church. Setting Sunday aside will free you up to worship by clearing your mind of other responsibilities. If you rush to church to get something out of the sermon and then rush out to the library before the last hymn is over, worship won't happen. Neither will some important relationships. Spend time getting to know your fellow parishioners, even if they're not part of the campus community. Your life will be enriched by interacting with people who are different than your peers.

Exercise. God wants us to take care of the bodies he's given us, and Sunday can be a great time to stretch out the muscles you haven't used all week. One word of caution: you might want to avoid activities that are too strenuous. If Sunday is so tiring that Monday finds you useless, you've missed the point.

Reach out. Sunday can also be a day for reaching out to others. The apostle James defines true religion as visiting the downtrodden in their distress (see 1:27). Maybe you don't know anyone who is sick, lonely or in prison. But if you hang around a local church for a while, you will meet them. And you can minister to them just by going to their house or hospital room for half an hour.

Practice the presence of God. Meditate on his presence in your life. And pray that God will cause the richness of that presence to overflow into the other days of the week.
—*Vance Hays*

PAYING GOD, CAESAR AND THE RENT

Linda Doll and Benny Walker

Payday. That marvelous time when you briefly get a feeling of great wealth.

Well, lie down till the feeling passes. There are probably more than enough bills and needed items to gobble up your whole paycheck. If you're not careful, it'll be instant poverty within twenty-four hours.

When you begin earning a regular income either with a part-time job at college or at a summer job, the inevitable question arises: What should I do with the money that God has entrusted to me?

In order to handle your money responsibly, you need a budget—a plan for realistic spending that will free you from guilt and worry. And learning to manage your small salary or part-time paycheck now will enable you to live responsibly when you're making more later on.

Here's a sensible plan for giving, saving and spending which begins with a basic teaching of Jesus: "Give to Caesar what is Caesar's and to God what is God's" (Mt 22:21).

Cutting the Pie

First of all, pay Caesar (that is, the government). Often you will have no choice; taxes are usually deducted from your paycheck before you ever see it. While a Christian has every right—and as a steward of God's money, a responsibility—to take all legitimate deductions, we must pay taxes to whom they are due. (Some Christians, as a matter of conscience, do decide to withhold all or some taxes to protest certain government policies, such as funding nuclear arms or abortions. They're also prepared to go to jail for it.)

Second, give to God what belongs to God: "Honor the Lord with your wealth, with the firstfruits of all your crops" (Prov 3:9). Why firstfruits? Because how and what we give reflects our values.

Immediately setting aside a segment of your income to give to God will help you put him first. Don't be like little Janie, whose mother gave her one quarter for the Sunday-school offering and another for ice cream on the way home. As one of the coins fell and rolled into the sidewalk grate, Janie exclaimed, "Oh no! There goes God's quarter!"

The longer you wait, the more likely you'll be to put your offerings toward textbooks or a pizza—"just this once."

You can give your money to a local church, missions board or other Christian organization, or to people you know with legitimate needs. (There are more worthwhile ministries than you can possibly support. It's better to regularly support a few people or organizations and to persistently pray for and interact with them, than to send a little money to more people than you can pray for.)

What about the spending money your folks have given you—should you be giving out of that portion, too? That depends on your parents. If you are still financially dependent on them, you are part of their household—and subject to playing by some of their rules, especially when it concerns *their* money.

Discuss your desire to give to God's work with them as openly as you can. They may be delighted that you want to share your spending money with others in need (as long as your own needs are being met, of course). Or they might intend only to give you as much as you need at school to survive and balk at the idea of you giving money away, even if you are willing to give sacrificially. Honor their wishes—but feel free to spend the money you earn on your time as God directs you. One friend of mine whose wealthy father, a non-Christian, forbade him to give any of his generous allowance to the church, typed papers to earn some cash he could give away.

Beyond Tithing

Tithing (giving away 10% of one's gross income) is a commonly cited biblical guideline. But be warned: ritualistically tithing your income may actually lure you into the trap of keeping 90% of what God gives you and being proud of it—regardless of how high your income is. Paul exhorts the Corinthians to give bountifully, "for God loves a cheerful giver" (2 Cor 9:7). The Greek word for *cheerful* is the root for the English word *hilarious.* So in a sense, Paul urges us to give "hilariously," with abandon. The Gospels portray several individuals who gave this way: Zacchaeus giving half his wealth to the poor; the widow casting all she had into the treasury.

One helpful principle for giving generously is the "graduated tithe." Without asking you to starve, this realistic principle lets you keep much of your surplus income while sharing some of it. It works by first figuring out how much you need to cover just your basic expenses. The idea is, you give 10% of your basic amount. Then, for each thousand you earn over that, you give an extra 5%. This means giving 15% of the next thousand, 20% of the next, and so on. Remember, you could survive without any of that surplus—but you're getting to keep most of it.

10-70-20

Now that you've paid God and country, figure out your remaining monthly total. Then set aside 10% of that amount for savings. "Pay yourself first" is not necessarily selfishness; it can be a principle to help you spend money more wisely. Think of saving as a balancing of present and future needs. By saving, you prepare for future purchases and thus avoid paying huge amounts of interest on loans

you'd have to take out later. In fact, you actually earn interest by letting your money earn more money for you.

Use the next 20% as a "cushion" to go toward large purchases, to cover unexpected costs such as a dead car battery and to pile up savings to help you avoid needing loans in the future. List the items that you expect to cover from this fund (you may want to have a separate bank account for it). Be realistic. Just a few large items can wipe out your whole account.

The remaining 70% in the formula goes for living expenses: rent, utilities, phone, food, debts, clothes, car, insurance, furniture, books, magazines, newspapers, educational costs, gifts, entertainment and so on. Write down a monthly amount for each expense. (Divide quarterly and annual expenses to arrive at a monthly amount to be budgeted.) Your monthly budget might look something like this:

Budget Guide
Month/year: _____

Income
Parents   _____
Savings   _____
Job (after taxes, tithing & saving) _____
Financial Aid   _____
Other _____   _____

Total   _____

Expenses
Tuition   _____
Fees   _____

Books and Supplies _____
Rent _____
Utilities (if off-campus) _____
Phone _____
Meals _____
Entertainment _____
Medical _____
Clothes/laundry _____
Travel _____
Auto maintenance _____
Insurance (prorated) _____
Other:

_____ _____
_____ _____
_____ _____
_____ _____
_____ _____

Total _____

If you receive money weekly, once a term or irregularly, you can still make a monthly budget (since that's when most bills come) and pay certain expenses out of each check you receive. If you overspend in one area in a certain month, be sure that you have some extra money in another category which can cover it, or else make plans to under-spend somewhere next month to make up the deficit.

Choosing a Lifestyle

Determine to live within your income, even if it involves some changes in lifestyle. In the words of Hebrews 13:5, "Keep your lives free from the love of money and be content with what you have." Paul put it this way: "I know what it is to be in need, and I know what it is

to have plenty. I have learned the secret of being content in any and every situation, whether well fed or hungry, whether living in plenty or in want" (Phil 4:12). Paul was content in plenty, not concerned about making more, more, more. You can deliberately buck the system too by deliberately choosing to live with less, which frees you up to give more.

But how do you do that?

Should you buy all generic brands of food and wear the tackiest clothes you can scrounge up from the local Goodwill or Salvation Army store? Not necessarily. Adopting a simpler lifestyle doesn't mean embracing a new legalism which says the measure of your spirituality is inversely proportional to the amount of money you spend. And it doesn't mean being miserly. Both of those approaches will stifle and enslave you.

Living with less means adopting a right attitude toward possessions and the job market. It involves resisting the temptation to define yourself by your car or the animal on your shirt, rather than as a follower of Christ.

Adjusting your lifestyle to reflect this attitude takes work. Instead of impulsively buying the latest personal computer (everybody else in the dorm has one!), you'll have to think about it. Is this a wise investment, or do you just want to be the first kid on the block with a computer that will accurately predict the future and start the coffee in the morning?

Living with less doesn't necessarily mean buying the cheapest goods. The cheapest shoes you can buy may only cost $10.99, but if they raise blisters on your feet and fall apart after a month, paying a little more would have been a better investment. Of course, that's no excuse to buy only the top brands. The best return on your dollar will often be a moderately priced yet reliable product.

Face it: a simple lifestyle isn't so simple. It takes time to make a mouth-watering meal of soybeans or lentils. And it takes time to sew together a new outfit, particularly if you're the type who throws away your jacket when a button comes off.

Cost-Cutting Tips

So what are some practical ways you can cut costs on campus?

As you plan your budget for the academic year, consider the two types of expenses you will encounter. Fixed expenses, such as tuition and fees, will not vary. Other expenses, such as room and board, transportation, books and supplies, and most importantly, personal expenses, you can control. Consider the following ways of doing more with less.

Housing. When selecting your housing, you should consider all the options available. Dormitories have varying rates. Linens may or may not be furnished. If you're living off-campus, utilities may or may not be included in your rent. If you choose to live off campus, try to find one or more roommates to share your house or apartment expenses. The university housing office can assist you in locating a room, an apartment or a roommate.

Food. Seven-day meal plans are availa- ble, but five-day meal plans and flexible ten-meal plans usually are too. (In my experience, the latter two save you money and allow you to eat out with friends occasionally without wasting money on prepaid meals you don't eat.) Check out the Greeks. Do any sorority or fraternity houses have meal plans you can get in on? You can save money by preparing your own meals, especially if you shop for bargains; but be aware that cooking and smart shopping will take time away from studies and social life.

Books. Books represent one of the most rapidly increasing educational costs. You can help offset these costs by taking advantage of student-sponsored book fairs or the used books section of the school bookstore. Don't be afraid to ask if softback editions of some expensive texts are available. Also, watch for opportunities in your school newspaper and bulletin boards to sell your old books; they may represent an unexpected source of income.

Personal expenses. Personal expenses are the most easily controlled part of your budget. When dating or going out with friends, for example, try campus-sponsored events (they're cheaper, and may even have some redeeming social value). Instead of getting a crowd together to go to the movies, split the cost of renting a VCR and some videos. Considering buying a stereo system? Perhaps you can get by with a radio—or moving in with some folks who are willing to share their sound system. Forsake the trendy salons just once and try getting your hair cut or permed at a beauty school in town; for a drastically reduced price, you can get your hair cut by someone who desperately aims to please and is being closely supervised.

Transportation. If you live on or near campus, a decent bicycle may be the best investment you ever made. If you're going to a large university, convenient public transportation may be available at low or no cost. Evaluate carefully whether you *need* a car at school; car maintenance at college can involve major time and money commitments (gas, oil, tires, insurance premiums, tune-ups, repairs, parking permits). If you commute, try car pooling. There is probably an office on your campus that can help you join or start a car pool. Minimize weekend trips back home. If you must fly, plan at least a month ahead to take advantage of super-saver rates. A good travel agent can save you hassles as well as money.

You'll find that these suggestions, coupled with the 10-20-70 plan will protect you from continually upping your tastes after college—and help you experience the joy of being in control of your finances and sharing more now.

—Some material in this article was adapted from Doing More with Less *by Benny Walker et al. (Southern Association of Student Financial Aid Administrators)—available at no cost through the Financial Aid Office of Furman University, Greenville, South Carolina 29613 or through your local financial aid director—and* How to Give Away Your Money *by Simon Webley (IVP).*

Your First Checking Account

You'll probably want to open a checking account at college. Even though you don't have a lot of bills to pay monthly, checks are easier to use than cash: they provide a record of where your money's going and prevent you from getting caught empty-pocketed. Besides, most bookstores, restaurants, clothes stores and other merchants near campus take checks if you have a student I.D.

To decide where to open an account, call several local banks ahead of time. Ask the customer service rep: "Do you offer a checking account which pays interest on all the money I have deposited, doesn't require that I keep a minimum balance, and costs me nothing except the price of a book of checks?" (Depending on where you live, you probably won't find a bank that meets all three criteria, but some will come closer than others.) Visit the two or three banks that look most promising. Which is most conveniently located? Which offers electronic tellers that dispense cash twenty-four hours a day? Which offers efficient and courteous service? Open your account there.

Keeping a checkbook is simple if you don't let it get away from you. Every time you write a check, immediately record the amount, date, check number and to whom it went. Ditto for electronic withdrawals. Subtract. Similarly, immediately record every deposit, as well as any interest reported on the monthly bank statement you receive. Add. Don't set yourself up for unpleasant surprises by forgetting to record a withdrawal. Banks commonly charge $15 for a single returned check—and when you've gone below zero, more than one check can bounce on the same day. (*Always* keep a cushion of $20 to $50 in your account, to offset check charges, returned check charges or service fees for letting your balance fall below their minimum balance requirement.)

When you receive your bank statement, note in your ledger each check that's come in, making sure that you recorded the amount of the check correctly. Adjust your current balance to compensate for any errors made along the way in your ledger. Then see whether the bank's total (*minus* any checks you've written that haven't yet reached the bank and *plus* any deposits you've made that aren't yet posted on your statement) matches your total balance. If not, check your ledger's addition and subtraction over the past month or so. Still confused? Go back to that nice customer service rep. He or she can detect a bank error or help you see what you're doing wrong.
—*Linda Doll*

The Fantastic Plastic Trap

One day during my junior year I found a letter from a major department store in my mailbox. It began something like this: "You have been selected to receive our charge card because we believe that you possess the characteristics of industry and responsibility we look for in our customers."

I was touched. This company wanted to offer *me*, a lowly student, a charge card! Didn't they know that my only assets were a wonderful disposition and a nearly completed education?

You can bet I accepted their offer.

I remember the first time I used that card. I entered the clothing department and felt like a man who had been in the desert without food or water for days. But the mirage I saw was big bucks—bucks to buy all the Polo sportswear I wanted.

My total charges on that first spree? $293.67. I left the store, drove home in my borrowed car and promptly burst into tears. *What am I going to do?* I thought, panic-stricken. I couldn't borrow from my parents—they were barely making ends meet themselves. I could take the clothes back— but I didn't want to admit to the salesman who so cheerily waited on me that I had used bad judgment.

I decided to keep the clothes and pray to God, the Eternal Banker, to send some monetary gift my way. He didn't. In the end I worked extra hours at my college job to pay the bill. My studies suffered.

Before you graduate, you'll probably be invited to enter the world of revolving credit by stores, banks and gasoline companies for the first time. And if you haven't had a lot of money, or if Mom and Dad have paid your college bills and sent you spending money, be prepared for a jolt if you say yes.

"Neither a borrower nor a lender be," Shakespeare wrote. But he never had to buy a car to get to his first job. Is his advice realistic in today's economy? How should a Christian approach the world of credit?

Christians wrestling with credit are really wrestling with two key spiritual issues: greed and priorities. Let's take a look at each.

Greed

As Christians, we struggle to reconcile some of our material wants with Jesus' commands to give generously. That chasm between what we want and what God wants for us can grow even wider when we're using credit to spend more money than we have.

"The love of money is a root of all kinds of evil," the apostle Paul wrote (1 Tim 6:7-10). Credit, I think, is the root of kinds of evil Paul could not have foreseen. Money is power—power to do good or evil. Credit is power too—but because it is used more often to acquire luxuries than to help others, it's more likely to encourage greed. Here are some greedbusters I've used when dealing with credit cards:

☐ *Treat credit cards like cash.* If I decide to use plastic, I go home and immediately write a check out to the bank-card company for the amount I charged; that way my balance accurately reflects what I have left to spend, and I'm more likely to use credit cards only as a handy money substitute when carrying cash is unsafe or inconvenient.

☐ *Leave home without it.* Don't take your credit cards if you're going somewhere you'll be tempted to spend frivolously. Keep them in an envelope at home where you'll consciously have to retrieve them when necessary.

☐ *Don't charge alone!* When possible, I shop with my wife or a friend who will help keep me accountable to spend money I have on items I really need.

Priorities

After experiencing the terrors of misusing credit, I learned to bring my money and credit line under God's control. This entailed identifying priorities and planning accordingly. As you sort through your priorities, keep these tips in mind:

☐ *Use priorities to determine goals.* As you prepare to leave school for That Great Job You've Always Wanted, do your financial goals reflect your priorities? My current goal is to free myself of dependence on ongoing credit within one year and be paid off in three. After I meet my family's needs (without using credit), my ultimate goal is to further support various ministries.

☐ *Use priorities and goals to write a budget.* Figure out how much of your income you feel you should be spending for housing, food, entertainment, church, etc. Then keep track of what you spend for several months. If you see big discrepancies between expectations and actual spending patterns, adjust accordingly.

☐ *Don't be afraid to go into debt if goals and timing demand it.* Fulfilling some goals may require more cash than you now have; and although you should seriously consider waiting until you've accumulated some savings to forge ahead with your plans, some purchases just can't wait. For an auto loan, school loan or mortgage, a good credit history (often built with the judicious use of credit cards) can help you get the cheapest loan available.

☐ *Avoid using credit cards for large purchases.* Although interest rates on loans have come down across the board, the interest rate on credit cards has remained high—often eighteen to twenty-two per cent! A good bank loan can be had much more cheaply, and borrowing a specific amount will help control your spending to a preset limit you can afford.

I'm still digging myself out of the quicksand of credit. The habit of spending what you don't have and buying what you don't need is easy to acquire when you're on your own for the first time at college—and hard to break. But having the power to make financial choices means much more than having something to worry about. It means learning another way to be a credit to our faith.

—*John Throop with Robert Kachur*

WINNING THE FINANCIAL AID GAME

Susan M. Zitzman

In some ways, getting financial aid is like playing a game—especially since federal funds for student aid have been cut. But you can pretty much count on getting some form of help in paying your school bills *if you know the rules.* You can get money for schooling whether you are rich or poor, at the top of the class or the bottom. Yet many students don't know they're eligible. Although it is true that the poorer you are the more student financial aid you should be able to get, the point is that there is something for everyone—with few exceptions. All you have to do is know how and when to move.

Of course, neither the government nor your college will give you any financial help without making you fill out a truckload of forms. The aid options are complex and confusing. But if you ask about them and work on them, you can find the resources to turn college from an impossible dream into reality.

Perhaps you're saying, "Well, if God wants me to go to this college, he'll provide the money." Your line of thinking is right, but God's provision probably doesn't mean he'll send you a $10,000 check in the mail every September. The Bible emphasizes earning and saving, thinking and planning. Yes, you can count on God to help you achieve the results he has planned for you. You may even get some miraculous funds along the way. But don't just sit back and wait for a handout. Use your head.

We thought we'd help you start "panning for gold" in the muddy stream of forms and terms. In this section you'll find answers to some of the basic questions students ask about financial aid.

What different types of financial aid are there?

There are three main types of aid: scholarships (or grants), loans and student employment. Scholarships and grants are outright gifts and do not have to be repaid. Loans are money that is borrowed by the student to be repaid from earnings after graduation. Colleges look upon loans as an appropriate way for students to invest in their own future. Employment is a job arranged for a student during the academic year to cover part of his or her college expenses.

What are the primary sources of the three types of aid?

There are four sources of aid: the colleges themselves, the federal government, your state government and private sources.

☐ Colleges provide all three types of aid (scholarships, loans and employment) from their own funds, while at the same time acting as the agent for channeling certain federal and state awards to students.

☐ The federal government has six large financial aid programs. Two of these give scholarships (or grants): the Pell Grant and the Supplemental Educational Opportunity Grant (SEOG). Three give loans: the Guaranteed Student Loan (GSL), the Perkins Loan Program (formerly the National Direct Student Loan or NDSL) and the Parents Loan for Undergraduate Students (PLUS) (formerly AIAS—Auxillary Loans to Assist Students). The sixth is a student employment program called College Work-Study (CWS). For more information about these federal programs, try The Department of Education's booklet, *The Student Guide,* which is available in

your school's financial aid office, public libraries, and from the department itself (write Dept. DEA-84, Public Documents Center, Pueblo, CO 81109). In addition, you can call the Federal Student Aid Information Center at (301) 984-4070, or, for $3.00, subscribe to Octameron Associates's "Update Service," which will keep you informed about any changes in federal programs (write P.O. Box 3437, Dept. 88, Alexandria, VA 22302-9990).

☐ Every state in the country has some form of aid for students attending college in their own state, and some even have awards for residents who enroll in other states. Almost all state aid is in the form of scholarships, although a few states also have work-study programs. Information about financial aid in your state can be obtained from your college's financial aid office, public libraries and your state's department of higher education.

☐ Private sources of aid consist primarily of scholarships that are awarded by corporations, unions, religious groups or denominations, and civic or fraternal associations. Information about private aid, particularly local scholarships, can be found in your college's financial aid office and in reference books in your public library.

Will I receive aid only if I need it?

Although the vast majority of aid awarded to college students is based on need, a sizable amount of money is awarded solely on merit—academic achievement, talent, athletic accomplishment, etc.

With few exceptions, the federal government's student aid programs are exclusively for students with need. The exceptions, however, are important. The non-need scholarship programs that are worth the most are a free education in one of the five service academies (West Point, Annapolis, the Air Force Academy, the Coast Guard Academy, the Merchant Marine Academy) and ROTC scholarships. In addition, veterans' benefits are given to those who have served in the military (the new G.I. bill) and to children of deceased or disabled veterans.

A Guaranteed Student Loan (currently available at 8% interest for the first four years of repayment and 10% for the fifth) is available without regard to need for students from families who earn less than $30,000 per year. And under the federally supported parents' loan program called PLUS, any family can borrow up to $4,000 per dependent undergraduate per year at a variable interest rate (3.75 points higher than Treasury bills, but no more than 12%).

State programs of student aid are quite similar to those that the federal government finances, and focus almost entirely on students with need. Once again, however, there are exceptions (the New York State Regents is one). Read your state's financial aid material carefully to see whether they offer merit scholarships for which you might qualify.

Probably the largest source of merit scholarships is the private sector. Scholarships available from this source range from large nationwide programs (such as National Merit, National Honor Society and Century III) to corporate scholarships for children of employees (such as the Grumman Corporation) to local awards given by such groups as the PTA and Rotary. Private sources also support a number of loan programs, such as the Disabled American Veterans loan program and American Society of Mechanical Engineers Auxiliary loan funds.

Finally, of course, needy and non-needy students alike can take jobs. Nearly every college town has private businesses that traditionally offer employment opportunities to students. If there are not sufficient jobs on campus, students can usually find work in the community.

How can I judge whether I will be eligible for aid?

Making an early estimate of whether you

qualify for need-based aid (or whether you must concentrate on the non-need sources mentioned above) involves two steps.

First, as best you can, carefully estimate your college expenses. Second, determine your expected family contribution toward college costs. Peterson's *College Money Handbook* and Anna Leider's *College Grants from Uncle Sam* provide tables with which to figure your parental contribution.

After you have figured out your estimated parental contribution, add to this number 35% of your own personal savings (for example, if you have $1,000 in your bank account, enter $350) and a $900 earnings assumption for the job that you will be expected to have for the summer before you enter college.

This total (parental contribution, student asset contribution and summer savings) is called the family contribution. Subtracting this from college costs shows whether you might have financial need. This preliminary estimate will give you some idea of whether you should concentrate on no-need types of financial aid or whether both kinds of aid, need and non-need, will be open to you.

If I think I might need aid, how do I apply for it?

First of all, read the "how to apply" sections in your school's catalog. Normally you will need to fill out two forms to apply. The first is your college's own aid application, which is returned directly to the college. The second is one of the two national "need-analysis" forms—the

Financial Aid Form (FAF) of the College Scholarship Service or the Family Financial Statement (FFS) of the American College Testing Program, depending on which one your college requires. The FAF or FFS is sent to the central office of the appropriate service. These forms are used to apply for college aid and also serve as applications for the federal Pell Grant program and most states' need-based awards.

All colleges will expect you to apply for all forms of state and federal government assistance as a first step in getting financial aid, and these funds will be figured into the financial aid package created for you by a college's financial aid office.

When should I apply for aid?

☐ In November, pick up need-analysis forms (FAF or FFS) from your college's aid office. Read them carefully and start assembling the financial records you will need.

☐ In January, complete your FAF or FFS. You will need to refer to at least a rough copy of your parents' most recent tax return. Apply for federal and state aid by following the instructions on the form for authorizing the release of your need-analysis information to these agencies.

☐ Two to three weeks after filing the FAF or FFS, you will receive an acknowledgment form that gives you the opportunity to correct data and get an early estimate of the family contribution figure that will be sent to your college.

☐ Four to six weeks after submitting your FAF or FFS, you should get a Student Aid Report (SAR) from the Pell

Grant processing center. Forward a copy of the SAR to the financial aid officer at that college.
☐ Be ready to send your school a copy of your parent's latest income tax return

to validate your aid request.
☐ File all forms as early as possible. The money runs out before the applicants do.

The Key Players

Here are the five key players in the financial aid game—and the rules they must play by.

The 1st Player—The Student

Students may see themselves as "A" students or "C" students, as freshmen or juniors, as jocks or BMOCs. Financial aid programs have their own classification system which defines students by dependency status. They are either *independent students* or *dependent students*.

A *dependent student* is one who is at least partially dependent on his or her parents for support. Financial aid programs use the income assets of both student and parents to develop the amount a family must contribute to college costs.

An *independent student* is not dependent on parental support. Only the student's income and assets (and that of any spouse) are evaluated to determine the contribution to college costs.

To be considered independent, under federal regulations, a student must meet one of the following conditions:

1. Be at least 24 years of age by December 31 of the award year.

2. Be an orphan, ward of the court, or a veteran of the Armed Forces.

3. Have legal dependents other than a spouse.

4. Be married, a professional student or a graduate student, and not be claimed as a tax exemption by his or her parents for the first calendar year of the award (for example, 1988 for the 1988/89 award year).

5. Be single with no dependents and not claimed as a dependent by his or her parents in either of the two calendar years preceding the award year (for example, 1986 and 1987 for the 1988/89 award year). Furthermore, a person in this category must demonstrate self-sufficiency by showing an income of at least $4,000 in each of those years.

6. Be judged independent by the financial aid officer based on unusual documented circumstances.

Establishing independence gives you an advantage: by not having to include parental income and assets on your financial aid application forms, your college contribution will most likely be lower and that will result in more student aid.

To preserve scarce aid funds, most states and almost all colleges have gone beyond the federal test to impose additional restrictions on your declaration of independence. These include written proof that the student's parents (or even grandparents) cannot provide any support whatsoever.

Now an important point: Once you have established independence, don't give it up. It will cost you money. George Webber, a young writer and truly independent student, decides to go back to college. He moves into his parents' home to save on room and board. What happened? He became dependent again. His parents, who thought they had picked up just another mouth to feed, found themselves again involved in footing tuition bills, only now the money came from their pension checks.

The 2nd Player—The Parents
Parents may be sweet, loving, caring, supportive role models. The financial aid process couldn't care less. Its main interest: are they married, separated, divorced? Is there a stepparent around who could foot the bill?

Here is the impact of marital status on financial aid:

Both Parents Are Alive and Married to Each Other. The income and assets of both parents are fair pickings for the financial aid computer.

Parents Are Divorced or Separated. Financial aid forms want to know the income and assets of the parent with whom the student lived for the majority of the calendar year preceding the academic year for which the aid is requested. The form is not interested in the other parent.

A Parent Remarries. If the parent with whom the student lived the greater part of the calendar year remarries, the stepparent automatically assumes partial responsibility for the student. His or her income and assets are evaluated for a contribution to college costs as though he or she were a natural parent.

The rules which we have described apply to federal aid and, generally, to state aid. The colleges, when they decide how to dispense their own money, do not necessarily follow these rules. They will frequently probe deeply into the resources of the divorced and absent parent who got off scot-free under federal regulations.

The 3rd Player—The Colleges
Colleges can be classified as either private or public. Private colleges can be more innovative in developing attractive college financing schemes and tuition assistance programs. They are not as circumscribed by red tape as are tax-supported schools. Private colleges also have more latitude in how to spend their money. Again, it's their money and not the taxpayer's money.

Public colleges, however, being tax-supported, usually cost less. As a general rule, students are seldom asked to pay more than 30% of actual tuition costs. The state pays the balance.

Also, public colleges have two sets of fee structures: a lower one for state residents and a higher one for out-of-state students. In the past, it used to be easy to establish state residency to qualify for the lower rate. Today, it's getting difficult. Most states have erected elaborate defense structures seemingly manned with beady-eyed, cold-hearted officials.

The 4th Player—The Need Analysis Services
Before the college can consider you for aid, they must know how much you can pay. The family that can pay $10,000 won't be eligible for as much aid as the family that can spare only $1,000.

The determination of how much you can safely pay without becoming a burden to your neighbors is called *need analysis.* Agencies known as *need analysis services* perform this job. Their tool: a long form called a financial aid application.

The chief need analysis services are the College Board's *College Scholarship Service* which serves schools on the East and West Coasts and the *American College Testing Program* which is big in the Midwest and the South.

The services use an identical evaluation technique in going over your family finances. You would gain nothing by submitting your data to one service rather than the other.

The 5th Player—The Financial Aid Officer

If money is water and you are a basin, the financial aid officer is the faucet. For the college-bound and those in college, the financial aid officer can be the most important person on campus.

The FAO can take the family contribution cranked out by the need analysis services and—ouch—increase it or—hurray—reduce it.

The FAO can draw on money that's under the college's control or certify the student's eligibility for money that is not under the school's direct control.

The FAO can decide on the contents of the student's assistance package. Is it to be scholarships and grants that do not have to be repaid? Or will it all be in loans?

In short, the FAO is the final arbiter of how much the family must contribute to college costs and how much outside help, and of what kind, the family will receive.

Get to know this player personally. He or she can make the difference between winning and losing.
—*Anna Leider*

This article is an excerpt from her very helpful book Don't Miss Out: The Ambitious Student's Guide to Financial Aid *(Octameron Associates, Inc., P.O. Box 3437, Alexandria, VA 22302—$5.25). Used by permission.*

Resource Books on Financial Aid

☐ *Don't Miss Out: The Ambitious Student's Guide to Financial Aid* (Octameron Associates, Inc., P.O. Box 3437, Alexandria, VA 22302) is, at only $5.25, one of the most concise and thorough resources available for more in-depth information and advice on obtaining financial aid. Look for it or one of the following helpful books at a local bookstore or library. (Most of these resources are updated regularly, so be sure you're getting the most current information.)

☐ *Applying for Financial Aid.* Free from ACT, Box 168, Iowa City, IA 52243.

☐ *The College Cost Book* by The College Board (College Board Publications).

☐ *The College Financial Aid Emergency Kit* by Joyce Lain Kennedy and Dr. Herm Davis (Sun Features).

☐ *The College Money* guides on financial aid sources by Anna J. Leider and others. For their list write to Octameron Associates, P.O. Box 3437, Alexandria, VA 22302.

☐ *The College Money Book* by Gene R. Hawes and David M. Brownstone (Bobbs-Merrill).

☐ *College Planning/Search Book* by ACT, Box 168, Iowa City, IA 52243. Loaded with worthwhile information.

☐ *Financing College Education* by Kenneth A. Kohl and Irene C. Kohl (Harper Colophon Books).

☐ *Five Federal Financial Aid Programs: The Student Guide.* Free from the U.S. Department of Education, Dept. DEA-84, Public Documents Center, Pueblo, CO 81109.

☐ *How to Beat the High Cost of Learning* by Leo L. Kornfeld, Gonnie McClung Siegel and William Laird Siegel (Rawson, Wade Publishers).

☐ *I Am Somebody* by Anna Leider (Octameron Associates). Focuses on the special needs of minority and disadvantaged students.

☐ *Making College Pay* by Jon E. Carson (Addison-Wesley). Innovative ways to earn money while in school.

☐ *Meeting College Costs.* Free from The College Board, Box 2815, Princeton, NJ 08541.

☐ *Mortgaged Futures: How to Graduate from School without Going Broke* by Marguerite J. Dennis (Hope Press). Excellent resource for short- and long-term planning.

☐ *Peterson's College Money Handbook,* ed. Karen C. Hegener (Peterson's Guides). Financial aid explanations plus a guide to costs and aid at 1,700 colleges.

☐ *Student Aid Annual* (Chronicle Guidance Publications). Up-to- date listing of aid opportunities.

—*Sue Zitzman*

Deciding Where to Live

John Throop

When we think of going off to college, most of us imagine living in a dorm. But more than ever before, students are freer to choose from a variety of options. Though some colleges still require students to live on campus all four years, most don't—many even push them out of the nest after freshman year due to the lack of on-campus housing. (Some students, of course, discover that they live in the library and have little to say about the matter; others live in the student union and keep Brazil's coffee prices high.)

What are the options? And what are the implications of each for your emotional, spiritual and physical well-being? Here are some pros and cons concerning the various campus living situations that you should consider:

Home Sweet Dorm

Pros: You are guaranteed to make instant acquaintances if not close friends. I met Bill the day I entered the University of Chicago. He, too, was a transfer student, and we discovered that we had a lot in common, including a bizarre sense of humor. He is still a friend over a decade later. In another case, in a dorm in a college in California, a guy named Dave befriended me. Through that friendship I became a Christian. Dorms, more than off-campus apartments, help create an atmosphere of community among the residents.

Dorm life can also provide options. Some dorms offer both double and single rooms connected to a main hallway; in others, rooms are clustered in suites centered around a common living area. In addition, you get the benefit of having a dorm manager or resident assistant (RA) who can usually help you with all kinds of things at all kinds of hours—sort of like a surrogate parent. You can't beat living so close to classes. And though dorm food can be lousy or great, at least it's there. (If nothing else, it gives you and your friends something to gripe about together.)

As a Christian, living in the dorm helps keep you in the mainstream of campus life, rather than in a little world of Christian fellowship and academics. It's easy to surround yourself with Christian friends and grow distant from the non-Christians you should be sharing your life and your faith with. The dorm is a microcosm of the world; living there will force you to deal with people who you might not gravitate toward otherwise.

Cons: Dorm life can be a real hassle, too. For instance, you want to sleep, but they want to have a water balloon fight in the suite's common living area. You want to study for a half-hour before going to sleep, but the Beastie Boys are blaring at you from across the hall. You want to clear your mind and pray, but the laughter, voices, footsteps and people knocking on your door are making it hard.

You give up privacy when you move into a dorm community. You also might have to compromise to accommodate your roommate's lifestyle. His slovenliness—or neatness—might drive you crazy. (A friend of mine lived with both extremes. Sophomore year he would wake up to the sound of his roommate shampooing the carpets; junior year he'd have to fling his roomie's clothes off the floor just to reach his bed.) More importantly, a roommate who doesn't share your values might want to use your room to get stoned—or have sex with his or her current love interest. You'll have to make some hard choices about where you can bend and where you have to stand firm.

These situations can stress you out, affecting your studies, sleep and spiritual life. Random computer selections don't automatically create community. You have to work at it.

Finally, dorm rates are sometimes relatively expensive, especially if you get burned out on roommates and opt for a single room.

A Place of Your Own

Pros: I lived off campus two years out of four, one year on my own and one year splitting an apartment with two roommates. I personally prefer the off-campus option—but then again, I always have been the independent type.

Living off campus gives you greater control over your study and social environment. For one thing, you'll have the freedom to have people over (especially nice if you want to cook your date dinner or host a small-group Bible study). You also have the freedom to establish rules for the apartment, such as no blasting the stereo after 10 P.M. And living off campus with roommates even gives you some semblance of family life, with several people able to share the duties of buying groceries, cooking meals, doing the dishes and cleaning up. Sharing an apartment saves on rent and food expenses, too.

If the dorm gives you a sense of community, living with one to three hand-picked people you want to get to know better provides a chance for building lifelong friendships. I remember special times late in the evening talking "heavy, deep and real" with apartment mates who were like brothers. As we got involved in each other's lives, we learned a lot about compassion, love and the power of prayer. We matured together as we took on adult responsibilities—opening a "house" checking account, paying bills, keeping food in the apartment, cleaning the bathroom every month (whether it needed it or not). In fact, when I did leap out into the big, bad world after graduation, I felt better prepared because I had been rowing my own boat off campus for a while.

Cons: If you have even the slightest tendency toward introversion, living off campus may not be the best option for you. You may withdraw. If, on the other hand, you do not like being alone, your sense of security may be threatened. And if an apartment mate who moves off campus with you doesn't like being alone, you may feel suffocated by that person's constant presence and demands that you spend more time at home.

You'll have to deal with landlords, who may not always make repairs or keep the place heated to your standards (a common problem in "student slums"). You'll still also have to deal with neighbors, who, depending on the layout of your building, can make a dent in your peaceful afternoon by cranking Springsteen.

Making a commitment to "family life" has its down side, too. If you have a problem with an apartment mate, you may have to live with it for a while. Unlike changing a roommate in a dorm, you can't very easily break a lease. Problems that may have come up in the dorm take on new proportions. Is Kent a slob? Now he'll be leaving his things all over your living room, kitchen and bathroom, as well as the bedroom. Did Laurie's boyfriend hang around the dorm a lot? Don't be surprised if he greets you coming out of the bathroom first thing in the morning.

My Christian apartment mate and I learned during the year that our third apartment mate was gay and suicidal. Talk about tension! We survived, and our friend made significant strides away from suicide and the gay lifestyle—but at the cost of many nights of sleep and a few notches in our GPAs.

Pros: Living on fraternity or sorority row can be a lot of fun. You're with people who have gone through the same **The Frat Race** pledging experience and have built ties. If you've decided to go Greek, there's no better way to get to know the brothers or sisters than living with them.

Greek houses vary widely, from opulent turn-of-the-century sorority houses to some fraternity houses that send all but the most strong-stomached running in the opposite direction. But living in most houses isn't a bad deal expense-wise. Rent is usually subsidized, to some degree, by dues (which you have to pay anyway) and the national organization. Often some of the housework is done by pledges or hired help. On top of that, the food might be great (depending on your house's cook) for less bucks than food services charges and less hassle than cooking for yourself.

If you're energized by being around people, rather than getting away from them, living in a Greek house may suit you. A friend of mine described living in the fraternity like living in a hotel, with lots of guests breezing in and out, a centrally located TV and fireplace where brothers gathered at all hours, and weekend entertainment.

As a Christian, living in the house might give you the best opportunity to love your brothers or sisters in practical ways—showing concern when they seem troubled, helping clean up around the house, affirming them and openly sharing your faith and values with them as you spend time together. Two friends of mine started a fraternity Bible study in their house which eventually drew several non-Christians to the Christian faith. Another became a Christian through a fraternity/sorority Bible study sponsored by Christians in various houses. These men and women knew little, if anything, about the Christian community at college. It took Christians committed to them—Christians inside the system—to reach them.

Cons: Greek life is tough on a Christian. Period.

Just joining a fraternity or sorority may require you to compromise your faith. Actually living in your house can stretch your faith to the limit, causing you to lose perspective on your own values and morals.

The Christians I knew who lived in Greek houses generally fell into one of two categories: those who had such strength and character that they earned the respect of others in the house, even while standing against some of what went on there; and those who compromised or even fell away from their faith for a while. By the very nature of the organization, life in a fraternity or sorority house may perpetuate elitism and hedonism. Be prepared for lots of little battles as you struggle to act Christlike in that atmosphere. (See Paul's admonition for believers not to return to old ways in Colossians 3:5-10.)

Some women who weren't too impressed with the fraternities at their university wrote an editorial in their school newspaper about how living in Greek houses seemed to change people. They likened some of the wilder fraternity houses on campus to brothels: to visit them now and then was bad enough, but *living* in one would warp your perspective on right and wrong. If you're not very strong in your faith (or even if you are), living in that kind of environment day in and out can wear you down morally.

Besides all that, Greek houses are not the most private places in the world. A friend of mine coped with the typical noise level by running a fan in his room, summer and winter, to block it out so he could read and sleep. And if you find it necessary to cope by spending time studying and socializing outside the house, you may get razzed for not being around enough (more than one guy with lots of interests outside the house has been nicknamed the "mystery brother").

Pros: One option on some campuses is to live in an intentional Christian community. Near my college campus several different groups of students decided to live together and devote themselves to shared duties, community prayer, building fellowship and encouraging each other in evangelism, spirituality, and peace and justice issues. They entered into these communities with clear expectations

Christian Communities

about what life was going to be like. Pooling resources to live together and encourage each other in the faith has, in fact, been part of the Christian experience from the beginning (see Acts 2:42-47).

For those who want a full on-campus experience but need a strong support group, living in Christian community might be the best option. Prayer groups and accountability are usually easy to build into the structure of family life. Generally a high level of trust in these communities brings a stability to college life that might otherwise be lacking.

Cons: You've really got to be committed to the idea of living in Christian community for it to work. Community life can be intense, especially if one or more of the members are working through deep-seated problems (which often may surface during the college years, when young adults are separated from their parents and home environment for the first time). Are you willing to be available to your brothers or sisters at odd hours or when you have something else to do?

As part of the community, you will probably be assigned some duties which you hate—but have to do as part of the rotation. And if your expectations of what community life will be like are too high, you're setting yourself up for big-time disappointments. Christians have problems and hang-ups just like everyone else. Alex is, basically, a slob. Janie hogs the telephone. It takes energy, nerve and patience to lovingly confront other Christians about these nitty-gritty issues while living with them on a day-to-day basis.

Finally, Christian communities can be *too* comfortable. You and your friends will continually be tempted to minister only to each other rather than to other Christians and non-Christians on your campus. After a few months you might find yourself so wrapped up in your community (with its particular concerns and jargon) that you are less and less able to relate to the outside world.

No Place Like Home

Pros: More students that ever before are choosing to live

with their parents and commute to school. With the high
cost of room and board, free rent and meals can't be beat.
What could be better than Mom's cooking? What could
beat the security of being near family while you're heading
off into new and untried realms of learning? While everything else is changing, your home remains a haven. You
don't have to adjust to a new roommates's idiosyncracies,
deal with landlords, do your own grocery shopping or (if
you're lucky) go to a laundromat.

Unlike your friends who go away to college, you'll be
able to further develop friendships in your hometown—
with high-school buddies and members of your local
church. Most important of all, living at home gives you the
opportunity to build your relationship with your parents at
a time when many become strangers to their parents. As
you grow and learn, you will have an easier time sharing
with them your thoughts, hurts and joys.

Cons: One of the purposes of going to college is to become more independent, to learn how to fend for yourself
after graduation. Living with your family, then, may thwart
an important part of your education. Granted, if you live in
a dorm, your needs for food and lodging (and sometimes
even maid service) are still met. But emotionally, you do
not operate out of the security of home.

College is also a time to explore a lot of new ideas and
integrate some of them with your faith in your own way.
Living at home, where everything you already believe is
probably reinforced (positively or negatively) by your parents, may either discourage you from seriously considering
new ideas, or cause conflict when you bring those ideas
home. Unless your parents are academically oriented and
open-minded, they may grow concerned about what you're
learning or just look at you with incomprehension when
you spout off on something you're excited about. I always
knew that my parents had tuned out on me whenever their
eyes began to glaze over and a sort of thin, wan smile
would form around the corners of their mouths. "That's in-

teresting, John," my father would say, then turn around and ask my mother what was for dessert. I never did get him to read my exciting paper on Marsiglio of Padua's political theory.

Furthermore, you may have to work through unrealistic expectations that your parents may place on you as a student living at home. While students who go away to college are usually free to determine their own schedules, students living at home may be expected to stick to curfews and other rules that they feel they've outgrown. They also may be expected to participate in as many household chores as before—even though they are taking a full course load, involved in a campus fellowship group and local church, working part-time and commuting. Resolving these issues with parental units may or may not be easy.

Socially, living at home can be a handicap. Dorms, fraternities and even off-campus housing all provide many opportunities for interaction with peers. While others are making friends by living in community and hanging out as they go about their daily business—studying, doing laundry, eating and so on—you will be home, surrounded by family and, perhaps, high-school friends. For many, college is a time to meet lifetime friends and a mate. Though you'll still meet and get to know other students through your classes, you'll have to work twice as hard as a resident student to build those kind of relationships. In addition, you may not have a "space of your own" to invite new friends over to. A little brother or sister hanging around can put a damper on an evening at home with your new friends.

Choosing where to live is a big decision. In most cases, you are probably best off living in the dorm your first year to familiarize yourself thoroughly with your new environment and begin learning how to take care of yourself. As you progress through school and make a new decision every spring about where you will live the next year, pray for wisdom and ask yourself some hard questions: Can I live this way and glorify God? Does this way of life prepare me

for life after graduation? Is my character strong enough to
handle the pitfalls and temptations this living situation may
bring? Will living in this situation enable me to use my
faith, time and money to its best advantage?

Living the Commuter Life

Andrés Tapia

While most people still picture a residential school when they think of college, the fastest growing group of students in the United States are commuter students.

The stats from a 1984 Carnegie Foundation study are surprising: Enrollment in community colleges rose 16% from 1970 to 1983, while in four-year institutions it rose only 3% during that same period. In 1984, more freshmen enrolled in two-year schools than in four-year schools for the first time. And at four-year schools the number of part-time and commuter students also increased sharply.

Despite the advantages, life as a commuter can be lonely and frustrating. Commuter students often find it difficult to juggle school with work and family responsibilities—and because of those "extracurricular" commitments, building community and school spirit is an uphill battle. Many deal with the added stress of asserting independence while still living at home with parents.

To find out how students were meeting the challenges of commuter life—time pressures, living with parents and the lack of community at their schools—I interviewed

Dorm Student

Commuter Student

commuters across the U.S. Here's what they had to say.

When Scott Volltrauer, a recent graduate, attended Triton
College (a community school near Chicago), he took sixteen credit hours plus a New Testament Greek class on
Monday nights at a nearby seminary. He worked forty hours
a week, and led his campus fellowship group, two Bible
studies and a children's club at his church. Every night he
ate dinner at home with his family—and averaged three
hours of sleep.

Time

Though most commuter students' schedules are not as
extreme as Scott's, many come close. Jim Andre, president
of his Christian fellowship and thirty-hour-a-week salesman, thought that taking classes only on Mondays, Wednesdays and Fridays would free up large blocks of time for
work. He found, however, that no one wanted to hire him
to work only on Tuesdays and Thursdays, and that his MWF
approach prevented him from keeping in tune with school

throughout the week. "Having classes every morning of the week has helped me concentrate better, be more involved in school and better approximate the four-year environment where I want to end up." Jim now works evenings.

Getting a job related to their field of study helped Tammy King and Jinny Cook, both from Triton, fight fragmentation. Tammy, who is studying restaurant management, worked as a cook. Jinny, an education major, is a day-care worker at a Montessori school. The best-laid plans, however, can be disrupted by time constraints. Tammy had to quit her job recently because the restaurant wanted her to work more hours than she could fit into her schedule.

Mastering the art of scheduling has helped many get control of their time. "I tend not to write things down," says Jim, "which has usually led to disaster. So I just purchased one of those personal planners to plot out my schedule." At the beginning of each semester he writes down all of his fellowship's activities and his work hours and then schedules his classes around them. "By putting in more planning time at the beginning, I can put all the pieces together better."

For Heriberto Reyes—computer technology major at Youngstown State University in Ohio, campus fellowship leader and church conga percussionist—strict scheduling is not as effective. "I never know how long it's going to take me to work out the bugs in a computer program," he says. "Instead I leave my weekends open for studying and catching up. I used to go out on weekends, but I don't as much anymore. I also study before going to work because after work I'm always too exhausted."

For Tammy, gaining control of her time meant postponing a few things. She explains: "I needed six more classes to graduate and planned to take them all next semester. But I've decided to take only four, so I'll have more time for homework, fellowship responsibilities and my part-time job." Before each semester Tammy also figures out the nonnegotiable things in her life. "I don't schedule any

classes for Wednesday nights, because that's when I have a
Bible study at my house," she says. "I also try to leave
Wednesday morning free to spend with my fellowship, and
so whatever job I get will have to work around that."

Several students found that they sometimes needed a
complete break from the hectic schedule. "I always want to
keep God first, but with all the pressures I lose sight of
that. Retreats with my campus fellowship help me get back
on track," says Dan Suiter.

"Students in residence halls have built-in support systems, both in terms of their peers, and in terms of parapro-
fessionals such as resident advisers," Barbara Jacoby, director of the Office of Commuter Affairs at the University of
Maryland—College Park, told *National On-Campus Report*.
"But students who live at home lack that kind of support.
They face typical college problems plus the need to cope
with parents who may not be ready for their changing role.
The parents may wonder why going to college classes is
any different from going to high school."

Jim Andre concurs: "You put up with some of the same

Parents

arguments you've been putting up with since you were five years old."

Even activities such as joining a Christian group can create tensions. When Nader Sahyouni—a Lebanese commuter student who attended Northwestern University in Evanston, Illinois—joined InterVarsity Christian Fellowship, his parents were pleased. "They saw changes in me as I grew in my faith," Nader says. "But their excitement decreased as my responsibilities in the fellowship grew and I spent less time at home."

For Nader, living at home was bittersweet. "At first we would not see eye to eye on things. But if I had moved out and lived on campus, we would never have faced those issues. . . . We would have grown further and further apart. But this way we've grown closer."

Randy Hoth, as a Triton College student, wanted to get closer to his parents, but didn't know how. He knew that his years as a commuter would probably be his last chance to spend so much time with them. "I began looking for ways to better participate in my parents' lives. They like to watch TV, especially when the Bears play. As I joined them, I found out that watching TV was a good time to ask my parents about their days, and for them to ask about mine. Once I began to relate to them on an everyday level, it became more natural for me to share more about myself."

For Sally Larrazabal, a Puerto Rican student at Hostos Community College in the Bronx, living at home has been much more difficult. "My parents fear that if I'm involved with the campus fellowship group that I won't study as much," she says.

Sally, raised in a conservative Hispanic family, has chosen to submit to her parents. "It's painful because they often say no. But obeying my parents has helped me mature. Lately I've been seeing that they trust me more than my siblings, and I know that it's because I have been living out my faith."

Others, however, feel they can't stay at home. Some

move out. Jim Andre would like to, but "I'm not making enough money to do that. In fact, it's already a bit sticky because I'm living at home without paying rent."

"It's hard to get real committed relationships because life is so fragmented," says Paul McNulty of Rock Valley College in Rockford, Illinois. A variety of factors contribute to the loneliness of many commuters: the high turnover rate at two-year schools, living off-campus instead of in a student community and hectic schedules. The Carnegie study revealed that only 47% of part-time students (most of whom commute) feel a sense of community at their colleges, as compared to 63% of full-time students.

Lack of Community

For most of the students we talked to, joining the Christian fellowship group on their campus proved instrumental in making them feel a sense of belonging. Says Jinny: "My involvement in the Triton Christian Fellowship helps me feel more part of the school. And as I go out and invite others to join our group, I get to meet more people."

Prayer, worship and Bible study as well as bowling, video parties and games, the students said, helped them get to know each other better. "We seek each other more because of all the pressures," says recent Elgin Community College graduate Kathy Besancon. "In the fellowship we encouraged one another about how God helped us deal with our hectic lives."

Heriberto, Jim and others help build community simply by hanging out before or after classes. Heriberto eats breakfast with friends at the student union. Jim goes to the cafeteria after class to meet and talk with people from his classes. "I try to eat lunch at the cafeteria a couple of times a week—even bring a lunch if I don't have the money—so I can get to know some people a little better."

The students I talked to made some more suggestions on how to overcome the challenges commuters face.

Ask yourself these questions: What are the most impor-

Moving Ahead

Dorm Student

Commuter Student

tant things to me? My studies? My family? My campus fellowship? Money? Does my use of time reflect my priorities?
Could I function better if I reduced my courses or work
hours? Do I have to make as much money as I do? Do I
really need to buy a car? Do I need to get an A in every
class? Do I need to spend more time with my friends and
less in studies? Or should I spend more time studying?

Get a calendar and let it reflect the priorities you've set.
While you're at it, make a calendar for your parents too—
listing all your activities (classes, work hours, campus fellowship meetings and events), midterms and finals. If they
know what to expect, they may be more understanding
when you're especially busy or stressed.

In addition to keeping your parents informed about your
life, keep them involved in your life. Think of activities that
can strengthen your relationship with them and even give
them a glimpse of school life. The fellowship group at
Trenton State College in New Jersey, for example, sponsors
an annual end-of-the-year banquet for parents and other
relatives.

Parties within the fellowship are also great community
builders. At Hostos the fellowship group participated in the

college's annual Christmas fair. They brought in a Christian
Latin American salsa band that was enthusiastically received. They also sponsored a retreat called Vacaciones con
Dios (Vacation with God) where many non-Christians
came and found a healthy atmosphere of community and
spiritual renewal.

At the University of Texas—El Paso, community life is
strengthened by moving activities off campus and using
people's houses to help bridge the gap between campus
activites and home life.

Students also said that prayer is a sure way to get involved in others' lives. Debbie Martinez, InterVarsity staff
worker at Pan-American University near the Texas-Mexico
border, has her small groups write up prayer lists that get
passed around to all the small groups. After a month or so,
when the small groups convene, getting acquainted is easy
because everyone's been praying for each other.

"Commuter schools are 'life laboratories,' " says InterVar-   **On the**
sity area director Sandy Beelen. "The age, ethnic diversity   **Cutting Edge**
and pace reflect our society. If commuters can learn to organize and balance the many demands on their lives, form
meaningful relationships and develop a Christian fellowship that positively influences the campus community, they
will be excellently equipped to tackle life after graduation."

An administrator in a Newark, New Jersey school made
up largely of commuter students agrees. "Those students
who drive to the campus, go to class and then go home are
wasting their time and money," he told *Administrator*
newsletter. "There is more to a college degree than sitting
in class. The technical knowledge they are learning today
represents only a fraction of what they will need. To survive a lifetime they must learn how to learn, to adapt, to
lead. They can only learn these things by involving themselves in the total university experience—both in and out
of the classroom."

Involving yourself in the total university experience as a

commuter is a tough balancing act. Those who do it well are disciplined and directed. It's not unlike the balancing act most people have to do to function efficiently out in the real world.

But then, most commuter students aren't preparing for the real world. They're already in it.

KNOWING WHEN TO CHANGE COLLEGES

Karen Wells

Iattended three schools my first three years of college. I moved from a community college my freshman year to a small Christian liberal arts school my sophomore year to a Big Ten university my junior year. I don't advise random college-jumping. But in my situation, every step was a positive one, a move to develop me academically, socially and spiritually.

Many students don't consider that they're free to change colleges—or that God may be encouraging them to do so. That realization can be reassuring or unsettling. Many times it's tough to try something new, even when God leads. (A lot of the friends I made in school were afraid to change majors, let alone colleges.)

Why bother changing colleges? Once you've settled into classes, teachers and friends, it's hard to pack everything into a U-Haul and move to another campus the next year. But it may be better than struggling through two or four years of a school that's not right for you. Speaking from experience, here are some solid reasons for transferring to another college;

☐ *Money.* For some, the financial burden of going to college is heavier than the academic load. Income from summer jobs and part-time work during the school year doesn't always cut it; government loans are becoming scarcer than 4.0 GPA's; and scholarship money has become less accessible to students who are brainy, brawny or both.

Money (or the lack of it) alone might not be a good reason to transfer. If you like where you are, seek out all possible sources at your school first. Knock on doors. Don't be afraid to ask for aid (a more diplomatic word than cash), or admit to school administration that you are having financial problems and need help. Most schools are willing to help you obtain loans, partial scholarships or part-time work. They may even help you find an internship which combines your major with practical, paid experience on the field.

As another alternative, consider taking a semester or two off to earn more tuition money.

☐ *New Direction.* Most students change majors after the first semester or year of school; some even later. One good reason for transferring is to take advantage of the best facilities or programs for your major. If you decide to major in journalism and you are attending an engineering school, it may be time to start looking for a school with a good journalism department.

☐ *Steppingstones.* After a year or two at a small school or local community college, you may be ready for the big leagues. You may need the broader scope of a larger school now that you've settled into a major. Or maybe after living at home and commuting to a local college, you have the financial ability to attend the school you really want. Sometimes an excellent GPA at a community college will give you a better chance to get into your favorite school than you would have had right out of high school. If your current college is a steppingstone, recognize it as such and move on.

☐ *Different Challenges.* After a semester or a year, some students discover they need more challenges . . . or fewer. Academically, you may be sinking or out in a desert. Socially, you may be overwhelmed or underwhelmed by the opportunities. Spiritually, you may need

the support of a Christian college or the challenge of attending a state university.

Pitfalls
Even if one or more of your reasons for changing colleges appears in the above list, examine your motives carefully. Analyze what you need in a college, then ask, "Is the school I'm now attending able to meet my needs?"

The grass is not always greener on another campus, although most brochures make it look that way. If you're not reasonably happy at one school, you might not be at the next either. A wallflower on one campus isn't usually transformed into the homecoming queen on another. (You can get to know new people on another campus, but it's often tougher, not easier, to break in as a newcomer.) And going to school in Vermont or Colorado doesn't guarantee that you'll be hitting the slopes every afternoon after classes. Do you want to transfer because of outward circumstances or an inner restlessness? Think about it. Pray about it. Don't just daydream.

Before you start filling out applications again, make sure you've exhausted all of the opportunities in your own backyard. If you're bored, getting involved in campus activities may help you channel untapped energies. If you want more academic challenges, you might be able to create your own interdisciplinary major (in which you combine courses from more than one department) or take a double major. My brother's small college, for instance, didn't have a program in commercial art.

Instead of switching schools, he double-majored in art and business. It worked out well. Sometimes you're better off waiting for new academic challenges until graduate school—particularly if you're considering switching colleges halfway into senior year.

You may have more trouble deciding whether and where to transfer than you had choosing a college in the first place. Transferring is serious business. I learned the hard way that you may lose credits, disrupt your education and have to extend your college career by a semester or two. But for me, not changing would have hurt in the long run. Transferring was part of growing—and well worth the hassle.

Tips on Transferring
While you're still just tossing around the idea of changing schools, here are some important steps to take before you decide.

Talk to your academic adviser or a trusted teacher about why you want to change schools. Be prepared to defend your reasons, but also be prepared to listen. Your decision could be short-sighted or rash, reacting to one circumstance (a bad roommate, a teacher who failed you, inedible food) instead of the overall situation. You may need a change, but not necessarily a change of school.

Talk to transfer students. (If you don't know any, your office of admissions may be able to direct you to some.) What were their reasons for transferring? What were their problems and how were they resolved? Are they glad they transferred? Was it worth the hassle?

Take a good look through college catalogs in the library. Is there another school that seems to suit your needs better? Write the college for facts, including information on transfer credits and application deadlines. Make it clear in your letter that you would be a transfer student; colleges usually set different application procedures, quotas and deadlines for transfer students.

Visit the school you're considering. Don't depend on the recommendation of a high-school chum on how good a college is. If you do, you may be in for some not-so-pleasant surprises. A high-school buddy may be lonely and want someone to commiserate with. Visit the school (and not just on homecoming weekend). Attend some classes in your major. Talk to recent alumni. Ask them about both the good and the bad characteristics of their alma mater. The situation may be no better than where you are now.

Pray about your plans. Then knock on different doors with confidence. God will do his part in leading you, often by opening some doors and closing others.

Start early—as soon as you become serious about transferring. Waiting until the end of the year postpones the inevitable and could preempt your chances of getting into the school of your dreams.

SOCIAL LIFE

When you're considering participating in any campus event—whether it's a party or a concert or the movies—the issue's the same: How do I live *in* the campus world without being *of* it? In the following pages you'll read about people like you who have sorted through the college social scene—and find help for setting your own guidelines.

Partying: Good Times or Compromise?

Robert M. Kachur

LILE DORM . . . WHERE THE FUN NEVER ENDS. I looked at that banner welcoming me to my fresh-man dorm and wondered what college social life would be like. I mean, I enjoyed social life in high school. I liked being with people and dancing and meeting girls. But was I ready for the big leagues?

I'd hardly had a chance to get oriented to my new campus or even get to know my roommate when fraternity rush began. Then, for the next six weeks, it consumed me. I had never taken partying so seriously. ("Don't dress *too* preppy," one Greek R.A. warned me. "Don't wear shorts. Don't get drunk. And don't *ever* refuse a beer.")

So began my initiation into the campus party scene. I got into a fraternity where the guys seemed, well, not too superficial. And I made close friends. During the week we worked hard; on weekends we played hard. Partying wasn't a moral issue for me. It wasn't an issue at all. Just part of life. If I occasionally drank too much, I could count on one of my friends to walk me back to the dorm, feed me two aspirin and take off my shoes when I dropped into bed. Life was good.

Then sophomore year I moved into the fraternity house, and my party life accelerated intensely. As a "brother," I felt obligated to go to every party we gave—"endless summer" parties in late August, freshman rush in September, the traditional "Hallograin" party in October, Homecoming pregame bloody-mary brunches, postgame keg parties, and on and on. I began to drink, dance and date more often than ever before.

Between my sophomore and junior years, a lot happened. My mom died of heart failure, and I went to live for the summer with an aunt and uncle. I felt empty inside and began to question what I was doing with my life. Through the influence of a Christian acquaintance, I started attending a campus fellowship group that fall and became a Christian halfway through my junior year. Suddenly I had a whole new crew of friends—Christian friends—who seemed to care about me a lot. My old friends cared too, but most didn't understand my new-found faith. Several who thought I was going off the deep end because of my mother's death even tried to talk me out of it.

New Perspective

Sometimes I felt uneasy around my non-Christian friends; I worried that they'd reject me if I stood up for my

beliefs. At the same time, I worried that I'd give in when they encouraged me to do things I now believed were wrong, such as drinking too much. So I gravitated toward Christian friends and Christian activities and decided to avoid situations where I was most tempted to go back to my old ways—namely, parties.

As senior year began, my new way of life seemed in place. Until I ran into Laura, an old friend, who startled me with her honesty.

"We never see you anymore. Is everything okay?"

"Oh, I'm fine," I said, avoiding any mention of change in my life. "Just real busy."

"You should go by and see Carol." Carol, who lived with Laura, had been one of my best friends since the first week of freshman year.

"Is she okay?" I asked.

"Oh, she's all right," Laura said, "Just hurt that you never talk to her anymore. You should come by the apartment."

My heart sank. That night I went to see Carol and apologized for not making time for her. I began to realize that a certain intimacy I'd once shared with her and other non-Christian friends was fading. By cutting back on my time with my old friends, I had been sending out signals that I didn't care anymore.

Keeping in Touch

I felt confused. On one hand, becoming a Christian seemed to mean making time in my schedule for new things (building friendships with the Christians I was meeting in my campus fellowship, praying, reading the Bible), as well as leaving behind some old things (like parties where drinking and casual sex were rampant). But the very people I hoped would notice a positive change in my life didn't see a thing, because I wasn't spending enough time with them. So should I make more time for old friends who didn't approve of my new faith? What would happen when our beliefs and values caused conflict? Would I have the strength not to back down?

I didn't know. But I also didn't want to lose my friends.
So I began to seek them out again—between classes, over
meals and even at parties.

I'd always felt comfortable at parties. As a Christian,
though, I knew I couldn't take part in everything that went
on there. So right away I set two rules for myself. If I started
feeling tempted to lust or gossip or sin in any other way
(including affirming others' sin by laughing or smiling at
it), I would simply leave. And I would never get drunk.

For a while everything went great. Friends who I hadn't
seen in a while welcomed me back warmly. I began to
build relationships again and talk about what was going on
in my life, including my faith. Friday and Saturday nights
seemed the best times to show my friends that Christians
knew how to have fun too—without hurting themselves or
anyone else.

But as fall progressed, two struggles surfaced that made
me more and more uneasy.

First, I worried about the unintentional messages I might
be sending out to my Christian friends. At one party, for instance, I was dancing up a storm when I spied Keith, a shy,
insecure freshman from my Bible study, guzzling beer and
standing with a rowdy group from his dorm. He was obviously compromising his standards in order to fit in. I
wanted to go up to him and tell him I accepted him as he
was, and that he didn't have to follow the crowd.

But then a thought struck me: *What impression am I giving Keith?* I had a beer in my hand (I had nursed the same
one all night), I was jumping up and down on the dance
floor, and at one point in the evening my drunk but otherwise wonderful friend Sandra ran up, gave me a big hug
and spilled beer all over me. I hadn't done anything wrong,
but I wondered what Keith was thinking: *My Bible study
leader drinks and hangs out with loose women—it must be
okay.* Also, a Bible verse I'd read nagged at me—the one
that said I should "abstain from all appearance of evil" (1
Thess 5:22 KJV). Did my going to a party give silent approv-

al to all that went on there?

Second, I still struggled to keep from slipping back into my old lifestyle.

At my girlfriend's sorority Christmas formal, I didn't know a soul and felt like an outsider. I half-consciously began drinking more than usual. Before I knew it I was drunk. Not rip-roaring drunk—just buzzed enough to think I could handle any situation. In a way it felt perfectly natural; in my first three years of college I had gone to lots of parties and gotten more intoxicated than this.

But it also felt strange. I hadn't been drunk in a long time. Even before the buzz wore off I felt guilt welling up. I was wrong to drink too much. I wanted to belong too— but instead of turning to God, or even my girlfriend, with my insecure feelings, I drank until I felt a false surge of confidence, just like during fraternity rush back in the old days. Maybe I shouldn't have gone to the party in the first place.

My Christian friends didn't have many good answers about how I should relate to others on campus. The only advice I received about the party scene was "Don't go." But sticking around Christians all the time and avoiding everyone else (or darting into the world for a few hours over the weekend to evangelize) didn't satisfy me. I needed to know how to conduct myself day by day in the real world, especially among those with whom I'd had the chance to build relationships. And for me, that meant learning how to approach the center of social life—parties—as a Christian.

My campus staff worker advised me that if I wanted my friends to see a change in me and be influenced to consider faith in Christ themselves, I shouldn't drink. Other than that, he assured me that Christians had always wrestled with how to relate to the world at large and urged me to look at some Bible passages.

Though it hadn't occurred to me that the Bible might have something to say about the party scene, I decided to

Jesus and Parties

check it out during the next several weeks. One passage in particular bothered me: "Do not be yoked together with unbelievers. For what do righteousness and wickedness have in common? Or what fellowship can light have with darkness? . . . What does a believer have in common with an unbeliever?" (2 Cor 6:14-16). I wondered, *Am I "yoking myself together with unbelievers" by going to parties?* I didn't know.

So I kept flipping through my New Testament, and zeroed in on how Jesus related to the people of his day. I noticed that he attended a local wedding reception (Jn 2). Not only did he attend, I discovered, but he changed 120 gallons of water into fine wine and had it delivered to the banquet master! Apparently Jesus didn't shy away from social gatherings and celebrations—places where some, the passage implies, drank too much. He even contributed to the party spirit.

However, Jesus' behavior raised the eyebrows of some of his pious contemporaries, who called him "a glutton and a drunkard" (Mt 11:19; Lk 7:34). It must have been so radical for a righteous teacher to keep the company Jesus kept that the Pharisees didn't know what to make of him. Yet he knew how to eat and drink and have a good time with sinners without sinning himself. He listened to them, sympathized with them, laughed with them—but consistently sought to influence rather than be influenced by them along the way.

Reflecting on those passages and my own party behavior, I realized that sometimes my friends, not I, did the influencing. When I didn't feel secure in my faith and desperately wanted my old friends to accept me, I would pretend that nothing had changed in our friendship or in my life. In contrast, Jesus not only accepted and spent time with nonreligious folk, but he stood out as a good man. He never compromised the truth. People saw that he was like them *and* that he was different. And many of their lives changed as a result.

Eventually I became convinced of a few things. Shutting myself off from all the non-Christian friends God had given me wasn't right. I also became confident, as I read through the Bible, that Jesus' command to be "in the world but not of it" (see Jn 17:14-18) was possible even on fraternity row. For some Christians who are secure in their faith and feel comfortable in the party scene, parties can be a good place to build friendships—and stand apart.

For other folk, I realized, the noise, music and crowds at parties were intimidating, or else offered too many irresistible temptations. But I later learned that many of the Christian friends I had criticized for avoiding fraternities and sororities were busy building bridges with non-Christians in other places—the student union, dorm lounges and intramural sports events, to name a few.

From my study of the Bible I also discovered that I was wrestling with a much bigger question than simply, "Should I go to parties?" I was really asking, "How should I live and act in this world, whether I'm at a party, in my dorm, in the cafeteria, on a date or anywhere?" To the first question, the Bible says very little; to the second, practical advice abounds.

"Speak truthfully," the apostle Paul says in Ephesians 4 and 5, "Do not let any unwholesome talk come out of your mouths. . . . Among you there must not be even a hint of sexual immorality, or any kind of impurity, or of greed. . . . Nor should there be obscenity, foolish talk or coarse joking. . . . For you were once darkness, but now you are light in the Lord. Live as children of light. . . . Do not get drunk on wine, which leads to debauchery."

A few words from Peter also helped: "Do not conform to the evil desires you had when you lived in ignorance. But just as he who called you is holy, so be holy in all you do" (1 Pet 1:14-15).

As my senior year progressed, I still didn't have answers to all my questions about relating to the social scene. And

Lessons for a Lifetime

at times I wondered if my struggles were worth it, since my college party-going days were drawing to a close.

But I realized that the past three years had taught me much more than the ethics of partying. I began to understand—sometimes the hard way—how to interact with people who don't share my most basic beliefs about God and life. I learned not to avoid them or the differences between us for fear of conflict. (Looking back, I would have saved myself some misunderstandings, even with Christian friends like Keith, if I'd talked more openly about my motives and observations.) I discovered personal weaknesses I have to guard against, such as my tendency to rely on alcohol or even other people to bolster my self-confidence. And finally, I learned that my struggle to live in the world without adopting the world's values would not end at graduation; it would continue for the rest of my life.

A few weeks before graduation, my girlfriend Susan and I attended my last fraternity formal. I enjoyed tying up loose ends with brothers I had spent time with over the years. As we reminisced and spun circles on the dance floor with our dates, I felt more relaxed than ever.

We talked about where we would be five years from then, why we would and wouldn't miss school, what we would have done differently. And we talked about our differences, even in matters of faith. I was able to explain how my Christian faith had altered my life goals.

Of course the party blared on as we had these conversations, but I didn't feel the need to participate in all that was going on. After accepting one drink, I had Diet Pepsi for the rest of the evening. And when a number of couples left early to go skinny-dipping, Susan and I kept dancing.

At one point, Jeff, an outspoken brother I had known since freshman year, approached me.

"You know," he said, "when you first got involved with Christianity I thought you had gone off the deep end. I think I even accused you of joining a cult."

I laughed. "Yeah, you did, didn't you?"

"Well, I just want to apologize for anything I said or did to make you uncomfortable," Jeff continued. "I should have respected your decision. It's obviously not some fly-by-night deal."

I was overwhelmed. Jeff had never apologized for anything.

"I really appreciate that," I said. "It's forgotten." I paused. "By the way, if you ever want to talk more about why I take it so seriously . . ."

"Not tonight," he said. "Maybe another time." I smiled as he walked away, thankful that he had seen something more in me than my insecurities. And for tonight, that was enough.

Should I Go?

Partying plays a big role in campus social life. But partying means different things to different people. How will you decide where you fit into the campus party scene? Here are a few suggestions:

☐ **Decide ahead of time what kinds of parties you'll attend.** Some parties are a good place to catch up with folks you might not see otherwise. Others are so wild that no Christian belongs at them: "For you have spent enough time in the past doing what pagans choose to do—living in debauchery, lust, drunkenness, orgies, carousing and detestable idolatry" (1 Pet 4:3). Establishing what's off limits now will make future choices easier.

☐ **Be honest.** Unless you're consistently up-front about your lifestyle and convictions as a Christian, people who see you having fun at a party may assume your presence lends a silent seal of approval to everything going on there. Stand firm about who you are.

☐ **Be realistic about your weaknesses.** Are you prone to drink too much, to flirt, to smoke pot? If so, limit your socializing to places where these temptations are reduced.

☐ **Be realistic about peer pressure.** Peer pressure on campus may be stronger at parties than anywhere else. If you find yourself compromising your beliefs to feel affirmed by others at parties, admit that you're letting others control you—and retreat to safer ground, at least for a while.

☐ **Be accountable to your friends.** Taking a friend along who knows and shares your beliefs can help keep you honest and clear-headed when you start losing perspective. Agree together that you will each warn the other if you think something's getting out of hand.

☐ **Avoid put-downs.** If you do decide to go to a party where you can't participate in everything happening, don't be judgmental. Declarations like "drinking is a sin" and "the Greek system is worldly" only make you sound superior to your friends and reinforce their mistaken idea that Christianity is nothing but dos and don'ts.

☐ **Be an influencer.** Don't go to parties thinking you're going to change your friends. Ultimately you're not responsible for anyone's actions but your own. Yet your refusal to participate in the excesses of partying may encourage other revelers to party more responsibly.

—*Robert M. Kachur*

DRINKING: HOW MUCH IS TOO MUCH?

David Neff with Robert Kachur

All the social chairman types griped when our college announced that flyers advertising campus events could no longer mention alcohol. It wasn't long, however, before a phrase one fraternity started using in their flyers caught on: "The usual beverage will be served."

That euphemism said it all. Like on most campuses, drinking at social events was a given.

As Christians on campus, my friends and I had to grapple with alcohol. Take my friend Jane. After becoming a Christian her sophomore year, she decided to make a radical break with the wild lifestyle she and her friends had shared by not drinking. With a few exceptions, her friends seemed to respect her decision. Some even wanted to know more about why she had changed, which gave her great opportunities to talk about her faith.

Then there's my friend Eddie, who could often be found at the student pub, sharing a sandwich, a beer and his faith with one of his close non-Christian friends over lunch. He had a way of breaking people's preconceived notions that Christianity was simply a list of dos and don'ts and getting them to understand the gospel.

As you can see, my friends and I took different stands on alcohol. On the way to our decisions, we each explored what the Bible has to say about drinking. For me, the question of whether I as a Christian on campus should drink or not boiled down to five issues.

Responsibilities

The Bible writers' primary concern about alcohol seems to be that drinking impairs judgment. That's why certain groups of people were asked not to touch it. In the Old Testament, those who served in the worship of God, such as priests, were instructed to avoid drinking when they had spiritual responsibilities: "You and your sons are not to drink wine or other fermented drink whenever you go into the tent of Meeting, or you will die. . . . You must distinguish between the holy and the common, between the unclean and the clean; and you must teach the Israelites" (Lev 10:9-11; see also Ezek 44:21).

Besides the priests there were the Nazirites, people called to take special vows of obedience and service to God. (You can read about them in Num 6:1-21; Judg 13:2-14; Amos 2:11-12; and Lk 1:15.) Kings, judges and other people in responsibility were advised to abstain, too: "It is . . . not for kings to drink wine, not for rulers to crave beer; lest they drink and forget what the law decrees, and deprive all the oppressed of their rights" (Prov 31:4-5). And in the New Testament, when Paul wrote to Timothy and Titus about selecting leaders for the infant church, he told them to choose men "not indulging in much wine" (1 Tim 3:8; see also Tit 1:7).

So people who claim to serve God must place their God-given responsibilities above their desire for a drink. My responsibilites on campus—to help a friend who needed me, to study, whatever—usually seemed less important than those of a king or priest. But, if I drank, would I be up to fulfilling them?

Priorities

With little cash in his pocket (and even less in his bank account), my friend Bob, who lives off-campus, went to buy enough groceries to last until the next paycheck.

At the checkout counter, he cringed as the clerk rang up the bill. He didn't have enough money. She could see it in his face.

"All right," she snapped. "What don't you want?"

Glancing at the people glowering in line behind him, Bob surveyed his groceries on the counter. The six-pack of Michelob almost shouted at him. He reluctantly pointed to the beer. Cheetos and doughnuts were next.

Fortunately, Bob was able to keep his alcohol and his pocketbook in perspective. Others can't. The Old Testament prophet Joel talks about those who sell children to buy drink (Joel 3:3). And Isaiah, taunting those who are heroes at drinking wine and mighty at mixing drinks, is appalled at their lack of concern for the poor (Is 5:8, 11-12, 20-23).

I knew I was not about to sell my firstborn into slavery for a drink. But when finances got tight, I needed to decide what would get squeezed out of my budget—booze, or those who needed the help I could provide with the money I would otherwise spend on booze?

Health

Hangovers, liver failure, D.T.s, hallucinations and alcholism are nothing new. "Who has needless bruises? Who has bloodshot eyes?" the writer of Proverbs asks. "Those who linger over wine, who go to sample bowls of mixed wine. . . . Your eyes will see strange sights and your mind imagine confusing things" (Prov 23:29-33). My body is a temple of the Holy Spirit. I knew God didn't want me destroying it with too much drink, food or anything else.

But I also realized that's only half the story. The Bible also portrays alcohol in moderation as a good gift from God.

Psalm 104:15 says that one reason God makes the plants grow is so that people may produce "wine that gladdens the heart of man." And in Deuteronomy 14:22-27, Moses tells the Israelites to honor the Lord by keeping an annual harvest festival, in which a tenth of what is produced—grain, wine, oil, the newborn animals—is to be set aside for a huge feast to be eaten in the Lord's presence. If an individual lived too far from the Israelite worship center to carry all that produce and meat, he was allowed to convert it into money and buy whatever he wanted to celebrate when he got there: "Use the silver to buy whatever you like: cattle, sheep, wine or other fermented drink, or anything you wish. Then you and your household shall eat there in the presence of the LORD your God and rejoice" (v. 26).

Relationships

Some Christian have trouble reconciling a divine command to celebrate with wine and strong drink in the Lord's presence with the picture of God they grew up with. But then Jesus was mistaken for a glutton and a drunkard (Mt 11:18-19)—and that didn't happen because he stayed away from places where people drank.

I began to realize that whether Jesus ever drank alcoholic beverages is an irrelevant question; the wine available to him was much less potent than what we have today and was customarily watered down as well. What's important is the company Jesus kept. Jesus got his reputation not because he drank too much, but because he spent time with people who drank too much—people who needed him.

One evening my friend Bob convinced his roommate Steve, a confirmed teetotaller, to have a beer with him in a local bar in celebration of their graduation the next day. During college Steve had shunned the nearby bars as a matter of principle, but he reluctantly accompanied Bob to Harrison's, a crowded, smoke-filled pub.

There they ran into Ashley, a mutual friend who had graduated a few years earlier. After reminiscing about the good ol' days, Ashley suddenly became very serious. "I haven't told anybody this, but I think I can tell you," he said. "I have to tell someone. My wife left me last week."

The news jolted them, but they listened as Ashley shared his struggles. After talking a while at the bar, they invited him back to Bob's apartment to talk further and pray. Ashley stayed until three in the morning.

After Ashley left, Steve turned to Bob. "You know, if we hadn't been at that bar, we would never have run into Ashley."

Of course, being with people who drink doesn't give us an excuse for compromising our own principles. But as a rule, most drinkers don't care what you're drinking. (As long as you don't make not drinking the point of your Christian witness, that is. "I don't drink. I'm a Christian," lacks the sensitivity Christ had for the people who needed him.) What matters is being with people at their point of need.

Your Situation

After reading Romans 14:21, I realized that if I decided to drink moderately, I'd have to be careful who I drank with: "It is good neither to eat meat nor drink wine nor do anything by which your brother stumbles, or is offended, or is made weak" (NKJV).

Even as a light drinker with excellent self-control, I would offend fellow Christians who lack self-control or have a history of alcohol abuse by drinking around them or offering them a drink. That's the kind of offense Paul writes about: causing a person who's weak in a certain area to sin.

But neither Paul nor Jesus worried about offending religious people who were firmly grounded in their beliefs. The question I started asking before I thought about taking a drink with others, then, changed from "What will these people think?" to "What do these people need?"

Some of my Christian friends chose not to drink for good reasons. Some couldn't handle alcohol. Others wanted to set a good example in a society where alcohol abuse contributes to a significant percentage of violent crimes, auto and industrial accidents, family breakups, debilitating disease and professional incompetence.

A few of my friends, however, chose not to drink for a bad reason: to get brownie points with God. Not drinking can be a practical help to a better relationship with God. But self-righteous teetotalling (or self-righteous anything) never seemed to impress Jesus much.

In the end, I realized that only I could decide whether I would drink. Could I do so without impairing my ability to carry out responsibilities, damaging my health, wasting my money or causing someone else to sin? Maybe. But one more piece of biblical advice kept me cautious: "So, if you think you are standing firm, be careful that you don't fall!" (1 Cor 10:12).

Going Greek

Elizabeth Riley

Idecided before I ever got to college that sororities weren't for me. After all, I didn't drink, I'd never approved of exclusive groups, and I had seen Christians drift away from their faith after joining the Greeks.

But as my first semester unfolded, some of my Christian friends and I began to wonder what we were missing. We heard sorority sisters talk about their special candlelighting ceremonies and close friendships. We observed the week-long excitement of fall formals. And we got tired of spending Saturday nights watching "Dance Fever" on the dorm TV.

The day rush was to start, my Christian friends and I quit debating, threw caution to the wind, and rushed over to the Inter-Sorority Council Office.

The Good News

Some people in my campus fellowship group were wary about my rushing sororities. One acquaintance told me that Christians should not be "yoked together with unbelievers" (2 Cor 6:14). But as "Bid Friday" grew closer and I prayed for God's guidance about whether to accept a bid if I got one, I kept being reminded of Jesus' command to love our neighbors as ourselves. I knew I would not be one in heart and spirit with every sorority sister, but I could, I thought, learn to love even those who were very different from me.

The bid came. I accepted it. And I never regretted it.

My sorority gave me rituals, symbols and a group identity to help mark my passage into adulthood. But most importantly, the Greeks taught me about people, relationships and love.

In the sorority I got to know people with different personalities, values and backgrounds, and I got to join them in common goals—planning a pledge formal, practicing for intramurals and raising money for a children's hospital, to name a few. Working, playing and just living together built trust and unified us.

Of course, Christians can experience this unity to an even greater degree with other believers in a campus fellowship group. But fraternities and sororities offered some of my Christian friends and I a golden opportunity to build lasting friendships with a number of non-Christians.

Not that Greeks and non-Christians are synonymous, of course. As it turned out, several of my sorority sisters were also my sisters in Christ. I loved having friends I could get silly with at a punk party—but with whom I could also share a prayer request board in the bathroom. Together we laughed about our euphemisms for questionable sorority mottoes, and together we found transportation home if the parties got out of hand. And eventually we had the privilege of seeing several of our sorority sisters become "twice sisters" in Christ.

Contrary to popular belief, my Greek friends and I found that some fraternities and sororities were open to activities with a spiritual focus. Many Greek organizations were founded on Christian principles; therefore, Christian rituals, symbols and service projects are part of the groups' traditions. Not only did our sorority sisters accept our reviving these activities, but they appreciated our making the traditions more meaningful.

For example, a couple other Christians and I encouraged

our sorority to elect a chaplain to give occasional prayers, to perform some of our initiation ritual, and to read inspirational poems or quotations before every meeting. The sisters welcomed the idea. This office, which I held for a year, became a natural avenue for Christians to share Bible passages and devotionals on friendship, character and love, especially God's love in Christ.

Another opportunity I found for spiritual growth and witness in the Greeks was an interfraternity/intersorority Bible study organized by folks from several houses. Our group struggled to learn what it means to be in the world but not of it, but we also laughed and shared the fun of Greek life.

This Bible study, the chaplaincy and the basic late night postmunchie dorm talks provided me with ample opportunity for verbal Christian witness. However, since I spent so much time with sorority sisters, my actions became just as important as my words.

By actions, I don't only mean not compromising on moral issues. For example, most fraternities and sororities have a seemingly endless list of minor chores: signs to be painted, decorations to be put up, decorations to be taken down, doughnuts to be sold, errands to be run. What better way for me to demonstrate Christ's teaching that "whoever would be great among you must be your servant" (Mk 10:43)? Sisters who couldn't have cared less about my regular church attendance took note that I never missed Saturday morning sign painting, and even expressed appreciation for my faithfulness.

Of course, I didn't give up my daily prayer times to earn the "Best Pledge" award. Rather, I prayed that faithfulness, humility, integrity and all the fruits of the Spirit would characterize my life among the non-Christians in my house.

The Bad News

John Stott once said that you do not blame the darkness for being dark; you blame the light for retreating. Yet whether Christians can permeate the haze better from inside or outside the Greek system is not always clear.

First of all, not every fraternity or sorority is created equal. Most campuses have their "Delta Drugs" or "Seagram's Sigs" reminiscent of *Animal House*. Nor are Greeks for everyone. Students who associate alcohol or even parties with their lives before they were Christians might be particularly susceptible to the wiles, or "wilds," of Greek life. The same team spirit that goes into preparing the house for a party can also generate seemingly insurmountable peer pressure to conform.

Yet even when I felt pressured (to gossip or attend a wild party or do anything else that compromised my standards), Paul's words proved true: "God is faithful, and he will not let you be tempted beyond your strength, but with the temptation will also provide the way of escape, that you may be able to endure it" (1 Cor 10:13).

Sometimes I escaped temptation by simply leaving a party or avoiding a bad situation. If the sisters invited me to a party or movie I thought would compromise my morals, I turned down the invitation—then acknowledged their offer of friendship by expressing my appreciation for being included.

Other times, such as when conversation about certain rushees turned to gossip at one of our late-night bull sessions, I reminded myself to fear God rather than people, prayed for strength not to compromise and tried to change the thrust of the conversation. That's where other Christians in the sorority came in. We encouraged each other, kept each other accountable and occasionally (such as when several sisters rallied to ban personal negative remarks about rushees) were able to change the momentum of the crowd.

Some of the Christian fraternity guys I knew were masters at showing other brothers how to have fun creatively, without vulgarity or alcohol. One friend, for example, became the first to join his fraternity's infamous and elite "100 Shot Club" by chugging 100 consecutive shots of Mountain Dew instead of beer—a feat his brothers deemed

no less remarkable. And my senior year one fraternity
staged a "Road Rally" with my sorority. Secret clues were
hidden at landmarks all over town. People got so excited
that they all but painted the campus road checkerboard
black and white, Indy 500 style.

Clever humor goes further than crudeness. And a little
originality goes a long way in a world of conformity.

My greatest struggles in a sorority, however, were not
with peer pressure concerning alcohol, sex and drugs, but
with the enticements of pride and social status. The Greek
system sets up a false caste system where a fraternity sweat-
shirt can do wonders for one's ego. I had to remind myself
constantly that my identity was in Christ, not in my sorority.
After all, "haughty eyes" are as great an abomination in the
Lord's sight as "feet that make haste to run to evil" (Prov
6:16-18).

For me, the ethical fog grew thickest during the blitz of
parties during rush, when we gave potential recruits the
once-over. How could I reconcile the rush system with Jesus' command to "judge not"?

My first year as a sister, I listened as the sisters rejected
rushees because of everything from the wrong clothes to
an unwitting date with the sorority president's boyfriend.
When I thought of James 2:1-4, where we are warned not
to make distinctions between ourselves on the basis of
wealth or clothing, I cringed. I realized that the real problem with rush is not that it exists, but that people often
base decisions on superficial attributes such as attractive-
ness and popularity instead of on common interests, enthusiasm and natural affinities.

Some of the sisters decided rush in our house didn't
have to stay that way. After a girl was rejected because
someone did not like her stationery, several girls got together and pushed for a new rule: no one could make negative personal comments about a rushee. It didn't do away
with all the problems rush presented. But this rule was en-
forced so strictly that we would have been afraid to bring

up a girl's reputation, even if she were rumored to be as notorious as "Dynasty's" Alexis Colby.

Christians have always been called to live in the tension between keeping themselves in the light and yet being light in the darkness, between keeping themselves unstained by the world and yet getting stained cleaning it up. The question of fraternities and sororities brings this tension to a head. Some feel the Greek system is irreconcilable with Christian principles. I believe it gives some Christians a great opportunity to share God's love with those who don't know him.

Yet I wouldn't be honest if I said my only motivation for joining a sorority was to evangelize my house. I also joined to make new friends, to be part of a group, and to have a lot of fun. I learned that "for everything there is a season" and that there is a season to dance. Long after I have forgotten my first-declension French nouns (in fact, I even had to look up how to spell declension), I know I'll remember declining them with my sorority sisters in the library "Zoo." And long after I've forgotten the Pythagorean theorem, I'll remember the words of every song we danced to at post-exam beach.

I shared with some of my sisters the love of the Creator. I know they helped me appreciate the joy of his creation.

Should I Rush?

The rush chairman grabbed my arm. "I'd like to talk with you upstairs for a minute."

Following him to the third floor of the fraternity house, I naively wondered what he wanted. Ten brothers looked up as he led me into a darkened bedroom and shut the door. Solemnly, one of them proceeded to explain that every year they offered a few really good guys early bids. My heart pounded.

"We'd like you to become a brother in this

house. Take some time to think about it if you want."

I had made it into the inner circle of a good fraternity. "I'm there!" I said without a thought. Suddenly I was a fraternity man!

Two-and-a-half years later I became a Christian and almost as suddenly found myself being welcomed into a campus fellowship group. Because I was one of the few Greeks (and the only fraternity man) there, freshmen soon began to ask me whether they should join a house or even rush at all. Unless I knew them well, I would always hesitate. Through the next two years, however, I developed some guidelines to offer them:

☐ Freshmen: Rush by all means but don't accept a bid, usually good for a year, in September. First impressions about houses often prove wrong.

☐ Make lifestyle decisions beforehand. If you drink occasionally, will you drink at par-ties and mixers? Will the possibly regular, quiet pressure to join in on drinks and drugs wear you down?

☐ Consider dues. Can you justify the costs of membership?

☐ Before you pledge, ask brothers or sisters with whom you feel close what the house expects pledges to do beyond answering phone calls and serving meals. Is there a "hell week"? After pledging for a year, few have the strength to refrain from objectionable initiation activities.

☐ Finally, check out Greek fellowship. My fraternity/sorority support group empathized in a way no one else could when conflicts between Greek and Christian life seemed insurmountable. Our motto sticks in my mind: "Paul preached to the Greeks. So can you!" True, but Paul had prayerful friends nearby who understood his mission.

—*Robert M. Kachur*

Don't Rush into It

I went Greek. And I got out. Never had I experienced such a hedonistic, exploitative and degrading atmosphere. Not all houses are like mine, but based on my own experience and reports from others, I have four objections to joining a fraternity or sorority.

The Greek system can be hedonistic and sexually exploitative. In addition to the alcohol which is the focal point of almost every social program, some fraternities show X-rated movies, hire stripteases for new pledges, and carry out initiation rites which demean the sexuality of the initiates or of unsuspecting women.

It can be racist. Some have been denied bids because of the color of their skin. A friend of mine had the courage to depledge when her house moved to keep a black woman out. How many minority students will be in your house?

It can be elitist. People are commonly favored for their looks, money or family connections. In a time when so many college students are on financial aid, high social dues automatically cut many out. Even if you can afford it, you should ask where your money goes. In most fraternities, at least, an exorbitant amount goes for booze. Is that good stewardship?

It can be hostile to Christians. Christians who objected to some practices have been ridiculed and discriminated against. At the University of Iowa, four women were asked to depledge because of their "born-again activities." And in some houses, the vestiges of Christian roots are parodied in the rituals and mocked by the members' behavior.

These objections are not the rule for every house. Daniel served in the court of the Babylonian empire. But Moses left his place of privilege to be with the outcasts. So if you join, be aware (and beware) of the system you're getting into.

—Andrés Tapia

FINDING GOLD ON THE SILVER SCREEN

Bob Bittner

Ask any four people on your campus what they thought of the most recent movie they saw, and you'll probably get predictable answers: "I really liked the special effects." "The dancing was fantastic." "It was hilarious." "Great photography." "Too much sex." "Boring." "Extremely violent." Short, easy critiques.

Our ability to be good movie critics, to sift relevant themes and constructive ideas from what we watch, has been weakened by half-watching television, skimming popular magazines and half-listening to Top 40 radio. We want to be entertained; we don't want to think. Let the critics be critical.

Becoming Critical Christians

But as Christians, we must be critical; everything we experience requires a Christian response. We can't drop off our faith back at the dorm and go unhin-dered into a darkened theater. If we casually stroll into *Chariots of Fire* or *The Color Purple,* Christ goes with us; if we blushingly tiptoe into *Debbie Does Dallas,* Jesus is there too. Whatever flashes across the screen must be seen through Christian eyes. What brings an audience to its feet might bring our Lord to tears.

Are movies really worth that much effort, especially with everything else there is to do on campus?

It depends on the movie. Some are poorly made or decidedly vulgar. Others have inconsequential stories with naive characters. But in the same way that incompetent authors shouldn't turn us away from literature or make us suspicious of Milton and Dostoyevsky, bad movies shouldn't make us shun all movies. There are some films we should walk out on. But others provide rich insight into our world and ourselves.

Despite peer pressure and your upbringing, it's up to you whether or not you're going to see a particular movie. And it's relatively easy to know what to expect from a movie before you buy your popcorn and take your seat. Ratings and advertisements offer basic clues about what to expect, though ratings are never an accurate measure of quality. Assume that as you move from G to R, the frequency of nudity, violence and strong language increases. Even though some films earn a stronger rating based on only one word or scene, it's better to assume excess on the part of the filmmakers; you'll save yourself the frustration of hating a movie you really shouldn't have seen in the first place.

Once you're seated in a dark theater, you might gasp, "But wait! I can't enjoy this. I have to be critical." Don't worry. A critical, Christian approach to movies will help you clarify what's happening on the screen so that you can enjoy them even more.

Here are five categories to consider while the film is rolling. (If you are ambitious, carry a small notebook to write in—just to keep things straight.)

Theme

No movie is purely entertainment. Every movie has a point to make or a controlling, underlying theme.

The theme is usually a view of life that can be expressed in a sentence or two: mankind is headed for self-destruction *(Silkwood)*; good can always outmaneuver evil (the James Bond films); every person has worth *(It's a Wonderful Life)*; or fantasy can come true *(Back to the Future)*. Sometimes the theme is simple *(Star Wars)*. Other times it's

complex. *Citizen Kane,* for example, has at least three themes: loving things more than people brings personal ruin; abandoning the joys of youth to achieve adult success ends in emptiness; and power corrupts. To determine a film's value, we must be able to discern its message.

Character

Characters must *do* something—reach a goal, effect change, learn some truth or teach a truth. Though a film may be technically proficient, something is wrong if the characters leave us cold.

Characters can't be much better than their dialogue. The words should reinforce the action and heighten the story. Are they realistic, expressing heartfelt emotions? Inane? With so much emphasis placed on big-screen visuals, don't sell dialogue short—sight *and* sound, images *and* words, are ideally combined into a cohesive whole. And only film can capture this.

Don't forget to determine characters' moral inclinations. Characters' morality affects their perceptions and actions. In *Being There,* Peter Sellers's innocent and amoral Chance accepts and imitates everything he sees. Edmund Gwenn's moral Kris Kringle in *Miracle on 34th Street* wholeheartedly believes in fairy tales and wants to convince an unbelieving world. Vivien Leigh's Scarlett O'Hara, though not completely immoral, would stun the unflappable Kris Kringle with her pouting avarice. Each character is different; each provides a unique glimpse into the human soul and human behavior.

Plot

Ask: Is the story line entertaining enough to hold my interest? Believable? Old hat? Innovative? Intriguing? Does the producer seem to care about the viewer? A drama—or any film—without conflict lacks its most basic element. A horror flick that exceeds our limits of belief leaves us tagging behind. The story should proceed logically within its own boundaries.

Tone

Tone creates the mood and is inseparably linked to theme, character and plot. Are the signals the movie sends consistent? Are we increasingly drawn into the story? Are we enchanted—or manipulated? Or is the movie simply visual and verbal assault, lacking tone altogether? If a film claims to be a comedy but doesn't make us laugh, something went wrong with its tone.

A film needn't be single-minded in tone, however. *Arsenic and Old Lace* and *Little Shop of Horrors* are good examples of films with two purposes—to make us jump and to make us laugh. They achieve a perfect balance between comedy and horror.

Offensive Language, Violence, Nudity

Since 1966, with the demise of the Hays Code of self-censorship, movies have progressively included more objectionable elements. Subsequently, moviegoers have found it harder to escape words, violence and sex scenes that offend.

So how do we avoid these situations? The most obvious solution is not to go to movies at all. For years conservative Christians considered this a given; today it is a legitimate response to the problem and should be considered.

But we must also be consistent. Books, TV, music and theater are also media that can be misused. Yet, like those other media, movies can bless us if we select and view them intelligently and with discernment.

If we are confronted with offensive elements in the theater, we should ask, What is the intent? Is the film just trying to shock? Titillate? Exploit? Or are the offensive items important to the story? In *The Exorcist,* vulgarity is offensive but essential. (We *are* watching the workings of a demon.) In *About Last Night,* though, the needless repetition of four-letter words is ridiculous. Likewise, *Rambo*'s violence exploits; *A Clockwork Orange*'s violence is integral.

As the curtain comes down and the lights come up we can add the finishing touches to our critique. Analyzing a movie with friends can be fun. Here are a few questions you can hash over in a group:

☐ Did the plot move the action toward a worthy climax or did it drag on?

☐ How were good and evil portrayed? How was God portrayed?

☐ Were the characters real people or stereotypes? Did they show strengths missing in your own life—or were they prime examples of what not to be?

☐ If the movie contained questionable scenes, what was the intent? Did they arouse and exploit the audience, or were they an integral element of the story?

☐ Which scenes were especially effective? Why?

If it was a good movie, all of the elements should fit into place like pieces in a puzzle.

Hollywood is out to make money by entertaining us. But all those flesh-and-blood human beings who make up the movie industry project their desires, prejudices and values onto the screen. To write off such a dynamic combination as "mere entertainment" is to miss its soul. Watching movies critically can help you see anew the world that Christ died for. To let a film wash thrillingly over you and then allow it to evaporate as you step into daylight is to relinquish what movies—both good and bad—are saying: I am a mirror of all the world.

TUNING IN: THE TRUTH ABOUT ROCK 'N' ROLL

Steve Lawhead

Mickey grew up in a family that thought rock 'n' roll was of the devil. Sometimes in high school some of the kids would get together and go hear a band who was in concert. They'd invite Mickey. But the answer was always the same: No. He wasn't even allowed to have a radio in the house. Later, as he grew older and entered college, Mickey was left to make those kinds of decisions on his own. Consequently, he listened to rock 'n' roll constantly.

One time during freshman year some friends invited him to go hear a local band. After the first amateurish, deafening set, I asked him, "What do you think?"

"Great," he said. When the second show was over he said, "Man, that was great, too."

"What are you saying?" I asked, shocked. "This band is the pits."

"Oh," was all he said. He couldn't tell the difference; all he knew was that he liked rock music. No one had ever taught him how to tell good music from bad music, which groups to listen to and which to stay away from. To him they were all the same.

Christians who have flatly condemned rock music as too weird, wanton

and wrongheaded for God to use have nurtured thousands of Mickeys—people who can't tell good rock from bad because they have no guidelines for judging it.

When you know what is good and how to recognize it, the choice is easy. However, when it comes to art (and when we talk about rock music we *are* talking about art), most people do not know what makes good art good, or how to recognize it.

Test #1: Is It Good?

Like all art, rock does not come affixed with a prepasted label which neatly lumps it into one of two categories: classic or garbage. Art exists on a continuum from excellent to awful. In general, good music must possess the qualities we have come to expect of good art.

Below are some questions which you could use to evaluate any kind of art. Try answering some of them about the music you listen to:

☐ Is it novel and inventive? Is it one of a kind?

☐ Is it skillfully written and performed? (Whether a rock song or a symphony, the work should say, "I was made by an expert.")

☐ Does it give you a glimpse into the mind of its creator? That is, rather than presenting a jumble of half-formed ideas, does this song reflect the artist's imaginative selecting, assembling and developing raw materials?

☐ Does it deliver all it promises? Is it complete and unified? (Good art must satisfy; there can be no loose ends or missing pieces.)

☐ Is it awkwardly patched together and forced sounding, or does it seem to flow naturally, as if it had a life of its own apart from the artist?

Test #2: Is It True?

In his book, *Art and the Bible,* Francis Schaeffer describes four categories of art: bad art with a true message; good art with a true message; bad art with a false message; and good art with a false message. These are what I call the four arts, and they abound in rock 'n' roll. Listen to any Top 40 radio station; you will hear from ten to fifteen different songs in an hour, some bad, some good and each with a different message.

When good music's combined with a false message, we can get confused. Catchy music and clever lyrics give false messages a credibility they would not ordinarily have. By naturally responding to the song's quality, we may suspend judgment and accept its false message, too.

Rockers don't try to trick us into believing lies; it just happens. As often as not, musicians are themselves ignorant of the truth and consequently in no position to communicate it to others. Many simply echo the myths of the modern world: "love's all you need," "you only live once; so grab for the gusto," "happiness is all that matters," and so on.

When it comes to communicating true messages, rock primarily falls short in the following areas:

Materialism. Although many songwriters point out that wealth and material things can never insure happiness, a good many more imply just the opposite. When Madonna bellows out that she's a material girl living in a material world, her tongue isn't completely in her cheek. Success is often presented stereotypically: obtaining more, getting your share, making your fortune, having it all.

Sex. "Love" usually means sex. Both men and women are presented as sexual objects existing solely to satisfy the desires of the other. Relationships in songs often focus on the sex act as the ultimate expression of love.

Hedonism. Pursuing the "good life" is a part of the rock myth. Personal pleasure is life's highest aim. The Christian value of service is foreign to most popular songs.

So, in the tangle of mixed messages presented by popular music, we have to decide what is true and what is false in a song, what to embrace and what to reject. If you're not used to paying close attention to what is being heard, you will have to make a conscious effort to discern a song's message as well as its emotional effect. Try asking these questions: Is this song's message consistent with the basic truths Christians live by? What kind of feelings does this song evoke in me? Are these feelings healthy?

Deciding that a song has a true message does not mean deciding that we agree with what is being said or that it makes us feel good. A song may have a true message yet make us uncomfortable. For example, the message of the Geldorf/Ure Band Aid anthem "Do They Know It's Christmas?", that millions of the world's people are starving, does not make anyone feel good. Yet it's true. On the other hand, a Christian song implying that "if you only trust Jesus he'll give you everything you want," might invoke good feelings, even though its message is false.

A song is not true just because it has the words *Jesus* or *God* in it. Neither is a song false because it omits those words.

Making Choices

If a song doesn't pass the tests of being good art and having a true message, should you refuse to listen to it? Though plenty of Christians are eager to dictate what we ought to listen to, only you can decide.

If, for example, a good song with a false message makes you doubt something you know to be right, then you should probably avoid it. But a word of warning: if we want the freedom to listen (or not to listen) to certain songs, then we must reserve judgment and allow others to make their own choices, too.

Rather than condemning rock, God's people should be in the position of encouraging whatever is good, worthy and true in popular music. And rather than blacklisting, condemning or otherwise shackling Christian rockers who don't fit our stereotypes of what Christian musicians should be, we must encourage them to higher achievement. The Christian community and the world at large desperately need the creativity, enthusiasm, courage and vision Christian artists can bring.

RELATIONSHIPS

Never will you meet as many people open to making friends as during your college years. And never again will relationships come, go and change so quickly. If you've never dated before, you might start now. And if you've never shared a bedroom before, you and your roomie are in for some surprises. Meanwhile, back at the ranch, your relationship with Mom and Dad will be changing, too. In this section we'll help you understand how to make the most of your key relationships over the next several years.

WINNING THE DATING GAME

Jean Stapleton and Richard Bright

The dating game—it's more than just a television show. College students have been playing it for years, with increasing subtleties and changes to accommodate such new inventions as the car and the telephone, as well as increasing affluence, greater independence for women and improved contraception.

But it has remained a game, one we begin to learn as small children, watching older brothers and sisters; reading fairy tales and, later, teen-age romances; and watching television and seeing movies. By the time we are old enough to start dating, we have our head full of oughts and shoulds and fuzzy romantic notions of what dating will be like. Even before we had found the first person we wanted to date, we knew from our early training who would do the asking, who would pay, who would attempt the first kiss, and who had the responsibility if the relationship became "too physical too fast."

A game is fun when you know it is a game and when you don't take it seriously. It is fun when it lasts for a few minutes or a few hours, when it has a definite ending, and when you might win.

A game wouldn't be much fun if the players didn't know it was a game, but mistook the other player's actions as reflecting his or her real feelings and thought the game was real life. It wouldn't be fun if the game lasted many years, if you were never quite sure how you were doing, and if in the end all the players lost. That's what the dating game is like. Most people aren't sure whether a date's actions are just part of the game or whether they spring from real emotion. Did she let him kiss her good night because she liked him or because she felt obligated after he spent all that money? Does he really think she looks nice, or is it just something he feels he must always tell his date when he picks her up?

But to get beyond the dating game and have the meaningful relationships we are really searching for, then we must analyze the rules or assumptions upon which the game is normally played. As we will see, these rules are based on assumptions that our society has made about the nature of men and women.

Men and Women
One assumption has been that men are "stronger" than women. From that assumption we have made man the protector, woman the protected. He has

been given the burden of carrying her books, opening doors, helping her with her coat. Men have also felt it their responsibility to ensure a woman's physical safety and to defend her honor.

Many women in turn have felt they needed to pay for this protection with their gratitude, with building up the man's ego, and with their own feigned weakness (or real weakness, since lack of use makes anyone's muscles flabby).

In truth, the difference between male and female strengths is not as much as we once imagined. And strength is not just muscle power. It is also the ability to endure pain, to endure stress, to survive—in all of which many women excel.

Another assumption that gives us rules for the dating game is that men are naturally more aggressive. It might be true that most men are more aggressive than women. But the rule that says men must initiate everything limits all of us. If a woman likes a man, she isn't allowed to take direct action, to ask for a date. Instead, she must give him special attention, flirt with him, dress up or wear a special perfume when he is going to be around. Then she can do nothing more—just wait for the telephone to ring or for him to get the courage to ask her for a date, or even for him to finally understand that she is interested.

Even after she has succeeded in interesting him and they have gone on a date, a woman in a traditional dating relationship has to wait for the man to decide to call for a second date. She mustn't seem too eager, according to the rules.

Under the same assumption, if the relationship becomes serious, it is the man who must propose marriage. The woman's role is only to say yes or no.

Equally Unfair
On the other hand, the man is forced to take all the risks. Asking someone for a date is an admission that "I like you." The woman doesn't have to go that far out on a limb. She can wait until he takes that risk and then turn him down—a very painful experience for him—or she can say yes, which says "I

like you too" but doesn't involve any risk, since the man has already made
his interest clear. The same is true for the second date and so on, up to the
marriage proposal: the man has to risk getting hurt every time.

The dating game assumes that men have steady income and that women
do not. Therefore, men pay for everything—meals, entertainment, travel expenses. But women are expected to pay men back for the expense of the
date through bolstering the man's ego and through sex. ("I spent fifty dollars
on you this evening, and all I get is a good-night kiss? I don't even get to
come into your apartment?") It is an unspoken bargain that men and women
have made for generations. But such an agreement makes them little more
than prostitute and customer. It interferes with their relating to each other as
persons.

Another assumption on which the dating game is based is that men are rational, women emotional. As a result, men must make the decisions; women
must accept the decisions. Men must be stoical; women may express all emotions except anger, the only emotion allowed men. The man makes the decisions about where the couple will go on a date, what they will do, what time
they will go, and whether there will be a next date, because both the man
and the woman have accepted all these myths about themselves and
members of the other sex. This is what makes dating a game. Games are fun,
you may respond; so what's wrong with the dating game?

The Problem with Games
In the end, the dating game has no winners, just people who drop out of the
game or graduate to the marriage game, and maybe go back to the dating
game after the marriage ends. Playing according to the rules certainly does
not guarantee a good relationship with another human being. In fact, it
makes it almost impossible to relate to the other person as a unique individual.

Most people get involved in the dating game in the first place because they
would like to have a healthy relationship with a member of the other sex.
Most of us want to be close to a person of the other sex, to be able to trust

that person with our secrets, our emotions, our faults, our accomplishments, and still to be loved and to know that our partner is cheering for us even when nobody else is. We want to be for our partner, to be trusted and allowed to love that person. We want to share affection and, to a growing degree, sex. That is what a good marriage is all about, and that is what most people really want, eventually.

Every relationship functions under rules. Most relationships function under unspoken rules, rules that have not been consciously chosen but that have developed between the two persons and that each is careful to observe. Neither party may be able to say what the rules are, neither may even admit that they exist, and so they are not intentionally chosen or thought about.

Unfortunately, the rules of the dating game tend to keep us from being real with each other, and so they make it difficult to ever get the kind of closeness with the other person that we want. Only by establishing a new set of rules, based on different assumptions that allow for individuality, can we form the kind of relationship that satisfies our need to be really close to another person.

New Rules

These are not rules about who pays for the meal or what time is off limits for phone calls or whether unannounced visits are welcome. Those are important, but they will be decided within the context of the rules we are talking about. The rules we are referring to set up the basic structure of the relationship. These have to do with the rights of each person, the relative status of each person, the power that each person has, and the leadership that each will allow the other. Really, they are rules that will lay a solid foundation for any friendship.

It is impossible for there to be no rules in a relationship. If a particular set of rules *is not* in operation, it just means that another set of rules *is* in operation, even though quite unconsciously. If we allow ourselves to drift into relationships, we will probably unconsciously choose the kind of relationships we see in our families, among our friends, on television, and in movies and books.

As you are setting up your relationship, it is wise to talk over the rules, and in the process each of you will discover whether the other is a person with whom you want a close relationship. If you want an equal relationship, your rules will probably include the following:

1. *No one is boss.* Decisions will generally be made by both persons. If an agreement cannot be reached, the decision should be postponed until both can come to an agreement. Neither person should have the final say-so on matters that affect both persons.

Only by making your decisions on an equal basis—where to go, how to pay, how much time to spend together, what your physical limits are, where the relationship will go next—will you be able to be open with each other and both take responsibility for decisions. When things go wrong, there isn't a boss to take the blame or an inferior to gloat about the boss's downfall. Equal decision-making is the basis for growing intimacy in a relationship.

2. *Each person can request anything.* The other person has the right to agree to the request, agree in part, or deny the request.

3. *Each person in a relationship has the right to be heard.* We've all had the experience of talking to someone who was reading a newspaper or watching television. The disinterested hmm's and uh-huh's tell us that the "listener" isn't listening, that we aren't being heard.

When your parents did that to you as a child you probably slipped in a "Can I have a hundred dollars to go to the movie, Mom?" or "I've decided to join the foreign legion, Dad," just to see if they'd react. An adult whose words are heard but not understood feels the same frustration, and failing to hear what the person really is saying may lead to a misunderstanding, a quarrel or even a breakup.

4. *Each person can freely express his or her feelings, and can expect the other person to accept those feelings as legitimate, no matter how hard they are to understand.* Sue turned down Tom's invitation to a party. "I'd feel guilty having fun while my brother is in the hospital," she explained.

"You can't help him. He's unconscious," Tom argued. "Your having fun isn't going to hurt him."

"I can't help it. That's the way I feel," Sue said.

"Well, it's a crazy way to feel. It's not rational."

Tom is unwilling to allow Sue to feel as she feels; he's trying to talk her out of feeling that way.

5. *On the other hand, while one cannot deny the legitimacy of the other's feelings, each person can freely challenge the other's opinions and conclusions.* Sam looked at Sally's new car with disdain. "I told you to get a Toyota if you wanted a good car for the money you had. Why did you buy that Chevette? You don't respect my opinion!"

"But my father and my aunt both love their Chevettes! They've always had good service from them," Sally replied.

Sam is confusing opinions with feelings and is hurt that Sally ignored his advice. But Sally had other evidence that she used in making her decision. She has the right to allow the experience of others and her own experience to determine her decision.

During discussions and disagreements, be sure to make a distinction between feelings, which should not be challenged, and information, which is subject to challenge.

6. *Chivalry is out; kindness is in.* The old roles are reinforced by chivalry. He must open the doors for her not because she needs help or because he wants to do something nice for her but because she is a woman. Kindness, however, is always appreciated. Anyone can appreciate another's caring enough to help with a coat or open a door when the other person is carrying something.

7. *Each person has the right to be alone or with other people for a while.* You don't have to be together all the time. It helps to keep your perspective on the relationship and to keep new interest in the relationship if you each spend time alone separately pursuing your own interests.

8. *You need to remain separate people, no matter how close you are.* Avoid using such terms as *we* and *us* until you know that you have agreed on the issue.

9. *Each person has the right not to have his or her mind read.* You can change your mind or seem inconsistent. Just because a person knows where you stood yesterday or knows where you stand on a number of issues doesn't mean that he or she can always tell what you are thinking.

10. *You each have the responsibility to allow the past to remain past.* The past should not be allowed to block out the future. People do change. Resentment over some long-ago wrong can spoil what you really have today; so if it isn't relevant, forget it.

11. *Above all, you each have the right to help determine the rules for this relationship.* This relationship is different from any you have ever had and any that has ever existed. Only you can decide what is right for you; and only in the negotiating, with both of you openly stating what you want, will the right combination be worked out so that both of you can be comfortable.

Handling Sex and Intimacy

Rebecca L. Propst

Seriously dating college-age couples yearn for intimacy and closeness. Many, however, confuse intimacy with sex, or mistakenly attempt to achieve intimacy through sex. Knowing the difference between the two will help us to develop some helpful biblical guidelines for maintaining both intimacy and sexual purity in dating relationships.

Characteristics of Intimacy

The essence of an intimate personal relationship is a mutually shared experience of the interior life. If only one person shares, there is not intimacy. Intimacy means knowing what is going on inside the other person—what makes her or him tick—and revealing in turn what is going on inside you.

What are the characteristics of intimacy? At least five descriptions are essential (see Thomas Oden, *Game Free: The Meaning of Intimacy,* published by Dell). First, an *intimate relationship is ordinarily sustained over a period of time.* There may be moments of greater intensity, but there must be a shared memory, a shared set of struggles and ecstasies. Often only time allows you to know someone well.

Jim, for example, may know a new aspect of Judy's trust-
worthiness when she defends him in a family feud.

Second, *an intimate relationship is characterized by
forthrightness.* Each person in an intimate relationship
knows what is expected. Both let the other person know
what they expect. These mutual expectations may constantly be shifting with no fear of working out new contracts.
Neither side is afraid to bring up unpopular ideas, because
both know the relationship won't cease to exist. Each can
lay the cards on the table because there is an established
bond. "I know that I can let it all hang out, and you won't
throw me out."

Third, *intimacy implies the ability to empathize.* If you do
not understand where the other person is coming from on
a certain issue, or why he or she feels that way, then you
do not have an intimate relationship. You need not, however, always agree with each other. In the religious sphere,
as we grow in our relationship with God, we come to understand him better. The same is true for our human relationships.

Fourth, *intimacy brings the ability to share both warmth
and conflict.* Can you both look honestly at disagreements,
or do you avoid them, hoping they will go away? When disagreements come up, do you negotiate and compromise?

Fifth, *intimacy encourages both partners to disclose themselves while allowing the other person some privacy.*

God's Intentions for Sex

A sexual relationship presupposes a high degree of intimacy. In Scripture, we find Paul constantly saying no to fornication *(porneia* in the Greek) as he lists it with other
sensuous sins he asks the early church to avoid.

For example, in 1 Corinthians 6:9-10 Paul writes, "Do not
be deceived; neither the immoral [the Greek word here is
pornoi, meaning fornicators], nor idolaters, nor adulterers,
nor sexual perverts, nor thieves, nor the greedy, nor drunk-
ards, nor revilers, nor robbers will inherit the kingdom of
God." Galatians 5:19 has a similar list which starts out with

fornication. *Porneia* means sexual intercourse outside the marriage relationship. There are also brief lists in Ephesians 5:3 and Colossians 3:5.

Why is Paul so negative? Divine law, though often expressed negatively, is rooted in a positive insight—that sexual intercourse involves two people in a life-uniting act. This is why Paul thought sexual intercourse by unmarried people was wrong: it violates the inner reality of the act. "Do you not know that he who joins himself to a prostitute becomes one body with her?" (1 Cor 6:16). Two people engage in a life-uniting act without a life-uniting intent.

The act of two becoming one may also signify the unique presence of God. Sexual intercourse may be considered a sacrament somewhat analogous to the Lord's Supper or baptism. That is, it can be seen as an outward and visible act that reflects an inward and spiritual reality. The physical manifestations of bread and wine represent the unique presence and memory of Christ for the individual. Likewise, sexual intercourse, in which male and female come together to become one, can also symbolize the presence of God. This analogy may be demonstrated in at least two ways.

First, Genesis 1:27 states that God created the human race in his own image: "male and female he created them." The complete image of God is male *and* female. We are all familiar with male imagery for God. But what about female imagery? An example is found in Isaiah 66:13. "As one whom his mother comforts, so I will comfort you," says God. And in Isaiah 46:3-4 Scripture describes the saving activity of God as a mother who gave birth to Israel. We can draw an analogy from this to suggest that when male and female become one, they form a special picture of the unity of God.

Second, sexual intercourse based on intimacy may also be a picture of God, in that both individuals in such a relationship will respond with something deeper than merely erotic love. In a relationship where both are known and

still accepted, love is present in a way that uniquely imitates God's love. Both spouses imitate Christ in their self-
giving love.

Such a selfless response is impossible, however, unless
both partners know each other deeply. (Christ knows us
and still chooses us.) Without this love, their oneness as an
image of God's love is absent, and sexual intercourse is in
violation of its own symbolism.

It is easy to say that sexual involvement outside marriage   **Intimate Hints**
is wrong. But it is difficult to maintain that standard in a
dating relationship, particularly when most of your friends
consider such standards prudish. At times it seems almost
impossible to develop intimacy in a dating relationship and
yet keep the sexual aspects of the relationship from taking
over. Here are some steps you can take.

First, you both must understand that sex by itself does
not lead to emotional intimacy. Deep relationships do not
magically materialize after marriage. Increased physical expression in dating will lead to less emotional intimacy.
Why is this so? I call it the mushroom-and-curry-powder
phenomenon. Mushrooms have very delicate flavor, where-
as curry powder is hot. Beside the experience of tasting
curry, the experience of tasting a mushroom is nothing. I
visited a Thai restaurant in Los Angeles a few years ago.
They served us the dishes one at a time, starting with the
one that was most delicate—black mushrooms. Each dish
was slightly more spicy. This was arranged so that we could
appreciate each dish and savor the delicacies, intricacies
and subtleties of the flavors. Each dish became slightly less
subtle than the preceding one, until we were hit over the
head with a hot curry. Some people with duller taste buds
may have missed the slight variations in the first few
dishes, but no one missed the last one!

Our feelings are like that. Instead of being in touch with
the more delicate feeling of contentment, or of discovery,
or even sadness, or irritation, you are overpowered by sex-

ual arousal. When you are separated, you don't think, "Ah, yes, I felt her despair, or irritation, or delight." You have sexual fantasies instead. Don't make the mistake of smothering mushrooms in curry powder. Talk this out. Make sure you both understand it.

The only way to develop emotional intimacy is to talk, to listen and to wait. Time is needed. I have found that Robert and Alice Fryling's *Handbook for Engaged Couples* (IVP) is a great aid for two people who want to become more intimate. (Couples do not even have to be engaged to use some of the chapters.) Each chapter has a discussion topic with space for written responses. You will soon learn what each thinks about important issues.

A Bible study in which you talk about the relevance of the passage for yourselves as a couple or individually may also provide a springboard for discussion. These techniques help you start talking about a vitally important topic, not just the weather or Aunt Mabel's apple pie. If it has been hard to refrain from physical contact, you can meet to talk in a more public place.

Good for the Soul

Confession can also help. If you have been having trouble controlling the physical aspect of your relationship, confess it to a pastor or Christian counselor each time you have difficulties. (I guarantee knowing you'll have to confess it again will make you think twice on your next date.) Friends, too, can help as they share with you their experiences and difficulties and what they've found helpful and not helpful. They can also challenge any of your behavior they think is unbecoming to a Christian. Let's face it—we live in a sexually supercharged era, and we need all the help we can get. You should also be willing to challenge other Christians if you feel their behavior is below par.

Finally, think about what you can do to improve your relationship with God. What is the focus of your attention? What do you want more than anything else in the world? Pause and think about that for a moment.

Many Christians would choose as a goal a satisfying intimate relationship in marriage. That is certainly not a bad goal. But Paul, in Philippians 3:7-8, states that he counted even good things as loss in order that he might gain Christ. Likewise in Philippians 1:21 he states, "For me to live is Christ, and to die is gain." Paul indeed had a passion for Christ that was stronger than a passion for any other person.

The biblical definition of chastity is not just sexual chastity; it means singleness of mind, undivided loyalty to a person's purpose. We must have a wholehearted allegiance to God. This wholehearted allegiance should be reflected in our romantic and dating relationships.

What steps can you take in your dating relationships right now to make them more appropriately reflect your love and passion for Christ?

Are You Addicted to Love?

Might as well face it. You're addicted to love," sings Robert Palmer in his Top 40 hit. "I'm addicted to you— you're a hard habit to break," Peter Cetera agrees in the Chicago single.

Finally, pop musicians are beginning to admit something many never knew was possible: You can be addicted not only to alcohol or drugs, but to a person—usually in a romantic context.

"When a person goes to another with the aim of filling a void in himself, the relationship quickly becomes the center of his or her life," Stanton Peele writes in his book *Love and Addiction*. "It offers him a solace that contrasts sharply with what he finds everywhere else, so he returns to it more and more, until he needs it to get through each day of his otherwise stressful and unpleasant existence. . . . Often, two people simultaneously engulf and are engulfed by each other. The result is a full-fledged addiction, where each partner draws the other back at any sign of a loosening of the bonds that hold them together."

Are you in love, or merely addicted to your romantic partner? Perhaps you'll know better after answering these questions about your relationship, offered by Peele in the same book:

☐ Do each of you have a secure belief in your own value?

☐ Are you both improved by the relationship? According to others, are you better, stronger, more accomplished or more sensitive individuals? Do you value the relationship for this very reason?

☐ Do you maintain serious interests outside the relationship, including other meaningful personal relationships?

☐ Is the relationship integrated into, rather than being set off from, the totality of your lives?

☐ Are you beyond being possessive or jealous of each other's growth and expansion of interests?

☐ Are you also friends? Would you seek each other out if you should cease to be primary partners?

Peele stresses that these standards are an ideal, a goal to strive for and a checklist to identify addictive, destructive aspects of any relationship.

"Mature love," Erich Fromm writes in his classic *The Art of Loving,* "is union under the condition of preserving one's integrity, one's individuality." One can only achieve love to the extent that one has become a whole and secure person—one who can freely choose to show "an active concern for the life and the growth" of the person loved.

The apostle Paul puts it this way: "Love is patient and kind; love is not jealous or boastful; it is not arrogant or rude. Love does not insist on its own way; it is not irritable or resentful; it does not rejoice at wrong, but rejoices in the right. Love bears all things, believes all things, hopes all things, endures all things" (1 Cor 13:4-7 RSV).

—*Verne Becker*

POPPING THE RIGHT QUESTIONS . . . BEFORE YOU MARRY

Alvin Lewis

Ron and Ruth, both seniors in college, are engaged to be married next year. Ron, the authoritarian, has an answer to almost any question that he and Ruth discuss and becomes irate when proven wrong. Although submissive, Ruth finds Ron's personality unbearable at times. She is afraid to confront him. Ruth keeps hoping that one day Ron will change. A confrontation, Ruth feels, would only intensify their problems—and maybe end their engagement.

Unlike Ron and Ruth, George and Jean get along peacefully. George has a college education and a good job. Being security minded, Jean said yes when

George popped the question. George loves Jean; Jean does not feel the same way about George. Jean thinks that love will grow with time.

Then there's John and Carmen. John was raised in a home where Mother picked up his clothes, cleaned his room and prepared his meals. John never had to do any household chores (such as cleaning and washing) that were considered women's work. Carmen, on the other hand, grew up in a home where household chores were shared by all family members. Carmen firmly believes in individual responsibility and equality for women.

John feels that Carmen is too competitive and does not understand her response to his views on the biblical role of wives. Carmen feels that John is too demanding and has a wrong view of a woman's role. In spite of their sharp differences, their commitment to marry remains unshaken.

Maybe you have known couples like these. They seem confused, angry and unsuited for each other. Yet they are determined to tie the knot no matter what. Engagement is a time of distress and discernment. It is a time for couples to evaluate their strengths and weaknesses, establish goals and make lifestyle decisions.

Marriage is a costly commitment. You have the responsibility to inquire intelligently before you invest your life. The questions below will help you and your future mate prepare for marriage. They are not a substitute for the direct help of your pastor or a marriage counselor; they are a supplement. Share with your premarital counselor any issues you aren't able to resolve while discussing these questions.

You and your future mate should answer all the following questions without consulting each other. Then find a quiet place to discuss your answers. Discuss each topic thoroughly. Do not rush through your discussion. If you reach an impasse on a question, go to the next one; then go back to the problem topic with a trusted friend or counselor present.

Maturity
What you are before marriage will remain the same after marriage. People who are emotionally and socially handicapped may find marriage to be a

threatening experience. When they face a crisis they react immaturely. Emotional and mental maturity will be tested as couples face struggles.

☐ If you do something wrong, how does your future spouse react?

☐ When there is a disagreement, how do each of you react?

☐ Do either of you have periods of depression? Why?

☐ When you argue, does one of you bring up past mistakes?

☐ How do you feel when you see your future spouse spending time with someone of the opposite sex? Why?

Commitment

Couples will sometimes get married because of parental prodding or peer pressure. Often, couples who marry because of outward pressure rather than inward persuasion are disappointed later on. A good marriage should be based on the deliberate choice of the two parties involved and not on the convictions or constraints of others.

☐ What are the advantages and disadvantages of being single? How hard will it be to give up the advantages?

☐ What are the benefits of settling down and being more responsible for your life? What concerns do you have about this?

☐ Are your parents or peers pressuring you to get married? How do you feel about that?

☐ What scares you about making a lifelong commitment? Why?

☐ How do you feel when your future spouse tells you what to do? Why?

Understanding

A sound marriage centers on a couple's knowledge of one another. There is no way to know everything about your future mate, but you should find out as much as you can before you say, "I do." Few of us would be willing to open the doors of our homes to a stranger without finding out some important facts.

☐ How long should the engagement period be? Why?

☐ How well do you know your future mate's family?

☐ How does that family make decisions?

☐ How does your future spouse communicate love? Anger? Disappointment? Hurt?

☐ What would you like to know about your future mate that you don't know now?

☐ When the two of you are alone, how does your future spouse like to spend the time? What do you like to do when it's just you two?

☐ What makes your future spouse feel loved?

☐ How does your future mate's family settle disputes and differences?

Finances

How much money you need before marriage will vary according to the lifestyle you choose.

Several years ago I was counseling an engaged couple. Both of them were twenty years old. During the counseling sessions I asked, "How do you intend to support yourselves when you are married?"

"We're going to find a job and move in with my mother," the man responded. Further counseling revealed that neither of them had a regular job, and that the young man's mother was not equipped to help them financially or with housing.

Insufficient financial resources can put much stress and strain on a marriage. Therefore, you and your future mate will want to talk about how you intend to acquire and manage your money.

☐ Do you have a job? How stable is it? Will your expenses match your income?

☐ How much money have you saved for marriage? What are you going to do with that money?

☐ What are your attitudes toward making money and spending it?

☐ How do you feel about spending money for food? Clothes? Entertainment? Vacations?

☐ Will you give to churches and other ministries? How much?

☐ How will the family's income be managed?

☐ Do you have debts? How large are they? How do you plan to pay them off?

Habits

There will be conflict over habits. Before you marry, take stock of the habits that might be offensive to your mate. As a marriage counselor, I have found that those habits excused in a future mate are seldom condoned after marriage. At the same time, you should not expect to perform radical surgery on your mate's habits after marriage. When you marry a person you also marry his or her habits.

☐ What habits does your future mate have that bother you?

☐ How do you plan to change your own habits which bother your future spouse?

☐ How do you react when you are told that a habit is offensive?

☐ Are you willing to accept your future mate with his or her present habits?

Marital Roles

Newlyweds often experience frustration over male and female roles. Many are deeply committed Christians who claim to draw their understanding of roles from the Bible. Other couples have emulated their parents.

Roles should be determined on the basis of mutual agreement and fairness. But you will discover that roles will shift as your lives change.

☐ What is the role of women in marriage? Of men?

☐ Who should make the final decision in case of an impasse?

☐ Will both of you work outside the home? If one spouse is offered a job in another state, whose job advancement will have priority?

☐ How do you differ and how do you agree with your parent's views about male and female roles?

☐ What household tasks did your father always do? Your mother?

☐ What do you believe the Bible teaches about the roles of husbands and wives?

☐ Who is going to shop? Clean the house? Do laundry? Cook? Take out the trash?

Religious Beliefs

Your beliefs about God, Jesus Christ, the Bible and the church are crucial in your marriage. Your religious beliefs are binoculars for viewing the world and those around you. So if you and your mate are poles apart in your convictions before marriage, you will not see eye to eye after marriage.

☐ What religious beliefs do you share?

☐ What beliefs do you differ on? What effect will these differences have on your marriage?

☐ How committed are each of you to a local church?

☐ What are the differences and similarities in your religious backgrounds?

☐ What will determine how you choose the church you will attend after marriage?

☐ Can you discuss religious issues without becoming angry and resentful? If not, why?

☐ If you have children, how will you pass your faith on to them?

So there it is. After this exercise I hope that you're still talking to each other. Struggling with these issues before you get married is crucial—once you tie the knot, there's no turning back.

Making Friends
for Life

Joan Wulff Duchossois

My friend and I are very different. She belongs to
an informal, familylike church and I'm a member
of a liturgical, traditional one. Her room is deco-
rated in pastels, florals, eyelet lace, quilts and wing chairs.
My taste leans toward things that are bright, solid and geo-
metric.

She loves mountain climbing, New England and Canada;
I'm addicted to summer and long, hot walks on the beach.
We voted for different presidential candidates.

Our friendship was "accidental." I didn't know her before our lives meshed for practical reasons. We ended up
living together and consequently became friends.

I've learned some new things about friendships since
I've been out of college. I've noticed that true friendship
has more to do with time spent together (and therefore experiences shared) than with things in common or even
personality compatibility.

In college I took an art course in which my classmates
and I wandered around a wonderful museum, holding little folding chairs in our hands. The instructor would stop at
a painting I knew nothing about, we would unfold, sit

down in front of it and listen to her talk about it, pointing out details and relating the history and life of the artist in a fascinating way. I went back to those paintings many more times in preparation for exams. They became familiar to me because I had spent so much time with them.

Now when I go back to that museum I go directly to the same paintings—to see my old friends. The rest of the paintings may be beautiful, perhaps better masterpieces than the ones I go to see. But they are strangers. I love my friends because I have spent time with them and I know them.

The folks you meet in college are *Very Important People.* You'll never have a better time for cultivating good friendships than you do now. Working on a biology project, planning a fellowship retreat, commiserating over a tough professor together—these are the best ways in the world to get to know people. Once you're out of college you won't have as many opportunities to build friendships. Yet it seems we spend much of our college years talking about our love lives instead of focusing on the vital elements of our "friend lives" which exist in all relationships, romantic or otherwise.

The Time Is Now

I got acquainted with a guy in college who is now a very good friend. When we met he was an unbelieving Jew who had grown up in Chicago and I was a Waspy Christian who knew nothing about unbelieving Jews from Chicago. Somehow we ended up together a lot—in the same dorm complex our freshman year, hanging around mutual friends our sophomore year, taking several classes together our junior year. We graduated the same semester and still, years later, get together to talk, talk, talk.

How could two people like us ever have discovered each other outside of a college setting? Our friendship would have been rather unlikely, I think, and I would have been that much poorer for it. Yet because we have been together we have an acceptance of one another, a real interest in what the other thinks, and a genuine respect. In college we were able to become friends, to keep it informal, to learn from each other without worrying about dating and all the tricky things associated with it.

Acquaintances, friends and romantic partners are three different levels of relating and are not clearly defined or self-contained. Friendships are an important part of and often exist beautifully in deeper relationships. My sisters are my siblings but they are also two of my closest friends, and I know of marriages where the partners are, after ten or thirty or fifty years, first and foremost friends.

**Making
Good Friends**

Yet some people are baffled by how to make friends and how to be a friend. Let's look at several things about friends that distinguish them from acquaintances:

Good friends respect each other. From this friendship principle stem all others. We may be very different, but we each like the kind of person the other is. Because we have spent time together, this respect is not founded on first impressions, but on knowing who the other really is.

In college I met a girl who was a transfer student. My impression of her was that she was one of those smiley, bubbly, friendly, ever-so-sweet types that people like me can easily get diabetes from. She was nice, I thought—but not my type; we were destined to be acquaintances. But that changed when, one rainy afternoon between classes, she talked me into having a cup of coffee with her. We discovered what each other was really like (so unlike the first impression), and had a talk that we still reminisce about. We eventually became roommates, and today I count her as one of my closest friends.

On the other hand, we have all met initially "impressive" people who gained our respect in the first meeting and dashed it as we got to know them. Good friends, however, know each other well enough that they don't have to worry about impressions. They have trouble hiding things from each other and are not easily embarrassed when the "real" person comes out.

Good friends learn from each other. When you respect someone and admire the qualities that person has, you find yourself wanting and trying to be more like him or her. That's one of the Holy Spirit's ways of making us like himself—by putting us in contact with godly people we can model ourselves after. We improve by being around them.

One thing I learned from my college roommate was how to pray. We'd get up in the morning, dress, and she'd go straight to her knees beside the bed. And not for one of those thirty-second prayers, either. I mean, this girl *prayed.* I used to laugh at her because when we'd leave for class she'd still have traces of a red mark on her forehead where her folded hands had pressed.

Good friends are confident of how the other feels about them. My roommate and I laughed and still laugh at each other a lot. We can do that because we don't walk on eggshells to avoid offending each other. Good friends don't constantly need to be evaluating what the other thinks of them, nor do they need to pretend to be what they are not. They feel free to disagree, respectfully, with each other.

During my junior year of college I was in a newswriting class and shared a typewriter table with a Christian guy I had known for a couple of years. We were in complete agreement in matters of faith. But this particular class dealt with many current events which often turned into political discussions, and he and I were surprised to discover how sharply we disagreed on not a few, but most issues. Secure in our mutual respect and being careful to avoid personal attacks, we had quite a few "lively" talks. But we always ended up laughing. He was a real friend—and we were still able to work together on both school and ministry-related projects.

Good friends speak highly of each other, even behind each other's backs. Have you ever accidentally overheard a friend say something nice about you to someone else on the telephone, or had a friend tell you that so-and-so thinks you're great? Good friends consider each other's reputation as important as their own.

Good friends confront each other. Friends can lovingly point out sins and weaknesses and challenge each other to higher standards of thought and behavior. You can't do this with acquaintances—not even with Christian "brothers and sisters" who are strangers. To do it successfully, you must trust each other's motives. This trust is gained over time.

Good friends (at some point) choose to be friends and actively continue their relationship. Martin E. Marty, a historian at the University of Chicago, writes in his book *Friendship:* "You can forget 999 of the 1,000 people you bump into in cafeteria lines, at concerts, in apartment hallways, or on tennis courts. There is no reason to become involved. Life's choices include the choice not to make friends, or not to relate to particular people. To make too many friends is to debase the coinage of friendship, since you could not devote yourself to the art if you defined it too broadly and spread yourself too thin. In making friends, you had the freedom to act—and you did."

Occasionally friends say to each other, "I really appreciate you—you are a great friend!" Some people need to hear that more often than others. But in general, friendship is manifested in small ways, such as courtesy to each other, a postcard sent, a birthday remembered.

Good friends graciously accept things from each other. My first roommate in college and I were nervous about doing something that would bother the other. The first few weeks we lived together we made a big deal out of using things the other had bought ("Do you mind too terribly much if I eat one of your apples?") or asking the other to do something for us ("Would it be too much trouble for you to drop me off at the bookstore since you're going that way anyway? I don't want to inconvenience you . . ."). That was evidence that we were still acquaintances.

Eventually I knew we had really become friends when she felt free enough to borrow a blouse of mine without asking a month in advance ("Let's see, what do we have for me to wear tonight?") and I felt free enough to rearrange the furniture ("I knew you'd love it this way!") while she was gone for the weekend.

Ultimately, this implies being willing to accept another's sacrifice. If a friend gives up a favorite television show to help you with your calculus, or listens to you even when it disrupts schedules or disturbs sleep, or pays for a long-distance call once in a while, you should accept these sacrifices and not feel compelled to keep apologizing for them.

John wrote that there is no greater display of love than sacrificing for friends, even to the point of laying down your life (Jn 15:13). Christ's death on the cross was a tremendous act of friendship because it reconciled enemies to each other and made friends of them (Rom 5:10-11). The Bible is a book about friendships. (Try reading one of the Gospels with this in mind and you'll see what I mean.)

Jesus, Friend Extraordinaire

In fact, Jesus' two great commandments call us to great acts of friendship. The first is becoming friends with God ("You shall love the Lord your God with all your heart, and with all your soul, and with all your mind") through reconciliation with him. The second is becoming friends with people ("You shall love your neighbor as yourself") through reconciliation with friend and enemy alike.

Of this second commandment, Martin E. Marty says, "We might as well say, 'what a Jesus we have in a friend.' Yet this is not as shocking as the first hearing suggests. Many Christian thinkers of the past spoke in such apparently scandalous terms. Some of them urged us to be not only as Christ to the neighbor, but to be a Christ to him or her. To be a Christ did not mean that we had climbed into the Godhead and achieved divine perfection. Being a Christ was conceivable because when God looked at us now, this looking occurred in Christ. God saw not us and our flaws but the perfection of Christ, which was the divine gift to us. . . . When a friend forgives us and recreates the basis of

friendship, something as deep as love has to be present. It
breaks the bounds of ordinary relations of the sort on
which friendship is built. That is why it is not nonsensical
to say 'what a Jesus we have in a friend.' "

There is something remarkably spiritual about being a
friend, about having a friend. To fail to be a friend, not to
let Christ be a friend through us, is a waste and a great loss.
And yet some let studies and other solo activities inhibit
the building of strong, deep friendships. They don't have
time to be friends, or they don't think it is very important,
or feel guilty whenever they spend time with people instead of studying. They may say, "I'll have time for people
when I get out of college—right now I'm concerned about
my personal walk with God and about getting a good job."
But getting along with people, being a friend, is vital to getting on well in life outside of college.

I've seen talented people whose "unfriendliness" made
them impossible to work with, and others whose lack of
friends made them lonely, which also affected their performance on the job. There is no point in having good
grades or a huge range of knowledge if you graduate without friends or the ability to be a friend. Once in the working world, you'll discover firsthand how unsatisfying even
the perfect job, salary, reputation and location can be.

It's relationships we humans seek. As Christians, especially, our contentedness in life does not ultimately rest on
these things, but on the quality of our relationship to God
and other people.

Making friends isn't always easy. There's no getting
around the hard "getting to know you" period. And you'll
be tempted to hang around old high-school buddies or
people of your same race, social group or brand of Christianity. Deep friendships with people who are different from
you take effort and time. So don't wait until you're out of
college to begin working on them. The friends you are
making in college will likely provide the core of your relationships for years to come. They will affect your job, your

present family, your future family and the rest of your life significantly.

Shun any hermit instincts you have when you arrive on campus. God desires to be a friend to us, and our priorities (the two great commandments) tell us that being a friend of people is the second half of being a friend of God.

Dealing with a Difficult Roommate

John Throop

One of my college roommates plunged into suicidal depression. Another constantly got stoned and threw impromptu parties at three in the morning. Roommates can make life tough. I know.

I wasn't a perfect roommate. No one's perfect. But some roommates have problems that can destroy you as well as them. What can you do when you're stuck in that situation?

Let me introduce you to four difficult roommates my friends and I have lived with—an emotionally disturbed roommate, a drug abuser, a clinging vine and a promiscuous roommate. The stories of my adventures with them follow. We made lots of mistakes, but eventually learned how to confront each other without losing our cool. You can too, whether you end up staying with that person or not. After the basics—praying for them and showing Christ's love—here are some steps you can take to turn an unpleasant or dangerous situation around.

Phil had not been sleeping well, and his whole body showed it. He looked haggard, hollow and oppressed by the weight of the world. He had become more remote in

The Emotionally Disturbed Roommate

recent months, harder to talk with, more passive and withdrawn. This wasn't the same Phil who had invited Carl and me to split a three-bedroom apartment with him a year earlier. Something was wrong.

Carl and I (both Christians) asked Phil whether he was having problems. He said no, but his demeanor said, "I don't want to tell you." Carefully, quietly, gently we attempted to draw out of him whatever it was that was troubling him. "Look," he replied, "I'm glad you're concerned. But there's nothing wrong."

That winter was long, hard and gray. Phil withdrew even more, staying in his room with the lights off, sleeping much of the time, avoiding common meals with the excuse that he wasn't hungry. Carl and I sensed that there was something deep within him that, if left unchecked, would lead him to take his life. All I need in my senior year, I thought to myself, is for my apartment mate to commit suicide. What could I do to help without losing my own balance or completely ignoring my studies and other friends?

Carl and I prayed about the matter and agreed about Phil's tendency toward suicide. Unfortunately, Phil was not taking classes at the time—he was working—so we could not refer him to our school's counseling service. We would personally have to intervene. We were the only ones who knew the depths of his symptoms.

Carl and I decided that we would talk as carefully and directly as we could with Phil about our concerns, and reassure him that nothing was too hard for us to bear if he would only open up. We wanted to help him release whatever was destroying him.

So one evening we confronted Phil. "We are sharing our lives with you, Phil," I said. "Something in you is tearing you apart, and we hurt to see you hurting like that. Please, for God's sake, what is it? We want to bear the burden with you!"

Phil thought for a long while, and then said flatly, "Well, if you really want to know: John, Carl, I'm gay and my lover has left me for someone else. I hate him, I hate my life, I hate myself, and I hurt so much that I can't take it anymore. I've been thinking about just ending it all." He looked at us with the saddest face I have ever seen. He looked at us to see how we would react.

We sat silently for a moment. Then I began, "Phil, we love you and care about you as you are." Carl nodded in ageement.

"We've been afraid that you would take your life. Nothing is so hard or so awful that you cannot work it out. Carl and I know that God has been keeping you close to him even though you didn't know that. We know it from our own lives. Will you let us help you? You know us. We'll stick with you."

"Yeah, I guess so," Phil said, with as much conviction as he could muster. That night, he shared his life—a child with alcoholic parents and a successful, egotistical brother who took every opportunity to undermine Phil's self-confidence, a confused homosexual damaged again and again by unstable relationships. That night was the beginning of a change in Phil's life, and a meeting with Jesus Christ some months later. He had a long way to go, but he began seeing a counselor and growing in his faith.

From this experience, Carl and I learned some tips on dealing with emotionally disturbed roommates.

☐ *Observe and listen first.* Don't just tell your roommate what he or she needs. Keep the lines of communication open.

☐ *Commit yourself to the person.* Be careful not to promise help or time that you can't give. Be ready to share tough times with them.

☐ *Suspend judgment.* You're trying to help the person see Christ through his difficulties, not condemn him for what he has done wrong. He knows that part of it full well. Encourage the person and hold out hope, not damnation.

☐ *Know who can help.* Most students don't know how to help others with deep-rooted psychological problems. Trying to do too much can rock your own equilibrium. Find out about the counseling resources that are available at your school or church, and encourage the person to seek professional help.

The Drug-Abusing Roommate

When I met Tom, he didn't seem too different from the other people Ken and I had interviewed to share our college suite. We agreed to let him share a bedroom with Jim, who had moved in a week earlier. Jim agreed to the arrangement, and we all settled in for our freshman year of college.

Within two weeks Ken, Jim and I knew we had made a mistake. A serious mistake. We had been woken up early in the morning when Tom returned with his friends to crank tunes and party. And there was this unpleasant odor wafting in from the living room. I went out to investigate.

Tom and his friends were smoking pot and snorting cocaine. "Hey, Throop!" Tom yelled. "Wanna lid?"

"No!" I said firmly. "Do you know what time it is—three in the morning—and we have classes tomorrow! Wrap this up and party somewhere else, okay?"

"Yeah, sure!" Tom laughed. "We will, don't worry."

I did worry. The party went on for another hour, even after another request from Ken to end it.

The pattern continued. Tom denied that anything strange was happening and claimed we were just hassling him. A steady stream of parties followed, some of them wild and out of control. Trying to persuade and then warn Tom did no good. And the dorm parents didn't want to get involved.

"You need to work out your problems," they said. "If there are parties that you don't like, then maybe you need to make other arrangements. Tom has rights too, you know." I was dumbfounded. Rights to use illegal drugs? Rights to throw parties when he wanted? Rights to trample over the needs of his three roommates for quiet and for sleep? Besides, we'd been in the apartment first and told Tom before he came the kind of guys we were.

As the days passed, I became more and more upset, anxious, tired and stressed from the noise and the drug use. "All I need," I thought, "is to be busted for having drugs in the apartment." I was at my wits' end. Jim had moved out, and Ken was as concerned as I was.

Eventually we began to notice people coming in with cash and out with little bags of leaves or powder. "Oh, Lord," I thought, "now he's selling the stuff." I prayed for guidance. What could I say or do?

I went to the university housing office and pleaded my case. The housing officer quietly and quickly moved Ken and me to other rooms in the dorm. Tom, who now had the apartment to himself, still sold drugs. But at least I was out. I prayed for Tom, but thanked God for my deliverance from a worsening situation. It was only after I had moved and later, when Tom had dropped out of school, that I learned how one weekend before I left, he had stabbed me to death in effigy.

You, as a roommate, may be closer to a drug or alcohol abuser than anyone on campus. Your life, your studies, your prayers, your friendships are all colored by his actions. You know his behavior, his patterns of denial, his destructive tendencies. You must make a choice. Do you want to attempt to encourage him to get help for his problem, or are the risks too great or the relationship too shallow to make the effort? Only you can decide. But here are a couple of points to remember.

☐ *You can't cure the person.* A drug or alcohol abuser has to choose to get help. You can guide them if you're willing to invest lots of emotional energy and time. Carefully decide if you can make the commitment. If you choose to stick it out, get help for yourself too; many campuses have an Al-Anon chapter for people close to folks with drug and alcohol problems. See if your school has treatment programs (or access to some) designed to help the drug abuser.

☐ *Know your limits.* Pray through what you can and can't

take. You can be a witness of Christ's love by setting limits on inappropriate or destructive behavior in your room and sticking to them—even if that eventually means leaving when all else fails.

"She's like my shadow," Debbie told me in frustration. "Wherever I go, she wants to go. Whatever I do, she wants to do. My friends are automatically her friends. Sometimes I feel like I'm being smothered!"

The Clinging-Vine Roommate

Debbie had described her roommate to me before. At first, she welcomed her roommate's desire to do things with her. But gradually Debbie felt that she couldn't lead her own life. "I know that as a Christian I'm supposed to help those who are lonely, hurting and in need of friends," she told me, "but her demands on me are getting out of control."

"She's like a clinging vine, right?" I asked.

"Exactly. She's growing alongside me, but strangling me as she goes. When she's done with me, I have the feeling she'll be the same way with someone else. She's a consumer of friendship."

Emotionally dependent roommates lack motivation and self-esteem—so much so that they can't bear to be by themselves very long. No one person can meet their enormous needs. So the dependent roommate latches on whoever happens to be close by for support, encouragement and cheer.

Clinging vines invariably become disappointed that no one person really understands them. They don't realize how oppressive their behavior comes across or even perceive their problems as lying within; their problem, as they see it, is that other people don't like them.

So what do you do if your roommate's like cellophane? First, remember that you're not responsible for their life. You're only responsible for your own. Then, if you choose to stay roommates, keep the following tips in mind.

☐ *Accept the person.* Accept dependent people for who

they are, not for who you want them to be. Don't try to organize their lives for them; make them learn responsibility
for their actions. Stand firm if they try to manipulate you
into feeling guilty for "not really caring."

☐ *Detach yourself.* Practice listening to the person, then
let them come to grips with their own problems. For example, say your roommate complains, "I have three papers to
write and a final in two days! I haven't prepared at all. What
am I going to do? Can you help me?" Instead of answering,
"Well, if you really need it, I can help type your papers.
You'll be fine. Now, on your first paper, if I were you, I
would . . . ," you need to say, "Well, you do have a problem. What are your choices?" That's detachment. Care, but
don't plunge in and try to solve every problem. Then you'll
preserve your freedom and theirs, freedom which you both
need.

☐ *Be firm.* If you really need to do something else when
the clinging vine comes to you with an "urgent" problem,
feel free to say you're sorry, you just can't help this minute,
but you'll be happy to help later. By not running to meet
every need on demand, you can help an overly dependent
friend grow.

☐ *Bring clingers to your fellowship or church.* Assure them
that people there will welcome and accept them. You don't
have to bear the burden of a dependent roommate alone.
Let the community of faith help the clinging vine find a
deeper relationship with the living Vine, Jesus Christ.

The Promiscuous Roommate

It's midnight. You've been working hard in the library,
trying to get that research paper done. Thoughts of your
warm, cozy bed lure you home. You make it across the
cold campus to your room, and for the fifth time in eight
weeks, there's a tie on the door—your roommate's code
for, "I've got someone special with me tonight, buddy.
Hope you find a comfortable place to sleep."

Few things threw me more than a surprise guest for the
night. Even when my roommate and his friend slept fully

clothed and didn't kick me out, I missed my privacy.

Face it. When your roommate takes someone to bed he has only himself in mind. Your needs take a back seat. So assert yourself—but remember that inside the promiscuous person lurks someone who's lonely and lacking self-respect. Someone who's wracked up a body count instead of seeking meaningful interpersonal relationships. Someone who probably avoids real intimacy.

If you choose to stay with a roommate who sleeps around, you'll have a hard time trying to change them. Maybe they come out of a strict home and are chafing at the bit to rebel. Or maybe they come from a home with few rules and little guidance. In either case, they may seem bent on cultivating a selfish get-what-you-can attitude.

Invite promiscuous roommates to taste the depth of a relationship by offering them one. Dare to love and guide them as much as they'll let you. Promiscuity gets old after a while; stable, meaningful relationships don't. You may be the one to break through your roommate's defenses. Here are some tips.

☐ *Voice your own needs without feeling guilty.* You both have to live by certain ground rules for health and well-being. You do not have to surrender your rights to a night's sleep in your own bed unless you choose to be someplace else. By sleeping on the dorm couch you're not bearing your cross—you're condoning sin. Be a martyr for something more worthy. As a Christian, you can be assertive without being demanding.

☐ *Set guidelines.* Decide together when guests need to leave, who may stay over and under what conditions, and so on. Be firm. Ask for the Holy Spirit's guidance and live by your conscience.

☐ *Model good relationships.* Show by your relationship with your roommate, friends and God that depth, stability and openness bring fulfillment. As you grow closer, you and your roommate will be able to talk quite naturally about what really matters in life.

Making a Good Roommate Relationship Better

A good roommate is a terrible thing to waste—yet roommate relationships are one of the greatest untapped resources on college campuses. Chances are that between orientation week and graduation you will have had three or more roommates.

Though the university housing computer had randomly matched us as roommates, Leroy Kim and I remained roommates through all four years of college. Because of the specialness of that relationship, the first thing that comes to mind when I think of college is Leroy.

College is a time of major decisions, change and growth. To have someone go through them with you is invaluable. Leroy was with me when I first fell in love with my future wife, and he saw me experience the ups and downs of that relationship. I saw Leroy nearly flunk out of school and then rally to make it into med school against all odds. He saw me adjust to a different culture far away from my family and friends. I saw him grow from an atheist to an effective leader in our fellowship group.

How can you make the best of a good roommate relationship? Here are some of the things we learned along the way.

☐ *Don't make unrealistic expectations.* It was important to allow the relationship to develop naturally. Talking about our hassles with the library or about our excitement with a class we were taking went a long way in deepening our friendship. We didn't set out to have a formal Bible study together once a week or become official prayer partners—yet prayer and Bible study happened as the need arose. Our relationship didn't necessarily work out because we were both Christians, but because we were both friends.

☐ *Keep lines of communication open.* No matter how well you get along, long-lasting roommate situations—like good marriages—don't happen by accident.

Our freshman year wasn't always fun for Leroy. Because I came from a culture where people borrow freely, I used Leroy's stuff as if it were my own. This made him mad. What he didn't know was that I expected him to do the same with my things. We finally talked about it and he was able to see that in Latin American culture my behavior would not be considered rude, and I learned something about life in these United States. So we agreed we would share everything. (A kink in the arrangement emerged when he saw that I didn't have much that he wanted to borrow. But we adjusted our agreement accordingly.)

Talking about our differences and feelings helped us understand where the other person was coming from, which buffered the anger of breaking the other person's rules.

It's also important not to expect yourself or your roommate to uphold a certain image. Sometimes rooming with another Christian creates obstacles to free communication because there might be pressure to maintain a spiritual image. Giving the "Christian" answers to everything does not build trust. Leroy and I were always open with each other about the doubts, struggles and bad attitudes we were having. Confession time was usually between 1 and 2 A.M. The next day we would stumble out of our beds—exhausted but better for the previous night's discussion.

☐ *Be committed to the relationship.* This means being willing to work out problems rather than letting them slide with the thought that "I'll only have to worry about this till the end of the year."

Rex Johnson, in *Solo* magazine, gives good guidelines to use in resolving conflicts with a roommate: (1) Listen more than you talk. (2) Define the problem. (3) Define your agreements and disagreements. (4) Identify your own contribution to the conflict (probably the most difficult step). (5) Suggest what you can do to help solve the conflict. (6) Suggest a way your roommate could help you or a way you could help your roommate. (7) Make a commitment to follow the solution or solutions you picked together. Make this commitment even if your roommate doesn't make one too.

Commitment also means spending time with each other. Meals, study sessions, sports and movies were always good opportunities for Leroy and me to see different sides of each other.

Our relationship never grew stale. We were always building on the past year. Eventually we learned what to expect; each year we had fewer issues to work out and fewer chances of getting irritated with each other. More than four years out of school we continue to build on our friendship.

I recently talked to Leroy about roommate relationships and he threw out a few more tips: accept roommates as they are; don't expect them to behave like you; be considerate; expect to be surprised or hurt sometimes; set a goal of encouraging the other person, yet don't demand that the other person encourage you; seek forgiveness for wrongs (even relatively insignificant ones) as soon as possible; and always be willing to forgive.

—*Andrés Tapia*

You Know It's Time to Change Roommates When . . .   *Rob Suggs*

. . . She hires waitresses and a nightly band for your dorm room.

. . . You're forced to swipe some of his underwear, only to find he's already swiped some of yours.

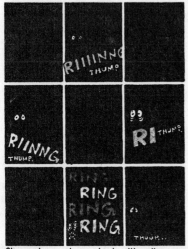

. . . She gets an alarm clock with a "snooze" button.

. . . His mother arrives with her suitcase.

. . . He starts working out for wrestling season.

. . . Her dog decides he likes *you* best.

. . . Her snoring begins to attract strange animals.

. . . He starts checking your mail for you.

REACHING OUT TO INTERNATIONAL STUDENTS

Jane Hopson and Andrés Tapia

"In Europe people get along with you very easily, but this is not true in the U.S.," says a Palestinian student studying in Illinois. "That's why we internationals feel so isolated. In class people are social, but outside of class nobody seems to care. It really hurts."

The World at Our Doorstep

This student echoes the complaint of many of the nearly 500,000 international students at U.S. and Canadian colleges and universities. The fast pace of campus life, along with financial difficulties (often due to unfavorable currency rates) and homesickness, adds to the tension of being in an alien cultural setting and having to operate in a foreign language.

Though you usually see them hanging out with other internationals, they are usually frustrated they don't spend more time with North Americans. After all,

that's one of the reasons they came. Many internationals return to their country never having entered a North American home, and with few *gringo* names in their address books.

Christians—because of their historical concern for the alien in their midst and their commitment to sharing the gospel to the ends of the earth—are among the best qualified to meet the needs of those students under the turbans, ponchos and saris.

Tips for Crossing the Cultural Gap

Here are some tips on building friendships with internationals that you may find helpful:

☐ Don't be afraid to take the initiative in establishing a relationship with an international student. Since they are often unsure about how things work and how one is supposed to behave in our culture, they are usually very open and appreciative when someone takes the time to befriend them.

☐ Ask questions about a person's culture and country. Since internationals miss their countries so much, they are eager to talk about them.

☐ Read about other parts of the world in your daily newspaper or weekly news magazine. Knowing about current events in an international's country can help open up conversations (you'll probably find that your friend knows more about international—and even North American—politics than you do).

☐ Keep your eye open for things that seem new to them and then offer to help. Many of these will be things you take for granted—using the library, taking the bus, ordering fast food at a drive-thru, using a laundromat, shopping for sales, opening up a checking account.

☐ Take them to events or places typically North American: Christmas caroling, a Fourth of July BBQ picnic, a pro football or ice hockey game, an automated car wash, a shopping mall.

☐ Take them to your home so they can see how a North American family lives or to family events such as a wedding, a baptism or Thanksgiving dinner. Or simply do routine things such as studying together.

☐ Pray often for your international friends. Most internationals, especially those from countries closed to missionaries, are curious about Christianity. Conversations about your faith will emerge naturally as your friendship develops, but don't make your friendship contingent on them becoming Christians.

A few cautions: let your motivation be a desire for friendship and welcoming someone to your country instead of a duty done out of obligation or to score some spiritual points; and due to different cultural assumptions and norms, it's usually better, at least initially, to befriend someone of the same sex.

For a bibliography of resources on international students write: Ned Hale, International Student Ministry, InterVarsity Christian Fellowship, 6400 Schroeder Rd., P.O. Box 7895, Madison, WI 53707-7895.

In the following story, Aye-Tee Teo Monaco, an international student from Singapore, talks about what the first few weeks of college in North America can be like for a foreigner—and how some Christian students made a difference.

Scared Stiff
in North America

Imagine starting freshman year during spring quarter, leaving home for the first time and being 11,000 miles away from family and friends. I was nervous, apprehensive and scared out of my wits. My well-known independent, adventurous, conquer-the-world attitude nearly lost out to my less-known anything-for-a-sheltered-lifestyle outlook. But my confident self did not allow me to back down. The decision had been made; I had been accepted at Northwestern University near Chicago, and was going to meet that challenge even if I died of loneliness and desperation in the attempt.

So I put on a tough front and requested a single room. I wasn't going to deal with any blond, blue-eyed, stereo-blasting, gum-chewing North American roommate. I built barriers to protect myself from my U.S. hosts and hostesses—contrary to my teenage desire to appreciate and adapt to a different culture. I'd always wanted to be a citizen of the world; studying abroad was a step in that direction. The school I chose would offer me a cross section of North Americans—the cosmopolitan urbanites, the neighborhood ethnics, the suburban preppies and the laid-back farmers. A perfect environment to pursue my dreams.

So why the walls? With my convictions, I should have wildly grabbed the first North American I saw on campus (female, of course) and invited her to be my roommate. But once on campus I stiffened in fear—fear of how my fellow students would accept my darker skin, my squinted eyes and my accent. Would they be snobby and ethnocentric, like some of the North Americans I had met in my country? Overnight my focus changed from wanting to understand and appreciate North American culture to wanting to be a hermit, bag my A's, return to my country and be a world-renowned economist.

For the first few days, I mutely went to my classes, hid in the library and my room, and ate silently in a cafeteria corner. The spunky girl I used to be couldn't muster the courage now even to start a conversation, much less initiate a friendship. Everybody fears being rejected, but to be disliked for what you are is much worse than to be rejected for who you are. (You can't change the color of your skin).

Friday night found me looking for a quiet corner in the library. In my search I caught sight of an extremely blond head smiling warmly in my direction. I wasn't sure he was smiling at me, but I liked the smile anyway. That smile somehow reminded me of a campus fellowship meeting that was going to be held at the student center that evening. I had asked about Christian groups on campus earlier, for I felt that if there was anyone with whom I had anything in common here, it would be those who shared the same belief in Christ. The warmth of that light-skinned face encouraged me to go to the meeting, scheduled for 7:30. When my watch registered 7:00, my courage failed me. I debated for the next forty-five minutes about going.

What finally stirred me from my seat were the faces of my Christian friends from high school and from my church, and the face of my brother. Those faces had watched me take off from the airport, encouraged me to seek out other campus Christians in the United States, and said they would be praying for me and writing to me. Then Isaiah 43:18-20 rang in my ears—"forget the former things; do not dwell on the past. See, I am doing a new thing! Now it springs up; do you not perceive it? I am making a way in the desert and streams in the wasteland."

Until then, I had been trapped by my fears and prejudices. I had tightly clung to memories of life on my island in the sun, crippling the new life of new friends in a new environment. With that realization, my gregarious, adventurous spirit revived within me. I grabbed my sweater, purse and books, and raced off to the meeting.

I entered quietly, slipping into a back-row seat. As I looked up, there was the beaming blond again! I smiled back at him, finally letting go of my prejudices and fears, and I sang the familiar songs and read the familiar Bible passages with those North Americans around me. I no longer felt like a foreigner; it was no longer them versus me. I was part of their group, and I knew that if I allowed them to, they could play an important role in my life during the next four years.

Fears and prejudices arise on both sides of any cross-cultural interaction. I had to decide to allow my U.S. counterparts into my daily existence in the same way that they had to decide to welcome me, not only to their country but also into their individual lives. The campus fellowship succeeded in this. They chose to take an interest in me for who I was and not for what I was. I appreciated being liked for being Aye-Tee Teo who happened to be a foreign student, instead of the foreign student to whom good Christians should minister.

—*Aye-Tee Teo Monaco*

Overcoming Racial Barriers

Bobby Gross

The black and white students at our fellowship's leadership conference seemed to be getting along well. Worship was lively and varied. I was caught off guard when some of the black students began expressing concern about undercurrents of racism: casual comments that hurt; racist jokes; segregated cliques.

I broached the subject in the small group I was leading. Almost immediately, Linda volunteered that she was free of prejudice: "When I look at people, I don't see black or white, I just see people." You could almost hear the retort in the minds of some of the others: "But my race and my ethnic heritage are part of who I am; if you don't see that, you don't fully see *me.*"

Another white student in the group tentatively asked the black members if they experienced much racism. Each had a story to tell.

Nancy grew up in the predominantly white Midwest. As she entered her teens, she saw her white childhood friends gradually pull away and her white teachers consistently ignore her. By the time she graduated from high school, the isolation had worn her out emotionally. Now, studying at a black college, she felt little desire to associate with whites.

Bill admitted that he had not spent much time with whites. Naturally shy, he was constantly worried that his way of relating to others would be misinterpreted as some sort of racism.

Then Leslie bravely shared from her past. As a little girl she had been sexually abused by a white teenager in her mostly white neighborhood. Only in recent years had she begun to deal with her deep fear and distrust of whites.

Others spoke up as well. Sid told of being spit on in Ft. Lauderdale because he was Jewish. Renee, half-Jewish, described similar experiences. And Emily, a Chinese American, mentioned the hurt she felt when people would ridicule her parents because they were different.

Racism on campus, contrary to current popular assumptions, is clearly alive and well.

The Illusion of Equality

The demise of public segregation, the increased presence of blacks in politics, sports and media, the growth of the black middle class, and the fading of the Civil Rights Movement have combined to give the illusion that we have made substantial progress in overcoming racism. Statistics for black income, unemployment, education, housing and health care, however, show exactly the opposite. In most of these areas, blacks now fare worse than in the sixties. The mood of frustration and despair prevalent in black communities reflects how much more progress needs to be made.

Black gains in the world of higher education are also eroding. For blacks, financial aid options have been slashed, enrollments are down, dropout rates are increasing, and blacks remain starkly underrepresented on faculties. "Black students know that at most colleges in this country, they are aliens and treated as aliens," remarks C. Eric Lincoln, noted black author and professor of religion and culture at Duke. Indeed, a spate of recent ugly racist incidents on a number of campuses have confirmed his assessment. What role can Christians play in such an environment?

Christians have the opportunity—indeed, the responsibility—to cut through illusions and learn to communicate across races. We can be peacemakers, ambassadors of reconciliation and agents of justice and love, because

Christ empowers us to become like him.

Me First

First, however, we must deal honestly with our own racism. God must heal us before we can help heal others. For a long time I thought that I was certainly not a racist. True, I had grown up white, Anglo-Saxon and Protestant in the heart of the segregated South. True, I knew only three blacks: our maid, our yard man, and Harold, the sole black student at my junior high. But I was no racist.

Racists were Ku Klux Klan members and those in angry mobs in the big cities. Racists hated blacks. But me? I was a Christian. I loved all people, "red and yellow, black and white," even my enemies. I never called black people "niggers." In fact, once I even got into an argument with my pastor about why blacks were not welcome to join our church.

In actuality, I *was* a racist. Since childhood, I had unknowingly conformed to a pattern of thought and action regarding race, especially the black race. Family, neighbors, peers, schools and the media did not explicitly teach me to hate or hurt blacks. Yet I picked up attitudes and understandings which made me unconsciously despise and indirectly injure blacks.

When I was little, it shocked me to see blacks eating in the same restaurant I was in. Blacks lived in their own part of town, ate in their own restaurants, had their own waiting rooms, used separate bathrooms and water fountains. *My* world was completely white: my school, my Little League, my neighborhood, my church, my shopping center. This, of course, was segregation. *Normal* for me meant *white*.

Sometimes certain people or situations made me feel uncomfortable. Whenever we drove our maid home, for example, she rode in the back seat, and as we approached her neighborhood, we would instinctively lock our car doors. I wondered now and then what her tiny apartment looked like inside and who took care of her daughter when she was taking care of us, especially during the weeks when she'd come to Florida to work for us during our vacations.

Whenever I voiced my uneasiness, I received the same gentle explanations: that blacks were less fortunate and that God had made them different; that I was to treat blacks with kindness but not go too far; that segregation was natural, in the best interest of both groups, and God's will. What I was really being taught was that blacks were *inferior.* We were to be nice and helpful to them, but not mix too much with them and certainly never marry one.

On Campus

Often racism is accompanied by patronizing smiles. When I entered the University of North Carolina in 1973, I had nothing against blacks. Like Linda, my motto was: "When I look at people, I don't see color—just people." I didn't give the whole racial subject much thought. But God did. And he launched me on an adventure of discovery, repentance and personal transformation that continues to this day.

During my last two years of college, God opened my eyes and challenged my thinking through my studies and his Word. In Sociology I learned the shocking economic statistics on life for blacks in the South between 1900 and 1940. Reading William Faulkner's *Go Down, Moses* for American Literature clothed these statistics with a bitter pathos: I saw myself in Faulkner's complex web of race, family, history and suffering. In American History I read a biography of Dr. Martin Luther King, Jr., which shook my false view of him.

"The Religious History of Southern Culture" challenged me most. We studied the history of evangelicalism in the South (imagine a final exam essay comparing these three Southerners: Martin Luther King, Billy Graham and Jimmy Carter!), which included the church's failure to help abolish slavery.

Most of the church had, in fact, actually justified and fought for slavery. I saw for the first time how racism had crippled the white church; but I also saw how God shaped a unique expression of his church to sustain blacks in their suffering. I felt both shame and joy.

In 1976, I attended the Urbana missions convention full of zeal for crossing seas and cultures to reach people for Christ. But in a seminar I attended,

Thom Hopler challenged the audience: "How can you talk about loving people of totally different cultures across the sea while you remain ignorant and uncaring about the black subculture just across town?"

That same year, God confronted me in my personal Bible study with one passage after another that speaks about justice, especially for the poor. These passages, plus others about love, penetrated my heart. God was calling me to repentance; he wanted a change of attitude and a renewal of obedience.

The First Step
When I moved to Gainesville, Florida, after college, I decided that I would actively cooperate with God in this process of transformation and mind renewal. My first step was easy: to read.

What Color Is Your God? (Salley & Behm, published by IVP) introduced me to racial issues from a Christian perspective. *Before the Mayflower* (Lerone Bennett, Jr., published by Johnson) began to fill the gaping holes in my knowledge of black history, while *The Autobiography of Malcolm X* (Grove) opened my eyes in other ways. John Perkins's story *Let Justice Roll Down* (Regal) offered me spiritual encouragement.

My next step was to attend some black-oriented events, especially on the nearby University of Florida campus. I listened to speeches by Julian Bond (Georgia state senator) and Benjamin Hooks (NAACP director), poetry by Gwendolyn Brooks, and the music of the college gospel choir. In addition to the cultural, intellectual and spiritual enrichment, I often experienced being a minority—a lone white face in a sea of black ones!

Another big step I took was to worship with black Christians. In addition to visiting a black campus fellowship, I periodically attended a nearby black church. Williams Temple Church of God in Christ wasn't like any church I had ever attended. At first, I felt extremely uncomfortable and confused; I wasn't prepared for either the emotional fervor of the worship or the length of the service. As the months passed, however, I felt more at home.

Another transforming experience I had occurred after the devastating riots in the black Liberty City section of Miami in May 1980. Blacks were outraged that an all-white jury acquitted white police officers who had beaten a black man to death. In Gainesville, black students organized a protest march to express solidarity with those in Miami. My wife, Charlene, and I decided to participate. It was eerie to walk through the rainy streets and be part of a throng made up of mostly black people shouting slogans for justice. I felt conspicuous and frightened.

I realized as never before that black Americans had been marching and struggling and suffering for justice for over three hundred years. I sensed a new freedom in myself that day. I had acted for justice. I marveled at how far God had brought me.

Your Turn

If Christian students can begin to come to grips with their own prejudices and establish friendships across racial and ethnic lines, seeds of societal change will have been planted. In the years after graduation, these seeds will sprout and take root and produce fruit. Men and women will have more vision for reconciliation and justice, more experience in communication and problem-solving, and more friends and resources to draw upon.

At Miami-Dade Community College the young InterVarsity group participated in the Black History Week activities a few years ago. Wearing specially designed T-shirts showing a black and white hand clasped, they marched in the campus parade under a bold banner: "United in Christ—Many Colors, One People!" Many students sought out their combination ethnic bakesale-outreach booktable, and many attended their seminar on racial reconciliation! Similar opportunities for creative growth and outreach are presented in campus events such as Hispanic Heritage Week, International Student Week, Chinese New Year and Jewish Passover.

God wants you to be an agent of reconciliation and justice also. As you step out in obedience to him, here are some guidelines to remember:

First, *recognize your enculturation.* Examine your attitudes toward those of different races. Think of both small matters, like taking a sip of Coke from the same glass, and larger ones, like interracial marriage. What in your early years influenced you? What influences you today? What racial stereotypes do you have? As you discover prejudice and ethnocentrism in yourself, acknowledge it and move beyond guilt to God's gracious forgiveness.

Second, *cooperate with God as he changes you.* Be willing to step out of your secure ethnic world into someone else's, whether through reading literature, attending events, visiting churches or simply making friends with people of other races.

Third, *take action as God gives you opportunity.* It is not enough to be *not against* blacks or other racial groups; we must also be *for* them, just as God is for them. Speak and act boldly, but also with the humility of one who is still learning. You may have opportunity to be a bridge, enabling folks from different races to come together in mutual respect and love, or a prophet, calling for repentance and change among those who are like you.

Finally, *persevere with others.* Racism is insidious and pervasive; the struggle to overcome it can overwhelm. Because the issues are complex and controversial, you may be rejected or opposed. You might be rebuffed in your sincere effort to make friends with someone of a different race and tempted to let that experience reinforce the negative impressions you already carry inside. Instead of attempting to be lone heroes, we need to struggle with other like-minded believers.

Keep in mind the hope God gives us in Revelation 7:9-10: One day a great multitude from every nation, tribe, people and language will stand before God and praise him—together.

LEARNING TO TALK TO YOUR PARENTS ABOUT . . .

John Throop

Talking to parents can be tough. College is a very different world than the one your family is in. Your priorities are different and your needs are changing. You need independence, yet you are probably still dependent on your parents for guidance, support, encouragement, love and (of course) money. On the other hand, it's a struggle for your parents to cut the apron strings. The tensions you're facing with your parents can actually provide opportunities for you to get to know them better and begin to relate to them as an adult. In the sections that follow, you'll find tips on how to talk to your parents about the classic touchy subjects.

Money

Every time a letter arrives from college, parents put the checkbook under armed guard. "How much is she going to ask for this time?" they ask defensively. And with reason. Some of my college friends hoped their care packages would arrive in armored trucks.

Whether you come from a rich, middle-class or poor family, you'll probably have problems talking about money with your parents. Colleges and graduate schools are expensive and increasing in cost much more quickly than everything else. Many parents have home mortgages, car loans, other children to clothe and feed, and all sorts of crazy bills to pay in addition to trying to put you through college.

Asking for money beyond what you need for books, housing, food, tuition and transportation to and from school can be asking for trouble. Asking your parents to pay for your entertainment can especially be a sore point. Do you really *have* to go to Fort Lauderdale during spring break? Do you *have* to have a stereo system and lots of records? Do you *have* to go to the Bruce Springsteen concert? Do you *have* to have a car? We're all for fun with friends, but what expenses are really necessary? You and your parents may have completely different perceptions of what your needs are, but by taking the initiative and following these steps you can bridge the gap.

☐ *Make a budget together.* List all the areas of your college education: tuition, room and board, transportation, clothing and cleaning, books, fees-for-use at college, entertainment and so on. Who will pay for what? Be specific. When you make a budget together, the give-and-take of a financial relationship with your parents can be ironed out.

☐ *Seek other sources.* Though your parents may be willing to provide you with an education, they don't owe you an education. You should aggressively seek private and public sources of financial aid such as scholarships, grants and loans. Your parents will be grateful that you've tried to ease their financial burden as much as you can.

☐ *Earn your own entertainment money.* You can do this by working while you're at school or saving some of your summer earnings. There is no such thing as a free lunch, though with ingenuity you can come close. I taught cooking lessons in the local supermarket while I was in college and got a free lunch in the class. With my paycheck I was able to buy concert series tickets and go to movies.

☐ *Give away some of your entertainment money.* Make the tithe (10%) the top priority of your earnings, and give to your church, campus fellowship or someone who doesn't have money to buy books. God will bless your giving, and you can learn how to live more simply with what's left over. You can also tithe unexpected gifts you receive—for they are truly gifts from God.

One set of parents I knew always looked forward to letters from their daughter at college. She never wrote asking for more money to spend. She often wrote telling how she was giving her money away.

Romance

Jeff fell in love with Becky, and he asked her to marry him. She accepted, and they announced their engagement to Becky's mother (her father was deceased) and to Jeff's parents. Becky's mother was very happy for her and promised to support her in any way she could. Jeff's parents, however, were hurt.

"Jeff, how could you do this to us? You didn't even bring her home before making this decision!" his mother said angrily. "We don't like Becky," she continued. "She's the wrong girl for you, and we think you should reconsider your decision. Wait a while and you'll see we're right."

Jeff was torn. He loved Becky but he also loved his parents and eagerly sought their approval. He wanted them to be happy, but his parents would not reason with him. His parents made it clear that he would be breaking his relationship with them if he married Becky, that he was disobeying Scripture by dishonoring them this way, and that neither one of them would be welcome in their home. What should he do?

Scripture is clear that marriage is a good thing. God's design for humankind is that "a man will leave his father and mother and be united to his wife, and they will become one flesh" (Gen 2:24). But it's a painful process, and talking to parents about romance can be difficult. Here are some thoughts about approaching them.

☐ *Give them the straight story.* If you are seriously dating someone but have no plans for marriage, say so. If you do plan to marry, give your parents ample warning so they can adjust. In either case, set up times when they can get to know him or her better.

☐ *Keep your parents' marriage in mind.* They will see your romance and marriage through the prism of their own experience. If they enjoy a good marriage, they most likely will be excited about your own romance. If their marriage is lousy, their reactions may vary from happiness for you (a sign of maturity and hope that you will do better) to dire warnings not to go forward with your plans (a sign of their own bitterness).

☐ *Listen to advice.* Whether you take it or leave it, at least listen to it. If your parents are telling you to wait, they might see something you, blinded by romantic emotion, cannot see—maybe the risk of marrying someone you've only known for a month, the difficulty of getting married before graduation, or the hard reality that you're going to have to give up a lifelong dream if you get married.

☐ *Make your own decision.* Your parents cannot live your life for you—you're the one who must live with the consequences of what you decide. After hearing them out, feel free to choose.

Faith

Coming home from my first year of college, I had exciting news that I couldn't wait to tell my parents.

At the dinner table that first evening home, I joyfully said to my parents, "Mom! Dad! I've become a Christian! I've never been happier in my life."

Both my mother and my father stared at me with incredulity. There was a long period of silence, after which my mother said, "I don't understand. You've always been a Christian. We've raised you as a Christian. What do you mean?"

"I accepted Jesus Christ as my Lord and Savior! I never knew Jesus before this year. I don't know where I've been—or where he's been."

My father spoke up. "We've taken you to church since you were little. We've raised you to be a good Roman Catholic. How can you say that you haven't been a Christian?" I didn't expect this turn in the conversation, but it was clear to me that my parents were confused and hurt. They thought that they had raised me as a Christian. Now I was telling them that I hadn't been one at all. I could see the wheels turning in their heads: "Where did we go wrong?"

The next Sunday was worse. "I'm not going to church with you this morning," I said defiantly. My mother's eyes widened. "You don't mean that. You're a good Roman Catholic, and you will go to church with us. You have to go to

Mass."

"I said that I am not going," I replied angrily. "I'm going somewhere where they preach the gospel of Jesus Christ." They let me go to the church of my choice, but for the next six months our family was a miniversion of Northern Ireland. Only by the time I was almost out of seminary seven years later had we finally reached a deep understanding about our walks of faith, and only after we all had grown and been stretched.

I handled my parents all wrong. Since then I've learned that, when approaching the folks about matters of faith, certain principles apply—whether you're from a Christian home, a religious home or a home in which you received little or no spiritual guidance.

□ *Be sensitive to your parents' beliefs.* Have you ever talked with your parents about personal faith before? If not (I hadn't), then first try to discern what their understanding of the Christian faith is. Let them articulate their beliefs in their own way. Perhaps no one has ever asked them to share their faith before.

□ *Affirm the faith they have.* Rather than correcting them where they are wrong (in your opinion), or getting angry at them for seeming to have no spiritual life, encourage them where they seem to be on the right track. You may be surprised at the depth they have in spiritual matters.

The greatest lesson I learned from talking about Christianity with my parents was not to be angry at them for not pressing me to commit myself to Christ. Initially I thought that they had goofed raising me. But with time I discovered that my parents had given me the spiritual foundations which allowed me, at the proper time, to be receptive to Christ.

□ *Encourage them by your example.* Your parents will be weighing your confession of faith with how you behave, particularly if you led a thoroughly sinful life before. As James says, "Do not merely listen to the word, and so deceive yourselves. Do what it says" (1:22). They will especially be watching to see how your newfound faith affects your relationship with them. Don't just tell them about your neat fellowship group and put Bible verses on your bulletin board. Prove that God has made a difference in your life by serving them when you're home—straightening up around the house, putting gas in the car, and taking your little sister and her friends out for ice cream so your parents can relax (even when you'd rather stay home yourself).

□ *Give them space.* You can't project your experience of faith onto your parents; you can only invite them to journey with you. Hard as it may be, they may choose not to come along.

Career

Charles's father was a New York attorney making big bucks in corporate law. Charles's grandfather had done the same. His great-grandfather had practiced civil law. Charles bore the same name as these men—he was Charles IV. He had always assumed that he, too, would be a lawyer.

But Charles did not enjoy law. He had no aptitude for it. He liked history and thought that he might want to teach it. He wasn't sure. On top of that, Charles had become a Christian in college and believed he was called to short-term missions as well. But Charles felt he owed his father something. It was his third year at college and he had to make a decision. What would he tell his father about his career plans? What would you say?

Parents frequently expect their children to do specific things when they grow up. Some parents, particularly those whose own lives are unhappy or unfulfilled, live through their children. Depending on whether they had bad or good work-related experiences, they may or may not want you to go into the same field they did. Other parents just can't let their children make their own decisions. Ultimately, you won't fit into any other mold than that which God has laid before you. You have the freedom not to be what your father or mother always wanted you to be. But how can you talk to your parents about career plans without creating conflict?

□ *Emphasize your responsibility.* Parents may help you make choices, but you have to live with them. Thank them for their concern, but gently remind them that you are responsible.

□ *Be knowledgeable about yourself and your anticipated career.* Do you know your gifts and abilities? Do you know your weaknesses? Do you know about your career track and your potential future in it? Will you need more schooling? These are all questions your parents will ask, particularly if they are not pleased with your career choice.

□ *Gain experience in your career.* Instead of going back to the ice-cream parlor to dish out double scoops all summer, try to get experience in the career field that interests you. Through your professors you can learn about paid internships and opportunities for volunteer work in the field. The more you expose yourself to a possible career, the more intelligently you can talk with your parents about it. If they see you taking steps to find out as much about that career as you can, your parents probably won't object as strenuously. They might even like your choice.

Holiday Plans

"Mom, it's too expensive to fly home for Thanksgiving." I was a freshman and Thanksgiving would be the first holiday that I had ever missed.

"So what are you going to do?" my mother asked.

"Well, Bambi and I are going to her parents' house for the holiday, but a few of us are going to Mexico first," I said nonchalantly.

"And *who* is *Bambi?*"

"Oh, she's a girl I know here at school," I answered innocently. And I was innocent. I had no designs on Bambi, nor she on me.

But you can imagine my mother's thoughts as she contemplated her son's first Thanksgiving away from home with a girl named Bambi. Then my father stepped in. I was to spend Thanksgiving with my aunt and uncle in Nowheresville, California. Period.

There are both wise and foolish ways to talk about holiday plans with your parents. I had been foolish. And I did go to Nowheresville that year.

Thanksgiving and Christmas are times when families expect to assemble. We may welcome those times, or dread them, but we must deal with them. Thanksgiving is usually the acid test, not only because it's the first holiday of the year you're away from home, but also because, with finals looming around the corner, you may be tense. So how can you discuss plans without your parents seeing red?

☐ *Pay your dues.* As a member of the family, you still have to be present for some functions and holidays. At first, if your presence is required, go willingly and enjoy yourself. As you become more independent the second, third and fourth year, family relationships change. You probably won't have to go home if you can't or don't want to be there.

If and when you marry, you will develop your own holiday traditions. College is a good time to move away slowly from what the family has always done.

☐ *Know when to go.* Do you have to be at home the entire Thanksgiving week, or just Thanksgiving Day? Just a few days at Christmas, or the entire winter break? You have some flexibility to make the most of your holiday breaks.

☐ *Count the cost.* How will it affect your relationship with your parents if you don't come home for a holiday? For some, spending time in the midst of family at holidays will be a return to a warm, loving, supportive environment; for others, it will be like spending a holiday in hell, but being there might be just what God is calling you to do.

Friends

Jim," his father said, "You are welcome home during your breaks from school, but your friend Doug is not."

Jim winced. "But Dad, why not?" They had had this irritating conversation before.

"Because Doug is a freeloader," Jim's father answered. "He raids the refrigerator, leaves his bed unmade and doesn't clean the bathroom up after himself. Besides, when he's here you and he stay out all night. I just don't like the guy."

Sound familiar? My parents live in the Chicago area, and they frequently accommodated my out-of-town friends who were making connections through the city. Friends can be unpredictable and irresponsible. One such friend arrived in the evening, went to a wild party in the area and never came back to our house. The next morning, my parents were worried. He finally called, returned as if nothing had happened, and left for school. My parents made it clear that he was not welcome back. No amount of persuasion could change their minds.

Dave, who led me to Christ, was another guest. Dave is well-mannered, but also opinionated and intelligent. At that time my younger brother was a self-proclaimed expert on dolphins. Somehow the dinner-table conversation turned to dolphins, and Dave, who knew something about dolphins, unwittingly demolished my younger brother's knowledge on the subject. A tough family argument erupted after Dave left.

It's natural to want to share friends with your parents—just make sure you know the rules. If you are going to bring a friend home with you, be sure to clear it well in advance with your parents. Tension will be high if a friend arrives unexpectedly for dinner, or, even worse, for spring break. And tell your friend the house rules on cleanliness, curfew and conversation (remember the dolphins).

The joy of sharing a good friendship with your family can help build trust between you and your parents. One friend of mine, Bill, became like one of the family after several visits—not because of the frequency of his visits, but because he was friendly and considerate. He came regularly to our home for holidays (his family, fragmented and divided, lived thousands of miles away), and even now calls my parents on holidays. He has become their friend too. Bill helped my parents see that (sometimes) I was wise in my estimation of people, and did more to smooth my relationship with them than anyone else I know.

Rules for Resolving Conflicts

Ironically, breaks and holidays—the times when you think you should be happiest—are tough for many students. Because you're growing, changing and becoming more independent, time home with Mom and Dad can create new (or resurrect old) tensions. Here are some tips to help you handle face-to-face conflict with your parents.

☐ *Talk it out.* Rather than run from conflicts and let resentment build, try to talk them out. Stress your forgiveness (if appropriate) and acceptance of them, and quickly admit and apologize for your mistakes. Before you approach them, ask God to take control of the situation and bring reconciliation to your household. If your parents don't feel comfortable talking openly about their feelings, try writing them a note expressing your feelings and asking them to respond. Once

you've resolved a conflict, don't resurrect it. Consider the matter closed.

☐ *Continue to express your love to them.* A hug, a squeeze, an "I love you," a bouquet of flowers or a card can bridge more gaps than you can imagine.

☐ *Look at their side of the story.* Get some perspective on why your parents act the way they do by putting yourself in their shoes. What was their upbringing like? If they unfairly take frustrations out on you, why are they frustrated? How would you react to the circumstances they've faced in life? Is there any way you can help them develop their potentials?

☐ *Learn to accept your parents as they are.* Their quirks may drive you crazy. But remember that no one's parents (and no parents' kids) are perfect. They've had forty years or more to establish their habits. You can't change them—but you can affirm the *good* attributes and interests they have.

☐ *Take an inventory of your own habits.* If your parents seem to nag you, try to see yourself as they see you. Do you, for example, do your share of the housework when you're home (cleaning your room, helping with dirty dishes, etc.)? If not, are you truly too busy with studies and other non-negotiable commitments? Or do you need to rearrange your priorities?

☐ *Give them your time.* Simply spending time with your parents when you can (over meals, running errands together, seeing a movie) will provide natural outlets to show them that they deserve your love and respect. You'll also have more chances to discuss some of the issues you're wrestling with in a less volatile setting.

☐ *Share your hurts with them.* Your parents may be tense or meddlesome because they fear that you don't need them anymore. Affirm them by letting them in on all aspects of your life, including your hurts and frustrations. They won't understand or be able to help every time. But you may be surprised at their wisdom and experience.

☐ *Be thankful.* No doubt about it—some people's parents spur more conflicts than others. But even if your parents made some mistakes and hurt you along the way, you probably have some good memories of their love and provision for you. Think on those things—then thank God for placing you in your family, trusting that he has placed you there for a purpose. (See Acts 17:26.) Finally, make a point of thanking your folks for their care.

—*Robert Burdett*

My Parents Got Divorced While I Was at College

One evening I sat down next to my mother and asked her what was wrong.

"Your father and I are going to get a divorce," she said.

I put my arms around her. "No you're not, Mom," I said. "No you're not."

The idea of my parents divorcing was so abhorrent that I refused to believe it could happen. I was sure God would never allow it.

As a child I didn't think much about my parents' relationship. My childhood was a happy one; Mom and Dad were loving parents and worked hard to hide their problems. Near my last year in high school, however, my parents' arguments—so well hidden for so long—came out in the open like an explosion, surprising and stunning us. They were married for exactly a quarter of a century. The year I was a junior in college they faced each other in divorce court on their twenty-fifth anniversary.

Long-Distance Denial

When I first went away to college, in a town thousands of miles away, I was very eager to leave home. I felt guilty about leaving my younger sister alone in a hostile environment. But I still believed God was on the verge of producing a miracle, of making my parents' marriage work out. Wasn't it God's will that married people stay married? Didn't my parents have three Christian daughters who prayed for them every day? It seemed obvious that if we prayed for something in God's will, he would do it.

My first semester at school, it was easy to imagine that my parents were working out their problems. Talking long-distance on the telephone, Mom and Dad sounded cheerful and my sister sounded unusually calm. I continued living the life of the good Sunday-school student: excelling in school, active in campus fellowship, counselor and adviser to all my friends. My freshman roommate had an alcoholic mother, and I spent hours discussing the problem with her, never admitting the seriousness of my own family's problems or of my own mother's excessive drinking. I felt that as long as I didn't admit my family's problems, they really wouldn't exist.

My parents' relationship continued to deteriorate, though I only recognized it during Christmas and summer breaks at home. While I was away at school, I kept praying for them and could fool myself into believing that the next time I went home everything would be fine. But by the summer after my sophomore year, my parents had separated.

God and Responsibility
That summer was the most unhappy period of my life. I got a job and stayed with my mother, who had just been released after several weeks in a crisis center. She had lost her appetite, and it frightened me to look at her thin arms and half-mast eyes. The West Coast heat I had always loved seemed oppressive; I dreaded coming home from work in the evening.

Even though I was dying inside, I assumed I had to maintain the role of the strong, "together" person in order to help my parents. I spent many emotional hours talking to each of them, listening to them, hearing them confide in me things I had never heard before, ugly stories of infidelities, drinking problems and deep-rooted emotional chaos.

Nothing helped. My father filed for divorce late in August, just as I was getting ready to go back to college.

On one hand, his decision didn't surprise any of us. Nothing had improved in my parents' relationship, despite all our efforts. But on the other hand, I still couldn't understand why God had not answered the prayers I had prayed so fervently for so many years, and had worked so hard to fulfill.

Desperately seeking direction for our next move, my sisters and I called a summit meeting late one night in the upstairs bedroom of my grandmother's house. We asked a thousand questions. What was God trying to do? How could he allow Mom and Dad to get divorced? Wasn't that against his will? How could our prayers have failed to keep them together? What did God want us to do now?

We talked and prayed for most of the night. Finally we came to some basic conclusions: though God wants every marriage to work, he won't automatically keep our parents' together if they move to end their marriage. We daughters cannot take reponsibility for our parents' marriage. God's will for us now is to love and honor our parents—not solve their problems for them. Instead of trying to decide which of them was right or wrong, we agreed to love them both.

As I dropped into bed after our meeting, I realized for the first time that I had to accept my parents as they are, along with their failed marriage. I couldn't change them; I could only change myself. For some reason these thoughts strengthened and encouraged me as I rolled over and fell asleep.

Rather than shattering our relationship, our eventual acceptance of our parents' failed marriage gave us strength and kept our family together through the difficult years following the divorce.

Coping with the Consequences
Back at school, I coped with the idea of the divorce mostly unconsciously, by avoiding thinking about it while throwing myself into my studies, friends and activities. I took down the family portrait that hung over my bed; it was too painful to look at our smiling faces, arms wrapped around each other as though we were the ideal family.

Although I didn't realize it at the time, I also coped with my parent's divorce by dating and later becoming briefly engaged to a fellow student. Randy was a dedicated Christian from the most Christian family I had ever met. The chaotic unhappiness of my family contrasted sharply with the loving security of his. It was my chance to be part of the perfect family, to have a perfect relationship that would be completely different from my parents'.

I also felt that our relationship would set

an example for my parents. One evening, while visiting my father, I announced that Randy and I would never get divorced.

"How can you be so sure?" my father asked, startled at my confidence.

"Because when you're Christians, you stay committed to each other."

My father, who was in no position to lecture me about what makes a good marriage, did not argue. But he looked pretty worried.

After graduating from college, I moved to a new town and started my first job. Randy came to visit often, but I never felt ready to set the date for our wedding. For some reason the initial thrill I had felt about Randy and his family began to fade. My roommates wondered out loud about my lack of enthusiasm for the wedding. Soon I began to wonder too.

It occurred to me that I had never truly considered whether Randy was right for me. He was a Christian; I would be part of a Christian family; everyone approved of the match. That seemed enough.

But as I got to know Randy and his family better, I began to notice their imperfections—some of which bothered me a great deal. I had never known that Christian families could have serious problems too. And though Randy and I both were Christians, we had very different interests and temperaments.

It wasn't until months after Randy and I broke up that I realized that our relationship had anything to do with my parent's divorce.

By that time my two sisters—living their lives in separate areas of the country—were both undergoing counseling to help them deal with the emotional havoc my parents' divorce created. One sister was seeing her pastor on a regular basis, the other a Christian psychologist.

I realized I needed outside help also. For me, "therapy" came in the form of a small

church prayer group I joined.

Members of this little Christian community met once a week to pray and study Scripture. At first I was hesitant to display my family's—and therefore my own—imperfections before the group. But I soon got over that feeling. When the members of this group talked about themselves and their families, they talked with great concern but absolutely no shame about divorce, wayward children, emotional distress. When I came to trust them enough to talk about my parents and their ongoing problems, I was amazed at how well they accepted them as part of life in an imperfect world.

Resolution

Four years after I graduated from college, and five years after my parents' divorce, Mom and Dad saw each other again for the first time. It was the day before my wedding, and we had gathered in the church for rehearsal. I was busy with other members of the bridal party, when, over my shoulder, I heard my mother speak first.

"Hello, Malcolm."

And then my father. "Hello, Sue."

Although I turned around quickly, I saw that they had already parted, and were heading in different directions down the aisle.

At that moment, I felt both sadness and relief simultaneously. It was kind of like seeing the casket at a funeral and realizing that the person is truly dead after a long, painful illness. The sadness came from knowing, as clearly as I had ever known it before, that my parents would never love each other again. The relief came from knowing that, on the eve of my own marriage, I could finally stop worrying about my parents' relationship and redirect my energy to new priorities in my life. It was something I should have done many years before.

FAITH AND FELLOWSHIP

Some people lose their faith at college. Others find it. Many muddle through without thinking about God too much. No doubt about it: your faith will be challenged during the next few years, but it will also have an excellent opportunity to grow among like-minded peers. In this section you'll find practical guidance on learning how to pray effectively, understand and apply the Bible and learn the ins and outs of finding and getting involved in a Christian student group and a church—as well as how to recognize one of the many different cults that recruit on campus. You'll discover the impact that a small, committed group of believers at school can have on your life. And we'll help you see ways you can express your faith on campus, from sharing your faith with a friend to taking a stand on social issues.

PRAYING (WHEN YOU HAVE A MILLION OTHER THINGS TO DO)

Chua Wee Hian

When I was a student, I was involved in a church which had a small circle of students who were actively praying for non-Christian friends. As we prayed, we were led to invite them to our rooms for supper and informal discussion. Hardly a week passed without someone turning to Christ! We learned the power of faithful prayer.

So why do so many of us on campus find it hard to make time for prayer? And how can we make prayer a dynamic part of our lives?

Most Christians on campus are "activists"; we immerse ourselves in planning and running endless activities. We believe that prayer is essential and important. But we struggle to be still and spend time with God in prayer. To be honest, we have to admit that we often only pay lip service to prayer.

Our prayerlessness and our inability to wait upon God for more than ten minutes a day are symptoms of spiritual uneasiness; we do not feel at home with God. We are missing the intimacy and joy the Psalmist testifies about: "You will fill me with joy in your presence, with eternal pleasures at your right hand" (Ps 16:11).

Jesus at Prayer

Luke, in his Gospel, records several key instances when the Lord prayed. Jesus' reliance on prayer shows how we can make prayer integral as we forge out a lifestyle in college. Let's look at five crucial occasions when Jesus took time out to pray:

1. During his busy ministry. Throughout his busy working life, our Lord did not neglect prayer. He often withdrew to remote and quiet places such as the wilderness (Lk 5:16), mountains and hills (Lk 6:12; 9:28) to be alone with the Father. The crowds sapped his energy as he taught, healed and fed them. His disciples needed constant attention—and besides, they were not an easy bunch to train! Yet Jesus never crowded prayer out of his life. Busyness was never an excuse for not praying. We can detect a rhythm in his life and ministry. It was always work/withdrawal, work/withdrawal. Withdrawing for prayer gives us fresh strength and perspective to accomplish God's work in our fellowship group, dorm room, fraternity house—wherever.

2. At his baptism. Before starting his public ministry, Jesus submitted himself to the baptism of John the Baptist. In the River Jordan, Christ openly identified himself with sinful men and women. For the sinless Jesus, this must have been a traumatic experience. But he prayed (Lk 3:21). His prayers were answered by the descent of the Holy Spirit and the voice of approval from his Father, "You are my Son, whom I love; with you I am well pleased" (v. 22). Preparing ourselves for God's work on campus clearly demands prayer.

3. Before the appointment of the disciples. Jesus had been announcing the advent of the kingdom and summoning his hearers to repent and believe the gospel. He had cast out demons and restored many to health. People flocked to hear him and many followed him. The time had come for him to select a smaller group of disciples with whom he could share his life and mission. What did he do? Did he go around canvassing the crowd, getting opinions as to the suitability of the prospective candidates? Did he hold open elections? No, our Lord devoted himself to a night of prayer before the appointment of the disciples (Lk 6:12-13).

Perhaps at no time will you have to make as many important decisions about your priorities, your relationships, your career and your future as during college. When making decisions with such far-reaching effects, we need to take time to call upon the Lord for wisdom and protection before we forge ahead.

4. *When teaching others.* Once when Jesus was praying alone, a disciple approached him with a specific request: "Lord, teach us to pray" (Lk 11:1). His response was embodied in what we call the Lord's Prayer. In this brief prayer of striking simplicity, we are taught first to focus our thoughts on God, his character, his kingdom and his will, and then to pray for basic human needs, both material and spiritual (Lk 11:2-4). So we learn that prayer should always be God-centered and that petitions should flow out of a deep sense of dependence on him.

Wouldn't it be great if a new Christian were to approach us with a similar request? "Will you please teach us to pray?" Many active Christians on campus are asked to share their secrets—their techniques of evangelism, program planning and leadership—but too few are asked to counsel others in cultivating a closer relationship with God in prayer. Our example will stimulate hunger in other students for communion with God when our lives reflect the joy and reality of constant meetings with him, rather than a packed schedule that crowds God out.

5. *In the face of suffering.* Toward the end of his earthly ministry, when the dark shadows of pain and suffering cast their pall on Jesus, there was every temptation for him to escape. Could there not be another route for the Lord's anointed than the way of suffering? An intense struggle took place in the garden of Gethsemane when he had to face his imminent crucifixion (Lk 22:41-44). This tension was so agonizing that Luke, the author-physician, describes Jesus' perspiration as being "like drops of blood falling to the ground" (v. 44). Doing God's will often involves hardship and suffering— from which we naturally shrink. Like Christ, we too can face up to these trials if we learn to wrestle with God in prayer.

On the cross, Jesus prayed for his tormentors: "Father, forgive them, for they do not know what they are doing" (Lk 23:34). What love in the midst of extreme suffering! Then his last breath was a prayer of committal to his Father: "Jesus called out with a loud voice, 'Father, into your hands I commit my spirit' " (v. 46). What confidence in the face of death! Without a life of prayer, how can we forgive those who unjustly wrong us or let us down? And how can we face death with absolute confidence in God?

In Acts, Luke reports the ways in which early-church leaders imitated their Master's habit of prayer. For instance, they prayed earnestly before appointing Matthias to replace Judas (Acts 1:14).

During the period of widespread turning to God after Pentecost, when thousands became Christians, prayer was a prominent feature in the life of the Jerusalem church. Members of this early community were instructed and encouraged to join the services and prayers of the Temple. Christians also participated in regular and spontaneous home prayer meetings (Acts 2:46-47). In times of persecution and harassment, the leaders led their people in prayer (Acts 4:24-31; 12:5). Stephen, the first martyr, prayed to God to forgive his persecutors and committed his spirit to the ascended Christ (Acts 7:59-60). His spirit of prayer enabled the church to proclaim the Word of God with boldness (Acts 4:31).

Quiet and Unhurried Moments

How can we make prayer central in our lives? On a personal level, we must learn to meditate. God has commanded us, "Be still, and know that I am God; I will be exalted among the nations, I will be exalted in the earth" (Ps 46:10). We are not to rush in and out of his presence. We must cultivate the habit of spending quiet and unhurried moments with him.

Christian meditation is very different from transcendental meditation. TM teaches people to empty their minds, to look inward and explore their inner consciousness. Christian meditation urges us to fill our minds with God. We gaze upward at the exalted Lord. The purpose of being still in his presence is to know him.

I have found it helpful to punctuate periods of silence by reading aloud

certain Psalms of praise and thanksgiving (Psalms 96—100: 145—150). Another alternative is to read and meditate on the classic passages in Isaiah 40—
66, which vividly depict God's glory and character. The singing or reading of
worshipful songs can also help us adore him.

Worshiping God transforms our lives (see 2 Cor 3:18). Those who spend
time in his presence are molded by their vision of the mighty God. As we be-
hold his majesty and holiness and ponder his steadfast love, we are "lost in
wonder, love and praise." Then as he discloses himself to us, we become
conscious of our sins. That stirs us to cry out to God for forgiveness and
cleansing (see Is 6:5 and Ps 51). And as we experience his forgiveness, we
appreciate his grace more and more. Finally, grace spurs us to attempt great
things for God and to accept others as God in Christ accepts us (see 1 Cor
15:10 and Rom 15:7).

Where Do I Begin?

The greatest obstacle to a vital prayer life is *getting started*. I used to believe
that prayer was a magical trip. I thought that any urge to pray would transport
me into a cloud-nine state. But that's not spiritual reality.

Someone might object: What about the glorious promise in Isaiah 40:31
that "those who hope in the LORD will renew their strength. They will soar on
wings like eagles; they will run and not grow weary, they will walk and not
be faint"?

I have always longed to soar into God's presence like an eagle. But how do
eagles mount up into the blue skies? A few months ago, some friends and I
were swimming in a secluded bay in Trinidad. We were held spellbound by
pelicans and eagles flying above us. Occasionally, a huge eagle would swoop
down into the sea to fish. To take off again it had to flap its wings furiously,
and only after strenuous exertion could it lift off.

For me, that visually captured prayer. Disciplined efforts at praying usually
precede being transported into God's holy presence. But just as the eagles
had the swirling air currents to help them soar to the heights, we as Christians have the Holy Spirit to assist and enable us. "In the same way, the Spirit

helps us in our weakness. We do not know what we ought to pray for, but the Spirit himself intercedes for us with groans that words cannot express" (Rom 8:26).

Prayer also includes intercession, bringing specific needs of others to God. One of the greatest intercessors in the Bible was the apostle Paul. In spite of his heavy schedule and the tremendous pressures he had to cope with as a church planter, apostle, teacher and pastor, he made time to pray for others (see Phil 1:3-9 and Col 1:3-4, 9-12). He asked others to pray for him (see Eph 6:18-19 and 2 Thess 3:1). Thus, to follow the example of Paul, we must set aside time to pray for others and to invite others to uphold us before God.

That may mean giving up other activities. But if we fail to pray, we are saying that we really believe we have all the resources we need within ourselves, or that we doubt God's power. Ponder a moment. Do your actions indicate foolish self-sufficiency or unbelief?

Prayer and Love
When we pray for others, we grow to love and understand them. Prayer helps us to relate people to God, to one another and to ourselves.

Be specific when praying for the needs of others—say, for a particular missionary, staff worker, situation or problem. When God answers your prayers tell others, so that they can rejoice with you.

Leaders in your campus fellowship should also meet regularly to pray together. This promotes harmony in personal and working relationships and provides the context for God to speak about the spiritual health and affairs of the fellowship. All campus fellowships exist in part to win fellow students to Christ. How are students converted? They must have the gospel clearly presented to them. This witness is effective when it is backed up by transformed lives and faithful intercession.

Share your prayer concerns about your fellowship with other students. Then ask God to help you make prayer central in your lives. He delights to answer us when we ask him to draw close.

The Art of Listening to God

You are ready to commit yourself to praying regularly. You realize how important prayer is and you really want to feel intimate with God. But how do you begin?

Silent Spots

Prayer usually goes best with quiet settings. But in today's noisy world, silence rarely finds us—we must actively seek it. Here are some suggestions for finding those special places.

☐ *Get up early.* Chances of finding a quiet spot on campus are greater at 6 or 6:30 A.M. than at 8 or 9. Look for a soft chair in the dorm lounge, a park bench, the campus chapel, a quiet cafe.

☐ *Take a walk.* A nearby park, forest pre-serve or lake can provide moments of rela-tive quiet. Even walking on seldom-traveled streets can give you time for silence and re-flection. In winter, bundle up and walk dur-ing a snowfall.

☐ *Go for a ride.* If you must drive to find woods or parks, take the back roads rather than expressways. Leave the radio off and en-joy the scenery. Better yet, ride your bike.

☐ *Sit in a church or cathedral.* Though God is everywhere, some sense his presence more easily in a church building. Many churches are open for prayer or meditation, and many offer daily or midweek services.

☐ *Avoid rush hours.* Many of the ordinary campus spots—your apartment or dorm room, the library, the student union—may be silent (or nearly so) during nonpeak hours.

Take advantage of these opportunities.

☐ *Schedule a personal retreat.* Plan a full day, or even a weekend, to get away by yourself. Take a long hike. Go wilderness camping. Spend a weekend alone at a family cottage. Plan an overnight bike trip.

How to Listen to God

Once you find silence, what do you do with it? Try some of these ideas:

☐ *Do nothing.* We are conditioned to think that every minute of our lives must be filled with "productive" activity. Why not simply enjoy the revitalizing effect and the life perspective that silent inactivity can provide?

☐ *Look around.* We look through our eyes sixteen hours each day. But how often do we truly see—see beyond what we expect to see or want to see? Can we look past the visual clamor that gluts our minds?

In silence, stare at the world around you, at the sky, at people, at yourself, at art. If you look closely with open eyes, you will see something new.

☐ *Keep a journal.* In a spiral notebook or a "blank book" write down your thoughts, feelings, hurts, dreams, doubts, joys, fantasies, struggles, prayers and poems—in other words, anything you want. Don't show your journal to anyone. Don't worry about writing style or grammar. And don't worry about what God will think.

☐ *Read the Psalms.* Forget any structured, systematic Bible study right now; simply allow the words of Scripture to speak to you, unencumbered by commentaries, handbooks and preachers. The Psalms and Proverbs are good places to start this kind of reading. Picture yourself in place of the writer. Paraphrase passages in your own words. Select a phrase or sentence and meditate on it for ten minutes, soaking up the meaning.

☐ *Pray conversationally.* Talk to God, silently or aloud, in the same way you'd talk to a friend, and with the same freedom that you'd write in the journal.

☐ *Sing.* Sing your favorite hymn, a "Scripture song," or any tune that turns your heart to God. If you belong to a liturgical church tradition, consider singing or reciting parts of your church's liturgy. A fresh setting may charge these oft-repeated words with new meaning.

☐ *Make a scrapbook.* Keep a list of people, places and things you are grateful to God for. Note prayers that are answered—and those that aren't yet. Collect inspiring paragraphs and quotes from magazine articles, books, the Bible, movies, TV shows and speakers. Categorize the quotes and reread them on occasion.

—*Verne Becker*

REDISCOVERING YOUR BIBLE

Tim Cummings

Swirling sand, a hot wind, an angry sun—deserts are typically dry places and not well liked by the general public. We call them wastelands or badlands or Death Valley.

Sometimes I open my Bible and hear the hollow, formless wind of the desert eroding my enthusiasm to read Scripture. The voice that reads to me in my head goes monotone, slows down and whispers, "This is boring."

Bible study boredom is a hard enemy to fight because we cannot see it. Where does it come from? Should I just wait for it to go away, or can I do something to fight it?

Finding Relief

As with the water beneath the desert, we can probe beneath that crusty, lifeless boredom to find the cool, life-giving water of Scripture. Here are some ways I have learned to combat Death Valley Quiet Times.

☐ *Examine your life.* Many times when the Bible goes bad on us, it is a symptom of something else in our life which is not right. Check it out. Is it dorm food? Bad mood? Relationship on the rocks? Too little sleep? GPA blues? Test anxiety? Sin? No one has unplugged your Bible. So first check your connections.

☐ *Pray for desire.* When I was a second-year Bible-college student, my personal Bible study bottomed out. Like others around me, I, too, wanted to enjoy poring over Scripture for hours on end. So I prayed. I told God my problem with boredom. And he answered. But not in one big zap.

I spent some time thinking about the place of Scripture in God's whole scheme of revealing himself, and was amazed to realize that our Creator has left us a diary of his activities and ac-

complishments! Through the pages of the Bible I began to take note of what God likes and dislikes, how he works in the lives of people and nations, what he says about the significance of the life of Christ, of the cross and of the empty tomb. Boring? My casual attitude toward the Bible gave way to excitement.

☐ *Cultivate a relationship with the Bible.* Exploration is the key to reading. When I have been taken on an adventure by means of a book, I sense an odd sort of friendship with it. C. S. Lewis fans talk about Narnia as if they have invested in real estate there. They've gone on an adventure. It can be that way with the Bible.

Try, for example, adopting one book of the Bible as your own. After attending an InterVarsity Christian Fellowship conference on inductive Bible study, I came home and began tearing into 1 Corinthians. I told myself there would be nothing in that book that I would not understand. I explored the book. It became

my book. Even five years later I have a sense of ownership toward 1 Corinthians.

The psalmist wrote of such a relationship in Psalm 119. Just look at the verbs he uses to describe his relationship with Scripture. Attitudes: I will treasure, have regard for, long for, wait for, esteem, stand in awe of, love, and rejoice in thy precepts. Action: I will walk in, observe, seek, keep diligently, look unto, learn, proclaim, meditate on, remember, cleave to, not turn aside from, turn my feet toward, believe in, diligently consider, perform, and sing of thy law. Each phrase becomes a challenge and a goal for me in my growing relationship with Scripture.

☐ *Chart your direction ahead of time.* I have found that my driest devotional times are when I'm between books. I don't know what to study next or what method to use. So I either read bits and pieces indifferently or lose my desire to read at all.

Try asking yourself: What books in the Bible do you know the least about? Which of those books would you find most intriguing to read right now? Then get started on that book. And before you finish that book, decide what you'll study next. Questions or interesting issues in your current study may lead you to another book. For example, while studying the book of Hebrews, I got interested in the Old Testament priesthood. So I tackled Leviticus next. While in Leviticus, I found myself in the middle of a larger story, and so I decided to study the five books of Moses (Genesis to Deuteronomy). I wasn't able to stop until I finished Joshua and Judges. I didn't have to worry about finding a starting place for five months!

☐ *Use a method of Bible study which taps your strengths.* Contrary to popular opinion, there is more than one way to study Scripture. Choose a method you feel comfortable with. You will find Bible study much more enjoyable if you capitalize on your abilities. (Some of these different methods will be described below.)

☐ *Add variety to your Bible study.* Change versions, methods, Testaments, even the place where you study. Part of the adventure of Bible study is in how we approach our task. Too much routine can breed boredom. If you know exactly what and exactly how you are going to study five years from now, you're in for it. Variety will help you stay out of the desert.

☐ *Put something down on paper.* One of my most cherished possessions is a green three-ring notebook which con-

tains almost five years' worth of various (and I mean various) types of studies I've done. I have used it as a resource on many occasions. Parts of it are typed, others are scrawled. Much of it is multi-colored.

Writing things down in study helps me to focus my thinking. Even when I am trying to cover lots of territory (like Genesis through Deuteronomy), I can pause long enough to think of the main thought in a chapter and jot a title down. Today could be the start of a cherished three-ring notebook for you.

Some Methods I Have Loved

As I mentioned above, trying different Bible study methods can rescue you from boredom. Here are my top nine:

Inductive Bible study. This method is fairly involved, but worth the effort. In three major steps—observing the facts (who, what, when, why, where and how), interpreting them (Why is this passage here? What can we conclude about it?) and making personal applications (What does this passage imply about my life?)—you can boil down the meaning of the text. In the process you may use some of the specific methods listed below. (InterVarsity Christian Fellowship offers a training weekend in this method called "Bible and Life Level 2".)

Paragraph and chapter titles. Simply list in your notebook a title for every paragraph you study, and then an overall title for the chapter. This method will help you center on main points in Scripture and remember in a fun way what goes on in a certain passage. Can you guess these different passages based on my titles? "Tablets' Second Printing"; "Rash Measures for Skin Disease"; "Here's Mud in Your Eye"; "Warning for Wilderness Christians."

Theme study. For this method you need a pack of color pencils and a Bible you're willing to mark up. As you read, look for different themes and shade relevant passages with different colors. Then trace recurrent themes in various books by underlining related passages in the appropriate color. For instance, in my Bible all the passages in the Gospel of John having something to do with the deity of Christ are underlined in orange. Other themes might be life, belief or signs. Themes in Jeremiah include chronology, reasons for judgment and idolatry.

Titles and themes—a combination of the second and third methods. Instead of underlining in a Bible, underline in your notebook the titles of the paragraphs which contain a recurring theme. (Repetition, of course, shows emphasis on something important.)

Book overview chart. Title the chapters. Then, depending on the nature of the book, add more graphs or maps. Mark off larger sections of the book as you notice major turning points. For Genesis, I added a list of the meanings of some of the names. You may wish to elaborate by highlighting key verses or the central theme of the book. My Joshua chart has a map of the progression which Israel made through the Promised Land. Judges has a chart which tells how long Israel was in bondage under different governments.

Journaling. Keep a journal of your own thoughts as you study a passage.

But beware of spiritualizing every pebble in the brook or bird in the sky. Some published devotionals get away with murdering the text. Stay as true to what the text actually says as possible.

Rereading short books. Occasionally I get burned out plowing through long books of the Bible. A few years back I decided to read the entire book of Colossians every morning for five days. A friend of mine who's a pastor read 1 Peter every day for a month. We were both amazed at the insights we gleaned from this concentrated survey.

Q & A. Write and try to answer seven questions for each chapter. You might ask why Matthew divides the genealogy into three sets of fourteen. Or what qualities Paul demonstrates as a discipler in 1 Thessalonians 2. I spent a week once chasing down Paul's thorn in the flesh. Although I didn't find a conclusive answer, I still remember the various speculations I ran across during my quest. You may want to use a Bible dictionary or commentary to help answer your questions.

Retelling and rewriting. Narratives, parables and Cecil-B.- DeMille events in Scripture lend themselves well to storytelling. For ideas, look for a book about how to tell stories, read a children's Bible, or read stories by good authors. Or try writing in your own words what's going on in the text you are reading. You might make some new connections or discover that you don't understand something as well as you thought you did.

Guidelines

When we unleash our imaginations during Bible study, we face the danger of running amuck. Don't be afraid to go a little wild and crazy, but make sure you can answer yes to these questions:

☐ *Am I absorbing content?* Keep your focus on God's truth as you study. If you pay too much attention to the exercise, you might forget its purpose.

☐ *Have I come to the Bible to be changed?* After you have understood a passage, make sure you understand what it means to you personally. Will you allow God's Word to shape your personality and lifestyle? Even questions like "What has Moses got that I haven't?" can open up applications for your life.

☐ *Am I communing with God?* Bible study can be an exercise in creativity or discipline. But it is not an end in itself. Your goal in Bible study is knowing God. Don't fall into the trap of ignoring God while reading Scripture.

☐ *Am I approaching the Bible as a student?* A student approaches his teaching material with humility and openness. Using the Bible to try to prove a point of view defeats learning. "Teach me thy ways; show me thy paths" should be the prayer on our lips as we approach God's Word.

I mentioned earlier the psalmist's attitudes toward Scripture. Psalm 119 also tells us what effects we can expect from God's Word. Our way becomes steadfast, we are kept pure, our weary soul is strengthened, our reverence for God increases. We gain wisdom, peace, stability and integrity. The list goes on.

Reading God's Word can be an adventure. It is not always fun. I still have week-long dry spells with Death Valley Quiet Times. But eventually the water of the Word surfaces. And the words in front of me come alive again.

Bible Study Resources

So you're all fired up to read the Bible—and this time you mean business. You open it up and begin to devour its contents. But some parts are hard to digest. You read about cherubim, Sadducees, tabernacles, Baal, Judea, Samaritans, sanctification, Babylon, Hittites and other things that aren't part of your average dorm discussion. How can you decipher what they all mean?

Because even the newest books in our Bible are almost 2,000 years old, they often take some special effort to understand. Thankfully, you can tap a number of resources to help you bridge the gaps:

☐ *Your Bible.* Choosing an accurate, understandable translation can save you time and confusion. Try the New International Version or the New American Standard. Other good modern versions include the Revised Standard Version, the New English Bible and the

Jerusalem Bible. (The King James Version uses archaic English and is not as accurate as these others.)

☐ *Your Bible.* No, this is not a misprint. Besides the text, many Bibles provide cross references, notes, essays, concordances, charts, maps and more. By using these resources, you can answer most of your questions without having to leave the book you're studying. Take care to remember, however, that these additional notes and charts are not divinely inspired; though they are helpful and generally dependable, they often represent the thinking of one person or one school of theological thought.

☐ *A Bible Dictionary.* A good Bible dictionary is the best reference tool you can own. Entries on people, places, events, books of the Bible, doctrines, tools, plants, wars and more provide background information that will help untangle most problem passages. *The New Bible Dictionary* (Tyndale) and *Harper's Bible Dictionary* (Harper & Row) rank among the best.

☐ *A Single-Volume Commentary.* Commentaries give verse-by-verse (or at least section-by-section) interpretations of Scripture. Buying a commentary is like inviting a Bible scholar to look over your shoulder as you read your Bible: it can show you things you never noticed, put things together in a way you never imagined—and tell you things you're not interested in knowing. Sometimes it may even be wrong. Nevertheless, a single-volume commentary such as *The New Bible Commentary* (Eerdmans) or *The Interna-*

tional Bible Commentary (Zondervan) will handle most of your concerns concisely. If you want more detailed information, you might pick up a commentary on an individual book of the Bible. Consult more than one person for their recommendations; there are many commentaries and not all of them are of the highest quality.

☐ *Bible Study Guides.* Having someone else ask the questions may force you to deal with issues and applications you may not have noticed on your own. Many people also appreciate the structure a study guide brings to their personal devotions. If this style of study appeals to you, consider LifeGuide Bible Studies (IVP), which offer questions on topics or single books of the Bible for either group or individual use. Other good series include LifeChange (NavPress), Fisherman (Harold Shaw) and Neighborhood (Tyndale) Bible Studies.

☐ *Other Helps.* As far as explaining general issues and giving you an overall approach to Scripture, you simply can't beat Gordon Fee and Douglas Stuart's *How to Read the Bible for All Its Worth* (Zondervan). It's packed with important information and fascinating tidbits.

This list certainly doesn't even touch on all the excellent resources for Bible study; atlases, concordances, handbooks, encyclopedias and more are available at your local Christian bookstore. Ask around. Find out what has been helpful to others. Enjoy the adventure!

—Mickey Maudlin

FINDING A FELLOWSHIP GROUP YOU CAN LOVE

Mike Basler

How does it feel to arrive at college without family, friends or a familiar church nearby? Lonely. As a freshman at Pasadena City College, I felt alone in a sea of 25,000 people. Before long I began to meet people in classes and make friends. But none of them were Christians who could understand my spiritual struggles. For reasons unknown even to me, I didn't seek out a campus fellowship group until sophomore year. I only wish I hadn't waited so long.

On the way to finding a group, I grew to realize that campus fellowships vary widely; each has its own personality, emphases and strengths. If you're new on campus, or wanting to grow spiritually for the first time, the choices can be confusing. From my experience and others', here are some guidelines for finding a campus fellowship group that will help you grow closer to God and to other people.

Make a List
Make a list of the characteristics you'd like to find in a group. People's priorities vary. But here are some characteristics any list should include:

Intimacy. I wanted to make some friends as soon as possible—so I looked for a fellowship group with a warm atmosphere. Some questions I asked my-self were: Are people cliquish? Do they seem eager to welcome and include visitors? Do people in the group hang out together before and after the struc-tured meeting starts? Does the group meet weekly (or at least bi-weekly)? Does the group encourage members to pair up with a prayer partner? Do people get together socially? Are people vulnerable about their hurts and struggles during prayer times? Does the larger fellowship include a network of small groups that encourage close relationships and accountability?

Sound teaching. Whoever addresses the group to share a testimony or teach doesn't have to be a theologian—but the message should jibe with Scripture. Ask one of the leaders if the group has a faith statement you can read. (They should. If a leader shrugs off your question with a vague claim like, "We teach what the Bible teaches," beware. Many groups with highly un-orthodox beliefs claim to teach the Bible.)

Then, after attending a few meetings, ask yourself: Does this group seem to have a good mix of teaching and testimony times led by students, mature Christian leaders and a campus staffworker or sponsor? Do speakers use the Bible as their primary resource? Do speakers welcome questions or concerns about what they are saying? What do other students in the fellowship have to say about the group's teaching? Is what I've heard consistent with the group's statement of belief?

Group enthusiasm and outreach. Some of the groups I visited felt stagnant; several people seemed to be doing all the work while everyone else watched. Look for a group where common interests and goals excite the whole group, where people support and pray for each other's outreach. Ask yourself: Will this group let me vegetate—or will they encourage me to use the gifts God has given me for the benefit of the group and others? Does there seem to be a place for me to serve God here? Is the group reaching out beyond itself to minister to others—encouraging members to share God's love and good news with non-Christians and to give money and time to the needy? Is anyone in the group considering short- or long-term missions work? If so, are others praying for and financially supporting them? Do members bring non-Christian friends to the group? If not, why?

Worshipful atmosphere. Worship styles vary widely—from staid prayers to hand-raising and speaking in tongues, from traditional hymns and a piano to contemporary choruses and electric guitars. Find a group whose style matches or complements your own. I was looking for a group whose relaxed atmosphere would encourage me to display more freedom in worship than the church I'd grown up in. Don't be afraid to visit widely different groups.

What if a group falls short in one of these areas, or in another area on your list? Like you and me, no group is perfect. Decide which characteristics you value most and make sure the group you choose exhibits those.

Visit the Various Groups

Visit the various groups on campus. Ask someone in the Student Activities Office which groups are officially registered on campus. Then look in your school paper and on bulletin boards around campus to find out meeting places and times.

Sort through your first impressions. They are not always (or even usually) correct. If the speaker's manner or message turned you off, don't assume that she accurately reflects the group. Ask other students what they thought of her. Then give the group another chance. Excellent groups have been known to host a bad speaker or two. (And, on the other hand, lifeless groups have been known to host a dynamic speaker or two.)

The first several meetings of the fellowship group that I attended were only fair—the students seemed great, but the speakers seemed to have little to say. As I got involved, however, I realized there was far more to the group than the speakers I had happened to hear. Similarly, at your first meeting you may meet a few students who rub you the wrong way. Don't write off the group until you've met a representative sample.

Evaluate and Commit

Evaluate the group in light of your list. As you try to determine which groups are a good fit, you may discover you don't know certain groups well enough to evaluate them honestly. Go back to those groups and get to better know one or two of the people you've already met. Ask them more about the group's leaders, background and goals.

Finally, commit yourself to one of your top choices. Ask God to lead you to the group where you will grow the most; then take a chance and get involved where you feel most comfortable. Go on the next retreat. Join a small group.

After a couple of months of fellowship-hopping, I found an InterVarsity Christian Fellowship group that was warm and offered solid, biblical teaching. They welcomed me and put me to work. I made friends. I felt wanted and needed.

I will never forget my experience with InterVarsity at Pasadena City College. I committed myself to the group and they committed themselves to me. In fact, they influenced about every area of my life.

One time a friend in the group confronted me about how I had been treating some other members. His honesty stung. If I hadn't been committed to the group, I might have left in a huff. But I knew he was committed to my growth, and eventually I followed his advice. God spoke to me through friends such as him in that fellowship group many times.

No one can make it through college alone and remain spiritually intact. God created us to be in fellowship with him and each other. Find and commit yourself to a campus fellowship that suits you. It may take time and effort—but you'll never be the same again.

Christian Organizations You Can Join

Look for one or more of these Christian student organizations on your campus, or write to their home offices for more information. Groups vary from campus to campus in their size, activities and theology. Use the principles discussed in the chapter "Finding a Fellowship Group You Can Love" in choosing which group is right for you.

Baptist Student Union, National Student Ministries, 127 Ninth Avenue North, Nashville, TN 37234.

Campus Crusade for Christ, Arrowhead Springs, San Bernardino, CA 92414.

Coalition for Christian Outreach (Pennsylvania, Ohio and West Virginia), 6740 Fifth Ave., Pittsburgh, PA 15208.

Episcopal Church Center, 815 Second Ave., New York, NY 10017.

Fellowship of Christian Athletes, 8701 Leeds Rd., Kansas City, MO 64129.

InterVarsity Christian Fellowship, 6400 Schroeder Rd., P.O. Box 7895, Madison, WI 53707-7895.

Lutheran Campus Ministries, 35 E. Wacker Dr., Suite 1847, Chicago, IL 60601.

Missouri Synod Office of Campus Ministry, 1333 S. Kirkwood Rd., St. Louis, MO 63122-7295.

Methodist Board of Higher Education in Ministry, P.O. Box 871, Nashville, TN 37202.

The Navigators, P.O. Box 6000, Colorado Springs, CO 80934.

Presbyterian Church U.S.A., Youth & Young Adults Program, 475 Riverside Dr., Rm. 1164, New York, NY 10115.

Sure-Fire Ways to Promote Your Campus Fellowship Group

Rob Suggs

Use of Persuasive Personalities for Recruiting

Relevant Themes

Banners in New Places

Big-Name Speakers

Popular Meeting Areas

Creative Campus Radio Announcements

Putting Together a Successful Small Group

Michael Wiebe

To achieve the degree of fellowship described in the New Testament—love, bearing burdens, encouragement, admonishment, sacrificial caring—becoming part of a small group of Christians is almost essential. It's almost impossible for large groups to have the needed intimacy for open and honest sharing. Small groups provide the context for close, long-term relationships in which the whole person can minister and be ministered to.

If you're interested in growing spiritually with others in a small group but can't find one, don't be afraid to begin one yourself. Successful small groups aren't started by committees but by people like you who are interested in growing closer to God and other people. Pray for the Holy Spirit to bring the people he wants to your small group. Here are a few suggestions to get you started.

Starting (and Maintaining) a Small Group

Don't worry about starting small. If you can find even one other person who is interested, just the two of you can begin meeting and ministering to each other, trusting God to increase the size of your group as he is ready.

Meet regularly, but be flexible. Once a week or once eve-

ry two weeks is good. Meeting less often makes communication difficult. Knowing someone's day-to-day burdens requires more than a monthly check-up.

Specify a trial period. Agree to meet for four to six weeks
initially. Then evaluate the group to see if people's needs
are being met and discuss whether you'd like to make
changes or even continue meeting at all.

Set goals. "If you aim at nothing, that's what you'll hit." At
the first group meeting spend some time discussing goals:
why each person came, and what he or she wants to get
out of the group. As the members discuss what goals the
group should have, try to be as specific as possible—not
just "to grow as Christians," but how? To grow in boldness
in order to share Jesus? To become more patient? To understand Scripture better? To feel more intimate with God
and other believers? To explore the role of the Holy Spirit
in your life?

Pray for God's wisdom and guidance before and after
you set your goals. And make sure they include experiencing deep, intimate fellowship—bearing one another's
burdens (Gal 6:2); encouraging each other (Heb 10:24);
building up each other (1 Thess 5:11); and so on. Because
each Christian has at least one spiritual gift given by God
for the good of others (1 Cor 12; Rom 12; Eph 4), discovering and exercising these gifts in the group might be a good
goal as well. (Members with leadership ability, for example, may want to learn how to lead a group with the long-
range goal of dividing to start several other groups, both
with other Christians and with non-Christians through
evangelistic Bible studies.)

An awareness of specific goals, both as individuals and
for the group as a whole, will help you decide what to
study, what to pray for, and how to spend your time together.

*Take time to get to know one another and build commu-
nity.* It's all too easy for a group to spend the beginning of
each meeting talking about a football game or favorite "Star

Trek" reruns and never really share their lives with each other. Good starter questions help:

"How did you become a Christian?"

"What person has had the most influence in your life?"

"Name one thing you really like about yourself."

"Name one thing you would like to change about yourself."

"What's the dumbest thing you ever did?"

Ask one of these questions and let people reveal as much or as little as they want to. Don't be afraid of a long silence—let people think. It's usually best not to go around the circle since this can put pressure on shy members before they are ready. Spontaneous sharing about experiences, struggles and joys will grow with time.

Study Scripture together. Choose a book or a topic in the Bible to see what you can learn together. (InterVarsity Press offers a series of practical and lively Bible studies called LifeGuides, which leaders might find useful.) Ask three basic questions as you look at a passage: "What does it say?" (gathering facts— who, where, when, what, how); "What does it mean?" (interpreting the facts); "What does it mean to me?" (applying the interpretation to our own lives). (For a more detailed discussion of Bible study methods, read *Leading Bible Discussions* by James Nyquist and Jack Kuhatschek [IVP].)

Pray aloud together. This provides a way for you to bear one another's burdens and seek God's guidance and blessing for your group. Using sentence prayers (in which people pray a sentence or so at a time as often as they want), give all the members an opportunity to pray for something without one person "exhausting" a prayer item at length. Praying for each other will help build unity and intimacy within the group.

Sing. Use a hymn or short chorus that everyone knows. If there's a piano or guitar handy, fine—but if not, just make a joyful noise together. You might even use singing as a launching pad for discussion about the meaning of a particular hymn or verse.

Encourage each other to memorize Scripture. Try starting each meeting with one person reciting a verse she memorized during the week and telling why that verse is important to her.

Encourage each other to reach out. Pray for and encourage each other in the areas of evangelism and social concern. A group that doesn't minister to others quickly becomes stagnant. Talking together about the joys and frustrations of telling others about Jesus will help the group see one of its ultimate purposes: to strengthen each other for carrying God's love to a dying world. Role playing in pairs (with one member of the group playing the part of a non-Christian and the other a Christian) can help you learn to present the gospel clearly, boldly and sensitively.

Another way you can encourage each other to serve people outside of your group is to jointly sponsor a needy child through World Vision, Compassion International or another reputable agency. Closer to home, you might volunteer to help rehabilitate a house for the poor one Saturday through a community agency, or rake an elderly person's leaves in the fall. The possibilities are endless.

Limit your group's size. When a small group grows over eight to ten members, some of the group's intimacy begins to disappear. You'll do better to break up into smaller groups at that point.

Finally, each member should have a clear idea of what is expected of him or her as a member of the group (see Lk 14:28-30). The expression of commitment to the group might take the form of a verbal or written covenant. As you toss around expectations, consider these areas:

Making a Covenant

Regular and prompt attendance. Habitually delaying the group meeting because of latecomers wastes the time of those who arrive promptly and shortens the actual meeting time.

Prayer for each other. Caring for each other doesn't stop

at the end of a meeting. Regular prayer not only brings
answers, but increases our awareness of and concern for
each other's welfare. Keep a group prayer request list that
members can use during the week to support each other in
prayer.

Meeting outside the group. We all look different in different settings. Meeting together outside the weekly sessions
is essential to know each other intimately. Sharing a meal,
playing volleyball or conducting an evangelistic outreach
together can enrich your relationships.

As long as it's not used legalistically, a covenant between
the group members incorporating some or all of these suggestions (and possibly more) will not only help members
know exactly what is expected of them, but what they can
expect from others in the group.

Any activity which seems to be a poor use of the hours   **Evaluating**
God has given us should be scrutinized carefully. This in-   **Your Group**
cludes small groups. After an initial trial period of four or
five meetings, and then at regular intervals every few
months, a group should spend part or all of a meeting to
evaluate its past experiences.

Start by asking questions about the goals that were established at the beginning. Have they been met? Has specific
progress been made toward them? Have the activities of
the group been directed toward these goals? Do the goals
still seem realistic? Do they need to be changed? What can
be done differently in the future to better meet the goals of
the group?

Are the members currently drawing strength from the
group to reach out to others? Has the group become a
clique, only interested in itself—or is there an atmosphere
of concern and prayer for sharing Jesus with non-Christians
and serving the needy? How is the group helping each person better minister to others in the church as a whole?

How would you describe relationships in the group? Is
everyone still wearing a mask? Is honest sharing taking

place? Do members feel free to disagree and prayerfully work out differences? Do people know each other better than they did a month ago? Are members praying for and otherwise supporting each other?

Talk about these questions and others that come to mind. Be sensitive to where different members of the group are at and to where God might be leading you as a whole.

If you are thinking about starting a small group of six or eight people, or if you're already leading a group, take time out to consider your role. As the leader you don't need to take control so much as to help the group meet the goals which the members have prayerfully established.

Leading a Small Group

Leaders must be flexible; it's easy to plod along with the same agenda even if that agenda isn't meeting people's needs—and that's a sure way to dry up a group. If things seem to be going stale, pray about changing the format and trying something different.

Some groups rotate the leadership weekly or monthly, giving each member a chance to lead the group using his or her own ideas. Others appoint two co-leaders who alternate from week to week. (One advantage of having more than one leader is that the group can easily divide if it gets too large.)

If there are several small groups meeting on your campus, the leaders may want to meet together regularly to discuss what's happening in their groups and to pray for each other. Also, all the small groups themselves may enjoy meeting together for "fun, food and fellowship" occasionally.

Whatever approach you take in leadership, remember: you are not to control the group—that's God's responsibility. Your responsibility is to serve the members by leading the group humbly and prayerfully (1 Pet 5:2).

Finally, be warned: Because a small group can be such a

Pitfalls

powerful atmosphere for God to work in, Satan may try to make your group ineffective.

For example, some or all of your group's members may continually feel too inhibited to get beyond the superficial. Although this is common at first, we must pray (both for ourselves and others) that the masks will be taken off so we can truly share one another's joys and struggles. Sometimes it takes only one person who dares to ask for help or share a problem to create an atmosphere for honest sharing. That person could be you.

And most groups go through what might be called the "third meeting slump." The first meeting is usually marked by the enthusiasm of a new adventure, and this may continue over into the second meeting. But often by the third time the group meets, many members feel the fellowship is not everything they expected. This meeting may be marked by disappointment or even antagonism.

Pray together about it. Trust God to get the group going again. The group that survives this experience and honestly discusses the problem will grow stronger as a result.

GETTING TO CHURCH: IS IT WORTH THE EFFORT?

Michael Pountney

"I love Christianity—it's the church I can't stand."

Many students have been turned off by organized religion. They've grown up within that Victorian redbrick on the corner of First and Main—you know, the one with the leaking roof and damp bathroom that seems to reflect the age and weariness of the congregation within. So many students see college as liberation. Some drop out of church entirely (at least for the school year). Others find an exciting, vibrant campus fellowship and try to make that their church. But both approaches fall short of what a Christian commitment intends. We all need a church. And whatever campus fellowships might be, they are *not* churches.

The English word *church* has its deepest roots in its Greek origin: the adjective *kyriakos* found in such New Testament phrases as *kyriakon doma,*

meaning "the Lord's house." Thus the word *church* means "of the Lord" and usually refers to a house or a building.

But our English word *church* usually stands for the New Testament word *ekklesia,* which comes from a verb meaning "to call out." So the people of the

ekklesia are people "called out" of the world into God's kingdom; this shifts our attention from church buildings to the people gathered in them. As Paul teaches, the church is the company of God's people, the body of Christ, the community of those who name Jesus as Lord and Savior.

This fellowship came into being after the crucifixion and resurrection of Jesus. It has no denominational or confessional barriers and is composed of all believers. It's membership is ultimately known only to God, who creates and sustains it.

Ekklesia also has a more particularized meaning. In pre-Christian writing, the word refers to an assembly of people gathered at a public place to deliberate. Later, the word appears in such places as 1 Corinthians 16:19 and Acts 5:11, where it describes a group of Jesus' followers who met regularly in a particular place, often a house. We therefore have the fellowship of all believers (Church with a capital C) and the particular, localized church (church with a small c).

Who Needs the Church?

Your membership in the Church, by virtue of your calling as a Christian, is guaranteed, automatic and maintained by the Spirit of God. You cannot become a Christian without becoming part of the Church at the same time; to become one is to become the other. They're as close as being born and joining the human race. It's when we come to joining particular churches and campus fellowships that problems arise.

Unfortunately, campus fellowship groups have had bad press concerning their relationships with churches. Some churches have accused campus fellowships of ignoring or downgrading the church, as well as of competing against the church for members by luring students away into fun-filled, with-it fellowship meetings (sort of the way a showgirl seduces a young man away from his mother). Once the fellowship's steak-and-shrimp meetings are tasted, they say, students are spoiled for life— never again will they be able to settle into the humdrum cheese sandwich of Trinity Presbyterian or First Baptist.

True, campus fellowships can be wonderfully rich: a fellowship of peers, educated and inquisitive people, surrounded by the human and physical resources of a university. But much as college is a training ground for life rather than a prototype of what is to come after college, campus groups are training grounds for fellowship and service in churches where students will serve long after graduation.

The Marks of a Church

Why do I say campus fellowship groups are training grounds for churches rather than substitutes for churches? Why do I, a former campus fellowship staff worker, strongly encourage students to join a church while they're in college?

Mostly because campus fellowships don't exhibit some of the permanent characteristics of a church as established in New Testament history. The biblical church, for example, contains a full age range in its membership and is socially diverse; unity in Christ is often the only glue that holds it together. (I am currently teaching a confirmation class with a sixty-year-old woman who cannot read or write, a twelve-year-old girl from Uganda, a hospital worker, a refugee from Sri Lanka, a pet shop owner and three teenagers from the Caribbean.) A campus fellowship's unity, on the other hand, is often founded on homogeneity—similarities in age, intelligence, culture and values.

Furthermore, the biblical church has an authority structure built on such New Testament categories as elder, bishop and deacon (churches use different titles to describe similar offices); leaders in student-run movements such as InterVarsity Christian Fellowship often lack the essential age, training and maturity necessary for such church leaders (see 1 Timothy 3:1-13). In addition, campus fellowships, with their fluctuating memberships and yearly turnovers, do not possess the stability required of a church.

True churches also administer the sacraments of baptism (to signify admission to Christ's Church) and Holy Communion (to remember and identify with Christ as we anticipate his return). Finally, a church also claims to be able to marry and bury people—a connection with the long-established traditional church, which traces its historical roots to the resurrection. Indeed, the church's strongest claim to authenticity remains tradition, that all-important connection with the first-century church gained from a continuous history of ordained ministry and faithfulness to the living and written Word.

The Marks of a Campus Fellowship
So where does your exciting, vital, challenging, fun-filled campus fellowship come in?

While on InterVarsity Christian Fellowship staff in Vancouver, I often found myself defending our campus fellowship against telephone callers who accused us of being anything from a cult to the occult. But campus fellowship groups are essentially missionary organizations. Many non-Christian students and faculty have so many misconceptions about Christianity that they'll never come to church. But they might listen to a Christian roommate or classmate. So campuses need organizations that will encourage and equip Christian students to grow in and share their faith in the unique college environment. This is where campus fellowship groups can help.

Of course, not every student has enough hours in the week to be both a campus "missionary" and a full participant in a church's many activities. John Alexander, former president of InterVarsity Christian Fellowship, writes: "Think of it this way. The Holy Spirit apparently calls some members of a local church to be *pillars*, others to be *missionaries*." Just as Barnabas and Saul were sent out from Antioch as missionaries (Acts 13), so too students are legitimately called to reach out to their peers through campus fellowships. But, as a result, church attendance should grow, rather than decline, as student missionaries, active in campus fellowship groups, bring interested friends along with them to church to worship.

Changing the Church

Like children taunting a weaker playmate, members of vital campus fellowships too easily mock the church for its
ineptness, failings, faults and weaknesses. Author Bruce Milne writes, "If
there is anything which can be virtually
guaranteed to turn the non-Christian
away from the Christian faith in our
times, it is precisely the church. . . . For
in the church they have found neither
personal piety nor communal concern,
neither God nor a brother" (*We Belong
Together,* IVP). The awful irony is that
the body of Christ—the people who are
called by his name, the shining community of saints, the recipients of the fire of
the Holy Spirit, the dazzling display of
love incarnate—is reduced in many students' minds to a bedraggled bunch of
half-hearted believers buried in the boring business of Sunday-morning banali-
ty.

To criticize the church is to criticize
the Church—which, in turn, is to criticize ourselves. We are the stuff of the
church. You and I. Like it or not, our lot
has already been thrown in; we have
joined. Therefore, we must make sure
that our contribution to the church is
part of the answer and not part of the
problem. Just as it only takes a spark to
get a fire going, a handful of on-fire believers can warm up the church.

Are Sunday mornings dull? Suggest an
improvement. Is Sunday school poorly
taught? Become a teacher. No one is
willing to lead the young people's
group? Get a couple of friends from
your fellowship group to help form a
leadership team. The possibilities are
endless. As a minister I know that campus fellowship groups can be an im-
mense source of inspiration, leadership,
talent, energy, enthusiasm and encouragement.

Who needs the church? You do . . .
and it needs you.

Choosing a Church

In choosing a church, there are three
things you should know. First, you
should have a thoroughly biblical understanding of the nature of the church,
what it really is. Second, you should be
aware that churches are imperfect; you
might encounter blandness, personality
conflicts, petty disputes about who owns
the dishes and a hundred other frustrations. Third, you should be able to
measure any local church against New
Testament benchmarks to assess its
strengths and weaknesses. Gordon Mac-
Donald, former pastor of Grace Chapel
in Lexington, Massachusetts, writes that
any church worth your involvement during college should meet certain standards:

"First, it should be faithful to the
Word of God and led by men and wom-
en who show evidence of living under
the lordship of Jesus Christ. Listen carefully to teaching that comes from the
pulpit and Christian education programs. Second, it should create an atmosphere of prayer and worship that fits
your temperament. Some feel they hear
God most forcefully in a liturgical setting; others gravitate toward a less formal, totally nonliturgical climate. We all
respond differently to different leaders,
different styles of worship and teaching,

different size congregations. And that's okay. . . .

"[Denominational] distinctives usually concern an emphasis on certain areas of Christian doctrine and a preference for one type of church government. [Before you join a church] ask two questions: How does this denomination represent the person of Jesus Christ? And, does it hold up the Word of God with integrity?

"One practical suggestion: take note of where a few mature Christian students who do things similarly to you worship. Chances are that if you follow them on the Lord's Day, you'll find what you're looking for."

In the New Testament the only prerequisite for joining the church is realiz-ing that you're bad; it is a club for sinners. But the sinners should be on the mend. Author John Stott's definition of the church is a good one: "a fellowship of consciously inadequate persons who gather together because they are weak, and scatter to serve because their unity with one another and with Christ has made them bold. . . . The Church is meant to be the company of people as committed to one another as to Christ!" (*One People,* IVP).

By all means use your college days to become involved in a campus fellowship. By all means use the years to broaden your experience a little; go to a Pentecostal church, take in a cathedral. But remember: your prime duty after joining the Church is to join a church.

Is Your Group a Cult?

When campus fellowship groups ask Christian author and lecturer James Sire to speak about cults, he often begins by reading aloud a *Chicago Tribune* article titled "How Groups Use Lies, Guilt, Terror to Capture Converts." In the article, Harvard psychiatrist and cult expert John G. Clark describes some of the characteristics of cults who recruit on campus:
☐ "From the first [potential converts typically experience] intense group pressure, lectures, . . . singing, chanting and a constant barrage of the kinds of rhetoric which catch young idealistic minds."

☐ "[During the conversion process] many promises are made of redemption or safety, in which time there will be enormous rewards or terrible punishments to believers or non-believers. . . . Preaching is constant from all sides."
☐ "Victims are induced to give up all familiar and loved past objects—parents, siblings, home, city. . . . Leaving the old familiar life, renouncing it for a new theology [and] accepting a new family with new definitions of love . . . leads an individual to think all bridges to the past are closed."

Many students are shocked to realize that

"We've got to deprogram Junior—he's run off and joined the Presbyterians."

some of Dr. Clark's descriptions seem to fit their own fellowship group. Indeed, even mainstream Christian groups have been accused of falling into cultic or aberrational practices—sometimes with good reason.

As long as cultic religious movements meet some of the same spiritual needs as Christianity, outward similarities to Christian groups will persist. But so will obvious differences. By definition, most "cults" are new religious groups who, according to Sire and Enroth, typically reject one or more of the following basic tenets of orthodox Christianity: the deity of Christ and the Holy Spirit, salvation by grace alone, and the final authority of Scripture.

Many of these groups can also display signs such as authoritarian leadership, control of members' day-to-day lives, overemphasis on giving money and possessions, twisted views about marriage and sex, and a distrust of normal human emotions and the intellect.

Doctrinally sound groups with unconventional practices, however, can be harder to evaluate. Writes LaVonne Neff in *A Guide to Cults & New Religions:* "Good results don't sanctify bad doctrine, but bad results can serve as warning lights, even where teaching appears sound." Below are some questions that any religious group you join should be able to answer affirmatively:

☐ Do they believe in the foundational Christian teachings upheld by believers throughout church history? (For example, does the group's doctrine contradict the Apostle's Creed or the Nicene Creed?)

☐ Do they value loyalty to Scripture's teachings and God's call more than loyalty to the organization and leadership?

☐ Do they believe that all forms of deception toward potential converts or others outside the group are wrong? Do they make everything they believe public, rather than foster an atmosphere of secrecy and privileged knowledge within the group?

☐ Do they encourage high moral standards? Do they affirm marriage and sexuality as gifts from God?

☐ Do they respect each member's privacy? Are wayward members confronted about their sin privately and lovingly, rather than subjected to physical punishment and public humiliation?

☐ Do they encourage members to give money and time to the group as God leads them, rather than setting strict, demanding rules? Do the leaders set godly examples by shunning self-indulgent extravagance?

☐ Do they serve and interact with the larger Christian community? Do they recognize that God is at work in the whole Christian church (not just in their group)?

☐ Do they allow outsiders to question the doctrines and leaders without accusing them of persecuting the group? Are members encouraged to think critically and voice doubts or objections?

☐ Do they encourage members to build healthy relationships with friends and family members?

☐ Are members allowed to leave the group without being made to feel guilty or fearful that God will punish them?

If the answer to any of the above questions is no, ask a mature Christian outside the group for guidance before committing yourself further.

—*Robert M. Kachur*

Christian Fringe Groups

Some groups that are labeled "cults" by people outside of evangelical circles are, in fact, student ministries whose doctrine is orthodox. These groups are more appropriately described as "ultrafundamentalist" and, according to Dr. R. E. Schecter, editor of the *Cult Observer,* they are "the most common kind of cultic group on and around campuses today." Though mostly orthodox in doctrine, they often practice "shepherding" and "discipleship" *to control recruits.*

These student groups operate under a variety of names and may differ in character from place to place; many, however, have certain potentially harmful practices in common—particularly an extremely authoritarian discipling process.

"Tim was a basket case when he came to us," says Mihae Yamamoto, a former InterVarsity staff worker at the University of Illinois—Chicago. "He was depressed and insecure after being involved in one group that's very hierarchical.

"Everyone in that group has a 'shepherd' to help them grow as a Christian," Yamamoto observes. "But that relationship becomes subtly controlling when there's no room to question your shepherd."

One young woman who joined a similar group shortly after flunking out of college remembers having to bare her soul to her "shepherdess" constantly: "It got to the point where I would tell her everything I had done during the day, and then private thoughts as well. When I'd say, 'I just want this to be between me and God,' she'd reply that [I should tell her anyway] since she had grown more in Christ and could pray better."

Chains of Authority

Shepherds themselves are usually under a chain of authority with one person on top. "In your average fundamentalist church, the standard of authority is the Bible," says Lowell Streiker, founder of the Freedom Counseling Center, which provides support for former cult members and their families. But in these extreme cases "one person sets himself above the group. Questioning him is questioning God."

Despite—or perhaps because of—this authoritarian structure, cult expert Dr. Ronald Enroth of Westmont College (who has watched many of these student organizations mushroom since their advent less than twenty years ago) says "these 'fringe' Christian groups seem, overall, to be experiencing the greatest growth of any religious movements on college campuses today." Adds Yamamoto: "For freshmen and commuter students still struggling with their independence, getting love, attention and structure is great—for a while. But then it's hard to pull out."

Mark, a former member of one group at the University of Illinois—Chicago, agrees. When he and a friend left their fellowship and spoke out against what they believe were destructive practices, group leaders "named us 'enemies of God' and wrote a letter slandering my name."

Former members of various groups report being threatened that leaving the group would mean leaving God's will—and suffering the consequences. Kathy, who left a shepherding group after three years of involvement, told *Christianity Today* that she did suffer from the emotional fallout of leaving: "I felt lost without a shepherdess to tell me if what I was doing was of God or of the Devil."

Spiritual Elitism

Critics of these groups are also disturbed by a strong emphasis on certain doctrines and a resulting spiritual elitism. "Students who are eager to please God but who don't know the Bible get confused when they're challenged about verses taken out of context," says John Roeckeman, InterVarsity staff worker at the University of Illinois—Champaign. "A girl I know who was a growing believer became convinced by members of one organization that she hadn't been baptized the right way and therefore wasn't a Christian at all; so she joined their group."

Adds Robert Burdett, an InterVarsity staff worker at Triton College: "There seems to be an attitude of 'Let's pull people out of these other Christian groups and get them into the right group,' rather than a real attempt to reach nonbelievers."

Burdett, Roeckeman and others worry about groups who foster what Enroth describes as "isolationist attitudes." Says Roeckeman: "They seem to think they have the perfect New Testament church. There's a real shortsighted attitude toward church history. It's as if they believe the church began in 1975 in Kansas."

Few deny, however, that these "fringe" groups do good: people become Christians and become geniunely excited about living for God. Even Mark admits that his experience made him "much more outgoing and serious about the Christian life." And campus workers who have complained about the time and energy it takes to counsel Christian students confused by dogmatic fringe groups have also pointed out that they've been forced to examine their own roles more closely. "Students obviously want the authority and direction these groups provide," says Burdett. "I'm struggling with how much I should give. It's hard to find a balance."

Still, Enroth fears for those who get burned: "Many who leave are plagued by depression and guilt. They have trouble adjusting, especially in the area of decision making." Kathy, for one, had so much trouble adjusting to life outside the group that she spent several months in counseling and even considered suicide. Adds Rob Decker, an InterVarsity staff worker at Loyola University in Chicago: "Students who leave one of these groups seem to have a hard time getting committed to any religious body."

—*Robert M. Kachur*

Telling the Truth: Evangelism on Campus

Terrell Smith

A friend of mine coaches a soccer team made up of six- to eight-year-old kids. During the new team's first two practices, he explained field positioning, the rules of the game, how to head the ball and the importance of passing. Halfway through the team's first game, he asked one of the players why he was letting the ball go by him all the time. "Oh," the little boy responded, "am I supposed to kick it?"

Often we get so caught up in the mechanics and strategies of doing something that we lose sight of the fundamentals. When it comes to evangelism—telling others about Christ—countless books have been published, seminars conducted, sermons preached. Somewhere along the line—often after several frustrated attempts—confusion, apathy and guilt set in, and soon we forget what evangelism is all about. Like the six-year-old soccer player, many of us have forgotten the basics.

Not only is knowing the basics of evangelism important, but it is also freeing. Let's look at what evangelism is *not* before we look at what it is.

There are five things that evangelism is not. First of all, *evangelism is not defined by positive response.* The essence of our role in evangelism is not to make converts—that is God's work. It may be fair to ask whether our evangelism is biblical if we see no fruit, but our responsibility is simply to faithfully proclaim the message. God convicts and brings spiritually dead people into new life. You can't say, for example, that in Acts 17 Paul was not evangelizing because some mocked him and some didn't believe.

Second, *evangelism is not something we can turn on and off or schedule into our week.* Evangelism often becomes something we do at a particular time. Jesus said, "You are the light of the world," but we try to turn it on and off like a light bulb. Evangelism should take place in our day-to-day interactions. Planned evangelistic events are important, but those should take place in the context of having built strong relationships with non-Christians on your campus. Biblical evangelism is a lifestyle.

Third, *evangelism is not deceitful.* Many Christians (me included) have invited non-Christian friends to a Christian meeting where the gospel was going to be preached, conveniently forgetting to tell them about the evangelistic part. Once they're there, the gospel is dumped on them.

God does not need these little tricks. Instead, when we are honest and open, God will draw people to himself. Paul wanted to make sure he came clean: "For the appeal we make does not spring from error or impure motives, nor are we trying to trick you" (1 Thess 2:3).

Fourth, *evangelism is not distorted.* It's tempting to tamper with God's Word to make it more attractive, leaving out "little things" such as turning from and forsaking sin. To tell people that becoming a Christian means all your troubles will evaporate is also a lie. (If it is true, there were not any Christians in the New Testament.) Paul again: "We do not use deception, nor do we distort the word of God" (2 Cor 4:2).

I knew of a girl who believed that in order to present a

clear picture of being a Christian she had to live a perfect, sparkling life before her roommate. She did it. She never let this roommate know that she had any problems or was struggling with anything. Her roommate eventually became a Christian and two weeks later committed suicide. She couldn't stand it. Her life still had problems which did not evaporate at conversion.

Fifth, *evangelism is not only for superevangelists.* Jesus did say, "Therefore go and make disciples of all nations . . . teaching them to obey everything I have commanded you" (Mt 28:19-20). But that doesn't mean we all have to become Billy Grahams. God has selected certain people in the church and given them gifts in evangelism, but he wants to use all his children in proclaiming his message. And he needs all types too. While it seems relatively easy for some extroverts to be aggressive in sharing their faith, their particular style may make it difficult for certain kinds of people to open up to them. Those people might be better ministered to by someone more shy and quiet.

Eloquence should not be a concern. Very often a shy person, an uneducated person or someone who just does not know how to say things with the right grammar or syntax can be very convincing because he speaks from his heart. Even though these people do not speak gracefully, they speak with such naturalness that everyone knows they are telling the truth.

So what *is* evangelism? First, *it's the proclamation of a relationship,* rather than the proclamation of a doctrine or a list of dos and don'ts. The good news is that God forgives our sins because of Christ's death and resurrection, and that we can enter into a friendship with him. Therefore, communicating that Christians are learning to love God and building a relationship with him is vital to effective evangelism.

What Evangelism Is

Second, *evangelism is done out of love rather than out of guilt.* As your relationship with God deepens, you will find yourself *wanting* to talk about him to others. How many have told themselves enthusiastically after hearing a dynamic speaker challenge the group about evangelism, "From now on, I'm going to be an excited evangelist. I'm going to go out and win the world." But within a few weeks all the zeal has seeped out—like an old, wrinkled helium balloon lying on the floor after being on the ceiling for a few days. Evangelism springs from the vitality of our relationship with God. No one suddenly says to herself, "I have decided that I am going to be excited about my fiancé." But many do exactly that with evangelism.

Evangelism is done not only out of love for God, but for other people. Of course, some people are less lovable than others. How do we learn to love the unlikable people, people who are annoying or who take up our time? One thing that always helps me are Jesus' words in Matthew 25 that when we serve the "least of these" we're also serving him. What a privilege! In addition, these "unlovables" end up teaching us a lot about love which we would never have imagined.

Third, *evangelism is hanging out with non-Christians.* Christians easily disengage themselves from much of non-Christian society. We dig our foxholes of fellowship so deep that we become like soldiers who have lost contact with the enemy. People have a need to be listened to, to be spoken to. Beneath the self-confidence and jokes lies a real person with emotional hurts and spiritual uncertainties. Someone who comes to people in openness, love and understanding is welcome.

Jesus said, "As the Father has sent me, I am sending you" (Jn 20:21). Jesus left his home in heaven to rub shoulders with promiscuous people and hedonists like us. Christians too have been sent by him. We need to leave our Christian ghettoes and rub shoulders with people.

Listen to people. When someone shares a problem, a curt "I'll pray for you" sounds trite. Ask that person, "How can I help you in this?" Perhaps she needs prayer, but we also need to get involved in her life.

Fourth, *evangelism is communicating the message clearly.* It is great to know God and be where the people are. But something else is needed to do evangelism—a message. The facts about the person of Christ, his life, his death and his resurrection need to be told. People must know that they need to respond to these facts, by choosing to change their lifestyles and by placing confidence in the Lord.

Plan to be used by God in evangelism. How? Pray, and in your prayers ask God for opportunities. Then expect God to open doors to good conversations.

Letting People Know

With a little thought and prayer, witnessing situations can be created. In conversations with friends, ask questions like, "What are your goals in life?" instead of just, "How was your weekend?" There are many questions which can lead to a discussion about spiritual things. If people know you are a Christian, they'll be watching you and opportunities will open up.

Sometimes Christians think they can witness without saying anything. On a summer job I had when I was in college I decided I would witness silently. While the other guys were telling dirty jokes during lunch hour, I went off and read my Bible. As a consequence, I never had one significant conversation with anyone. I heard of another Christian student who used to play hymns on his fraternity's piano while his frat brothers were drinking at the bar. He never said anything. He just played and left, every night.

Paul asks (perhaps a bit sarcastically), "How, then, can they call on the one they have not believed in? And how can they believe in the one of whom they have not heard? And how can they hear without someone preaching to them? . . . Consequently, faith comes from hearing the message, and the message is heard through the word of Christ" (Rom 10:14, 17).

As a friend of mine, Jack, was unpacking his books on

the first day of his freshman year at college, he laid his Bible down on his desk. His new roommate saw it and said, "You're not some kind of a Christian, are you?" Actually he used words a little stronger than that. Jack was not sure how to answer. But just because Jack took his Bible out and laid it there, his Christianity became visible. And because his roommate knew that Jack was a Christian, he watched him.

Amazingly, the roommate talked to other guys. In Jack's dorm there were two hundred guys. Guys he had never seen before would stop him and say, "Hey, I hear you're some kind of religious person. Tell me about it." Jack's non-Christian roommate opened many doors just because of that Bible Jack unpacked.

God will open many more if you simply ask him.

Launching an Evangelistic Bible Study

You're near the start of a new term on campus. Perhaps you've resolved to be more vocal about sharing your faith. Perhaps you're even considering leading an investigative Bible study.

During my junior year in college, my roommate, Barb, and I had a remarkable camaraderie with the other women in our dorm that grew into just such an investigative study. Here are some principles we learned.

1. *Reach out with a friend.* There are times and places to be a lone voice crying in the wilderness. An investigative study in your dorm or fraternity house is not one of them. It's great to share the joys and the problems of reaching out with a Christian friend, someone with whom you can plan and pray.

It also gives the people in your study a chance to see the varieties of religious faith and to see that they don't have to be or act a certain way (namely, just like you) to seriously consider the claims of Christ.

2. *Talk and dream.* Barb and I had spent the first semester building our own friendship as well as reaching out to others on our corridor. And as we talked before the second semester began, we decided to consider forming a group study.

We agreed almost immediately on at least three girls whom God seemed to be leading us to invite: Diane, who needed some encouragement to rekindle her childhood faith; her roommate, Lynn, who challenged, yet seemed curious about, our religious beliefs; and Sara, who joked about being overweight but indirectly asked questions about whether God loved her. We invited them to the study during the first week of the semester, and nearly everyone accepted eagerly. If you have these kinds of relationships on campus, you'll realize as we did how much genuine friendship and vulnerability they'll bring to your Bible study.

3. *Invite people to investigate.* Sharing your love for Jesus can be the natural next step to take. When you talk with people, don't be defensive about whom you're introducing. But don't be pushy either, and respect the fact that the group setting, timing or other factors might prevent someone from accepting the invitation. Be sure not to make anyone feel like a second-class citizen for turning you down; don't offer conditional friendship.

4. *Choose a good study guide.* You can, of course, make up your own discussion questions as you go, but a carefully chosen guidebook can free you from many hours of preparation, ensuring that your friendships (and your studies) don't get pushed aside.

Many fine study guides are available. Choose one that seems appropriate in tone, topic and time commitment for your group. We decided on an eight-week study of the Gospel of John, using the IVP study guide *Jesus the Life Changer* by Ada Lum. The study began during the second week of classes.

5. *Keep being a friend.* We were glad that our study became a normal part of the week, not an awkward shifting of gears that communicates, "Now it's time to act religious." Be understanding about fluctuations in attendance—exams and papers press in on even the best intentioned.

Avoid the trap of being the perfectly pious one now that you're leading a Bible study. You don't have to have all the answers during your discussion time. Be yourself and be open to your friends and to God. For us, being ourselves meant continuing our comedy

routines at dorm functions and putting a sign on our door offering writing and math help.

6. *Be faithful, and leave the results to God.* The success of your study will not be measured by lightning-bolt conversions or the startling sermons that you preach during the studies. In fact, a sure sign of a fading study is if you find yourself talking too much.

Instead, enjoy opening yourself to your friends and reinvestigating Jesus' claims with them.

What happened to our study? Nothing earthshaking, but Diane renewed her faith and became active in our InterVarsity campus fellowship group. And all of them expressed appreciation for what they'd learned in the Bible and what they'd seen in Barb's and my friendship for each other and for them. Meanwhile, bookings for our comedy routine increased sharply.

What might God have in store for you and your friends this term?

—*Betsy Rossen Elliot*

TRANSLATING YOUR FAITH INTO SOCIAL ACTION

Tony Campolo

When I speak to Christian students, I see a lot of people who want, deep down inside, to be heroes, who long to change the world for God. But many get burned out because they don't feel one person can make a difference.

I want to make this as clear as I know how: Jesus saved you so that he could work through you to accomplish things that he wants to have done in this world. Jesus saved you in order that you might be an agent for his revolution in the world.

I know that the Christians in college today could change the world. But that's not going to happen. Why? Not because they're not committed to Christ, but because they don't see how they could effect change. Commitment without a methodology to carry it through is ineffective.

Whether you now realize it or not, on campus you will actually have more opportunities than ever before to get involved in social action of some kind—perhaps through a Christian organization or perhaps side by side with non-Christians through a secular nonprofit agency. University and college campuses are a focal point for young, idealistic people to organize and try to effect change.

Unfortunately, many Christian students feel too busy with homework, small group Bible studies and other campus fellowship activities to get involved in social action. Why should a Christian student be concerned about social action, anyway? Aren't evangelism and Bible study more important?

Jesus Came to Transform Society

Jesus wasn't only interested in saving individuals so that they could go to heaven when they died. Jesus broke into history with a declaration that he had come to initiate the kingdom of God. Many of his parables were given to teach us some of the principles upon which this kingdom was to be developed. The Sermon on the Mount provided the ethic for this kingdom. When Jesus taught us how to pray he encouraged us to yearn that the kingdom might exist on earth as it already exists in heaven.

Jesus wants to create a revolutionary new society. Once we grasp that, we can begin to understand why he was crucified. The custodians of the status quo, who had a vested interest in maintaining the established social order with all of its oppression and injustice, predictably opposed this man who called for the creation of a new regime. While his adversaries may have been blind to the fact that Jesus was the Son of God, they clearly recognized that he was socially dangerous. The accusations that they leveled at him as he moved toward the crucifixion expressed their fear of him. They said, "He stirs up the people," and that "It is necessary for this man to die, that Israel (the established social order) might be saved."

I am not attempting to reduce Christianity to some simplistic social gospel. God's kingdom does not become a reality simply by facilitating a few positive social changes with the expectation that all will be well if we can just eliminate corrupt institutional structures. On the contrary, there will be no kingdom unless it is populated by people who incarnate the nature and the values of the King.

People need to be saved from sin. They need to be made into new creatures before they can effect the institutional changes which are essential if the kingdom is to come "on earth as it is in heaven."

Jesus calls us to move beyond a desire for personal piety to a desire to serve others, especially those who are desperately poor. The contrast between these two emphases became brilliantly clear to me as I listened to a bright student deliver a talk at a college chapel service. He opened by saying, "Last night, according to U.N. statistics, approximately ten thousand people starved to death. Furthermore, most of you don't give a shit. What is worse, most of you are more upset with the fact that I just said 'shit' than you are over the fact that ten thousand people starved to death last night. That's what I want to talk to you about—your morality."

To be a Christian is to have your heart broken by the things that break the heart of God. To be a Christian is to be filled with righteous indignation over the fact that we affluent North Americans live with a high level of indifference to the unjust privations of people around the world. The Jesus of Scripture beckons us to change a world in which 500 million people suffer from malnutrition while the rich in other nations suffer from overweight. He calls us to transform it into a world in which the needs of all people are satisfied.

I was once with a group of college students who had just completed a month of exhausting labor rebuilding a Third World village which had been destroyed by a hurricane. On the day we were to leave the village the people threw a party for us. There was singing and dancing. Laughter abounded everywhere. As I stood at the edge of the party, looking on with pleasure and satisfaction, an old man of the village pulled me aside and said, "You can tell me now. You're a Communist, aren't you? You and your friends are Communists. Right?"

I said, "No, of course not. I oppose Communism. I'm a Christian. What makes you think that I or my students are Communists?"

He said, "You care about poor people."

His response upset me more than I can say. Why aren't Christians known as the ones who are most concerned about the poor and the oppressed people of the world? Perhaps it's because we haven't been the most concerned.

Of course, God's kingdom is his to create; it will not be ushered in through our efforts. Actually, the kingdom of God will never become a complete social, historical reality until the Lord Himself returns. But he continues to build it through *us*.

Feeling Powerless?

But you say, "What can *I* do? I mean, I'm just a college student struggling to get through history, let alone change the course of it. I feel powerless to change anything."

In a sense, you're right. As a college student, you are relatively powerless. And the world believes that only the powerful can bring about social change. They think that the powerless count for nothing. But the Bible reminds us— through the lives of Jesus, John the Baptist, Mary, the prophets, the disciples and others—that it is through the powerless that the works of the powerful are brought to nothing.

In my own efforts to bring about social change, I have witnessed the effectiveness of powerlessness. A group of my students from Eastern College became very upset with one large corporation, Gulf and Western Industries, while we were doing missionary work in the Dominican Republic.* We became aware that this multinational corporation was taking land that should have been used to grow food for needy people in that poor country and using that land to grow sugar.

As you know, sugar is bad for you. So is coffee. So is tobacco. You may not know that if all of the land in the world that is presently being used to grow sugar, coffee and tobacco were used to grow food, we could cut malnutrition in the Third World by almost 50%.

Anyway, we were upset with Gulf and Western because we saw that they were growing sugar for people in the United States on land that we felt should have been used to grow food for needy Dominican peasants.

There were eleven of us, and each of us bought one share of stock in the company. I don't know how many millions of shares of stock there are in Gulf and Western, but we owned eleven of them. And you only need one share to go to the annual stockholders meeting. So each of us "stockholders" went to the meeting and said our piece.

We were a bit arrogant about it, but we really laid into them: "Hey! We don't like the way you are running this company! This company belongs to God." In private confrontations following that meeting, we met with some of the company's top executives and told Jesus' story of a man who had a vineyard. The man went away on a long trip, but the people he left in charge of the vineyard didn't run it right. He sent messengers, but they wouldn't listen to the messengers. Then he sent his son, but the people put him to death. Jesus ends that parable with this question, "What then should the owner of the vineyard do to the unfaithful stewards when he returns?"

We told all of that and more to those guys. "You are God's stewards. He doesn't like the way you are running the company, and so we have come as messengers. You had better listen to us, or God is going to come and get you."

Looking back on our behavior I have to admit we weren't Christlike or even fair. But what followed those encounters was incredible. We found out that the leaders of that company weren't bad men. In our talks with them they convinced us that they wanted Gulf and Western to be an instrument for good in the Dominican Republic.

About a year and a half after our discussions with Gulf and Western began, I got a call from one of its executives. He said, "Tomorrow we're going to have a press conference, and part of the reason we're holding it is to make an announcement about some of the issues we discussed with you. We want you to be among the first to know what's going to happen."

And as I sat there dumbfounded, that executive told me that Gulf and Western was going to do the following: first, they would test the soil that made up their landholdings in the Dominican Republic, determine what land could be used to grow food, and shift that land from sugar to food production. Second, the company would make a commitment to build forty thousand new housing units for the sugar workers so that they would no longer have to live in the slums. Third, Gulf and Western would provide educational and health programs, particularly in the eastern half of the country where their operations were located. The spokesman went on to say that his corporation had made a commitment of $100 million dollars to be spent over the next five years in order to make all the promises a reality. Now *that's* incredible.

Don't tell me college students can't effect change. Christians on campus need to be willing to stand up and make things happen.

Ways *You* Can Make a Difference

So how can you make a difference? Here are some ways you and your Christian friends can begin to bring peace and justice to your campus, community, country and world in the name of Jesus.

The first and best kind of social action is a Christian response to individuals in need: feeding the hungry, clothing the naked, healing the sick, and visiting those who are in prison. People have needs; Christian students become aware of those needs; Christian students do what Jesus would do—meet those needs.

One warning: if you are not trying to share the love of Christ with those on or near your campus, you have no legitimate right to move on to other types of social action. It is easy to become so concerned with the social injustices that are inherent in our political and economic systems that we pass over the suffering of people who confront us face to face in daily living. Jesus would remind us that if we cannot respond to those whom we can see, it is impossible to respond to a God whom we cannot see.

Some ideas:

☐ *Adopt a Grandparent.* Call a convalescent home and find out at what times visitors are welcome. Then mingle and talk with some of the people there. Choose one or two elderly people to visit on a regular basis, to remember on special occasions, to take on short trips now and then—to just be a friend to. If you are doing this in a group, take time periodically to share joys, difficulties or concerns with each other and pray for your "grandparents."

☐ *Big Brothers, Big Sisters.* You may want to become a "big brother" or "big sister" to children in your church or college town who don't have older brothers or sisters. This would simply involve getting to know them by name and making a point to welcome them each Sunday at church, visit them at home on a regular basis, do special things with them, or pick them up for Sunday school.

☐ *Christmas Gifts for the Needy.* Usually the Salvation Army or local welfare department will be aware of particularly needy families in your area. Find out their names, ages, clothing sizes and so on. Then get some friends together and pool some money you'd spend on yourselves to buy a gift for each member of the family or families you've chosen. Later, go Christmas caroling and deliver the gifts.

☐ *Creative Canned Food Drives.* Gather your fellowship group, divide them into teams and send them into nearby neighborhoods for a "scavenger food hunt." Give everyone a list of nonperishable food items to find and bring back within a given time limit (one hour or so). They can't buy them—they must get them donated by other people. Each item can be worth points according to the difficulty of finding that item.

☐ *Hospital Visitations.* Many patients get very few visitors. Get permission from a hospital administrator to visit some of these people on a regular basis. Nurses on duty can clue you in on which patients are most willing to have visitors, as well as the basics of hospital etiquette (don't lay down on the patient's bed to take a nap, etc.).

☐ *Migrant Ministry.* You can get information regarding migrant workers in your area by contacting local farmers, community service agencies or the local farm bureau. Meet the young people of the migrant camp and plan some activites with them. You and your friends can take them to movies, organize soccer games or do other fun things with these kids whose lives are often drab and wearisome.

☐ *Ministry to the Retarded.* In most cases, institutions which care for the mentally retarded are understaffed. Here are a few things that you or your fellowship group can do with retarded persons who are institutionalized: perform music for them; play games with them; bring some arts and crafts projects and work on them together; develop a close friendship with one person; go on walks; take one or two residents to a shopping mall; participate in a "Special Olympics"; or bring a few retarded young people to your campus fellowship group meetings.

☐ *Prison Ministry.* One of the specific instructions Jesus gave the church was to minister to the needs of prisoners. The following ideas, suggested by Chuck Workman of Bravo Ministries in San Diego, are just a few of the ways you and your campus fellowship can minister to prisoners: sponsor a "book drive" to provide used books for the prison library; become an inmate's "big brother" or "big sister"; write inmates letters; bring in a group to play a game against an institutional team; or raise money to buy something to make the institution more livable (such as a sound system or sports equipment).

☐ *Sponsor a Child.* Agencies such as World Vision and Compassion International try to find financial sponsors for needy children overseas. You give a certain amount of money to provide food, clothing and shelter for a particular child each month, and receive detailed information about that boy or girl, including a photo and occasional hand-written notes from the child.

☐ *Summer Workcamps and Missions Projects.* You'll be surprised at how much you can contribute and learn in one short summer, doing anything from evangelism and leading Bible studies to helping build orphanages and adminster health care.

Political Action
This kind of social action should not be seen as a substitute for service projects that minister directly to the needs of hurting people. Your highest priority should be to minister to those who are suffering. But, in the long run, it does little good to minister to the victims of an evil system while doing nothing at all to change the system so that it produces fewer victims.

Ron Sider, a popular author and leader of Evangelicals for Social Action, tells the following parable:

A group of devout Christians once lived in a small village at the foot of a

mountain. A winding, slippery road with hairpin curves and steep preci-
pices without guard rails wound its way up one side of the mountain and
down the other. There were frequent fatal accidents. Deeply saddened by
the injured people who were pulled from the wrecked cars, the Christians
decided to act. They pooled their resources and purchased an ambulance.
Over the years they saved many lives, although some victims remained
crippled for life.

Then one day a young college student came to town. Puzzled, he asked
why they did not close the road over the mountain and build a tunnel instead. Startled at first, the ambulance volunteers quickly pointed out that
this approach (although technically quite possible) was not realistic or ad-
visable. After all, the narrow mountain road had been there for a long time.
Besides, the mayor would bitterly oppose the idea. (He owned a large restaurant and service station halfway up the mountain.)

The student was shocked that the mayor's economic interests mattered
more to these Christians than the many human casualties. Somewhat hesi-
tantly, he suggested that perhaps the churches ought to speak to the
mayor, an elder in the oldest church in town. Perhaps they should even
elect a different mayor if he proved stubborn and unconcerned. Now the
Christians were shocked. With rising indignation and righteous conviction
they informed the young radical that the church dare not become involved
in politics. The church is called to preach the gospel and give a cup of
cold water. Its mission is not to dabble in worldly things like social and
political structure.

Perplexed and bitter, the college student left. Is it really more spiritual,
he wondered, to operate the ambulances which pick up the victims of destructive social structures than to try to change the structures themselves?
Here are some ways you and your fellowship group can begin to change un-
godly social structures:

☐ *Campaign Workers.* Contact the candidate of your choice and volunteer to
work in the upcoming campaign—delivering literature, making phone calls,
developing position papers, making posters, whatever. Party people will be

willing to listen to you; they may even be willing to significantly modify party plans and programs to bring them into accord with your viewpoints.

☐ *Guerrilla Theater.* To protest a great social injustice, a group from your campus fellowship can develop "guerrilla theater"—a short play or skit performed in the street, on the steps of the state capitol, or at city hall. Guerrilla theater dramatizes the injustice you want corrected. A few years ago, some Eastern College students opposed to torture in Iran got a permit to stage a demonstration on the steps of the Capitol building in Washington. They then dramatized the kinds of torture that were being employed by the government of Iran against political dissidents. The demonstration appeared in the newspapers and got significant public recognition.

☐ *Letters to the Editor.* On crucial political issues, write letters to the editor of your local newspaper. These are usually published and read by hundreds, sometimes thousands of people—including candidates and policy-makers.

☐ *Letter-Writing Campaigns.* Never underestimate the impact of organizing a letter-writing campaign on an important issue. A hundred letters on a particular issue can easily sway the opinion of a Congressman or Congresswoman who does not have strong convictions on a particular matter. (Every letter should address the issue and state whether you are for or against a particular piece of legislation, but each person who writes should do so individually.)

☐ *Pickets for Christ.* Every political party has gatherings of some sort. If your party has ignored or taken what you understand to be an unchristian position on a social issue of great concern, then picket that gathering. Get your group together, map out a strategy, spend a day making signs and banners, print up some press releases, and take a stand. You will probably get coverage on radio, television and the newspapers—giving you a chance to explain why your Christian commitment has led you to your position.

☐ *Position-Paper Writers.* New candidates for state or national office do not usually have staffs to help them develop position papers on crucial issues. A group of sharp Christian college students can present themselves to a candi-

date and offer to serve in that capacity. Can you imagine actually formulating
the position that a candidate will assume in crucial legislation?

☐ *School-Board Meetings*. Very few citizens ever attend these meetings, and a
group of Christian college students who express their views will be able to
influence the decision-making process.

*This story is taken from *You Can Make a Difference* by Tony Campolo (Waco, Tex.: Word,
1984), pp. 60-63.

Help Wanted: Social Action Organizations Who Need You

Wondering what you can do to help
serve others and effect godly
change in society during your college years? Besides writing letters to your
senators and representatives (and in Canada
to your members of parliament), you can
hook up with a number of organizations
committed to social action, some of which
are listed below:

AMNESTY INTERNATIONAL
National Office
322 8th Ave.
New York, NY 10001
(212) 807-8400

633 Shatto Place
Room 213
Los Angeles, CA 90005
(213) 388-1237

A recipient of the Nobel Peace Prize in 1977,
Amnesty International is "a worldwide movement of people working for the release of
prisoners of conscience, for fair trials for political prisoners, and for an end to torture
and the death penalty."

AMOR INDUSTRIES
Aiding Mexican Orphanages and Refugees
2500 E. Nutwood Ave., Ste. 121A
Fullerton, CA 92631
(714) 680-6402

AMOR, an evangelical mission agency with
ministries in Mexico and inner cities of the
U.S., provides cross-cultural opportunities in
which fellowship groups and individuals may
serve during the summer, vacations and on
weekends.

BREAD FOR THE WORLD
802 Rhode Island Ave. N.E.
Washington, DC 20018
(202) 269-0200

Bread for the World is "a Christian Citizen's
Movement" formed to help enact public pol-

icy and legislation that is in the best interests of the poor and needy of the world.

CARE
660 First Avenue
New York, NY 10016
(212) 686-3110

CARE is probably the largest relief agency in the world, having provided over three billion dollars in aid to people in over 80 countries since it was founded in 1946. Its goals today are the same: to feed the hungry, to provide emergency aid, to establish self-help programs, and to offer health assistance to the poor and needy all over the world.

COMPASSION INTERNATIONAL
P.O. Box 7000
Colorado Springs, CO 80933
(303) 594-9900

Compassion International, a relief and educational ministry founded by Rev. Everett Swansor in Korea, co-labors with more than sixty evangelical church and mission organizations and sponsors over 70,000 children in more than 30 countries.

EVANGELICAL ASSOCIATION FOR THE PROMOTION OF EDUCATION
P.O. Box 238
St. Davids, PA 19087
(217) 341-1722

E.A.P.E. is a nonprofit corporation founded in 1967 by Tony Campolo. It is involved in educational, medical and economic programs in the Dominican Republic, Haiti and Niger, as well as U.S. urban centers.

EVANGELICALS FOR SOCIAL ACTION
712 G St. S.E.
P.O. Box 76560
Washington, DC 20013
(202) 543-5330

A national movement of evangelicals committed to "dynamic Biblical justice," ESA offers members resources to become meaningfully informed and actively involved in such issues as peace, nuclear disarmament, abortion, poverty, the family, racial and sex discrimination, human rights, protection of the environment, and others.

FOOD FOR THE HUNGRY
7729 East Greenway Road
Scottsdale, AZ 85260
(602) 998-3100

Food for the Hungry, a nonprofit, nondenominational organization committed to disaster relief and long-range, self-help assistance to the poor of the world, enlists volunteers (21 or over) who work overseas in their "Hunger Corps."

MEALS FOR MILLIONS HDQ
P.O. Box 2000
1644 DaVinca Ct.
Davis, CA 95617
(916) 758-6200

Meals for Millions is a nonprofit organization fighting hunger and malnutrition through programs which aim to strengthen the capabilities of developing communities to solve their own food and nutrition problems.

MENNONITE CENTRAL COMMITTEE
21 South Twelfth Street
Akron, PA 17501
(717) 859-1151

The Mennonite Central Committee (the international service and relief agency of the Mennonite and Brethern in Christ churches in the United States and Canada) has over 750 personnel serving two to three-year assignments in agriculture, economic and technical development, education, health, and social services in about 45 countries overseas as well as North America.

OXFAM AMERICA
115 Broadway
Boston, MA 02116
(617) 482-1211

Oxfam America is an international agency that funds self-help development projects and disaster relief in poor countries in Asia, Africa and Latin America, and also prepares and distributes educational materials for Americans on issues of development and hunger. If there's not a chapter at your campus, be the folks to start one.

PRISON FELLOWSHIP
P.O. Box 17500
Washington, DC 20041
(703) 478-0100

Chuck Colson, following his own prison term in the aftermath of the Watergate Conspiracy, founded Prison Fellowship in 1976 to provide hope and Christian friendship to inmates all over the United States. The organization is active in the prison reform movement and can provide you with literature and ideas on how to become more involved in prison reform.

SALVATION ARMY
National Headquarters
799 Bloomfield Avenue
Verona, NJ 07044
(201) 239-0606

This well-known Christian social service agency assists the poor and does important evangelistic work all over the world.

UNICEF
The United Nations Children's Fund
866 U.N. Plaza
NY, NY 10017
(212) 415-8000

UNICEF directs contributions to the essential needs and problems of children, primarily those in the developing world.

VOICE OF CALVARY MINISTRIES
P.O. Box 10562
1655 St. Charles
Jackson, MS 39209
(601) 353-1635

Voice of Calvary Ministries, founded in 1960 by John Perkins, ministers to needy blacks in the South.

WORLD CONCERN
Box 33000
19303 Fremont Ave., N.
Seattle, WA 98133
(206) 546-7201

World Concern, a Christian humanitarian relief and development agency working in Third World countries, assists refugees and others recovering from disaster.

World Concern has a very fine program for groups called "Refugee Camp," which is similar to a hunger fast but with a unique twist. During this project, groups raise money for refugees by setting up and living in their own simulated Refugee Camp for 24 hours.

WORLD RELIEF
P.O. Box WRC
Wheaton, IL 60189
(312) 665-0235 or (800) 431-2808

World Relief, the international relief and development arm of the National Association of Evangelicals, works for disaster relief and rehabilitation, self-help programs to combat hunger and poverty, and refugee resettlement.

In addition, World Relief sponsors an overseas volunteer program for students called "Open Hands," which sends teams of young people into areas of the world where there is great need. Participants in this program may receive up to three semester hours of academic credit through a program offered by Eastern College in St. Davids, Pennsylvania, under the supervision of Dr. Tony Campolo.

WORLD VISION
919 W. Huntington Dr.
Monrovia, CA 91016
(818) 357-1111

World Vision, a well-known Christian humanitarian agency, has been a pioneer in famine and disaster relief, refugee resettlement, and the establishment of missions, schools and orphanages in Third World countries. World Vision offers an excellent program for student groups called "Planned Famine," in which participants fast for 30 hours to help hungry people. In addition, you or your small group can sponsor a foster child overseas through World Vision.

FUTURE PLANS

You don't have to be a college senior to wonder about God's will for your life. Throughout college you'll have to make important choices—about your relationships, your major, your summers—that will make you ask, "What does God want me to do, anyway?" That's what this section is about: discovering God's will for all the far-reaching decisions leading up to graduation. You'll find counsel on finding and trusting God's plan for your life. And for those getting ready to step out into the "real world," there's practical advice on preparing for the job market.

TRUSTING GOD'S WILL

Paul Little

If the Lord were to grant you the answer to one question, what would you ask?

My guess is that it would probably relate to his will for your life as you think about your senior year and beyond. Our peace and satisfaction depend on knowing that God is guiding us.

But we have a problem because we are confused about what the will of God is. Most people speak of God's will as something you have or you don't have. "Have you discovered God's will for your life?" someone may ask you. In asking this question they usually mean, Have you discovered God's *blueprint* for your life? The fact is that God seldom reveals an entire blueprint, and if you are looking for that blueprint, you are likely to be disappointed. What he does most frequently, however, is to reveal the next step to you.

A sensational plus to being a Christian is knowing that God has a plan for your life. "For we are God's workmanship, created in Christ Jesus to do good works, which God prepared in advance for us to do" (Eph 2:10).

And he has promised to reveal his will to us. "Trust in the LORD with all your heart, and lean not on your own understanding; in all your ways acknowledge him, and he will make your paths straight" (Prov 3:5-6).

Two Sides of God's Will

God's will has two sides: the side where he has already revealed exactly what he wants in his Word; and the side where he has not set down specific guidelines.

Has it ever struck you that most of God's will has already been revealed in Scripture? These are the aspects of his will which apply to every Christian. We are commanded by our Lord to go into all the world and preach the gospel to every creature. God tells us in unmistakable terms in 2 Corinthians 6:14 that we are not to be unequally yoked together with unbelievers. (Are you praying for guidance about whether you should marry a non-Christian? Save your breath.) Try making a list of all the commands that apply to you from the book of James. You'll have a good beginning in knowing God's will for you in many areas.

The late A. W. Tozer pointed out that we should never seek guidance about what God has already forbidden. Nor should we ever seek guidance in the areas where he has already said yes and given us a command. He then points

out that in most things God has no preference. He really doesn't have a great preference whether you eat steak or chicken. He's not desperately concerned about whether you wear a green shirt or a blue shirt. In many areas of life, to use Tozer's phrase, God invites us to consult our own sanctified preferences.

Then Tozer points out that there is, on the other hand, the second side of God's will, those areas where we need special guidance. The Lord spoke to the prophet Isaiah (48:17): "I am the LORD your God, who teaches you what is best for you, who directs you in the way you should go." In these areas of life there is no specific statement like "John Jones shalt be an engineer in Cincinnati," or, "Thou Mary Smith shalt marry Fred Grotzenheimer." No verse in the Bible will give you those kind of details about your life.

By recognizing the two aspects of God's will—that which is already revealed in his Word and those areas about which he is not specific—you get away from the static concept of the blueprint. The will of God is not a package let down from heaven on a string. We can't grope after it in desperation and hope that sometime in the future we'll be able to clasp it to our hearts, and know we have the will of God because we've got the magic package.

The will of God is far more like a scroll that unrolls every day. God has a will for you and me today, tomorrow and the next day and the day after that. Every one of us continues to seek the will of God throughout the whole of our lives. Now it may well be that a decision which you make will commit you for three months, or two years, or five or ten years or a lifetime. But the fact still remains that the will of God is something to be discerned and lived out every day of our lives. It is not something to be grasped once and for all.

Because of this, our call is not basically to a plan, a blueprint, a place or a work, but our call is basically to follow the Lord Jesus Christ.

Prerequisites

So what are the prerequisites for knowing the will of God in the unspecified areas of our lives? The first is *to be a child of God.* One day some people asked Jesus directly, "What must we do to be doing the works of God?" And Jesus answered, "The work of God is this: to believe in the one he has sent"

(Jn 6:29). We must first come to the Lord Jesus Christ in a commitment of faith to him as Savior and Lord. Then we are God's children and can be guided by him as our Father.

A second prerequisite for finding God's will is that *we need to be obeying God where we know his will.* What's the point of God guiding us in areas where he's not been specific when we're apparently unconcerned about areas where he is specific? Mark Twain wryly observed that it wasn't the parts of the Bible he didn't understand that bothered him, but the parts he did understand.

We need to begin to obey what we already know to be the will of God. We know we ought to be meeting with the Lord every day in prayer. "But you don't know my schedule this year. I've got eighteen hours." All of us have twenty-four hours to spend. It's a matter of setting priorities. If you're going to meet with God every day, it means you decide when you're going to bed, when you're getting up and how much time you can spend in prayer in the morning. Commit yourself to God now to do certain things you already know are his will.

The third prerequisite is that *we must be willing to accept the will of God in these unspecified areas of our lives without knowing what it is.* For most of us, I suspect, this is where the real problem lies. If we're honest, most of us would have to admit that our attitude is, "Lord, show me what your will is so I can decide whether it fits in with what I have in mind and whether I want to do it or not."

That attitude reflects the fact that we do not trust God to know best what will work out for our lives. We don't believe that he has our good at heart. We're saying, "I think I know better, God, what will make me happy, and I'm afraid that if I trust my life to you, you're going to shortchange me." Have you ever felt that? It's a solemn thing to realize. We make the tragic mistake of thinking that the choice is between doing what we want to do and being happy, and doing what God wants us to do and being miserable. We think the will of God is some terrible thing that he shoves under our nose and says, "Are you willing, are you willing?" We think that if we could just get out from under his clammy hands, we could really swing. We see God as a celestial Scrooge who leans down over the balcony of heaven trying to find anybody who's enjoying life, and says, "Now, cut it out."

Celestial Scrooge

Nothing could be further from the truth.

It's a slur on the character of God that those ideas even cross our minds. We need to have the tremendous truth of Romans 8:32 deeply planted in our hearts: "He who did not spare his own Son but gave him up for us all—how will he not also, along with him, graciously give us all things?" If you can get hold of that verse and allow it to get hold of you, you will have solved ninety per cent of your problem about desiring the will of God. You'll realize that the God who loved you and me enough to die for us when we didn't care about him is not about to shortchange us when we give our lives to him.

I have two children, a daughter, Debbie, and a son, Paul. My children come to me and say, "Daddy, I love you." Do I respond by saying, "Ah, children, that's just what I've been waiting to hear. Now into the closet for three weeks. Bread and water. I've just been waiting for you to tell me you love me so I can make your life miserable."

No. Just the opposite. They can get almost anything they want out of me at that point.

Heavenly Father

Do you think that God is any less loving than a human father? God's love so far transcends any love that we humans have that it can never be expressed. The Lord is constantly drawing contrasts between human love and our heavenly Father's love. If you, being evil, he says in Luke 11:13, know how to give good gifts to your children, how much more shall your heavenly Father give the Holy Spirit when you ask him. When we come to God and say, "I love you and I'm prepared to do your will, whatever you want me to do," we can be sure that God rejoices and fits our lives into his pattern for us, that place where he in his omniscience and love knows we will fit hand and glove. He is our Creator, and knows us better than we will ever know ourselves.

As you look to your last years of college and life after graduation, will you affirm God's will with confidence, joy and deep satisfaction? This is a very crucial prerequisite to knowing his will. And you won't be able to hold out any area or relationship in your life. You can't qualify it or say, "I'll go anywhere, Lord, but . . ." or, "I'll go and do anything, but it's got to be with so-and-so."

Rather, say, "Lord, you've created me and I belong to you. You loved me enough to die for me when I couldn't have cared less for you. Everything I am and have belongs to you. I'm not my own; I'm bought with a price, with your precious blood. I consciously and joyfully commit myself to you. Do with me what you choose."

And when you come to that place, you'll be able to say in the depths of your heart with Paul, "To me to live is Christ."

Discovering Your Vocation

Tom Sine

When it comes time for choosing a major or seeking work experience or some other activity that involves our future, an often asked question is, "Is it God's will?" But when we try to find God's will for the private, particular desires of our lives, we may in that very effort miss the whole point of his will.

I was startled recently to find no examples or teachings in the New Testament on how to discern the will of God regarding occupations, marriage partners or living accommodations for a particular individual.

Even though a number of Paul's prayers are recorded in the Epistles, we never hear him praying about the kinds of things that tend to fill our prayers: "Father, show me whether I should get a job tentmaking next week. And show Timothy whether he should get married or not." Even in his extensive teaching on singleness and marriage, Paul offers absolutely no advice on how to find the particular will of God in marriage.

Does this mean that God has no intentions for our lives? No. But to discover his will we must start with a very different question.

Instead of asking what kind of occupation, spouse, house or lifestyle God wants us to pursue, we will have a better chance of finding God's will by asking, "What is God's *vocation* for my life?"

By vocation I don't mean job. I mean those specific ways God wants to use our lives, gifts and education *to be a part of his loving initiative in changing the world.*

We see from Scripture that, since the Fall, God has intended to bring in a new age of righteousness, justice and peace for all peoples. So when we pray "Thy kingdom come, thy will be done on earth as it is in heaven," we are praying a radical prayer. We are praying that the future transformation of our world that will occur when Christ returns will begin now.

As Christians, we must seek to understand how we fit into God's plan to transform the world. But *how* do you discern God's vocation or call to ministry for you? Here are six key ways God speaks to us:

Asking the Right Questions

As soon as we ask the question, "What is God's agenda for his people?" we are driven to his Word to find answers.

From the Bible

The Bible gives example after example of individuals who heard God's call and either responded positively or went their own way. Notice the ways he dramatically changed the priorities of those who responded. Listen for God's call to you as you study his Word. Keep a journal and list all the impressions you receive in your biblical study—especially of specific areas of service into which God may be calling you.

As Dan and Caroline studied the Scriptures they were especially moved by the passages that underlined the international character of the church's mission. This study led them to begin working with international students in Seattle. Since they were both working full time, the best they could do was free up one evening a week to work with internationals.

As they prayed over God's call to this ministry, they con-

cluded that one evening a week wasn't enough. No sooner
had they made this decision than their church offered them
a half-time position in church administration in which they
each worked ten hours a week. Dan quit his job as a teacher and Caroline quit her job as a secretary, and they moved
into a Christian community where sharing food, housing
and material possessions reduced their expenses consider-
ably. Now, instead of having one evening free a week for
working with internationals, they have thirty hours a week
for their vocation.

The Scriptures teach that Jesus is incarnated in the lives   **In the Lives of**
of the poor, suffering and forgotten peoples (Mt 25:31-46).   **Needy**
Therefore, if we listen, we can hear God calling us through   **Persons**
the pain and suffering of a hungry child in Saõ Paulo, Bra-
zil; the alienation and loneliness of seniors in a retirement
home in Atlanta; the despair of a young drug addict in San
Francisco; the fear of abused and neglected children in
your own community.

Read newspapers, news magazines and mission newslet-
ters. Watch films and TV specials on human concerns. What
areas of human suffering and need particularly grip your
heart? List them in your journal, pray over them, discuss
them with friends. Jesus may be calling you through a specific area of spiritual, emotional or physical need into an
area of compassionate service.

Denny and Jean Grindal only visited Africa to take a vacation from their flower shop and look at the animals. But
they got more than they bargained for when they decided
to visit a small Presbyterian mission among the Masai (a
nomadic tribe of tall warriors who make their living by raising cattle). When the Grindals visited the Masai, they were
appalled. The land was barren. A drought had killed
hundreds of cattle, and thousands of Masai were struggling
for their very survival.

Denny and Jean returned to the United States, but God
wouldn't let them forget what they had seen. So Denny

went to the library and spent several months researching earth-filled dams. Then he and Jean took some money out of savings and returned to Kenya. They worked with tribal leaders to construct the first of a series of huge earth-filled dams. In one night of torrential rain the dam—the size of three football fields—was filled.

When the Grindals heard the call of God through the lives of a people in need, they responded and discovered a whole new vocational ministry for themselves. Now they spend six months each year in their flower shop and six months with their new friends in Kenya.

God gave us gifts for a purpose. Those gifts were not given to be squandered aimlessly on increasing the profit margin of a corporation, the bureaucracy of government or the prestige of a religious organization. Make a running list in your journal of your natural and spiritual gifts and how you have already used them.   **In Your Gifts**

Al had sensed God calling him through his interest and ability in engineering. After he got his B.S. in engineering, he had a wide range of jobs to choose from. One was a position designing missiles for Boeing. But he believed strongly that there are no neutral jobs for Christians; the time and creativity we invest in our jobs either improve the human condition or make it worse. So Al turned down the missile job in favor of designing better cardiology equipment.

Al later heard God speak to him through the needs of some kids with cerebral palsy. When he visited an institution for physically and neurologically disabled children, he learned that many victims of cerebral palsy feel helplessly trapped in bodies that won't move or communicate in the way they want. All of a sudden it came together for Al. He is now using his engineering skills to design—as a ministry for God's kingdom—innovative ways for these children to get around and communicate.

Christian author and speaker Blaine Smith tells a story about his friend Malcolm, who hated being a housepainter. One day he lamented to Blaine that he would love to be an English teacher, except for one thing: "I know that God doesn't want me teaching. I'd enjoy the experience too much. The affirmation of students would be more than I could handle." Then, Blaine writes, he added the clincher: He was sure that God wanted him painting houses, for he thoroughly disliked his work!

Blaine continues: "While Scripture has much to say about the dangers of following our desires, . . . it also proclaims that God himself creates certain desires within us who follow Christ, in order to guide us in certain directions. Paul stresses this in Phillipians 2:13: 'It is God who works in you to will and to act according to his good purpose.' Literally translated, Paul means, 'God is *energizing* you.' God, in other words, is giving us motivation and desire to do what he wants us to do.

"But how does this reconcile with the frequent biblical admonitions to *deny* our desires? Part of the answer lies in where my heart is before God. If I'm taking my relationship with Christ seriously and doing what I need to do to keep spiritual growth alive, then I can be confident that many of the desires I'm experiencing are being inspired by him. And many I might otherwise feel are not coming to the surface."

Spend time noting some of your deepest desires in your journal. Then lift them up to God and ask him to show you if and why he's placed them there.

Open yourself up to dreaming new dreams for your vocation and your future. Invite God's Spirit to flood your imagination. Brainstorm new ways in which everything you've written in your journal could be orchestrated into vocational opportunities. Don't be constrained by traditional categories or even by the lack of income to support your dream. Pray over your ideas and begin to do research on

In Your Desires

By Using Your Imagination

people already involved in related areas of ministry.

Finally, take the various dreams God is giving you to a group of brothers and sisters to find his confirmation. Richard Foster has pointed out, in *Celebration of Discipline* (Harper & Row), that the call of God was not a private, individualistic matter in the early church. Paul and Barnabas's missionary call came through the community. We hear God's voice best in the midst of those who have a shared sense of seriousness for his kingdom.

Through Other Christians

Once you have a clear sense of God's vocational call on your life, you have the best criterion possible for deciding where you should work and live (places that directly or indirectly enable you to participate in your ministry), as well as whom you should marry (someone who shares or enthusiastically supports your calling, and vice versa). If you genuinely seek his kingdom first, the message of Matthew 6:33 is clear: he will provide for your essential needs.

UNDERSTANDING WHAT MAKES A JOB "CHRISTIAN": FIVE MYTHS

Dave Veerman

Choosing a career is serious business, especially for Christian students who want to serve God with their lives. But many carry around mistaken ideas of what it means to follow Christ in one's career. Here are the top five myths I've heard:

Myth #1: Very few career options are suitable for Christians.
Some people believe God wants Christians to avoid "secular" careers because they are "worldly." Certainly God has given guidelines and principles in the Bible that must inform one's career choice—for example, obey the government, do not steal, lie, murder or commit adultery. But what career fields do these guidelines eliminate other than becoming a Christian thief, a Christian con artist, a Christian hit man, a Christian prostitute or a Christian drug dealer?

It's not as simple as that, of course.

While very few careers are inherently evil, individual jobs or companies may at times expect a person to misrepresent the truth, circumvent the law, or in some way contribute to larger goals that are morally questionable. But just because an accountant is asked to distort figures for the IRS doesn't mean he or she should abandon an accounting career. A better bet is to look for another employer—one with integrity.

Myth #2: The only true Christian careers are becoming a pastor, a missionary, or pursuing "full-time Christian service." All other careers are second class.
While many Christians decide to serve God by starting churches or introducing others to the faith, people sometimes forget that these occupations, while very important, are only one part of life. The whole earth is the Lord's (Ps 24:1), and

Christians are to do *everything* for the glory of God (Col 3:17). God wants people to serve him in a multitude of arenas, not just the spiritual. In his eyes, any vocation is spiritual if it contributes to his greater purpose of "reconciling the world to himself" (Col 1:20). And in that sense, all Christians should pursue "full-time Christian service" whether they're church-planting or corn-planting.

But don't some occupations matter more than others? Don't presidents change the world more than paperboys? Yes, but in terms of the inherent worth or "Christian-ness" of the work itself, both jobs are consistent with Christ's command to serve other people (Jn 13:12-17).

One way to consider whether a particular occupation is Christian is to ask, "What if there weren't any?" That is, if no one were pursuing this career, would the world be worse or better off? Think about it. What if there weren't any garbage collectors? Carpenters? Professional football players? Accountants? Stock brokers? Fashion color analyzers? Computer programmers? Championship wrestlers? Artists? The answers aren't always clear. But asking the question can help a person identify how a career may or may not further God's purposes in the world.

Myth #3: I shouldn't pursue any career unless I feel a specific call from God.
The feeling of being called can be important. Without it one may lose all motivation, drive and energy to serve God meaningfully in the marketplace. Those who sense a call from God should confirm the feeling with concrete evidence that they are suited for a particular career. But those who don't feel a supernatural call need not fret: God often simply expects us to put our interests, gifts and talents to use in working out his will.

Either way, answering a few questions may help clarify whether a particular career is for you:

How does this occupation fit with my personal goals and priorities? Will it tap my God-given interests and gifts and help me to become the person God wants me to be? Are the pressures and time demands so great that they'll adversely affect my relationships with God, my family, my friends? Are the requirements of this job compatible with my view of marriage (if I choose to marry)? Does it make the world a better place or contribute to that end? Do other Christians who know me well feel that this career suits me?

Myth #4: The career choices one makes during college are permanent and irrevocable.
Studies have shown that the average adult changes careers at least twice before he or she turns sixty. Career choices made during college must be taken seriously, but, on the other hand, things can change—one's interests, one's family situation, the economy, the job market and so on. Any of these changes could lead to a career switch later on.

But a career change isn't the end of the world; it's possible to honor God in more than one field of work. Though some may never have to wrestle with a career-change decision, statistics indicate that most people will. Just knowing that fact should reduce some of the pressure you're feeling now.

Myth #5: All I can do to serve God in a "secular" profession is to share my faith with coworkers.

This view assumes that faith and work are completely separate, unrelated parts of life. The biblical view is quite different: in God's eyes, work itself is an outgrowth of one's faith, a tangible expression of service to God and other people (Gen 1:27-30).

But it's not enough to simply say that work itself is Christian. Even while on the job, one needs to continually ask, What does it take to make *this* job Christian? The answer has more to do with one's attitude than one's job description.

First, we are to approach our jobs as though we were working for God and not just for employers (Col 3:23). Enthusiasm, creativity, integrity and service—not greed, dishonesty or doing the absolute minimum—should mark followers of God.

Second, we make our job Christian by modeling Christ's love as we relate to managers, coworkers and clients—the people who see us day to day and under pressure.

Third, we must evaluate how the company we work for affects society. Are its products beneficial? Are its methods fair to the poor? Do its goals promote justice? Do its by-products harm the environment? The answers may not be clear cut, but we need to weigh these and other factors as we decide whether our job is Christian or not.

Fourth, we can honor God by what we do with our salary. That first paycheck can bring great satisfaction. But it also brings power: power to do good by giving generously to the church and to those in need, or power to do evil by squandering God's resources on things we don't need.

Making a job or career "Christian" demands more than leaving Bible verses on our desks or sharing our faith over coffee breaks. The actual work itself, as well as our behavior on the job, may or may not be Christian. Our attitude can make all the difference.

Getting Started in a Missionary Career

W. Terry Whalin

Ah, the first sign of spring—job recruiters descending on campus. Those men and women with big smiles and leather briefcases represent many career tracks. But chances are that one option you may be considering won't be represented at all: cross-cultural missions.

You've probably at least thought about missions. You may have even jotted down the names of a few mission boards you've heard good things about. But how do you really get started exploring the vast range of missions opportunities?

You might begin with *World Christian* magazine (P.O. Box 5199, Chatsworth, CA 91313). For twelve dollars a year, you get just about as much practical information on missions organizations, as well as other cultures, as you can digest. Each issue includes a postcard to send for more info from the mission agencies that advertise in the magazine—a quick way to contact a number of organizations with one stamp. (Average response is seven weeks.)

You can also make key contacts (and narrow down possibilities more quickly) through Intercristo, a Christian placement network that's been helping Christians find jobs since 1967. You fill out a profile identifying your education, interests, skills and preference of job location. And for $35 Intercristo taps their computer database, holding over 35,000 service opportunities, to give you names and addresses of Christian organizations (and commercial businesses serving the Christian community) with job openings matching your interests. Fifty per cent of Intercristo's job listings are overseas. To get an application, you can either call Intercristo toll-free at 1-800-426-1342 (in Washington, Hawaii, Alaska or Canada, call 206-546-7330) or write Box 33487, Seattle, WA 98133.

The Missions department of InterVarsity Christian Fellowship has recently begun similar services—free of charge. Qualified men and women in their Missions Counseling Service can help you sort out your plans, goals and confusing number of options; and their Missions Placement Service can match you with an agency that can help you carry out the plans and goals you identify. For more information, call InterVarsity Missions at 1-800-DECLARE or write 6400 Schroeder Rd., P.O. Box 7895, Madison, WI 53707-7895.

The Big Questions

Once you decide what kind of cross-cultural career you're interested in, try to speak with people from different organizations who are pursuing that kind of work. Most denominational and independent mission boards have missionary representatives who travel the United States and Canada speaking at churches and missions conventions.

Ask the organizations which interest you how you can meet with one of their missionaries. If you still haven't narrowed down which groups look good to you, mull over the possibilities at **Urbana,** InterVarsity's triennial student missions convention, which attracts hundreds of missionary representatives. (For more information, write InterVarsity Missions at the address above.)

Once you corner a missionary from a board which appeals to you, what do you ask? Here are eleven critical concerns to discuss:

1. What kind of ministry does your missions board emphasize: Church planting? Bible translation and literacy? Reaching children or college students? Inner-city evangelism? Helping start businesses that create jobs in the Third World?

2. How can your organization use my skills? Considering my major, will I work in that field or need to be retrained?

3. Do you pay a salary? Do I need to raise financial support through friends and churches? If so, how long has the initial fund-raising process taken most of your missionaries? How much time will I probably have to spend raising support in later years? Will you train me and provide resources to help me get going in this area? How much will I be able to do with your organization before my full support is raised?

4. Where does your organization send people? Can I choose an area or country to work in?

5. What kind of training do you provide before I start working in a cross-cultural situation?

6. What's your organization's turnover rate in personnel? Why do people leave the field? (You might cite Ada Lum in *A Hitchhiker's Guide to Missions* [IVP]: "It's no secret that thirty-five to fifty per cent of first-term missionaries return early or do not return after their first term.")

7. What time commitment do you ask your missionaries to make?

8. What language will I use in my overseas assignment—English or a national language? How much time and training will the mission give me to learn a new language?

9. What kind of experience and schooling do I need to do the kind of work I'm interested in?

10. Tell me about the history of your organization's formation and how it has changed through the years. (Try to discern if the organization is wedded to traditions and rigid procedures, or if it changes as needed with the times.)

What is your stand on women in ministry? Different styles of worship? Trying new approaches to reaching people with the gospel? Is your goal to work yourself out of a job by training nationals to lead? Do you discourage or prohibit missionaries from taking stands on the political issues of the area they're working in? What percentage of your missionaries are minorities or nationals?

11. Are you excited about your involvement with this organization? Why?

A word of caution: Ask the representative's counsel about any concerns you have, but don't ever feel pressured by him or her to sign up. Listen to what God may he saying to you—and get input from a variety of different people.

What next? One good way to process everything you've learned from literature and missionary contacts is to participate in a short-term missions program that exposes you to cross-cultural work (and, usually, fund-raising) without pressuring you to make a long-term commitment.

Getting Experience

CAM International's Practical Missionary Training (PMT) has been taking college students to Central America for over thirty-five years. Their four-week program, which costs about $1200 (plus transportation), focuses on starting churches in urban areas. For more information, write the PMT Director, CAM International, Box 28005, Dallas, TX 75228.

InterVarsity Christian Fellowship offers a wide variety of short-term missions experiences through their Overseas Training Camp (OTC) programs. OTC sends teams of students to places such as Kenya, Brazil, Guatemala, China/ Hong Kong, Western Europe, Eastern Europe, India, Malta, the Middle East and the Philippines. The programs last between six and eight weeks and cost anywhere from $1200 to $3000. To get more information about OTC —or to receive a very helpful, comprehensive list of other organizations' summer missions programs that InterVarsity has compiled—call the Missions department toll-free at 1-800-

DECLARE or write 6400 Schroeder Rd., P.O. Box 7895, Madison, WI 53707-7895.

Even if you can't travel overseas this summer, you might be able to attend Quest, a four-week program offered by Wycliffe Bible Translators. Quest sessions, limited to forty participants, are held year-round in three locations in the United States. "Questers" stretch themselves in simulated cross-cultural exercises, test their aptitude in linguistics and other skills, get to know themselves better through a class called Personal Growth, and interact with others who are also seeking God's guidance about missions work. Not all Questers are expected to join Wycliffe; in fact, forty per cent of the Quest alumni do not. The cost is about $500 per person. For more information, write: Quest, Wycliffe Bible Translators, Huntington Beach, CA 92647.

Can't go on Quest or short-term missions? Still feel compelled to prepare for job interviews? Here's one more opportunity: work overseas with a secular corporation. Depending on your education and skills, you may be able to work, make friends and witness in a country where traditional "missionaries" are barred and few Christians live. For more information about this type of overseas experience, contact Tentmakers International at Box 33836, Seattle, WA 98813 or Global Opportunities at 1600 Elizabeth, Pasadena, CA 91104.

No doubt about it: those job recruiters who visit your campus make pursuing safe, well-paying careers with their companies easy. But if God is calling you to a career in cross-cultural missions, opportunities to explore your options abound—and in the long-term, you won't be as fulfilled anywhere else.

SNAGGING YOUR FIRST JOB: RÉSUMÉS, LETTERS AND INTERVIEWS

Dick Staub and Jeff Trautman

his chapter is adapted from Intercristo's Career Kit. *Intercristo is a non-profit service organization dedicated to helping Christian men and women integrate their faith and work. Through their self-study program,* Career Kit, *nationwide career-building seminars and one-on-one career counseling, Intercristo teaches Christians how to interpret the role of work from a biblical perspective, while also equipping them to be effective stewards of their God-given abilities in the marketplace. In addition, Intercristo's Christian Placement Network helps Christians find jobs that match their abilities in Christian organizations. For more information on any of Intercristo's services, call toll-free, 1-800-426-1342 (in Hawaii, Washington and Canada, call 1-206-546-7330) or write Intercristo, The Career and Human Resource Specialists, 19303 Fremont Avenue North, Seattle, WA 98133.*

Job seekers who can't or who won't promote themselves don't progress. It's as simple as that. As a job-seeker, you have a responsibility to give an employer a reason for deciding to hire you; employers aren't in the business of giving away jobs.

The Résumé

Your promotion effort is bound to take two forms during your job search—verbal and written. Although the most effective form of promotion is one-to-one communication with the employer, you'll probably need to develop and distribute written communication that can be reviewed by prospective employers. A résumé is a written advertisement designed to attract potential employers. It is one tool to help you get a job interview—nothing more, nothing less.

The marketplace is loaded with books on résumé writing. Rather than over whelming you with all the alternatives and procedures out there, let's summarize the best effective wisdom reflected in many of these writings:

In general, the shorter the résumé the better. Advertisements are short, easy to read and to the point. As an advertisement, your résumé should follow suit. With few exceptions, keep your résumé to one or two pages. An employer doesn't have the time to wade through pages on your personal background.

Focus your résumé to a particular job. The one-size-fits-all résumé is practically worthless. You should have a different résumé for each specific position you seek. This means work, but it's worth it.

Writing a good résumé takes time. No one writes an effective advertisement in one sitting. Most promotional literature goes through at least two or three drafts before it's finalized. Expect to rework your résumé a few times in order to make it effective.

A good résumé reflects accomplishment—and results. Most résumé writers overwork their features and say little about their benefits. An effective résumé is geared toward the employer's expectations and needs, not your past history. Your past is only significant as it relates to your future.

Avoid including any information on your résumé that could initially work against you. These are referred to as "knockout" factors, and include age, marital status, religious affiliations, height, weight, personal photos, race and any handicaps. Don't include one or more of these items unless you're sure it will work to your advantage.

Make it eye-catching. Use a format that accents the part of your past that will appeal most to a potential employer. Basically, there are two formats—chronological and functional. (See examples.) The information should be appealing to the eye and easy to find. This is accomplished in several ways. First, provide enough white space on paper so that the information does not look cluttered or wordy. Second, use capital letters, bullets, underlines and/or typesetting to accent critical information. Third, eliminate any abbreviations or words that are confusing, vague, or not widely accepted by the average reader. Finally, be sure to photocopy your résumé on quality paper. Contact a copy center or graphics firm to help you. We suggest using any ivory, off-white, beige or gray colored paper.

Make it generate reader interest. Here are some basic strategies for generating interest through a written résumé: First, have a written or unwritten job objective. Focus on the skills, achievements and experience that specifically relate to that objective. Second, utilize facts and figures to accent your accomplishments (for example, "Supervised 50 employees and increased revenue by 25%"). Third, note your accomplishments through action verbs (for example, "organized," "directed," "supported"). Fourth, include an appealing testimonial (for example, "One of the hardest-working employees I've ever had."—Vice President of Accounting, Sunset System, Inc.).

Cover Letters
In most cases, you should accompany

John Doe
1000 Any Name Avenue
Any City, State, zip
(800) 555-8000

OBJECTIVE: Entry level/trainee position in sales and marketing leading to a career in financial services/international business.

EDUCATION:

| Bachelor of Arts | University of Washington
Economics Major - 3.4 GPA
With an emphasis in Chinese studies | December
1987 |
| | Grinnell College, Grinnell, Iowa | 1984 - 1986 |

STRENGTHS   EXPERIENCE

Setting realistic but ambitious goals	As walk-on college soccer player, set progressively ambitious goals of (1) making the team, (2) obtaining starting position and (3) becoming team captain. Accomplished all goals by junior year.
Exceeding quotas for sales	As organizer for fundraising telethon, responsible for soliciting $32,000 in donations. Raised additional $16,000 when project ended. In next telethon, raised $182,000 when quota was set at $160,000.
Training and motivating others to achieve goals . .	As defensive captain for the soccer team, trained 8 players in defense strategies and skills to limit opponent scoring. Efforts resulted in team achieving lowest "scored against" rating in the division.
Researching data to gain favorable position	Conducted a 2-month economic research project that resulted in presenting findings and a proposal at a 3-day conference in Washington, D.C., attended by 20 other university representatives. Succeeded in getting proposal approved by committee and passed by the delegates.

EMPLOYMENT HISTORY:

Intern/Assistant	Johnson and Higgins of Washington Seattle, Washington	Summers 1984 - 1986
	During 3 summers with insurance brokerage firm, serviced small accounts, researched tort law, claims, and international insurance, and assisted on large accounts. Presented an internship proposal to the firm which was accepted.	
Production Director/ Publicity Director	KDIC Radio Grinnell, Iowa	Part-time 1986
	Produced public service announcements and promotional tapes for campus station.	

Functional résumé: Use this format to emphasize strengths not used in recent jobs.

Susan Doe
1000 Any Street
Resume City, WA 98000
(206) 555-5454

OBJECTIVE: Seeking a position in Sports Information/Administration.

PROFESSIONAL EXPERIENCE:

Recreation Leader   Redmond Parks and Recreation   1985 – Present
                       Redmond, Washington

                       Responsible for planning, promoting, leading, and
                       evaluating athletic events and leagues that involve
                       over 4,000 participants.

                       ACCOMPLISHMENTS

                       * Ran a successful 3-month winter basketball program
                         involving 300 youth. Received frequent comments
                         from coaches on improved efficiency of program due
                         to better organization and communication.

                       * Administered a 57-team weekday softball league.
                         Coordinated over 50 rainouts with minimal
                         disruption to master schedule. Excelled in
                         tracking league statistics.

                       * Accomplished all program goals at 20% under
                         $200,000 budgeted.

Athletic Director/   Camarillo Christian School   1983 – 1985
Instructor   Camarillo, California

                       Planned, developed, promoted, and monitored after-
                       school sports program for 500 students.

                       ACCOMPLISHMENTS

                       * Through writing press releases and securing press
                         coverage, designing and distributing flyers, and
                         creating more lively events, increased attendance
                         at home games 3 times over previous years.

                       * Proposed and acquired funds for securing uniforms,
                         facilities, transportation and concessions.
                         Improved quality of program became selling point
                         for school and increased transfers into the school.

                       * Taught 6 co-ed Physical Education classes daily.
                         Creatively developed and adapted programs to
                         accommodate minimal facilities and wide range of
                         ages in same class.

EDUCATION: Bachelor's Degree   Pacific Christian College   1983
                                 Fullerton, California

Chronological résumé: Use this format when your job history is impressive or applicable.

your résumé with a cover letter. A cover letter helps personalize your communication and attract the employer's interest in your résumé. Here are the five basics of an effective cover letter:

1. *Target it to a specific person.* No "to whom it may concern" titles or introductions. What if I don't know the name of the person doing the hiring? Then call the organization and find out.

2. *Appeal to the interests of the employer.* Don't load your cover letter with "I wants." Rather fill it with employer needs, interests and concerns.

3. *Make the first line an "attention grabber."* Here are five basic ways to use a grabber.

□ *Refer to a mutual acquaintance.* Example: "Dick Strand, operations manager for Miller Industries, suggested it would be beneficial for the two of us to meet. Let me explain. . . ."

□ *Tell an employment story.* Example: "While teaching mathematics to underprivileged children, I was able to raise student test scores by more than an average of 20%. The persistent and creative instructional methods I used became a model for similar classes within the district. . . ."

□ *Ask a question.* Example: "Can you use a mechanical engineer with the ability to maintain tight control over multifaceted problems, analyze complex problems and arrive quickly at some solutions? I have these talents, as demonstrated in the enclosed résumé."

□ *Give a compliment.* Example: "I have used your products for years, and have been impressed recently with the new current line. Your 'Does It Easy' cleaner ·

is everything you advertise it to be—and more. I am writing you because I want to put my knowledge of your products to greater use."

□ *Promise a benefit.* Example: "Throughout my ten years of sales training, I have consistently increased my students' sales volume by more than 30% within their first nine months of employment. Chances are I can bring this same level of success to your organization. . . ."

4. *Answer the question "Why should I hire you?"*

5. *Ask for an interview and take the initiative to follow up the cover letter to set an interview time.*

Take the time to write a personalized, effective, business-like cover letter. And be sure to keep copies of every cover letter you send. You need to know what you've said when it's time to follow up and pursue an interview.

"R & R" Interviews

The most successful strategy we at Intercristo know for getting the exposure needed for finding work is called the "R & R" interview. In this interview you simply schedule brief appointments with a potential hiring manager. Your objective is not to ask him or her for a job but to talk about your interests and strengths, and to solicit any advice or suggestions he or she may have for your job search.

The two Rs stand for "Be Remembered" and "Be Referred." The genius of this approach is that it gives a potential employer sufficient exposure to you so you'll be remembered for immediate or future openings. In addition, you may also be referred to other hiring managers who may have an interest in meeting with you.

Taking the initiative to contact hiring managers can lead to job possibilities. The greater the number of hiring managers who become exposed to your background and potential, the greater will be your chances of landing a job that fits you. This strategy provides a painless means for contacting hiring managers who have no apparent job openings, and for gaining solid advice, counsel and direction from individuals who have the knowledge and perspective you need.

So where do you start? Effective R&R interviews involve four steps:

Step #1: Targeting Potential Hiring Managers. Generally speaking, there are three groups of people in your world to contact. The first is made up of individuals who have direct experience in, or knowledge of, the industry or field in which you're seeking employment. Regardless of their respective positions, these individuals have inside knowledge that can be very valuable.

A second group to contact includes individuals who, though not directly involved in the type of work you're pursuing, tend to know a lot of people. These folks are constantly making contact with a wide variety of people. They may include your dentist, Aunt Laura, a college roommate, or your aerobics instructor.

There is a third group of contacts you should pursue. Those are acquaintances who don't fit into the two previous groups, but who may know someone who could help. You could overlook such people because they have no obvious connection to your job objective. Maybe your neighbor has a cousin who hires for the very position you seek. Mine these contacts for leads, and you'll be surprised at the treasure you'll uncover.

On the average, you have the potential to generate 250 names from these three groups. We suggest you identify your 50 best contacts and start networking with them to identify hiring managers.

Step #2: Contacting Potential Hiring Managers. Once you've identified the hiring manager for the position you're pursuing, there are three ways to contact him or her.

The first way is in person. Another name for this approach is "cold calling." It means walking into an organization without any previous introduction and asking to speak with the hiring manager. The challenge in cold calling is to initiate a conversation that results in an immediate appointment.

A second way to contact a potential hiring manager is by phone. It's less time consuming than an in-person contact, but still provides direct communication with the hiring manager. Here is one example of a phone contact: "Good morning, Mr. Schwartz. My name is Jan Matthews. I'm calling to seek your professional advice. As a paralegal pursuing a job change, I would like to meet briefly with you, for 30 minutes—no longer. I'm not expecting you to have a job for me, but would appreciate any direction you could give in my job search. Could we schedule a time to meet this week?"

The introductory letter is a third effective way of setting up a referral interview. It has two major advantages: First, a letter goes directly to your contact. You eliminate the work of going through a secretary to make initial contact. Second, a letter paves the way when you phone to make the actual appointment since you've already established contact with the hiring manager.

Once you've succeeded in getting a 30-minute appointment with the hiring manager, you need to make the most of this time. And since you initiated the contact, it's up to you to structure the half hour.

Step #3: Conducting the R & R Interview. To maximize your appointment you must consider what you want to get out of the interview. Essentially, you'll want the hiring manager to like you, see your potential, offer suggestions for improving your presentation (résumé, appearance, communication, etc.) and refer you to other hiring managers who may have an interest in you.

How can you achieve these goals? You can make a favorable impression on the hiring managers by giving them the chance to talk about their own career. Simply ask how they got into the field, and what part of the job is most enjoyable. By learning how they got where they are, you may find some common ground. Also, try to find a point of common interest. Look for clues in the manager's office. Magazines, pictures, trophies can become targets for building common ground. Don't hesitate to use them.

Here are some more tips for the interview: Arrive ten minutes early for your appointment. This gives you time for any last-minute preparation or unexpected delays. Look sharp. Your interviewer could be a potential employer. Be sure to have extra copies of your résumé. Be prepared. Write out your agenda and questions on a 3 x 5 card to use as a reference during the interview. As much as possible, stick within the time frame you agreed upon. Usually this will be 20 to 30 minutes. If the manager wants to spend more time with you, fine, but be sure it's her decision.

When someone gives you a referral, be sure you have permission to use his name as the referral source. Also, gather as much information about contacting the referral as seems appropriate. This will include a job title and phone number. After the interview, take a few minutes to review what you did and didn't learn. Jot down suggestions for future interviews; learn from each encounter.

Step #4: Saying "Thanks." After every interview, it's wise to send a thank-you note. This can be handwritten or typed. Make it brief and complimentary. Remember, getting a job means building positive relationships. A thank-you note is another step in that direction.

On the average, you'll receive one job interview for every twenty-five R & R interviews you conduct. This means you should expect to talk to a number of hiring managers and walk away with no definite employment prospects. Don't be discouraged. Every time this happens you're still one step closer to a job interview.

Acknowledgments

The chapter "Surviving the First Week" by Andy LePeau was originally published as "How to Keep From Committing Suicide After Your First Week on Campus" in HIS magazine, October 1975. Copyright © 1975 Andy Le Peau. Used by permission.

The chapter "Ten Sure-Fire Ways to Have a Lousy Time in College" by Greg Spencer was originally published in HIS magazine, January 1986. Copyright © 1986 Greg Spencer. Used by permission.

The chapter "When to Drop a Class" by Joan Wallner was originally published as "Dropping a Class" in U magazine, February 1987. Copyright © 1987 Joan Wallner. Used by permission.

The chapter "Easing the Pain of Studying" by Jeanne Doering Zornes was originally published as "How to Ease the Pain of Studying" in HIS magazine, October 1983. Copyright © 1983 Jeanne Doering Zornes. Used by permission.

The chapter "Reference Books You Can't Live Without" by Betsy Rossen Elliot and Shirley Kostka was originally published as "Say Hello to Some Good Reference Books" in HIS magazine, October 1986. Copyright © 1986 Betsy Rossen Elliot and Shirley Kostka. Used by permission.

The chapter "Six Ways to Weasel Out of an Exam" by Rob Suggs was originally published in HIS magazine, December 1983. Copyright © 1983 Rob Suggs. Used by permission.

The chapter "Taking Your Faith to Class" by Brian Walsh was originally published as "How to Think Your Way through College" in HIS magazine, November 1983. Copyright © 1983 Brian Walsh. Used by permission.

The chapter "Making the Most of Religion Courses" by John Duff was originally published as "Religion Courses: Take 'em or leave 'em (with your faith still intact)" in HIS magazine, December 1982. Copyright © 1982 John Duff. Used by permission.

The chapter "Managing Your Time" contains three sections by three different authors. "Setting Priorities" by Alice Fryling is adapted from "Beating Burnout" and "Am I Doing Too Much?" originally published in HIS magazine, October 1986; copyright © 1986 Alice Fryling; used by permission. "Making Plans" by Alan Lakein is excerpted from *How to Get Control of Your Time and Your Life* by Alan Lakein (New York: Random House, 1973); copyright © 1973 Alan Lakein; used by permission. "Tracking Your Time" by Merrill E. Douglass and Donna N. Douglass was adapted from *Manage Your Time, Manage Your Work, Manage Yourself* by Merrill E. Douglass and Donna N. Douglass (New York: AMACOM, 1980); copyright © 1980

Merrill E. Douglass and Donna N. Douglass; used by permission.

The chapter "Setting Christian Priorities" by Rich Lamb was originally published as "First Things First" in HIS magazine, October 1985. Copyright © 1985 Rich Lamb. Used by permission.

The chapter "Sunday: This Day's For You" by Vance Hays was originally published in HIS magazine, October 1985. Copyright © 1985 Vance Hays. Used by permission.

The chapter "Paying God, Caesar and the Rent" by Linda Doll was originally published in U magazine, January 1987. Copyright © 1987 Linda Doll. Used by permission.

The chapter "The Fantastic Plastic Trap" by John Throop and Robert M. Kachur was originally published in HIS magazine, November 1986. Copyright © 1986 John Throop and Robert M. Kachur. Used by permission.

The chapters "Winning the Financial Aid Game" and "Resource Books on Financial Aid" by Susan M. Zitzman were originally published as "Making Your Way through the Financial Aid Maze" in Campus Life magazine, November 1984. Copyright © 1984 Campus Life magazine. Used by permission.

The chapter "The Key Players" by Anna Leider is excerpted from Don't Miss Out: The Ambitious Student's Guide to Financial Aid by Anna Leider (Alexandria, Va.: Octameron Associates, 1987). Copyright © 1987 by Anna Leider. Used by permission.

The chapter "Living the Commuter Life" by Andrés Tapia was originally published as "The New Commuters: Living on the Edge" in U magazine, March 1987. Copyright © 1987 Andrés Tapia. Used by permission.

The chapter "Knowing When to Change Colleges" by Karen Wells was originally published as "Should You Change Colleges?" in HIS magazine, December 1985. Copyright © 1985 Karen Wells. Used by permission.

The chapters "Partying: Good Times or Compromise?" and "Should I Go?" by Robert M. Kachur were originally published as "Party Politics: Could I Whoop It Up With Friends Without Compromising My Standards?" in HIS magazine, October 1986. Used by permission.

The chapter "Drinking: How Much Is Too Much" by David Neff with Robert M. Kachur was originally published as "To Drink or Not to Drink: Now That's a Tricky Question" in HIS magazine, April 1982. Copyright © 1982 David Neff. Used by permission.

The chapter "Going Greek," by Elizabeth Riley was originally published as "Going Greek: Should Christians join fraternities and sororities?" in HIS magazine, October 1984. Copyright © 1984 Elizabeth Riley. Used by permission.

The chapter "Should I Rush?" by Robert M. Kachur was originally published as "I Took the Pledge" in HIS magazine, October 1984. Copyright © 1984 Robert M. Kachur. Used by permission.

The chapter "Don't Rush into It" by Andrés Tapia was originally published in HIS magazine, October 1984. Copyright © 1984 Andrés Tapia. Used by permission.

The chapter "Finding Gold on the Silver Screen" by Bob Bittner was originally published as "How to Find Gold on the Silver Screen" in HIS magazine, March 1985. Copyright © 1985 Bob Bittner. Used by permission.

The chapter "Tuning in: The Truth about Rock 'n' Roll" by Steve Lawhead is adapted from *Rock of This Age* by Steve Lawhead (Downers Grove, Ill.: InterVarsity Press, 1987). Copyright © 1987 Steve Lawhead. Used by permission.

The chapter "Winning the Dating Game" by Jean Stapleton and Richard Bright was excerpted from *Equal Dating* by Jean Stapleton and Richard Bright (Nashville, Tenn.: Abingdon Press, 1979). Copyright © 1979 Abingdon Press. Used by permission.

The chapter "Handling Sex and Intimacy" by Rebecca L. Propst was originally published as "Sex and Intimacy" in HIS magazine, January 1983. Copyright © 1983 Rebecca L. Propst. Used by permission.

The chapter "Are You Addicted to Love?" by Verne Becker was originally published in HIS magazine, December 1986. Copyright © 1986 Verne Becker. Used by permission.

The chapter "Popping the Right Questions . . . Before You Marry" by Alvin Lewis was originally published as "Popping the Right Questions . . . Before You Tie the Knot" in HIS magazine, March 1985. Copyright © 1985 Alvin Lewis. Used by permission.

The chapter "Making Friends for Life" by Joan Wulff Duchossois was originally published as "How's Your Friend Life?" in HIS magazine, October 1981. Copyright © 1981 Joan Wulff Duchossois. Used by permission.

The chapter "Dealing with a Difficult Roommate" by John Throop was originally published as "Clash of the Roommates" in HIS magazine, February 1986. Copyright © 1986 John Throop. Used by permission.

The chapter "Making a Good Roommate Relationship Better" by Andrés Tapia was originally published as "Making a Good Relationship Better" in HIS magazine, February 1986. Copyright © 1986 Andrés Tapia. Used by permission.

The chapter "You Know It's Time to Change Roommates When . . ." by Rob Suggs was originally published in HIS magazine, February 1986. Copyright © 1986 Rob Suggs. Used by permission.

The chapter "Reaching Out to International Students" by Jane Hopson and Andrés Tapia was originally published as "The World on Your Campus" in U magazine, February 1987. Copyright © 1987 Jane Hopson and Andrés Tapia. Used by permission.

The chapter "Scared Stiff in North America" by Aye-Tee Teo Monaco was originally published in HIS magazine, November 1985. Copyright © 1985 Aye-Tee Teo Monaco. Used by permission.

The chapter "Overcoming Racial Barriers" by Bobby Gross was originally published as "Racism with a Smile" in HIS magazine, February 1985. Copyright © 1985 Bobby Gross. Used by permission.

The chapter "Learning to Talk to Your Parents About . . ." by John Throop was originally published as "How to Talk to Your Parents About . . ." in HIS magazine, January 1986. Copyright © 1986 John Throop. Used by permission.

The chapter "Rules for Resolving Conflicts" by Robert Burdett was originally published as "Resolving Conflicts with Your Parents" in HIS magazine, December 1986. Copyright © 1986 Robert Burdett. Used by permission.

The chapter "Praying (When You Have a Million Other Things to Do)" by Chua Wee Hian was originally published as "Shall We Pray?" in HIS magazine, November 1981. Copyright © 1981 Chua Wee Hian. Used by permission.

The chapter "The Art of Listening to God" by Verne Becker was originally published as two articles, "Silent Spots" and "How to Listen," in HIS magazine, December 1986. Copyright © 1986 Verne Becker. Used by permission.

The chapter "Rediscovering Your Bible" by Tim Cummings was originally published as "Reading Scripture Won't Change Your Life—But Applying It Will" in HIS magazine, May 1984. Copyright © 1984 Tim Cummings. Used by permission.

The chapter "Sure-Fire Ways to Promote Your Fellowship Group" by Rob Suggs was originally published in HIS magazine, October 1983. Copyright © 1983 Rob Suggs. Used by permission.

The chapter "Putting Together a Successful Small Group" by Michael Wiebe was originally published as "The Anatomy of a Small Group" in HIS magazine, May 1976. Copyright © 1976 Michael Wiebe. Used by permission.

The chapter "Getting to Church: Is It Worth the Effort?" by Michael Pountney was originally published as "Who Needs the Church at First and Main? (When Your Campus Fellowship Is So Much Fun)" in HIS magazine, January 1985. Copyright © 1985 Michael Pountney. Used by permission.

The chapters "Is Your Group a Cult?" and "Christian Fringe Groups" by Robert M. Kachur were originally published in U magazine, May 1987. Copyright © 1987 Robert M. Kachur. Used by permission.

The chapter "Telling the Truth: Evangelism on Campus" by Terrell Smith was originally published as "How to Develop an Evangelistic Lifestyle" in HIS Guide to Evangelism (Downers Grove, Ill.: InterVarsity Press, 1977). Copyright © 1977 InterVarsity Christian Fellowship of the USA. Used by permission.

The chapter "Launching an Evangelistic Bible Study" by Betsy Rossen Elliot was originally published in U magazine, January 1987. Copyright © 1987 Betsy Rossen Elliot. Used by permission.

The chapters "Translating Your Faith into Social Action" and "Help Wanted: Social Action Organizations Who Need You" by Anthony Campolo are taken from Ideas for Social Action by Anthony Campolo (Grand Rapids, Mich.: Zondervan, 1983). Copyright © 1983 Youth Specialities. Used by permission.

The chapter "Trusting God's Will" by Paul Little is taken from the booklet Affirming God's Will by Paul Little (Downers Grove, Ill.: InterVarsity Press, 1971). Copyright © 1971 Paul Little. Used by permission.

The chapter "Discovering Your Vocation" by Tom Sine was originally published as "Get with the Program!" in HIS magazine, October 1982. Copyright © 1982 Tom Sine. Used by permission.

The chapter "Understanding What Makes a Job 'Christian': Five Myths" by Dave Veerman was originally published in HIS magazine, October 1986. Copyright © 1986 Dave Veerman. Used by permission.

The chapter "Getting Started in a Missionary Career" by W. Terry Whalin was originally published as "Missionary Careers: Getting Started" in **U** magazine, February 1987. Copyright © 1987 W. Terry Whalin. Used by permission.

The chapter "Snagging Your First Job: Résumés, Letters and Interviews" by Dick Staub and Jeff Trautman was adapted from Intercristo's *Career Kit*. (For more information on Intercristo, call toll-free 1-800-426-1342, or write Intercristo, The Career and Human Resource Specialists, 19303 Fremont Avenue North, Seattle, WA 98133.) Used by permission.

A

her beauty spots. And Carlitos was suffering because of that, he thinks, his anguish, his serenity all depended on that.

"She made me sleep on the rug," Santiago said. "My body doesn't ache from the accident but from that hard floor you've got at your place."

Carlitos and China stayed and chatted for about an hour, and as soon as they left the nurse came in. She had a malicious smile hovering on her lips, and a devilish look.

"Well, well, such girl friends as you've got," she said as she arranged the pillows. "Isn't that María Antonieta Pons who was just here one of the Bim-Bam-Booms?"

"Don't tell me that you've seen the Bim-Bam-Booms too?" Santiago said.

"I've seen pictures of them," she said; and let out a little serpentine laugh. "Is that Ada Rosa another one of the Bim-Bam-Booms?"

"Ah, you were spying on us." Santiago laughed. "Did we use a lot of dirty words?"

"A whole lot, especially that María Antonieta Pons. I had to cover my ears," the nurse said. "And your little friend, the one who made you sleep on the floor, does she have the same kind of garbage-can mouth?"

"Even worse than this one," Santiago said. "She's nothing to me, she didn't give me a tumble."

"With that saintly little face, no one would have ever thought you were a wild one," she said, breaking up with laughter.

"Are they going to discharge me tomorrow?" Santiago asked. "I don't feel like spending Saturday and Sunday here."

"Don't you like my company?" she asked. "I'll stay with you, what more could you want. I'm on duty this weekend. But now that I see you hang out with chorus girls, I don't trust you anymore."

"And what have you got against chorus girls?" Santiago asked. "Aren't they women just like any others?"

"Are they?" she said, her eyes sparkling. "What are chorus girls like, what do they do? Tell me, you know them so well."

It had started like that, gone on like that, Zavalita: jokes, games. You thought what a flirt she is, lucky to have her there, she helped kill time, you thought too bad she isn't prettier. Why her, Zavalita? She kept

497

coming into the room, bringing meals, and she would stay and chat until the head nurse or nun came and then she would start adjusting the sheets or would stick the thermometer into your mouth and put on a comical professional expression. She would laugh, she loved to tease you, Zavalita. It was impossible to know if her terrible, universal curiosity— how did a person get to be a newspaperman, what was it like being a newspaperman, how were stories written—was sincere or strategic, if her flirting was disinterested and sporting or if she really had zeroed in on you or whether you, the way she was with you, were only helping her kill time. She'd been born in Ica, she lived near the Plaza Bolognesi, she'd finished nursing school a few months before, she was serving her internship at La Maison de Santé. She was talkative and obliging, she sneaked him cigarettes and loaned him newspapers. On Friday the doctor said that the tests were not satisfactory and that the specialist was going to have a look at him. The name of the specialist was Mascaró, and after glancing apathetically at the x-ray pictures, he said they're no good, take some new ones. Carlitos appeared at dusk on Saturday with a package under his arm, sober and very sad: yes, they'd had a fight, this time it's over for good. He'd brought some Chinese food, Zavalita, they wouldn't throw him out, would they? The nurse got them some plates and silverware, chatted with them and even tried a little of the fried rice. When visiting hours were over, she let Carlitos stay a while longer and offered to sneak him out. Carlitos had also brought some liquor in a small bottle without a label, and with the second drink he began to curse *La Crónica,* China, Lima and the world and Ana was looking at him scandalized. At ten o'clock she made him leave. But she came back to take the plates away and, as she left, she winked at him from the door: I hope you dream about me. She left and Santiago could hear her laughing in the hall. On Monday the specialist examined the new x-rays and said disappointedly you're healthier than I am. Ana was off that day. You'd left her a note at the desk, Zavalita. Thanks so much for everything, he thinks, I'll give you a call one of these days.

6

"But what was that Don Hilario like?" Santiago asks. "Besides being a thief, I mean."

Ambrosio had come back a little tight from his first talk with Don Hilario Morales. The guy had acted stuck-up at first, he'd told Amalia, he saw my color and thought I didn't have a cent to my name. It hadn't occurred to him that Ambrosio was going to propose a business deal between equals, but that he'd come to beg for some little job. But maybe the man had come back tired from Tingo María, Ambrosio, maybe that's why he didn't give you a good reception. Maybe, Amalia: the first thing he'd done when he saw Ambrosio was to tell him, panting like a toad and pouring out curses, that the truck he brought back from Tingo María had been stopped eight times by washouts after the storm, and that the trip, God damn it, had taken thirty-five hours. Anyone else would have taken the initiative and said come on, I'll buy you a beer, but not Don Hilario, Amalia; although in that, Ambrosio had screwed him. Maybe the man didn't like to drink, Amalia had consoled him.

"A man of about fifty, son," Ambrosio says. "He was always picking his teeth."

Don Hilario had received him in his ancient spotted office on the Plaza de Armas without even telling him to have a seat. He'd left him waiting on his feet while he read the letter from Ludovico that Ambrosio had handed him, and only after he had finished reading it had he pointed to a chair, without friendliness, with resignation. He had looked him up and down and finally had deigned to open his mouth: how was that rascal of a Ludovico?

"Doing fine now, sir," Ambrosio had said. "After dreaming for so many years about getting on the regular list, he's finally made it. He's been going up the ladder and now he's subchief of the Homicide Division."

But Don Hilario didn't seem the least bit enthusiastic about the news, Amalia. He'd shrugged his shoulders, he'd scratched a black tooth with the nail of his little finger, which he kept very long, spat, and murmured who can figure him out. Because even though he was his nephew, Ludovico had been born dumb and a failure.

"And a stud horse, son," Ambrosio says. "Three homes in Pucallpa, each with its own woman and a mob of kids in all three of them."

"Well, tell me what I can do for you," Don Hilario had finally muttered. "What brings you to Pucallpa?"

499

"Looking for work, like Ludovico says in the letter," Ambrosio had said.

Don Hilario laughed with the croak of a parrot, shaking all over.

"Are you out of your mind?" he had said, scratching his tooth furiously. "This is the last place on earth to come to looking for work. Haven't you seen all those guys walking up and down the street with their hands in their pockets? Eighty percent of the people here are unemployed, there's no work to be had. Unless you want to go work with a hoe on some farm or work as a day laborer for the army men who are building the highway. But it's not easy and they're jobs that don't give you enough to eat. There's no future here. Get back to Lima as fast as you can go."

Ambrosio had felt like telling him to go to hell, Amalia, but he'd held back, smiled amiably, and that was where he'd screwed him: would he like to go somewhere and have a beer, sir? It was hot, why couldn't they have a little talk while they were drinking something cool, sir. He'd left him surprised with that invitation, Amalia, he'd realized that Ambrosio wasn't what he thought he was. They'd gone to the Calle Comercio, taken a small table at El Gallo de Oro, ordered two ice-cold beers.

"I didn't come to ask you for a job, sir," Ambrosio had said after the first sip, "But to make you a business proposition."

Don Hilario had drunk slowly, looking at him attentively. He'd put his glass down on the table, scratched the back of his neck with its greasy creases, spat into the street, watched the thirsty ground swallow his saliva.

"Aha," he had said slowly, nodding, and as if speaking to the halo of buzzing flies. "But in order to do business you need capital, my friend."

"I know that, sir," Ambrosio had said. "I've got a little money saved up. I wanted to see if you could help me invest it in something good. Ludovico told me my Uncle Hilario is a fox when it comes to business."

"You screwed him again there," Amalia had said, laughing.

"He became a different person," Ambrosio had said. "He began to treat me like a human being."

"Oh, that Ludovico," Don Hilario had rasped with a sudden good-natured air. "He told you the absolute truth. Some people are born to be aviators, others to be singers. I was born for business."

500

He'd smiled roguishly at Ambrosio: he was wise to have come to him, he would pilot him. They would find something where they could make a little money. And out of the blue: let's go to a Chinese restaurant, he was beginning to get hungry, how about it? All of a sudden as smooth as silk, see the way people are, Amalia?

"He lived in all three of them at the same time," Ambrosio says. "And later on I found out that he had a wife and kids in Tingo María too, just imagine, son."

"But you still haven't told me how much you've got saved up," Amalia had dared to ask.

"Twenty thousand soles," Don Fermín had said. "Yes, yours, for you. It will help you get started again, help you disappear, you poor devil. No crying, Ambrosio. Go on, on your way. God bless you, Ambrosio."

"He bought me a big meal and we had half a dozen beers," Ambrosio had said. "He paid for everything, Amalia."

"In business, the first thing is to know what you're dealing with," Don Hilario had said. "The same as in war. You have to know what forces you have to send into battle."

"My forces right now are fifteen thousand soles," Ambrosio had said. "I have more in Lima, and if the deal suits me, I can get that money later."

"It isn't too much," Don Hilario had reflected, two greedy fingers in his mouth. "But something can be done."

"With all that family I'm not surprised he was a thief," Santiago says.

Ambrosio would have liked something related to the Morales Transportation Co., sir, because he'd been a chauffeur, that was his field. Don Hilario had smiled, Amalia, encouraging him. He explained that the company had been started five years before with two vans, and that now it had two small trucks and three vans, the first for cargo and the second for passengers, which made up the Tingo María–Pucallpa line. Hard work, Ambrosio: the highway a disaster, it ruined tires and motors. But as he could see, he'd brought the business along.

"I was thinking about a secondhand pickup. I've got the down payment, the rest I'll pay off as I work."

"That's out, because you'd be in competition with me," Don Hilario had said with a friendly chuckle.

501

"Nothing is set yet," Ambrosio had said. "He said we've made the first contacts. We'll talk again tomorrow."

They'd seen each other the next day and the next and the one after that, and each time Ambrosio had come back to the cabin tight and with the smell of beer, stating that this Don Hilario turned out to be quite a boozer! At the end of a week they'd reached an agreement, Amalia: Ambrosio would drive one of Morales Transportation's buses with a base salary of five hundred plus ten percent of the fares, and he would go in as Don Hilario's partner in a little deal that was a sure thing. And Amalia, seeing that he was hesitating, what little deal?

"Limbo Coffins," Ambrosio had said, a little drunk. "We bought it for thirty thousand, Don Hilario says the price was a giveaway. I won't even have to look at the dead people, he's going to run the funeral parlor and give me my share of the profits every six months. Why are you making that face, what's wrong with it?"

"There's probably nothing wrong with it, but I have a funny feeling," Amalia had said. "Especially since the dead people are children."

"We'll make boxes for old people too," Ambrosio had said. "Don Hilario says it's the safest thing there is because people are always dying. We'll go fifty-fifty on the profits. He'll run the place and won't collect anything for that. What more could I want, isn't that so?"

"So you'll be traveling to Tingo María all the time now," Amalia had said.

"Yes, and I won't be able to keep an eye on the business," Ambrosio had answered. "You'll have to keep your eyes wide open, count all the coffins that come out. It's good we're so close by. You can keep an eye on it without leaving the house."

"All right," Amalia had said. "But it gives me a funny feeling."

"All in all, for months on end I did nothing but start up, put on the brakes, pick up speed," Ambrosio said. "I was driving the oldest thing on wheels in the world, son. It was called The Jungle Flash."

3

"So you were the first one to get married, son," Ambrosio says. "You set the example for your brother and sister."

From La Maison de Santé he went to the boardinghouse in Barranco to shave and change his clothes and then to Miraflores. It was only three in the afternoon, but he saw Don Fermín's car parked by the outside door. The butler received him with a grave face: the master and mistress had been worried because he hadn't come to lunch on Sunday, master. Teté and Sparky weren't there. He found Señora Zoila watching television in the little room she had fixed up under the stairway for the young people's Thursday canasta parties.

"It's about time," she muttered, raising her furrowed brow. "Have you come to see if we're still alive?"

He tried to break through her annoyance with jokes—you were in a good mood, Zavalita, free after being shut up in the hospital—but she, while she cast continuous involuntary glances at her soap opera, kept scolding him: they'd set a place for him on Sunday, Teté and Popeye and Sparky and Cary had waited until three o'clock for you, you ought to be more considerate to your father, who's not well. Knowing that he counts the days until he can see you, he thinks, knowing how upset he gets when you don't come. He thinks: he'd listened to the doctors, he wasn't going to the office, he was resting, you thought he was completely recovered. And still that afternoon you could see he wasn't, Zavalita. He

503

was in the study, alone, a blanket over his knees, sitting in the usual easy chair. He was thumbing through a magazine and when he saw Santiago come in he smiled at him with affectionate crossness. His skin, still tanned from the summer, had grown old, a strange tic had appeared on his face, and it was as if in a few days he had lost twenty pounds. He was tieless, with a corduroy jacket, and tufts of grayish fuzz peeped through the open collar of his shirt. Santiago sat down beside him.

"You're looking very well, papa," he said, kissing him. "How do you feel?"

"Better, but your mother and Sparky make me feel so useless," Don Fermín complained. "They only let me go to the office for a little while and make me take naps and spend hours here like an invalid."

"Only until you're completely recovered," Santiago said. "Then you can let yourself go, papa."

"I warned them that I'll only put up with this fossil routine until the end of the month," Don Fermín said. "On the first I'm going back to my normal life. Right now I don't even know how things are going."

"Let Sparky take care of them, papa," Santiago said. "He's doing all right, isn't he?"

"Yes, he's doing fine," Don Fermín said, nodding. "He practically runs everything. He's serious, he's got a good head on his shoulders. It's just that I can't resign myself to being a mummy."

"Who would have thought that Sparky would end up as a full-fledged businessman." Santiago laughed. "The way things turned out, it was a lucky thing he was kicked out of the Naval Academy."

"The one who's not doing so well is you, Skinny," Don Fermín said with the same affectionate tone and a touch of weariness. "Yesterday I stopped by your boardinghouse and Señora Lucía told me you hadn't been home to sleep for several days."

"I was in Trujillo, papa." He'd lowered his voice, he thinks, made a gesture as if saying just between you and me, your mother doesn't know anything. "They sent me off on an assignment. I was sent off in a hurry and didn't have time to let you know."

"You're too big for me to scold you or give you advice," Don Fermín said, with a softness both affectionate and sorrowful. "Besides, I know it wouldn't do any good."

504

"You can't think that I've set out purposely to live a bad life, papa," Santiago said, smiling.

"I've been getting alarming reports for some time," Don Fermín said, without changing his expression. "That you're seen in bars, nightclubs. And not the best places in Lima. But since you're so sensitive, I haven't dared ask you anything, Skinny."

"I go once in a while, like anybody else," Santiago said. "You know I'm not a carouser, papa. Don't you remember how mama used to have to force me to go to parties when I was a kid?"

"A kid?" Don Fermín laughed. "Do you feel so very old now?"

"You shouldn't pay any attention to people's gossip," Santiago said. "I may be a lot of things, but not that, papa."

"That's what I thought, Skinny," Don Fermín said after a long pause. "At first I thought let him have a little fun, it might even be good for him. But now it's been so many times that they come and tell me we saw him here, there, drinking, with the worst kind of people."

"I haven't got either the time or the money to go off on toots," Santiago said. "It's absurd, papa."

"I don't know what to think, Skinny." He'd grown serious, Zavalita, his voice had become grave. "You go from one extreme to the other, it's hard to understand you. Look, I think I'd rather have you end up as a Communist than as a drunkard and a carouser."

"Neither one, papa, you can rest assured," Santiago said. "It's been years since I've known what politics is all about. I read all the newspaper except for the political news. I don't know who's a minister or who's a senator. I even asked them not to send me out to cover political stories."

"You say that with a terrible resentment," Don Fermín murmured. "Are you that disturbed at not having dedicated yourself to bomb-throwing? Don't reproach me for it. I just gave you a piece of advice, that's all, and remember that you've been going against me all your life. If you didn't become a Communist it's because deep down you weren't so sure about it."

"You're right, papa," Santiago said. "Nothing bothers me, I never think about all that. I was just trying to calm you down. Neither a Communist nor a carouser, don't worry about it."

They talked about other things in the warm atmosphere of books and

505

wooden shelves in the study, watching the sun set, rarefied by the first mists of winter, listening to the voices from the soap opera in the distance, and, little by little, Don Fermín was mustering his courage to bring up the eternal theme and repeat the ceremony celebrated so many times: come back home, get your law degree, come to work for me.

"I know you don't like me to talk about it." It was the last time he tried, Zavalita. "I know I'm running the risk of driving you away from home again if I talk about it."

"Don't talk nonsense, papa," Santiago said.

"Aren't four years enough, Skinny?" Had he become resigned from that point on, Zavalita? "Haven't you done enough damage to yourself already, haven't you hurt us enough?"

"But I am registered, papa," Santiago said. "This year . . ."

"This year you're going to do a lot of talking, just like in past years." Or had he been cherishing to the bitter end, secretly, the hope that you'd come back, Zavalita? "I don't believe you anymore, Skinny. You register, but you don't set foot in the university or take any exams."

"I've been very busy the past few years," Santiago insisted. "But now I'm going to start going to classes. I have my schedule all made out so I can get to bed early and . . ."

"You've got used to staying up late, to your paltry little salary, to your carousing friends on the newspaper, and that's your life." Without anger, without bitterness, Zavalita, with a tender affliction. "How can I stop repeating to you that it can't be, Skinny? You're not what you're trying to show yourself as being. You can't go on being a mediocrity, son."

"You've got to believe me, papa," Santiago said. "I swear that this time it's true. I'll go to class, I'll take the exams."

"I'm not asking it for your sake now, but for mine." Don Fermín leaned over, put his hand on his arm. "Let's arrange a schedule which will let you study and you'll make more than at *La Crónica*. It's time you got to know all about things. I might drop dead anytime and then you and Sparky will have to keep things going at the office. Your father needs you, Santiago."

He wasn't furious or hopeful or anxious as on other occasions, Zavalita. He was depressed, he thinks, he repeated the standard phrases out of routine or stubbornness, like someone betting his last reserves on

506

one last hand, knowing that he's going to lose that one too. He had a disheartened glow in his eyes and clasped his hands together under the blanket.

"I'd only get in your way at the office, papa," Santiago said. "It would be a real problem for you and Sparky. I'd feel that you were paying me a salary as a favor. Besides, stop talking about dropping dead. You told me yourself that you never felt better."

Don Fermín lowered his head for a few seconds, then he raised his face and smiled, in a resigned way: it was all right, he didn't want to try your patience anymore by harping on the same thing, Skinny. He thinks: just to tell you that it would be the happiest moment of my life if one day you came through that door and told me I've quit my job at the paper, papa. But he stopped talking because Señora Zoila had come in, pushing a little wagon with toast and tea. Well, the soap opera was over at last, and she began to talk about Popeye and Teté. She was concerned, he thinks, Popeye wanted to get married the following year but Teté was still a child, she advised them to wait a little while longer. Your old mother doesn't want to be a grandmother yet, Don Fermín joked. What about Sparky and his girl friend, mama? Ah, Cary was very nice, charming, she lived in La Punta, she could speak English. And so serious, so proper. They were talking about getting married next year too.

"At least, in spite of all your crazy things, you haven't got there yet," Señora Zoila said cautiously. "I don't imagine that you're thinking about getting married, are you?"

"But you probably have a girl friend," Don Fermín said. "Who is she? Tell us. We won't say anything to Teté so she won't drive you crazy."

"I don't, papa," Santiago said. "I swear I don't."

"But you ought to, what are you waiting for?" Don Fermín said. "You don't want to end up an old bachelor like poor Clodomiro."

"Teté got married a few months after I did," Santiago says. "Sparky a little over a year later."

19

I knew he'd come, Queta thought. But she thought it incredible that he would have dared. It was after midnight, impossible to move. Malvina was drunk and Robertito was sweating. Hazy in the half-light, poisoned

507

by smoke and cha-cha-cha, the couples were swaying in place. From time to time, Queta could catch the saucy laughter of Malvina at different places along the bar or in the small parlor or in the upstairs rooms. He stayed in the doorway, large and frightened, with his loud, striped brown jacket and his red tie, his eyes going back and forth. Looking for you, Queta thought, amused.

"Madame doesn't allow niggers in here," Martha said beside her. "Get him out, Robertito."

"He's Bermúdez' strong-arm man," Robertito said. "I'll go see. Madame will decide."

"Get him out, whoever he is," Martha said. "It'll give the place a bad name. Get him out of here."

The boy with a shadow of a mustache and a fancy vest who had asked her to dance three times in a row without saying a word to her came back over to Queta and managed to say with anguish shall we go up? Yes, pay me for the room and go on up, it was number twelve, she'd get the key. She made her way through the people dancing, faced the black man and saw his eyes: burning, frightened. What did he want, who had sent him here? He looked away, looked at her again, and all she heard was good evening.

"Señora Hortensia," he whispered, with a shamed voice, averting his eyes. "She's been waiting for you to call her."

"I've been busy." She didn't send you, he didn't know how to lie, you came because of me. "Tell her I'll call tomorrow."

She took half a turn, went upstairs, and while she was asking Ivonne for the key to number twelve, she thought he'll go away but he'll be back. He'd be waiting for her in the street, one day he'd follow her, finally he'd get his courage up and he'd come over, trembling. She came down a half hour later and saw him sitting at the bar with his back to the couples in the salon. He was drinking, looking at the figures with protuberant breasts that Robertito had sketched on the walls with colored chalk; his white eyes were rolling around in the shadows, bright and intimidated, and the nails on the hand that held the glass of beer seemed phosphorescent. He dared, Queta thought. She didn't feel surprised, she didn't care. But Martha did, she was dancing and grunted did you see? when Queta passed by her, now they're letting niggers in. She said good-bye at the door to the boy in the vest, went back to the bar and Robertito was serving the black man another beer. There were still a lot of men without partners, crowded together and standing, looking, and Malvina couldn't be heard anymore. She crossed the dance floor, a hand pinched her on the hip and she smiled without stopping, but before she reached the bar, a puffy face with musty eyes and shaggy brows was interposed: let's dance.

"The lady's with me, mister," the black man's strangled voice mumbled; he was beside the lamp and the shade with its green stars was touching his shoulder.

"I got there first." The other one hesitated, looking at the long, motionless body. "But it's O.K., let's not fight over her."

"I'm not with him, I'm with you," Queta said, taking the man by the hand. "Come on, let's dance."

She pulled him onto the dance floor, laughing inside, thinking how many beers to get his courage up? thinking I'm going to teach you a lesson, you'll see, you'll see. She danced and felt her partner stumbling, unable to follow the music, and she saw the musty eyes out of control as they watched the black man, who, still standing, was now looking carefully at the drawings on the wall and the people in the corners. The number was over and the man wanted to withdraw. He couldn't be afraid of the darky, could he? they could dance another one. Let go, it had gotten late, he had to leave. Queta laughed, let go of him, went to sit on one of the bar stools and an instant later the black man was beside her. Without looking at him, she felt his face falling apart with confusion, his thick lips opening.

"Is it my turn yet?" he said heavily. "Could we dance now?"

She looked into his eyes, serious, and saw him lower his head at once.

"And what happens if I tell Cayo Shithead?" Queta asked.

"He's not here," he babbled, without looking up, without moving. "He's gone on a trip to the South."

"And what happens if, when he gets back, I tell him you came and wanted to get involved with me?" Queta insisted patiently.

"I don't know," the black man said softly. "Probably nothing. Or he'll fire me. Or he'll have me arrested or something worse."

He looked up for a second, as if begging spit on me if you want to, but don't tell him, Queta thought and he looked away. Was it a lie, then, that the crazy woman had sent him on that errand?

"It's the truth," the black man said; he hesitated a moment and added, still hanging his head, "But she didn't tell me to stay."

Queta began to laugh and the black man raised his eyes: burning, white, hopeful, startled. Robertito had come over and mutely questioned Queta by pursing his lips; she told him with a look that everything was all right.

"If you want to talk to me you have to order something," she said and ordered. "Vermouth for me."

"Bring the lady a vermouth," the black man repeated. "For me the same as before."

Queta saw Robertito's half-smile as he went away and she caught Martha at the other end of the dance floor, looking at her in indignation over the shoulder of her partner, and she saw the excited and censorious eyes of the single men in the corner fastened on her and the black man. Robertito brought the beer and the glass of weak tea and as he left he winked at her as if telling her I'm sorry for you or don't blame me.

"I can see," the black man murmured, "you don't like me at all."

"Not because you're black, I don't give a damn about that," Queta said. "It's because you're a servant of that disgusting Cayo Shithead."

"I'm not anybody's servant," the black man said calmly. "I'm only his chauffeur."

"His strong-arm man," Queta said. "Does the other fellow in the car with you belong to the police? Do you belong to the police too?"

"Yes, Hinostroza belongs to the police," the black man said. "But I'm only his chauffeur."

"If you want, you can go tell Cayo Shithead that I say he's disgusting." Queta smiled.

"He wouldn't like that," he said slowly, with respectful humor. "Don Cayo is very proud. I won't tell him, don't you tell him I came either and that way we'll be even."

Queta let out a loud laugh: burning, white, greedy, relieved but still insecure and fearful. What was his name? Ambrosio Pardo and he knew that her name was Queta.

"Is it true that Cayo Shithead and old Ivonne are partners now?"

510

Queta asked. "That your boss owns all this too now?"

"How should I know?" he murmured; and insisted, with soft firmness, "He's not my boss, he's my employer."

Queta drank a sip of cold tea, made a face of disgust, quickly emptied the glass on the floor, took the glass of beer and while Ambrosio's eyes spun toward her in surprise, took a little drink.

"I'm going to tell you something," Queta said. "I shit on your boss. I'm not afraid of him. I shit on Cayo Shithead."

"Not even if you had diarrhea," he dared whisper. "We'd better not talk about Don Cayo, this conversation is getting dangerous."

"Have you gone to bed with that crazy woman Hortensia?" Queta asked and saw terror suddenly flower in the black man's eyes.

"How could you think such a thing," he babbled, stupefied. "Don't repeat that even as a joke."

"Then how do you dare to want to go to bed with me?" Queta asked, looking for his eyes.

"Because you," Ambrosio stammered, and his voice was cut off; he put his beer down, confused. "Do you want another vermouth?"

"How many beers did it take to get your courage up?" Queta asked, amused.

"A lot, I lost count." Queta heard him chuckle, speak in a more intimate voice. "Not only beers, even *capitanes.* I came last night too, but I didn't come in. Today I did because the mistress gave me that errand."

"All right," Queta said. "Order me another vermouth and leave. You'd better not come back."

Ambrosio rolled his eyes at Robertito: another vermouth, mister. Queta saw Robertito holding back his laughter, and in the distance, the faces of Ivonne and Malvina looking at her with curiosity.

"Negroes are good dancers, I hope you are too," Queta said. "For one single time in your life, let me do you the honor of dancing with you."

He helped her off the stool. He was looking into her eyes now with a doglike and almost weepy gratitude. He barely put his arm around her and didn't try to get close. No, he didn't know how to dance, or he couldn't, he barely moved and he had no rhythm. Queta felt the experienced fingertips on her back, his arm holding her with fearful care.

511

"Don't hold me so tight," she joked, amused. "Dance like a human being."

But he didn't understand and instead of getting closer, he drew back an inch or two more, murmuring something. What a coward he is, Queta thought, almost with feeling. While she was spinning, humming, moving her hands in the air and changing step, he, rocking gracelessly where he stood, had an expression as amusing as the carnival masks that Robertito had hung from the ceiling. They went back to the bar and she ordered another vermouth.

"It wasn't very bright of you to come here," Queta said in a friendly way. "Ivonne or Robertito or somebody will tell Cayo Shithead and you'll probably get into trouble."

"Do you think so?" he whispered, looking around with a stupid expression. The poor idiot had figured everything out except that, Queta thought, you've ruined his night.

"Of course," she said. "Can't you see that they all tremble in front of him the way you do? Can't you see that it seems that he's Ivonne's partner now? Are you so dumb that that didn't occur to you?"

"I wanted to go upstairs with you," he stammered: his eyes burning, sparkling in the leaden face, over the broad nose with wide-open nostrils, his lips parted, the very white teeth gleaming, his voice run through with fright. "Could we?" And getting even more frightened: "How much would it cost?"

"You'd have to work for months to be able to go to bed with me." Queta smiled and looked at him with compassion.

"What if I did," he insisted. "What if it was just once. Could we?"

"We could for five hundred soles," Queta said, looking him over, making him lower his eyes, smiling. "Plus the room, which is fifty. You can see, it's out of range of your pocket."

The whites of his eyes rolled for a second, his lips tightened together, crushed. But the big hand rose up and pointed pitifully at Robertito, who was at the other end of the bar: that fellow had said the price was two hundred.

"The price of the other girls. I've got my own price," Queta said. "But if you've got two hundred you can go upstairs with any of them. Except

512

Martha, the one in yellow. She doesn't like blacks. Well, pay your bill and go ahead."

She saw him remove some bills from his wallet, pay Robertito and take the change with a remorseful and meditative face.

"Tell the madwoman I'll call her," Queta said in a friendly way. "Go ahead, go to bed with one of those, they charge two hundred. Don't be afraid, I'll talk to Ivonne and she won't say anything to Cayo Shithead."

"I don't want to go to bed with any of them," he murmured. "I'd rather leave."

She accompanied him to the small garden by the entrance and there he suddenly stopped, turned around, and in the reddish light of the street lamp, Queta saw him hesitate, raise, lower and raise his eyes, struggle with his tongue until he managed to babble: he still had two hundred soles left.

"If you keep on insisting, I'm going to get mad," Queta said. "Go on, get on your way."

"For a kiss?" he choked, confused. "Could we?"

He waved his long arms as if he were going to hang from a tree, put one hand into his pocket, drew a quick circle and Queta saw the bills. She saw them come down to her hand and without her knowing how, they were already there, wrinkled and crushed between her own fingers. He cast a glance inside and she saw him lean his heavy head over and felt a sticky sucker fish on her throat. He embraced her furiously but didn't try to kiss her on the mouth, and as soon as he felt her resist, he drew back.

"All right, it was worth it," she heard him say, smiling, and she recognized the two white coals dancing in his eye sockets. "Someday I'm going to get that five hundred."

He opened the gate and left and Queta remained for a moment looking in astonishment at the two blue banknotes that were dancing about between her fingers.

9

Rough drafts written up and thrown into the wastebasket, he thinks, weeks and months that were rough drafts and thrown into . . . There they

513

were, Zavalita: the static city room with its recurrent gab and gossip, the swirling conversations with Carlitos in the Negro-Negro, the thieflike visits to nightclub bars. How many times had Carlitos and China become friends, quarreled and made up? When had Carlitos' drunken benders become one single chronic bender? In that gelatin of days, those jellyfish months, those liquid years that slithered out of his memory, only a very thin thread to cling to. He thinks: Ana. They'd gone out together a week after Santiago had left La Maison de Santé and they went to the Cine San Martín to see a movie with Columba Domínguez and Pedro Armendáriz and ate some sausages at a German restaurant on Colmena; the following Thursday, chili con carne at the Cream Rica on the Jirón de la Unión and a bullfighting movie at the Excelsior. Then everything fell apart and became confused, Zavalita, tea near the Palace of Justice, walks through Parque de la Exposición, until, suddenly, in a winter of fine mist and sticky fog, that anodyne relationship made up of cheap menus and Mexican melodramas and plays on words had taken on a vague stability. There was the Neptuno, Zavalita: the dim locale of dream-walking rhythms, its ominous couples dancing in the shadows, the phosphorescent little stars on the walls, its smell of drinks and adultery. You were worried about the bill, you made your glass endure like a miser, you were calculating. There you kissed for the first time, pushed by the lack of light, he thinks, the music and the silhouettes feeling each other in the shadows: I love you, Anita. There your surprise on feeling her body letting itself go against yours, I love you too, Santiago, there the juvenile avidity of her mouth and the desire that swallowed you up. They kissed at length as they danced, they kept on kissing at the table, and in the taxi, when he took her home, Ana let her breasts be fondled without protesting. No wisecracks the whole night, he thinks. It had been a listless and semiclandestine romance, Zavalita. Ana insisted on your coming to her home for lunch and you never were able, you had a story to cover, a meeting, next week, another day. One evening Carlitos ran into them in the Haití on the Plaza de Armas and he looked surprised at seeing them holding hands and Ana leaning on Santiago's shoulder. It had been their first fight, Zavalita. Why hadn't you introduced her to your family, why don't you want to meet mine, why haven't you even said anything to your best friend, are you ashamed to be going with me?

They were at the door of La Maison de Santé and it was cold and you felt bored: now I know why you like Mexican melodramas so much, Anita. She gave a half-turn and went into the hospital without saying good-bye.

The first days after that fight he'd felt a vague unrest, a quiet nostalgia. Love, Zavalita? Then you'd never been in love with Aída, he thinks. Or had that worm in the guts you felt years ago been love? He thinks: never with Ana then, Zavalita. He started going out with Carlitos and Milton and Solórzano and Norwin again: one night he joked with them about his affair with Ana and made up the story that they were going to bed together. Then one day, before going to the paper, he got off the bus at the stop by the Palace of Justice and made an appearance at the hospital. Without premeditation, he thinks, as if by chance. They made up in the entranceway, among people who were coming and going, without even touching hands, talking in secret, looking into each other's eyes. I was wrong Anita, I was the one who was wrong, Santiago, you don't know how upset I've Anita, and I cried every Santiago. They met again at nightfall in a Chinese café with drunks and a sawdust-covered tile floor, and they talked for hours without letting go of their hands over the untouched cups of coffee. But you should have told her before, Santiago, how was she to know that you weren't getting along with your family, and he told her again, the university, the group, *La Crónica,* the tight cordiality with his parents and his brother and sister. Everything except about Aída, Zavalita, except about Ambrosio, about the Muse. Why had you told her your life story? From then on they saw each other almost every day and they'd made love a week or a month after, one night, at a shack-up house in the Margaritas development. There was her body, so thin you could count the bones of her back, her frightened eyes, her shame and your confusion when you discovered she was a virgin. He'll never take you here again Anita, he loved you Anita. From then on they made love at the boardinghouse in Barranco, once a week on the afternoon that Doña Lucía went visiting. There that anxious frightened love on Wednesdays, Ana's weeping remorse every time she remade the bed, Zavalita.

Don Fermín was putting in an occasional appearance at the office again and Santiago lunched with them on Sundays. Señora Zoila had

515

allowed Popeye and Teté to announce their engagement and Santiago promised to come to the party. It was Saturday, his day off at *La Crónica*, Ana was on duty. He sent his most presentable suit out to be cleaned, he shined his own shoes, put on a clean shirt, and at eight-thirty a taxi took him to Miraflores. A sound of voices and music poured over the garden wall and came into the street, maids in shawls were looking into the inside of the house from neighboring balconies. Cars were parked on both sides of the street, some on the sidewalk, and you went ahead hugging the wall, avoiding the door, suddenly undecided, lacking the urge to ring the bell or to leave. Through the garage gate he saw a corner of the garden: a small table with a white cloth, a butler standing guard, couples chatting around the pool. But the main body of guests were in the living room and the dining room and through the window shades one could make out their figures. The music and talking was coming from inside. He recognized the face of that aunt, this cousin, and faces that looked ghostly. Suddenly Uncle Clodomiro appeared and went to sit in the rocker in the garden, alone. There he was, hands and knees together, looking at the girls in high heels, the boys with neckties who were starting to come up to the table with the white cloth. They passed in front of him and he smiled at them eagerly. What were you doing there, Uncle Clodomiro, why did you come where nobody knew you, where those who did know you didn't like you? To show that in spite of the snubs they gave you that you were a member of the family, that you had a family? he thinks. He thinks: in spite of everything, did the family matter to you, did you love the family that didn't love you? Or was solitude even worse than humiliation, uncle? He had already decided not to go in, but he didn't leave. A car stopped by the door and he saw two girls get out, holding onto their coiffures and waiting for the one driving to park and come along. You knew him, he thinks: Tony, the same little dancing brush on his forehead, the same parrot laugh. The three of them went into the house laughing and there the absurd impression that they were laughing at you, Zavalita. There those sudden savage desires to see Ana. From the store on the corner he explained to Teté by phone that he couldn't get away from *La Crónica*: he'd come by tomorrow and give my brother-in-law a hug for me. Oh, you're always such a wet blanket, Superbrain, how could you pull a stunt like that on them. He called Ana, went to see her, and they talked for a while at the entrance to La Maison de Santé.

A few days later she had called *La Crónica* with a hesitant voice: she had some bad news for you, Santiago. He waited for her at a Chinese café and saw her coming all huddled up in a coat over her uniform, her face long: they were moving to Ica, love. Her father had been named director of a school system there, maybe she could get a job at the Workers' Hospital there. It hadn't seemed so serious to you, Zavalita, and you had consoled her: you'd go see her every week, she could come here too, Ica was so close by.

19

The first day he went to work as a driver for Morales Transportation, before leaving for Tingo María Ambrosio had taken Amalia and Amalita Hortensia for a little drive through the bumpy streets of Pucallpa in the dented little blue truck that was all patched up, with mudguards and bumpers tied on with ropes so they wouldn't say good-bye at some pothole.

"Compared to the cars I've driven here it was something to weep over," Ambrosio says. "And still, the months I drove The Jungle Flash were happy ones, son."

The Jungle Flash had been fitted out with wooden benches and there was room for twelve passengers if they squeezed together. The lazy life of the first weeks had been replaced by an active routine from then on: Amalia would feed him, put his lunch in the glove compartment of the vehicle and Ambrosio, wearing a T-shirt, a visor cap, ragged pants and rubber-soled sandals, would leave for Tingo María at eight in the morning. Since he'd been traveling, Amalia had picked up on religion again after so many years, pushed a little by Doña Lupe, who had given her some holy pictures for the walls and had dragged her off to Sunday mass. If there wasn't any flooding and the vehicle didn't break down, Ambrosio would get to Tingo María at six in the afternoon; he would sleep on a mattress under the counter at Morales Transportation, and the next day he would leave for Pucallpa at eight o'clock. But that schedule had rarely been kept, he was always getting stuck on the road and there were trips that took all day. The engine was tired, Amalia, it kept stopping to get

517

its strength back. He would arrive home covered with dirt from head to toe and weary unto death. He would flop down on the bed and, while she got him his dinner, he, smoking, using one arm as a pillow, peaceful, exhausted, would tell her about his wiles in fixing the motor, the passengers he'd carried, and the bills he was going to give to Don Hilario. And what he enjoyed most, Amalia, his bets with Pantaleón. Thanks to those bets the trips were less boring, even though the passengers were pissing with fright. Pantaleón drove The Highway Superman, a bus that belonged to Pucallpa Transport, the rival company of Morales Transportation. They left at the same time and they raced, not just to win the ten soles of the wager, but, most of all, to get ahead and pick up passengers who were going from one village to the next, traveling between farms along the way.

"Those passengers who don't buy any tickets," he'd told Amalia, "the ones who aren't customers of Morales Transportation but of Ambrosio Pardo Transportation."

"What if Don Hilario finds out about it someday?" Amalia had asked him.

"Bosses know how things are," Pantaleón had explained to him, Amalia. "And they play dumb because they get their revenge by paying us starvation wages. A thief robbing from a thief will never run on a reef, brother, you know all about it."

In Tingo María Pantaleón had gotten himself a widow who didn't know he had a wife and three children in Pucallpa, but sometimes he didn't go to the widow's but ate with Ambrosio in a cheap restaurant called La Luz del Día, and sometimes afterward to a brothel with skeletons who charged three soles. Ambrosio went with him out of friendship, he couldn't understand why Pantaleón liked those women, he wouldn't have got mixed up with them even if they'd paid him. Really, Ambrosio? Really, Amalia: squat, fat-bellied, ugly. Besides, he was so tired when he got there that even if he wanted to cheat on you, his body wouldn't respond, Amalia.

During the early days Amalia had been very serious in spying on Limbo Coffins. Nothing had changed since the funeral parlor changed hands. Don Hilario never went to the place; the same employee as before was still there, a boy with a sickly-looking face who spent the day sitting on the porch looking stupidly at the buzzards who were sunning themselves on the roofs of the hospital and the morgue. The single room of the funeral parlor was filled with coffins, most of them small and white. They were rough, rustic, only an occasional one planed down and waxed. During the first week one coffin had been sold. A barefoot man without a jacket but with a black tie and a remorseful face went into Limbo Coffins and came out a short time later carrying a little box on his shoulder. He passed by Amalia and she crossed herself. The second week there hadn't been a sale; the third week a couple, one for a child and one for an adult. It didn't seem like much of a business, Amalia. Ambrosio had begun to grow uneasy.

After a month Amalia had grown careless in her vigilance. She wasn't going to spend her life in the cabin door with Amalita Hortensia in her arms, especially since coffins were carried away so rarely. She'd made friends with Doña Lupe, they would spend hours chatting, they ate lunch and dinner together, took strolls around the square, along the Calle Comercio, by the docks. On the hottest days they went down to the river to swim in their nightgowns and then had shaved ice at Wong's Ice Cream Parlor. Ambrosio relaxed on Sundays: he slept all morning and after lunch he would go out with Pantaleón to watch the soccer games in the stadium on the road to Yarinacocha. At night they would leave Amalita Hortensia with Señora Lupe and go to the movies. People on the street already knew them and said hello. Doña Lupe came and went in the cabin as if she owned it; once she'd caught Ambrosio naked, having a bucket bath in the backyard, and Amalia had died laughing. They also went to Doña Lupe's whenever they wanted to, they loaned each other things. When he came to Pucallpa, Doña Lupe's husband would come out and sit by the street with them at night to get some air. He was an old man who only opened his mouth to talk about his little farm and his debts to the Land Bank.

"I think I'm happy now," Amalia had told Ambrosio one day. "I've already gotten used to it here. And you don't seem as grumpy as you were at the start."

"You can see that you're used to it," Ambrosio had answered. "You go around barefoot and with your umbrella, you're already a jungle girl. Yes, I'm happy too."

519

"Happy because I don't think about Lima very much anymore," Amalia had said. "I almost never dream about the mistress anymore, I almost never think about the police."

"When you first got here, I thought how can she live with him," Doña Lupe had said one day. "Now I can tell you that you were lucky to get him. All the women in the neighborhood would like to have him for a husband, black as he is."

Amalia had laughed: it was true, he was behaving very well with her, much better than in Lima, and he even showed his affection for Amalita Hortensia. His spirits had become very merry of late and she hadn't had a fight with him since they'd been in Pucallpa.

"Happy, but only to a point," Ambrosio says. "What wasn't working out was the money question, son."

Ambrosio had thought that thanks to the extras he was getting without Don Hilario's knowing it, they'd get through the month. But no, in the first place, there weren't many passengers, and in the second place, Don Hilario had come up with the idea that the cost of repairs should be split between the company and the driver. Don Hilario had gone crazy, Amalia, if he accepted that he'd be left without any pay. They'd argued and it was left at Ambrosio's paying ten percent of the repair bills. But Don Hilario had deducted fifteen the second month and when the spare tire was stolen, he'd wanted Ambrosio to pay for a new one. But that's awful, Don Hilario, how could he think of such a thing. Don Hilario had looked at him steadily: you better not complain, there was a lot that could be told about him, wasn't he picking up a few soles behind his back? Ambrosio hadn't known what to say, but Don Hilario had shaken his hand: friends again. They'd begun to get through the month with loans and advances that Don Hilario himself made grudgingly. Pantaleón, seeing that they were having trouble, had advised them to stop paying rent and come live in the settlement and build a cabin next to mine.

"No, Amalia," Ambrosio had said. "I don't want you to be alone when I'm on the road, with all the bums there are in the settlement. Besides, you couldn't keep an eye on Limbo Coffins from there."

4

"THE WISDOM OF WOMEN," Carlitos said. "If Ana had thought about it, it wouldn't have turned out so well for her. But she didn't think about it, women never premeditate these things. They let themselves be guided by instinct and it never lets them down, Zavalita."

Was it that benign, intermittent feeling of uneasiness that reappeared when Ana moved to Ica, Zavalita, that soft restlessness that would surprise you on buses as you figured out how many days left till Sunday? He had to change the luncheon dates at his parents' to Saturday. On Sunday he would leave very early in a group taxi that came by to pick him up at the boardinghouse. He would sleep the whole trip, he stayed with Ana until nightfall, and he would come back. Those weekly trips were bankrupting him, he thinks, Carlitos always paid for the beers at the Negro-Negro now. Was that love, Zavalita?

"Have it your own way, have it your own way," Carlitos said. "Have it your own way the both of you, Zavalita."

He'd finally met Ana's parents. Her father was a fat, loquacious Huancayan who had spent his life teaching history and Spanish in national high schools, and her mother was an aggressively pleasant mulatto woman. They had a house near the chipped stone courtyards of the Educational Unit and they received him with a noisy and affected hospitality. There were the bountiful lunches they inflicted on you on Sundays, there the anguished looks you exchanged with Ana, wondering when the

521

parade of courses was going to stop. When it was over, he and Ana would go out to stroll through the straight and always sunny streets, go into some movie to neck, have some refreshments on the square, come home to chat and exchange quick kisses in the little parlor filled with Indian pottery. Sometimes Ana would come to spend the weekend with relatives and they could go to bed together for a few hours in some small hotel downtown.

"I know that you're not asking me for advice," Carlitos said. "That's why I won't give you any."

It had been during one of those quick trips of Ana's to Lima, at the end of the afternoon by the entrance to the Cine Roxy. She was biting her lips, he thinks, her nostrils were quivering, there was fright in her eyes, she was babbling: I know that you were careful, love, I was always careful too, love, I don't know what could have happened, love. Santiago took her arm and, instead of the movies, they went to a café. They had talked quite calmly and Ana had accepted the fact that it couldn't be born. But there were tears in her eyes and she talked a lot about how afraid she was of her parents and said good-bye with grief and rancor.

"I'm not asking you because I already know what it will be," Santiago said. "Don't get married."

In two days Carlitos had got the name of a woman and Santiago went to see her in a run-down brick house in Barrios Altos. She was heavy-set, dirty and mistrustful and sent him away rudely: you were very much mistaken, young man, she didn't commit crimes. It had been a week of exasperating running around, with a bad taste in his mouth and a continuous fright, of heated conversations with Carlitos and wakeful dawns at the boardinghouse: she was a nurse, she knew all kinds of midwives, doctors, she didn't want to, it was a trap she was setting for him. Finally Norwin had found a doctor who didn't have too many patients and, after devious evasions, he accepted. He wanted fifteen hundred soles and it took Santiago, Carlitos and Norwin three days among them to get it together. He called Ana on the telephone: it's all set, all arranged, she should come to Lima as soon as possible. Making her see by the tone of your voice that you were putting the blame on her, he thinks, and that you weren't forgiving her.

"Yes, that has to be it, but out of pure selfishness," Carlitos said. "Not

522

so much for your sake as for mine. I won't have anyone to tell me his troubles anymore, anyone to watch the sun rise with in a dive. Have it your own way, Zavalita."

On Thursday someone who was coming from Ica left Ana's letter at the boardinghouse in Barranco: you can sleep peacefully, love. The heavy, asphyxiating sadness of bourgeois words, he thinks, she'd convinced a doctor and it was all over, the Mexican movies, all very painful and sad and now she was in bed and had had to invent a thousand lies so that mama and papa won't know what's going on, but even the misspellings had moved you so much, Zavalita. He thinks: what made her happy in the midst of her sorrow was the fact that she'd taken such a great worry off your back, love. She'd discovered that you didn't love her, that she was just a toy for you, she couldn't bear the idea because she did love you, she wasn't going to see any more of you, time would help her forget you. That Friday and Saturday you'd felt relieved but not happy, Zavalita, and at night the upset would come along with peaceful feelings of remorse. Not the little worm, he thinks, not the knives. On Sunday, in the group taxi to Ica, he hadn't shut his eyes.

"You made up your mind when you got the letter, you masochist," Carlitos said.

He walked so fast from the square that he was out of breath when he got there. Her mother opened the door and her eyes were blinking and sensitive: Anita was ill, a terrible attack of colic, she'd given them a scare. She had him come into the living room and he had to wait some time until her mother returned and told him go up. That dizzy tender feeling when he saw her in her yellow pajamas, he thinks, pale and combing her hair hurriedly as he came in. She let go of the comb, the mirror; she began to cry.

"Not when the letter arrived, but right then," Santiago said. "We called her mother, we announced it to her, and the three of us celebrated the engagement with coffee and tarts."

They would be married in Ica, with no guests or ceremony, they would return to Lima and, until they found an inexpensive apartment, they would live at the boardinghouse. Maybe Ana could get a job in a hospital, both their salaries would be enough if they tightened their belts: there, Zavalita?

"We're going to give you a bachelor party that will go down in the annals of Lima journalism," Norwin said.

She went to fix her makeup in Malvina's little room, she came back down, and when she passed the little parlor she ran into Martha, furious: now they were letting anybody in here, this place has turned into a dung heap. Anyone who could pay could come here, Flora was saying, ask old Ivonne and she'd see, Martha. Queta saw him through the door to the bar, from the back, like the first time, up on a stool, wrapped in a dark suit, his curly hair gleaming, his elbows on the bar. Robertito was serving him a beer. He was the first to arrive in spite of its being after nine o'clock, and there were four women chatting around the phonograph, pretending not to notice him. She went over to the bar, still not knowing whether or not it bothered her to see him there.

"The gentleman was asking for you," Robertito said with a sarcastic smile. "I told him it would be a miracle if he found you, Quetita."

Robertito slipped catlike to the other end of the bar and Queta turned to look at him. Not like coals, not frightened, not like a dog: impatient, rather. His mouth was closed and it was moving as if chewing on a bit: his expression was not servile or respectful or even cordial, just vehement.

"So you came back to life," Queta said. "I didn't think we'd ever see you around here again."

"I've got them in my wallet," he muttered quickly. "Shall we go up?"

"In your wallet?" Queta began to smile, but he was still very serious, his tight jaws throbbing. "What's eating you?"

"Has the price gone up over the last few months?" he asked, not sarcastically but with an impersonal tone, still in a hurry. "How much has it gone up?"

"You're in a bad mood," Queta said, startled by him and by the fact that she wasn't annoyed at the changes she saw in him. He was wearing a red necktie, a white shirt, a cardigan sweater; his cheeks and chin were lighter than the quiet hands on the bar. "What kind of a way to act is this? What's come over you during all this time?"

"I want to know if you're coming up with me," he said with a deadly calm in his voice now. But there was still that savage haste in his eyes. "Yes and we'll go on up, no and I'll leave."

What had changed so much in so little time? Not that he was any fatter or thinner, not that he'd become insolent. He's like furious, Queta thought, but not with me or anyone, with himself.

"Or are you scared?" she said, making fun. "You're not Cayo Shithead's servant anymore, now you can come here whenever you feel like it. Or has Gold Ball forbidden you to go out at night?"

He didn't get enraged, he didn't get upset. He blinked just once and didn't answer anything for a few minutes, slowly, pondering, searching for words.

"If I've wasted a trip, I'd better leave," he finally said, looking into her eyes without fear. "Tell me right out."

"Buy me a drink." Queta got up on one of the stools and leaned against the wall, irritated now. "I can order a whiskey, I imagine."

"You can order anything you want, but upstairs," he said softly, very serious. "Shall we go up, or do you want me to leave?"

"You've learned bad manners with Gold Ball," Queta said dryly.

"You mean the answer is no," he muttered, getting off the stool. "Good night, then."

But Queta's hand held him back when he had already turned half around. She saw him stop, turn and look at her silently with his urgent eyes. Why? she thought, startled and furious, was it out of curiosity, was it because . . . ? He was waiting like a statue. Five hundred, plus sixty for the room and for one time, and she heard and barely recognized her own voice, was it because . . . ? did he understand? And he, nodding his head slightly: he understood. She asked him for the room money, ordered him to go up and wait for her in number twelve and when he disappeared up the stairs there was Robertito, a malefic, bittersweet smile on his smooth face, clinking the little key against the bar. Queta threw the money into his hands.

"Well, well, Quetita, I can't believe my eyes," he said slowly, with exquisite pleasure, squinting his eyes. "So you're going to take care of the darky."

"Give me the key," Queta said. "And don't talk to me, fag, you know I can't hear you."

525

"How pushy you've become since you've joined the Bermúdez family," Robertito said, laughing. "You don't come around much and when you do, you treat us like dogs, Quetita."

She snatched the key. Halfway up the stairs she ran into Malvina, who was coming down dying with laughter: the black sambo from last year was there, Queta. She pointed upstairs and all of a sudden her eyes lighted up, ah, he'd come for you, and she clapped her hands. But what was the matter, Quetita.

"That piece of shit of a Robertito," Queta said. "I can't stand his insolence anymore."

"He must be jealous, don't pay any attention to him." Malvina laughed. "Everybody's jealous of you now, Quetita. So much the better for you, silly."

He was there waiting by the door to number twelve. Queta opened it and he went in and sat down on the corner of the bed. She locked the door, went to the washstand, drew the curtains, turned on the lights and then put her head into the room. She saw him, quiet, serious under the light bulb with its bulging shade, dark on the pink bedcover.

"Are you waiting for me to undress you?" she asked in a nasty way. "Come here and let me wash you."

She saw him get up and come over without taking his eyes off her, his look had lost the aplomb and haste and had taken on the docility of the first time. When he was in front of her, he put his hand into his pocket with a quick and almost reckless motion, as if he remembered something essential. He handed her the bills, reaching out a hand that was slow and somewhat shameful, you paid in advance, didn't you? as if he were handing her a letter with bad news in it: there it was, she could count it.

"You see, this whim is costing you a lot of money," Queta said, shrugging her shoulders. "Well, you know what you're doing. Take off your pants, let me get you washed up."

He seemed undecided for a few seconds. He went toward a chair with a prudence that betrayed his embarrassment, and Queta, from the washstand, saw him sit down, take off his shoes, his jacket, his sweater, his pants, and fold them with extreme slowness. He took off his tie. He came toward her, walking with the same cautious step as before, his long tense

526

legs moving rhythmically below the white shirt. When he was beside her he dropped his shorts and, after holding them in his hands for an instant, threw them at the chair, missing it. While she grasped his sex tightly and soaped and washed it, he didn't try to touch her. She felt him stiff beside her, his hip rubbing against her, breathing deeply and regularly. She handed him the toilet paper to dry himself and he did it in a meticulous way, as if he wanted to take time.

"Now it's my turn," Queta said. "Go wait for me."

He nodded, and she saw a reticent serenity in his eyes, a fleeting shame. She drew the curtain and, while she was filling the basin with hot water, she heard his long, even steps on the wooden floor and the creaking of the bed as it received him. The shitass has affected me with his sadness, she thought. She washed herself, dried, went into the room and, as she passed by the bed and saw him lying on his back, his arms crossed over his eyes, his shirt still on, half his body naked under the cone of light, she thought of an operating room, a body waiting for the scalpel. She took off her skirt and blouse and went over to the bed with her shoes on; he was still motionless. She looked at his stomach: beneath the tangle of hair was the blackness which just barely stood out against the skin, shiny with the recent water, and there his sex, which lay small and limp between his legs. She went over to turn out the lights. She came back and lay down beside him.

"Such a hurry to come upstairs, to pay me what you don't have," she said when she saw him making no move. "All for this?"

"You're not treating me right," his voice said, thick and cowardly. "You don't even pretend. I'm not an animal, I've got my pride."

"Take your shirt off and stop your nonsense," Queta said. "Do you think you disgust me? With you or with the King of Rome, it's all the same to me, black boy."

She felt him sit up, sensed his obedient movements in the dark, saw in the air the white splotch of the shirt that he threw at the chair, visible in the threads of light coming through the window. The naked body fell down beside her again. She heard his more agitated breathing, smelled his desire, felt him touching her. She lay on her back, opened her arms, and an instant later received his crushing, sweaty flesh on her body. He was breathing anxiously beside her ear, his damp hands ran over her skin, and she felt his sex enter her softly. He was trying to take off her bra and she helped him by rolling to one side. She felt his wet mouth on her neck and shoulders and heard him panting and moving; she wrapped her legs around him and kneaded his back, his perspiring buttocks. She let him kiss her on the mouth but kept her teeth together. She heard him come with short, panting moans. She pushed him aside and felt him roll over like a dead man. She put her shoes on in the dark, went to the washbasin, and when she came back into the room and turned on the light, she saw him on his back again, his arms crossed over his face.

"I've been dreaming about this for a long time," she heard him say as she was putting on her bra.

"Now you're sorry about your five hundred soles," Queta said.

"What do you mean, sorry?" She heard him laugh, still hiding his eyes. "No money was ever better spent."

While she was putting on her skirt, she heard him laugh again, and the sincerity of his laugh surprised her.

"Did I really treat you bad?" Queta asked. "It wasn't because of you, it was because of Robertito. He gets me on edge all the time."

"Can I smoke a cigarette like this?" he asked. "Or do I have to leave now?"

"You can smoke three, if you want to," Queta said. "But go wash up first."

       9

A send-off that would go down in history: it would start at noon in the Rinconcito Cajamarquino with a native lunch attended only by Carlitos, Norwin, Solórzano, Periquito, Milton and Darío; they would drag him around to a lot of bars in the afternoon, and at seven o'clock there'd be a cocktail party with nighttime butterflies and reporters from other papers at China's apartment (she and Carlitos were back together again, for a while); Carlitos, Norwin and Santiago, just they, would top off the day at a whorehouse. But on the eve of the day set for the send-off, at nightfall, when Carlitos and Santiago were getting back to the city room after eating in *La Crónica*'s canteen, they saw Becerrita collapse on his desk, letting out a desperate God damn it to hell. There was his square, chubby little body falling apart, there the writers running over. They

528

picked him up: his face was wrinkled in a grimace of infinite displeasure and his skin was purple. They rubbed him with alcohol, loosened his tie, fanned him. He was lying with his lungs congested, inanimate and exhaling an intermittent grunt. Arispe and two writers from the police page took him to the hospital in the van; a couple of hours later they called to tell them that he'd died of a stroke. Arispe wrote the obituary, which appeared edged in black: With his boots on, he thinks. The police reporters had written biographical sketches and apologies: his restless spirit, his contribution to the development of Peruvian journalism, a pioneer in police reporting and chronicles, a quarter of a century in the journalistic trenches.

Instead of the bachelor's party you had a wake, he thinks. They spent the following night at Becerrita's house, on a back alley in Barrios Altos, sitting up with him. There was that tragicomic night, Zavalita, that cheap farce. The reporters from the police page were mournful and there were women sighing beside the coffin in that small parlor with miserable furniture and old oval photographs that had been darkened with black ribbons. Sometime after midnight a woman in mourning and a boy came into the place like a chill, in the midst of whispers of alarm: oh dammy, Becerrita's other wife; oh dammy, Becerrita's other son. There'd been the start of an argument, insults mingled with weeping between the family of the house and the new arrivals. Those present had to intervene, negotiate, calm the rival families down. The two women seemed to be the same age, he thinks, they had the same face, and the boy was identical to the male children in the house. Both families had remained there standing guard on opposite sides of the bier, exchanging looks of hate over the corpse. All through the night long-haired newspapermen from days gone by wandered through the house, strange individuals with threadbare suits and mufflers, and on the following day, at the burial, there was a wild gathering of mournful relatives and hoodlumish and nighttime faces, police and plainclothesmen and old retired whores with smeared and weepy eyes. Arispe read a speech and then an official from Investigations and there they discovered that Becerrita had been working for the police for twenty years. When they left the cemetery, yawning and with aching bones, Carlitos, Norwin and Santiago ate in a lunchroom in Santo Cristo, near the Police Academy, and had some tamales, darkened

529

by the ghost of Becerrita, who kept coming up in the conversation.

"Arispe promised me he won't print anything, but I don't trust him," Santiago said. "You take care of it, Carlitos. Don't let any joker do his thing."

"They're going to find out sooner or later at home that you got married," Carlitos said. "But all right, I'll take care of it."

"I'd rather they found out from me, not through the newspaper," Santiago said. "I'll talk with the old folks when I get back from Ica. I don't want any trouble before the honeymoon."

That night, the eve of his wedding, Carlitos and Santiago had talked for a while in the Negro-Negro after work. They were joking, they'd remembered the times they'd come to this spot, at this same time, to this same table, and he was a little downcast, Zavalita, as if you were going away on a trip for good. He thinks: that night he didn't get drunk, didn't snuff coke. At the boardinghouse you spent the hours remaining until dawn smoking, Zavalita, remembering Señora Lucía's stupefied face when you told her the news, trying to imagine what life would be like in the little room with another person, whether it wouldn't be too promiscuous and asphyxiating, how your folks would react. When the sun came up, he packed his bag carefully. He looked the little room over pensively, the bed, the small shelf with books. The group taxi stopped by for him at eight o'clock. Señora Lucía came out in her bathrobe to see him off, still numb with surprise, yes, she swore to him that she wouldn't say anything to his papa, and she'd given him a hug and kissed him on the forehead. He got to Ica at eleven in the morning and, before going to Ana's house, he called the Huacachina Hotel to confirm their reservation. The dark suit that he had taken out of the cleaners the day before had become wrinkled in the suitcase and Ana's mother pressed it for him. Reluctantly, Ana's parents had done what he had requested: no guests. Only on that condition would you consent to be married in the church, Ana had warned them, he thinks. At four o'clock they went to City Hall, then to the church, and an hour later they were having something to eat at the Tourist Hotel. The mother was whispering to Ana, the father was stringing stories together and drinking, in a very sad mood. And there was Ana, Zavalita: her white dress, her happy face. When they were about to get into the taxi that was taking them to

Huacachina, her mother broke into tears. There, the three days of honeymoon beside the green, stinking waters of the lagoon, Zavalita. Walks through the dunes, he thinks, inane conversations with other honeymoon couples, long siestas, the games of Ping-Pong that Ana always won.

9

"I was counting the days for the six months to be up," Ambrosio says. "So, after six months exactly, I dropped in on him very early."

One day by the river, Amalia had realized that she was even more accustomed to Pucallpa than she had thought. They'd gone swimming with Doña Lupe, and while Amalita Hortensia was sleeping under the umbrella stuck in the sand, two men had come over. One was the nephew of Doña Lupe's husband, the other a traveling salesman who had arrived from Huánuco the day before. His name was Leoncio Paniagua and he had sat down beside Amalia. He had been telling her how much he'd traveled all through Peru because of his job and told her what was the same and what was different about Huancayo, Cerro de Pasco, Ayacucho. He's trying to impress me with his travels, Amalia had thought, laughing inside. She'd let him put on the airs of a world traveler for a good spell and finally she'd told him: I'm from Lima. From Lima? Leoncio Paniagua wouldn't have believed it: because she talked like the people from here, she had the singsong accent and the expressions and everything.

"You haven't lost your mind, have you?" Don Hilario had looked at him with astonishment. "The business is going well but, as is logical, up till now it's a total loss of money. Do you think that after six months there'll be any profit left over?"

Back at the house Amalia had asked Doña Lupe if it was true what Leoncio Paniagua had told her: yes, of course it is, she was already talking like a jungle girl, you should be proud. Amalia had thought how surprised the people she knew in Lima would be if they could hear her: her aunt, Señora Rosario, Carlota and Símula. But she hadn't noticed any change in the way she talked, Doña Lupe, and Doña Lupe, smiling slyly: the man from Huánuco had been flirting with you, Amalia. Yes, Doña Lupe, and just imagine, he'd even invited her to the movies, but naturally Amalia hadn't accepted. Instead of being scandalized, Doña

531

Lupe had scolded her: bah, silly. You should have accepted, Amalia was young, she had a right to have some fun, didn't she think that Ambrosio was doing just as he pleased the nights he spent in Tingo María? Amalia, rather, had been the one who was scandalized.

"He went over the accounts with me holding the papers in his hand," Ambrosio says. "He left me dizzy with all those figures."

"Taxes, stamps, a commission for the shyster who drew up the transfer." Don Hilario kept rummaging through the bills and passing them to me, Amalia. "All very clear. Are you satisfied?"

"Not really, Don Hilario," Ambrosio had said. "I'm kind of tight and I was hoping to get something, sir."

"And here are the payments for the half-wit," Don Hilario had concluded. "I don't collect for running the business, but you wouldn't want me to sell coffins myself, would you? And I don't imagine you'll say I pay him too much. A hundred a month is dirt, even for a half-wit."

"Then the business isn't doing as well as you thought, sir," Ambrosio had said.

"It's doing better." Don Hilario moved his head as if saying make an effort, try to understand. "In the beginning a business is all loss. Then it starts picking up and the returns start coming in."

Not long after, one night when Ambrosio had just got back from Tingo María and was washing his face in the back room, where they had a washbasin on a sawhorse, Amalia had seen Leoncio Paniagua appear by the corner of the cabin, his hair combed and wearing a tie: he was coming right here. She had almost dropped Amalita Hortensia. Confused, she'd run into the garden and crouched among the plants, holding the child close to her breast. He was going to go in, he was going to run into Ambrosio. Ambrosio was going to kill him. But she hadn't heard anything alarming: just Ambrosio's whistling, the splash of the water, the crickets singing in the darkness. Finally she had heard Ambrosio asking for his dinner. She'd gone in to cook trembling, and even for a long while after everything kept dropping out of her hands.

"And when another six months were up, a year, that is, I dropped in on him very early," Ambrosio says. "And Don Hilario? You're not going to tell me that there still hasn't been any profit."

"How could there be, the business is in bad shape," Don Hilario had

532

said. "That's precisely what I wanted to talk to you about."

The next day Amalia, furious, had gone to Doña Lupe's to tell her: just imagine, how fresh, just imagine what would have happened if Ambrosio . . . Doña Lupe had covered her mouth, telling her I know all about it. The man from Huánuco had come to her house and had opened up his heart to her, Señora Lupe: ever since I met Amalia I've been a different man, your friend is like no one else in the world. He didn't intend going into your house, Amalia, he wasn't that stupid, he just wanted to see you from a distance. You've made a conquest, Amalia, you've got the man from Huánuco crazy about you, Amalia. She'd felt very strange: still furious, but flattered now as well. That afternoon she'd gone to the small beach thinking if he says the least thing to me I'll insult him. But Leoncio Paniagua had not made the slightest insinuation to her; very well-mannered, he cleaned the sand for her to sit down, he invited her to have an ice cream cone, and when she looked into his eyes he lowered his, bashful and sighing.

"Yes, just what you heard, I've studied it very carefully," Don Hilario had said. "The money's just lying there waiting for us to pick it up. All that's needed is a little injection of capital."

Leoncio Paniagua came to Pucallpa every month, for just a couple of days, and Amalia had come to like the way he treated her, his terrible timidity. She'd grown used to finding him at the beach every four weeks, with his shirt and collar, heavy shoes, ceremonious and sweltering, wiping his wet face with a colored handkerchief. He never went swimming, he sat between Doña Lupe and her and they chatted, and when they went into the water, he took care of Amalita Hortensia. Nothing had ever happened, he'd never said anything to her; he would look at her, sigh, and the most he ever dared was to say what a shame I have to leave Pucallpa tomorrow or I kept thinking about Pucallpa all this month or why is it I like coming to Pucallpa so much. He was awfully bashful, wasn't he, Doña Lupe? And Doña Lupe: no, it's more that he's a dreamer.

"The big deal he thought of was buying another funeral parlor, Amalia," Ambrosio had said. "The Model."

"The one with the best reputation, the one that's taking all our business away," Don Hilario had said. "Not another word. Get hold of that

533

money you've got in Lima and we'll set up a monopoly, Ambrosio."

The farthest she'd gone, after a few months and more to please Doña Lupe than him, was to go to a Chinese restaurant and then to the movies with Leoncio Paniagua. They'd gone at night, through deserted streets, to the restaurant with the fewest people, and had gone in after the show had started and left before it was over. Leoncio Paniagua had been more considerate than ever, not only had he not tried to take advantage of being alone with her, but he nearly didn't say a word all night long. He says because he was feeling so emotional, Amalia, he says he lost his tongue because he was so happy. But did he really like her that much, Doña Lupe? Really, Amalia: the nights he was in Pucallpa he would stop by Doña Lupe's cabin and talk for hours on end about you and even cry. But why hadn't he ever said anything to her, then, Doña Lupe? Because he was a dreamer, Amalia.

"I've barely got enough to feed us and you're asking for another fifteen thousand soles." Don Hilario had believed the lie I told him, Amalia. "Even if I was crazy, I wouldn't get mixed up in another funeral parlor deal, no, sir."

"It's not another one, it's the same one, only bigger, and a chance to get it all sewed up," Don Hilario had insisted. "Think it over and you'll see I'm right."

And once two months had gone by and the man from Huánuco hadn't shown up in Pucallpa. Amalia had almost forgotten about him the afternoon she found him sitting on the beach by the river, his jacket and tie carefully folded on a newspaper and with a toy for Amalita Hortensia in his hand. What had he been doing? And he, trembling as if he had malaria: he wasn't coming back to Pucallpa anymore, could she talk to him alone for a minute? Doña Lupe had moved away with Amalita Hortensia and they talked for almost two hours. He wasn't a traveling salesman anymore, he'd inherited a small store from an uncle and that was what he came to talk to her about. He'd looked so frightened to her, beating around the bush so much and stammering so much, asking her to go away with him, marry him, that she had even felt a little sorry to tell him he was crazy, Doña Lupe. Now you can see that he really loved you and it wasn't a passing affair, Amalia. Leoncio Paniagua had not

534

insisted, he'd remained silent, like an idiot, and when Amalia had advised him to forget about her and look for another woman back in Huánuco, he shook his head sorrowfully and whispered never. The fool had even made her feel nasty, Doña Lupe. She'd seen him for the last time that afternoon, crossing the square on the way to his small hotel and staggering like a drunkard.

"And when we were most short of money, Amalia finds out she was pregnant," Ambrosio says. "The two bad things at the same time, son."

But the news had made him happy: a little playmate for Amalia Hortensia, a jungle-boy son. Pantaleón and Doña Lupe had come to the cabin that night and they had drunk beer into the small hours: Amalia was pregnant, what did they think of that. They'd had a fairly good time and Amalia had got sick to her stomach and done crazy things: she danced all by herself, sang, said dirty words. The next day she'd awakened weak and vomiting and Ambrosio had made her feel ashamed: the child would be born a drunkard with the bath you gave it last night, Amalia.

"If the doctor had said she might die, I would have had her get an abortion," Ambrosio says. "It's easy there, a whole raft of old women who know all the herbs for it. But no, she felt fine and that's why we didn't worry about anything."

One Saturday, during the first month of her pregnancy, Amalia had gone with Doña Lupe to spend the day in Yarinacocha. All morning they'd sat under a canopy looking at the lagoon where people were swimming, the round eye of the sun was burning in a crystal-clear sky. At noon they had untied their bundles and eaten under a tree, and then they'd heard two women having soft drinks saying awful things about Hilario Morales: he was this, he was that, he'd cheated, he'd robbed, if there was any justice left he'd have been dead or in prison. It's probably nothing but gossip, Doña Lupe had said, but that night Amalia had told Ambrosio.

"I've heard worse things about him, and not just here, in Tingo María too," Ambrosio had told her. "What I can't understand is why he doesn't pull one of his tricks so our business will start showing some profit."

"Because he's most likely pulling the tricks on you, dope," Amalia had said.

"She put the doubt in me," Ambrosio says. "The poor thing had the nose of a hound, son."

From then on, every night when he got back from Pucallpa, even before he brushed off the red dust of the road, he'd asked Amalia anxiously: how many big ones, how many small ones? He had copied down everything that had been sold in a notebook and he had come back every day with stories of new tricks he'd heard concerning Don Hilario in Tingo María and Pucallpa.

"If you mistrust him that much, I've got an idea," Pantaleón had told him. "Tell him to give you back your money and we'll go into something together."

Ever since that Saturday in Yarinacocha she'd kept a scrupulous watch on the customers at Limbo Coffins. This pregnancy hadn't been at all like the earlier one, not even like the first one, Doña Lupe: no nausea, no vomiting, not even thirsty, almost. She hadn't lost her strength, she could do the housework as well as ever. One morning she'd gone to the hospital with Ambrosio and had to stand in a long line. They'd killed time with a game where they tried to guess the number of buzzards they saw sunning themselves on nearby roofs, and when their turn came, Amalia was half asleep. The doctor had given her a very quick examination and said get dressed, you're fine, come back in a couple of months. Amalia had got dressed and only when she was about to leave had she remembered:

"At the Maternity Hospital in Lima they told me that I could die if I had another baby, doctor."

"Then you should have paid attention and taken precautions," the doctor had grumbled; but then, when he saw she was frightened, he forced a smile. "Don't be scared, take good care of yourself and nothing will happen to you."

A short time later another six months had passed and Ambrosio, before going to Don Hilario's office, had called her over with a devilish look: come here, I've got a secret. What is it? He was going to tell him that he didn't want to be his partner anymore or his driver either, Amalia, that he could stick The Jungle Flash and Limbo Coffins where it best suited him. Amalia had looked at him with surprise and he: it was a surprise he was saving for you, Amalia. He and Pantaleón had been making plans all that time and they'd come up with a great one. They'd fill their pockets at Don Hilario's expense, Amalia, that was the funniest part of it. There was a small used truck for sale and Pantaleón had taken it apart and cleaned it up right down to its soul: it worked. They were letting it go for eighty thousand and would take a thirty thousand down payment and the rest on time. Pantaleón would ask for his severance pay and he would move heaven and earth to get his fifteen thousand back and they'd buy it on halves and drive it on halves and charge less and take customers away from the Morales and the Pucallpa companies.

"All dreams," Ambrosio says. "I was trying to end up where I should have started when I got to Pucallpa."

5

THEY CAME STRAIGHT BACK to Lima from Huacachina in the car of
another newlywed couple. Señora Lucía received them with sighs at the
door of the boardinghouse and, after embracing Ana, dried her eyes with
her apron. She'd put flowers in the room, washed the curtains and
changed the sheets, and bought a bottle of port wine to toast their
happiness. When Ana began to unpack the suitcases, she called Santiago
aside and gave him an envelope with a mysterious smile: his little sister
had dropped it off yesterday. Teté's Miraflores handwriting, Zavalita,
you devil, we found out about your getting married! her Gothic syntax,
and reading about it in the paper! Everybody was furious with you (don't
you believe it, Superbrain) and dying to meet my sister-in-law. They
should run right over to the house, they were going to look for you
morning and night because they were dying to meet her. You were such
a nut, Superbrain, and a thousand kisses from Teté.

"Don't turn so pale." Ana laughed. "What difference does it make if
they did find out, were we going to keep it a secret marriage?"

"It's not that," Santiago said. "It's just, well, you're right, I'm acting
stupid."

"Of course you are." Ana laughed again. "Call them and get it over
with or, if you want, let's go face them. You'd think they were ogres,
love."

"Yes, we'd better get it over with," Santiago said. "I'll tell them we'll come by tonight."

With an earthworm tickle in his body, he went down to phone and no sooner had he said hello? than he heard Teté's triumphant shout: Superbrain was on the phone, papa! There was her gushing voice, but how could you have done this, you crazy nut! her euphoria, did you really get married? who to, you madman? her impatience, when and how and where, her giggle, but why didn't you even tell them you had a sweetheart, her questions, had you kidnapped my sister-in-law, had they eloped, was she underage? Tell me, come on, tell me all about it.

"First give me a chance to speak," Santiago said. "I can't answer everything at once."

"Her name is Ana?" Teté burst out again. "What's she like, where's she from, what's her last name, do I know her, how old is she?"

"Look, maybe you'd better ask her all that," Santiago said. "Will you all be home tonight?"

"Why tonight, idiot?" Teté shouted. "Come over right now. Can't you see that we're dying with curiosity?"

"We'll come by around seven o'clock," Santiago said. "For dinner, O.K. So long, Teté."

She had fixed herself up for that visit more than for the wedding, Zavalita. She'd gone to a hairdresser, asked Doña Lucía to help her iron a blouse, had tried on all her dresses and shoes and looked and looked again in the mirror and took an hour to put her makeup on and do her nails. He thinks: poor skinny little thing. She'd been so sure of herself all afternoon, while she got things ready and decided on what to wear, all smiles, asking questions about Don Fermín and Señora Zoila and Sparky and Teté, but at dusk, when she walked in front of Santiago, how does this look, love, do you prefer this other one, love? she was already too loquacious, her ease was too artificial, and there were those little sparks of anguish in her eyes. In the taxi on the way to Miraflores, she'd been silent and serious, uneasiness stamped on her mouth.

"They're going to look me over the way they would a man from Mars, aren't they?" she said suddenly.

"A woman from Mars, more likely," Santiago said. "What do you care?"

But she did care, Zavalita. When he rang the bell he felt her clutch his arm, saw her protect her coiffure with her free hand. It was absurd, what were they doing here, why did they have to go through that examination: you'd felt furious, Zavalita. There was Teté, dressed for a party, at the door, leaping up and down. She kissed Santiago, embraced and kissed Ana, said things, squealed, and there were Teté's little eyes, and a moment later Sparky's little eyes and the eyes of his parents, looking her over, running up and down her, an autopsy. In the midst of the laughter, Teté's squeals and embraces, there was that pair of eyes. Teté took each one by the arm, crossed the garden with them, talking incessantly, pulling them along in her whirlwind of exclamations and questions and congratulations and still casting the inevitable quick glances out of the corner of her eye at Ana, who was stumbling. The whole family was gathered in the living room. The Tribunal, Zavalita. There it was: including Popeye, including Cary, Sparky's fiancée, all of them dressed for a party. Five pairs of rifles, he thinks, all aiming and firing at Ana at the same time. He thinks: mama's face. You didn't know mama very well, Zavalita, you thought she had better control of herself, more ease, more restraint. But she didn't hide her annoyance or her stupefaction or her disappointment: only her rage, at first and halfway. She was the last to come over to them, like a penitent dragging chains, flushed. She kissed Santiago, murmuring something you couldn't catch —her lips were trembling, he thinks, her eyes were wide—and then and with effort, she turned to Ana, who was opening her arms. But she didn't embrace her, she didn't smile at her; she leaned over and barely touched cheeks with Ana and drew away immediately: hello Ana. Her face grew harder still, she turned to Santiago and Santiago looked at Ana: she'd suddenly turned red and now Don Fermín was trying to smooth things over. He'd rushed over to Ana, so this was his daughter-in-law, had embraced her again, this is the secret that Skinny kept hidden from us. Sparky embraced Ana wearing the smile of a hippopotamus and gave Santiago a clap on the back, exclaiming curtly you really kept it secret. He too showed the same embarrassed and funereal expression at times that Don Fermín had when he was careless with his face for a second

540

and forgot to smile. Only Popeye seemed happy and relaxed. Petite, blond, with her little bird voice and her crepe dress, Cary, before they sat down, had begun to ask questions with an innocent, flaky little laugh. But Teté had behaved well, Zavalita, she'd done the impossible to fill the gaps with shreds of conversation, to sweeten the bitter drink that mama, on purpose or unwittingly, served Ana during those two hours. She had spoken to her a single time, and when Don Fermín, anxiously merry, opened a bottle of champagne and hors d'oeuvres were served, she forgot to pass Ana the plate of cheese chunks with toothpicks. And she remained stiff and neutral—her lips still trembling, her eyes wide and staring—while Ana, badgered by Cary and Teté, explained, making mistakes and contradicting herself, how and when they had been married. In private, no attendants, no wedding party, you crazy nuts, Teté said, and Cary how simple, how nice, and she looked at Sparky. From time to time, as if remembering that he was supposed to, Don Fermín would emerge from his silence with a little start, lean forward in his chair and say something affectionate to Ana. How uncomfortable he looked, Zavalita, how difficult that naturalness, that familiarity was for him. More hors d'oeuvres had been brought, Don Fermín poured a second round of champagne, and for the few seconds they were drinking there was a fleeting relaxation of tensions. From the corner of his eye Santiago saw Ana's efforts to swallow the things Teté was passing her, and she was responding as best she could to the jokes—which were getting more and more timid, more false—that Popeye was telling her. It seemed as if the atmosphere was going to burst into flames, he thinks, that a blaze would spring up in the middle of the group. Imperturbably, tenaciously, healthily, Cary kept putting her foot in it at every moment. She would open her mouth, what school did you go to, Ana? and the atmosphere would thicken, María Parado de Bellido was a public school, wasn't it? and add tics and tremors, oh, she'd studied nursing! to his mother's face, not as a volunteer gray lady but as a professional? So you knew how to give shots, Ana, so you'd worked at La Maison de Santé, at the Workers' Hospital in Ica. There your mother, Zavalita, blinking, biting her lips, wiggling in her chair as if she were sitting on an ant hill. There your father, his eyes on the tip of his shoe, listening, raising his head and struggling to smile at you and Ana. Huddled in her chair, a piece of toast

541

with anchovies dancing in her fingers, Ana was looking at Cary like a frightened student at her examiner. A moment later she got up, went over to Teté and whispered in her ear in the midst of an electrified silence. Of course, Teté said, come with me. They left, disappeared up the stairs, and Santiago looked at Señora Zoila. She wasn't saying anything yet, Zavalita. Her brow was wrinkled, her lips were trembling, she was looking at you. You thought it won't matter to her that Popeye and Cary are here, he thinks, it's stronger than she is, she won't be able to stand it.

"Aren't you ashamed of yourself?" Her voice was hard and deep, her eyes were turning red, she was wringing her hands as she spoke. "Getting married in secret like that? Passing the shame on to your parents, your brother and sister?"

Don Fermín still had his head down, absorbed in his shoes, and Popeye's smile had frozen and he looked like an idiot. Cary was looking from one person to another, discovering that something was happening, asking with her eyes what's going on, and Sparky had folded his arms and was looking at Santiago severely.

"This isn't the time, mama," Santiago said. "If I'd known it was going to upset you like this I wouldn't have come."

"I would have preferred a thousand times that you hadn't come," Señora Zoila said, raising her voice. "Do you hear me? Do you hear me? A thousand times not to see you rather than see you married like this, you lunatic."

"Be quiet, Zoila." Don Fermín had taken her arm, Popeye and Sparky were looking apprehensively toward the stairs, Cary had opened her mouth. "Please, girl."

"Can't you see who he's married?" Señora Zoila sobbed. "Don't you realize, can't you see? How can I accept it, how can I see my son married to someone who could be his servant?"

"Zoila, don't be an idiot." He was pale too, Zavalita, he was terrified too. "You're saying stupid things, dear. The girl might hear you. She's Santiago's wife, Zoila."

Papa's hoarse and stumbling voice, Zavalita, his efforts and those of Sparky to calm mama down as she shouted and sobbed. Popeye's face

542

was freckled and crimson, Cary had huddled in her chair as if there were a polar wind blowing.

"You'll never see her again, but be quiet now, mama," Santiago said finally. "I won't let you insult her. She hasn't done anything to you and . . ."

"She hasn't done anything to me, anything to me?" Señora Zoila roared, trying to break away from Don Fermín and Sparky. "She wheedled you, she turned your head, and that little social climber hasn't done anything to me?"

A Mexican movie, he thinks, one of the kind you like. He thinks: mariachis and charros were the only things missing, love. Sparky and Don Fermín had finally led Señora Zoila, almost dragging her, into the study and Santiago was standing up. You were looking at the stairs, Zavalita, you were locating the bathroom, calculating the distance: yes, she'd heard. There was that indignation you hadn't felt for years, that holy wrath from the days of Cahuide and the revolution, Zavalita. His mother's moans could be heard inside, his father's desolate and recriminatory voice. Sparky had come back to the living room a moment later, flushed, incredibly furious.

"You've given mama an attack." He furious, he thinks, Sparky furious, poor Sparky furious. "A person can't live in peace around here because of your crazy tricks, it would seem that you haven't got anything better to do than make the folks fly into a rage."

"Please, Sparky," Cary peeped, getting up. "Sparky, please, please."

"It's all right, love," Sparky said. "Just that this nut always does things the wrong way. Papa in such delicate health and this one here . . ."

"I can take certain things from mama, but not from you," Santiago said. "Not from you, Sparky, I'm warning you."

"You're warning me?" Sparky said, but Cary and Popeye had got hold of him now and were pulling him back: what are you laughing at, son? Ambrosio asks. You weren't laughing, Zavalita, you were looking at the stairs and over your shoulder you heard Popeye's strangled voice: don't get all worked up, man, it's all over, man. Was she crying and was that why she didn't come down, should you go up to get her or wait? They finally appeared at the top of the stairs and Teté was looking as if there were ghosts or demons in the living room, but you carried yourself splendidly, sweet, he thinks, better than María Félix in such-and-such, better than Libertad Lamarque in the other one. She came downstairs slowly, holding the banister, looking only at Santiago, and when she got to him she said in a steady voice:

"It's getting late, isn't it? We have to leave now, don't we, love?"

"Yes," Santiago said. "We can get a taxi over by the square."

"We'll take you," Popeye said, almost shouting. "We'll take them, won't we, Teté?"

"Of course," Teté babbled. "We'll take a little drive."

Ana said good-bye, walked past Sparky and Cary without shaking hands, and went rapidly into the garden, followed by Santiago, who hadn't said good-bye. Popeye got ahead of them by leaps and bounds to open the gate to the street and let Ana through; then he ran as if someone were chasing him and brought up his car and jumped out to open the door for Ana: poor Freckle Face. At first they didn't say anything. Santiago started to smoke, Popeye started to smoke, Ana, very stiff in her seat, was looking out the window.

"You know, Ana, give me a call," Teté said with a voice that was still wounded, when they said good-bye at the door of the boardinghouse. "So I can help you find an apartment, anything."

"Yes, of course," Ana said. "So you can help me find an apartment. Yes, of course."

"The four of us ought to go out together sometime, Skinny," Popeye said, smiling with his whole mouth and blinking furiously. "To eat, to the movies. Whenever you say, brother."

"Yes, of course," Santiago said. "I'll call you one of these days, Freckle Face."

In the room, Ana began to weep so hard that Doña Lucía came to ask what was the matter. Santiago was calming her down, caressing her, explaining to her, and Ana had finally dried her eyes. Then she began to protest and to insult them: she was never going to see them again, she detested them, she hated them. Santiago agreed with her: yes sweet, of course love. She didn't know why she hadn't come downstairs and slapped that old woman, that stupid old woman: yes sweet. Even though she was your mother, even though she was an older woman, so she would learn what it meant to call her a social climber, so she would see: of course love.

9

"All right," Ambrosio said. "I've washed, I'm clean now."

"All right," Queta said. "What happened? Wasn't I at that little party?"

"No," Ambrosio said. "It was meant to be a little party and it wasn't. Something happened and a lot of guests didn't show up. Only three or four and him among them. The mistress was furious, they've snubbed me, she said."

"The madwoman thinks Cayo Shithead gives those little parties so she can have a good time," Queta said. "He gives them to keep his buddies happy."

She was stretched out on the bed, lying on her back like him, both dressed now, both smoking. They were putting the ashes in an empty matchbox that he held on his chest; the cone of light fell on their feet, their faces were in the shadows. No music or talking could be heard; only the distant creak of a lock or the rumble of a vehicle on the street from time to time.

"I'd already realized that those little parties had some reason behind them," Ambrosio said. "Do you think that's the only reason he keeps the mistress? To entertain his friends with her?"

"Not just for that." Queta laughed with a spaced and ironic chuckle, looking at the smoke that she was letting out. "Because the madwoman is pretty too and she tolerates his vices. What was it that happened?"

"You tolerate them too," he said respectfully, not turning to look at her.

"I tolerate them?" Queta asked slowly; she waited a few seconds while she crushed the butt of her cigarette and laughed again with the same slow, mocking laugh. "Yours too, right? It's been expensive for you to come and spend a couple of hours here, hasn't it?"

"It cost me more at the whorehouse," Ambrosio said; and he added, as if in secret, "You don't charge me for the room."

"Well, it costs him a lot more than you, don't you see?" Queta said.

545

"I'm not the same as her. The madwoman doesn't do it for money, or because she's looking after her interests. Or because she loves him, naturally. She does it because she's naïve. I'm like the second lady of Peru, Quetita. Ambassadors, ministers come here. Poor madwoman. She doesn't seem to realize that they go to San Miguel as if they were going to a whorehouse. She thinks they're her friends, that they come because of her."

"Don Cayo does realize it," Ambrosio murmured. "They don't consider me their equal, those sons of bitches, he says. He used to say that to me lots of times when I worked for him. And that they fawn on him because they have to."

"He's the one who fawns on them," Queta said and, without pausing, "What was it, how did it happen? That night, that party."

"I'd seen him there a few times," Ambrosio said, and there was a slight change in his voice: a kind of fleeting retractile movement. "I knew that he used the familiar form with the mistress, for example. Ever since I started working for Don Cayo his face was familiar to me. I'd seen him twenty times maybe. But I don't think he'd ever seen me. Until that party, that time."

"Why did they have you come in?" Quetita seemed distracted. "Had they had you join other parties?"

"Just once, just that time," Ambrosio said. "Ludovico was sick and Don Cayo had sent him home to sleep. I was in the car, knowing that I'd be on my behind all night long, and then the mistress came out and told me to come help."

"The madwoman?" Queta asked, laughing. "Help?"

"Really help, they'd fired the maid or she'd left or something," Ambrosio said. "To help pass the plates around, open bottles, get more ice. I'd never done anything like that, you can imagine." He stopped speaking and laughed. "I helped, but I wasn't very good. I broke two glasses."

"Who was there?" Queta asked. "China, Lucy, Carmincha? How come none of them realized?"

"I don't know their names," Ambrosio said. "No, there weren't any women. Only three or four men. And him, I'd been watching him when I came in with the plates of things and the ice. He was having his drinks but he wasn't falling off his horse like the others. He didn't get drunk. Or he didn't look it."

"He's elegant, his gray hair suits him," Queta said. "He must have been a good-looking boy when he was young. But there's something annoying about him. He thinks he's an emperor."

"No," Ambrosio insisted firmly. "He didn't do anything crazy, he didn't carry on. He had his drinks and that's all. I was watching him. No, he wasn't at all stuck-up. I know him, I know."

"But what caught your attention?" Queta asked. "What was strange about the way he looked at you?"

"Nothing strange," Ambrosio murmured, as if apologizing. His voice had grown faint and was intimate and thick. He explained slowly: "He must have looked at me a hundred times before, but all of a sudden you could see that he was looking at me. Not like at a wall anymore. You see?"

"The madwoman must have been falling all over herself, she didn't notice," Queta said distractedly. "She was very surprised when she found out you were going to go to work for him. Was she falling all over herself?"

"I would go into the living room and right away I could see that he'd started looking at me," Ambrosio whispered. "His eyes were half laughing, half shining. As if he was telling me something, you know?"

"And you still didn't realize?" Queta said. "I'll bet you Cayo Shithead did."

"I realized that way of looking at me was strange," Ambrosio murmured. "On the sly. He'd lift his glass so Don Cayo would think he was going to sip his drink and I realized that wasn't why. He'd put his eyes on me and wouldn't take them off until I was out of the room."

Queta started laughing and he stopped immediately. He waited, not moving, for her to stop laughing. Now they were both smoking again, lying on their backs, and he'd put his hand on her knee. He wasn't stroking it, he was letting it rest there, peacefully. It wasn't hot, but sweat had broken out on the portion of naked skin where their arms touched. A voice was heard going down the hall. Then a car with a whining motor. Queta looked at the clock on the night table. It was two o'clock.

547

"One of those times I asked him if he wanted more ice." Ambrosio murmured. "The other guests had gone, the party was almost over, he was the only one left. He didn't answer me. He closed and opened his eyes in a funny way that's hard to explain. Half as a challenge, half making fun, you know?"

"And you still hadn't caught on?" Queta insisted. "You're dumb."

"I am," Ambrosio said. "I thought he was acting drunk, I thought he probably is and wants to have some fun at my expense. I'd had my few drinks in the kitchen and thought I'm probably drunk myself and only think that's what it is. But the next time I came in I said no, what's eating him. It must have been two or three o'clock, how should I know. I came in to empty an ashtray, I think. That's when he spoke to me."

"Sit down for a bit," Don Fermín said. "Have a drink with us."

"It wasn't an invitation, it was more like an order," Ambrosio murmured. "He didn't know my name. In spite of the fact that he'd heard Don Cayo say it a hundred times, he didn't know it. He told me later on."

Queta started to laugh, he fell silent and waited. A halo of light was reaching the chair and lighting up his jumbled clothes. The smoke was flattening out over them, spreading, breaking up into stealthy rhythmical swirls. Two cars passed in rapid succession as if racing.

"What about her?" Queta asked, now just barely laughing. "What about Hortensia?"

Ambrosio's eyes rolled around in a sea of confusion: Don Cayo didn't seem either displeased or surprised. He looked at him for an instant seriously and then nodded yes to him, do what he says, sit down. The ashtray was dancing stupidly in Ambrosio's uplifted hand.

"She'd fallen asleep," Ambrosio said. "Stretched out in the easy chair. She must have had a lot to drink. I didn't feel right there, sitting on the edge of the chair. Strange, ashamed, my stomach upset."

He rubbed his hands and finally, with a ceremonious solemnity, said here's how without looking at anyone and drank. Queta had turned to look at his face: his eyes were closed, his lips tight together, and he was perspiring.

"At that pace you're going to get sick on us." Don Fermín started to laugh. "Go ahead, have another drink."

548

"Playing with you like a cat with a mouse," Queta murmured with disgust. "You like that, I've come to see it. Being the mouse. Letting them step on you, treat you badly. If I hadn't treated you badly, you wouldn't have got the money together to come up here and tell me your troubles. Your troubles? The first few times I thought so, now I don't. You enjoy everything that happens to you."

"Sitting there like an equal, having a drink," he said with the same opaque, rarefied, distant tone of voice. "Don Cayo didn't seem to mind or he was pretending he didn't. And he wouldn't let me leave, you know?"

"Where are you going there, stay," Don Fermín joked, ordered for the tenth time. "Stay there, where are you off to?"

"He was different from all the other times I'd seen him," Ambrosio said. "Those times he hadn't seen me. By his way of looking and talking too. He was talking without stopping, about anything under the sun, and all of a sudden he said a dirty word. He, who seemed to have such good manners and with that look of a . . ."

He hesitated and Queta turned her head a bit to observe him: look of what?

"Of a fine gentleman," Ambrosio said very quickly. "Of a president, how should I know."

Queta let out a curious and impertinent merry little laugh, stretched, and as she moved her hip she rubbed against his: she instantly felt Ambrosio's hand come to life on her knee, come up under her skirt and anxiously look for her thigh, she felt his arm pressing on her up and down, down and up. She didn't scold him, didn't stop him, and she heard her own merry little laugh again.

"He was softening you up with drinks," she said. "What about the madwoman, what about her?"

She kept lifting her face every so often, as if she were coming out of the water, looking around the room with eyes that were wild, moist, sleepwalking, she picked up her glass, raised it to her mouth and drank, murmuring something unintelligible, and submerged again. What about Cayo Shithead, what about him? He was drinking steadily, joining in the conversation with monosyllables and acting as if it were the most natural thing in the world for Ambrosio to be sitting there and drinking with them.

"That's how it went," Ambrosio said: his hand calmed down, returned to her knee. "The drinks made me less bashful and I was already bearing up under his little look and answering his jokes. Yes I like whiskey sir, of course it's not the first time I've drunk whiskey sir."

But now Don Fermín wasn't listening to him or so it seemed: he had him photographed in his eyes, Ambrosio looked at them and he saw himself, did she see? Queta nodded, and all of a sudden Don Fermín tossed down what was left in his glass and stood up: he was tired, Don Cayo, it was time to go. Cayo Bermúdez also got up.

"Let Ambrosio take you, Don Fermín," he said, holding back a yawn with his fist. "I won't need the car until tomorrow."

"It means that he didn't only know," Queta said, moving about. "Of course, of course. It means that Cayo Shithead had planned it all."

"I don't know," Ambrosio cut in, rolling over, his voice suddenly agitated, looking at her. He paused, fell onto his back again. "I don't know if he knew, if he planned it. I'd like to know. He says he didn't know either. You, hasn't he . . . ?"

"He knows now, that's the only thing I know." Queta laughed. "But neither the madwoman nor I have been able to get out of him whether he planned it or not. When he wants to be, he's as silent as a tomb."

"I don't know," Ambrosio repeated. His voice sank into a well and came back up weak and hazy. "He doesn't know either. Sometimes he says yes, he has to know; other times no, maybe he doesn't know. I've seen Don Cayo a lot of times and there's been nothing about him that tells me he knows."

"You're completely out of your mind," Queta said. "Of course he knows now. Who doesn't know now?"

He accompanied them to the street, ordered Ambrosio tomorrow at ten o'clock, shook hands with Don Fermín and went back into the house, crossing through the garden. Dawn was about to break, small strips of blue were peeping through across the sky and the policemen on the corner murmured good night with voices that were cracked from being up all night and from so many cigarettes.

"And then there was that funny thing," Ambrosio whispered. "He

550

didn't sit in back the way he should have, but next to me. That was when I had my suspicions, but I couldn't believe that was it. It couldn't be, not in the case of someone like him."

"Not in the case of someone like him," Queta said slowly, with disgust. She turned over: "Why are you so servile, so . . . ?"

"I thought it was just to show me a little friendship," Ambrosio whispered. "I treated you like an equal back there, now I'm still doing the same thing. I thought sometimes he likes the common touch, to be on familiar footing with the people. No, I don't know what I thought."

"Yes," Don Fermín said, closing the door carefully and not looking at him. "Let's go to Ancón."

"I looked at his face and it seemed the same as ever, so elegant, so proper," Ambrosio said in a complaining way. "I got very nervous, you know. You said Ancón, sir?"

"Yes. Ancón." Don Fermín nodded, looking out the window at the faint light in the sky. "Have you got enough gas?"

"I knew where he lived, I'd driven him home from Don Cayo's office once," Ambrosio complained. "I started up and on the Avenida Brasil I got up the courage to ask him. Aren't you going to your house in Miraflores, sir?"

"No, I'm going to Ancón," Don Fermín said, looking straight ahead now; but a moment later he turned to look at him and he was a different person, you know? "Are you afraid of going to Ancón alone with me? Are you afraid something will happen to you on the way?"

"And he began to laugh," Ambrosio whispered. "And I did too, but it didn't come out. It couldn't. I was so nervous, I knew then."

Queta didn't laugh: she'd turned over, resting on her elbow, and she looked at him. He was still on his back, not moving, he'd stopped smoking and his hand lay dead on her bare knee. A car passed and a dog barked. Ambrosio had closed his eyes and was breathing with his nostrils opened wide. His chest was slowly going up and down.

"Was that the first time?" Queta asked. "Had there ever been anyone before for you?"

"Yes, I was afraid," he complained. "I went up Brasil, along Alfonso Ugarte, crossed the Puente del Ejército and both of us quiet. Yes, the first time. There wasn't a soul on the streets. On the highway I had to turn

551

my bright lights on because there was fog. I was so nervous that I started driving faster. All of a sudden the needle was at sixty, seventy, you know? It was there. But I didn't run into anything."

"The street lights have already gone out," Queta said distractedly for an instant, and turned back. "What was it you felt?"

"But I didn't crash, I didn't crash," he repeated furiously, clutching her knee. "I felt myself waking up, I felt . . . but I was able to put the brakes on."

Suddenly, as if a truck, a donkey, a tree, a man had appeared out of nowhere on the wet pavement, the car skidded, squealing savagely and whipping from left to right, zigzagging, but it didn't leave the road. Rolling, creaking, it recovered its balance just when it appeared it would turn over and now Ambrosio slowed down, trembling.

"Do you think that with the braking, with the skid he let go of me?" Ambrosio complained, hesitating. "His hand stayed right there, like this."

"Who told you to stop," Don Fermín's voice said. "I said Ancón."

"And his hand there, right here," Ambrosio whispered. "I couldn't think and I started up again and, I don't know. I don't know. You know? All of a sudden sixty, seventy on the needle again. He hadn't let go of me. His hand was still like this."

"He had your number as soon as he saw you," Queta murmured, turning over on her back. "One look and he saw that you'd evaporate if you were treated badly. He looked at you and saw that if someone got on your good side, you'd be putty in his hands."

"I thought I'm going to crash and I went faster," Ambrosio complained, panting. "I went faster, you know."

"He saw that you'd die of fright," Queta said dryly, without compassion. "That you wouldn't do anything, that he could do whatever he wanted with you."

"I'm going to crash, I'm going to crash." Ambrosio panted. "And I pushed my foot farther down. Yes, I was afraid, you know?"

"You were afraid because you're servile," Queta said with disgust. "Because he's white and you're not, because he's rich and you're not. Because you're used to having people do whatever they want to with you."

552

"All I had room for in my head was that," Ambrosio whispered, more agitated. "If he doesn't let go, I'm going to crash. And his hand here, like this, see? Just like that all the way to Ancón."

Ambrosio had come back from Morales Transportation with a face that right away made Amalia think it went bad for him. She hadn't asked him anything. She'd seen him pass her without looking, go out into the garden, sit down on the chair that had no seat, take off his shoes, light a cigarette, scratching the match angrily, and start looking at the grass with murder in his eyes.

"That time there wasn't any foo yong or foo beer," Ambrosio says. "I went into his office and right off he held me back with a look that meant you can stew in your own juice, nigger."

Besides that, he'd run the index finger of his right hand across his neck and then raised it to his temple: bang, Ambrosio. But still smiling with his wide face and his wily bulging eyes. He was fanning himself with a newspaper: it's bad, boy, a total loss. They practically hadn't sold a single coffin and for those last two months he'd had to pay the rent out of his own pocket, as well as the pittance for the half-wit and what they owed the carpenters: there were the bills, Ambrosio had fingered them without looking, Amalia, and had sat down across the desk: that was awful news he was giving him, Don Hilario.

"Worse than awful," he'd admitted. "The times are so bad that people can't even afford to die."

"I just want to say one thing, Don Hilario," Ambrosio had said after a moment, with complete respect. "Look, you're right, of course. Of course the business will show a profit in a little while."

"Absolutely," Don Hilario had said. "The world belongs to people who are patient."

"But I've got money trouble and my wife is expecting another child," Ambrosio had continued. "So even if I wanted to be patient, I can't."

An intricate and surprised smile had filled out Don Hilario's face as he continued fanning himself with one hand and had begun to pick his tooth with the other: two children were nothing, the trick was to reach a dozen, like him, Ambrosio.

"So I'm going to let you have Limbo Coffins all to yourself," Ambrosio had explained. "I'd rather have my share back. To work with it on my own, sir. Maybe I'll have better luck."

That's when he started his cackling, Amalia, and Ambrosio had fallen silent, as if concentrating on killing everything close by: the grass, the trees, Amalita Hortensia, the sky. He hadn't laughed. He'd watched Don Hilario wriggling in his chair, fanning himself rapidly, and he'd waited with a tight seriousness for him to stop laughing.

"Did you think it was some kind of savings account?" he'd finally thundered, drying the perspiration on his forehead, and the laugh got the better of him again. "That you can put your money in and take it out whenever you feel like it?"

"Cluck, cluck, cock-a-doodle-doo," Ambrosio says. "He was crying, he was laughing so hard, he turned red from laughing, he was worn out from laughing. And I was waiting peacefully."

"It's not stupidity, it's not trickery, I don't know what it is." Don Hilario pounded on the table, flushed and wet. "Tell me what you think I am. A fool, an imbecile, what am I?"

"First you laugh and then you get mad," Ambrosio had said. "I don't know what's wrong with you, sir."

"When I tell you the business is going under, what do you think it is that's going under?" He started to talk in riddles, Amalia, and he'd looked at Ambrosio with pity. "If you and I put fifteen thousand soles each into a boat and the boat sinks in the river, what sinks along with the boat?"

"Limbo Coffins hasn't sunk," Ambrosio had stated. "It's right there as large as life across from my house."

"You want to sell it, transfer it?" Don Hilario had asked. "I'd be delighted, right now. Except that first you've got to find some easy mark who'd be willing to take on the corpse. Not someone who'd give you back the thirty thousand we put in, not even a lunatic would do that. Someone who'd accept it as a gift and be willing to take care of the half-wit and pay the carpenters."

"Do you mean I'm never going to see a single one of the fifteen thousand soles I gave you?" Ambrosio had said.

"Someone who would at least give me back the extra money I advanced you," Don Hilario had said. "Twelve hundred now, here are the receipts. Or have you forgotten already?"

"Go to the police, file a complaint against him," Amalia had said. "Have them make him give you back your money."

That afternoon, while Ambrosio was smoking one cigarette after another on the chair without a seat, Amalia had felt that burning that was hard to locate, that acid emptiness at the mouth of her stomach from her worst moments with Trinidad: was bad luck going to start all over again for her here? They'd eaten in silence and then Doña Lupe had come by to chat, but when she saw them so serious, she'd left at once. At night, in bed, Amalia had asked him what are you going to do. He didn't know yet, Amalia, he was thinking. The next day Ambrosio had left very early without taking his lunch for the trip. Amalia had felt nauseous and when Doña Lupe came in, around ten o'clock, she'd found her vomiting. She was telling her what had been happening when Ambrosio arrived: what's up, hadn't he gone to Tingo? No, The Jungle Flash was being repaired in the garage. He'd gone out to sit in the garden, spent the whole morning there thinking. At noontime Amalia had called him in for lunch and they were eating when the man had come in, almost on the run. He'd come to attention in front of Ambrosio, who hadn't even thought to stand up: Don Hilario.

"You were spreading insolent stories around town this morning." Purple with rage, Doña Lupe, raising his voice so much that Amalita Hortensia had waked up crying. "Saying on the street that Hilario Morales had stolen your money."

Amalia had felt the breakfast-time nausea coming back. Ambrosio hadn't budged: why didn't he stand up, why didn't he answer him? Nothing of the sort, he'd remained seated, looking at the little fat man who was roaring.

"Besides being a fool, you don't trust people and you're a blabbermouth," shouting, shouting. "So you told people you're going to put the screws on me with the police? Fine, everything out in the open. Get up, let's go, right now."

"I'm eating," Ambrosio had barely murmured. "Where was it you wanted me to go, sir?"

"To the police," Don Hilario had bellowed. "To set things straight in the presence of the Major. To see who owes money to who, you ingrate."

"Don't act like that, Don Hilario," Ambrosio had begged him. "They've been telling lies to you. How can you believe a bunch of gossips. Have a seat, sir, let me get you a beer."

Amalia had looked at Ambrosio in astonishment: he was smiling at him, offering him a seat. She'd stood up in a leap, run out into the yard, and vomited on the manioc plants. From there she'd heard Don Hilario: he wasn't in the mood for any beer, he'd come to dot a few *i*'s, he should get up, let's go see the Major. And Ambrosio's voice, getting more and more faint and fawning: how could he mistrust him, sir, he'd only been complaining about his bad luck, sir.

"So no more threats or loose talk in the future, then," Don Hilario had said, calming down a bit. "You be careful about going around smearing my good name."

Amalia had seen him take a half-turn, go to the door, turn around and give one last shout: he didn't want to see him at the business anymore, he didn't want to have an ingrate like you as a driver, he could come by Monday and pick up his wages. Yes, it had started up again. But she'd felt more rage against Ambrosio than against Don Hilario and she came running into the room.

"Why did you let yourself be treated like that, why did you knuckle under? Why didn't you go to the police and make a complaint?"

"Because of you," Ambrosio had said, looking at her sorrowfully. "Thinking about you. Have you forgotten so soon? Don't you remember anymore why we're in Pucallpa? I didn't go to the police because of you, I knuckled under because of you."

She'd started to cry, asked his forgiveness, and she had vomited again at night.

"He gave me six hundred soles severance pay," Ambrosio says. "With it we got by for a month, I don't know how. I spent the month looking for work. In Pucallpa it's easier to find gold than a job. Finally I got a starvation job driving a group taxi to Yarinacocha. And after a little while the final blow came, son."

6

DURING THOSE FIRST MONTHS of marriage without seeing your parents or your brother and sister, almost without hearing anything about them, had you been happy, Zavalita? Months of privation and debts, but you've forgotten about them and bad times are never forgotten, he thinks. He thinks: you probably had been, Zavalita. Most likely that monotony with a tight belt was happiness, that discreet lack of conviction and exaltation and ambition, most likely it was that bland mediocrity about everything. Even in bed, he thinks. From the very beginning the boardinghouse was uncomfortable for them. Doña Lucía had allowed Ana to use the kitchen on the condition that it didn't interfere with her schedule, so Ana and Santiago had to have lunch and dinner very early or very late. Then Ana and Doña Lucía started having arguments over the bathroom and the ironing board, the use of dusters and brooms and the wearing out of curtains and sheets. Ana had tried to get back into La Maison de Santé but there wasn't any opening and they had to get through two or three months before she got a part-time job at the Delgado Clinic. Then they began looking for an apartment. When he got back from *La Crónica,* Santiago would find Ana awake, looking through the classified ads, and while he got undressed, she would tell him about her activities and her walks. It was her happiness, Zavalita, marking ads, making phone calls, asking questions and haggling, visiting five or six of them when she left the clinic. And yet, it had been Santiago who just by chance discovered the elf houses on Porta. He'd gone to interview someone who lived on Benavides, and as he was going up toward the Diagonal he found them. There they were: the reddish façade, the little pygmy houses lined up around the small gravel rectangle, the windows with grillwork and the corbels and pots of geraniums. There was a sign: apartments for rent. They'd hesitated, eight hundred was a lot of money. But they were already sick of the inconveniences of the boardinghouse and the arguments with Doña Lucía and they took it. Little by little they started filling the empty little rooms with cheap furniture that they bought on time.

If Ana had her shift at the Delgado Clinic in the morning, when Santiago woke up at noon he would find breakfast all ready to be warmed up. He would stay reading until it was time to go to the paper or out on some assignment, and Ana would get back around three o'clock. They'd have lunch, he'd leave for work at five and come back at two in the morning. Ana would be thumbing through a magazine, listening to the radio, or playing cards with their neighbor, the German woman with mythomaniacal duties (one day she was an agent of Interpol, the next a political exile, another time the representative of a European consortium who had come to Peru on a mysterious mission) who lived alone and on bright days she would go out in a bathing suit to sun herself in the rectangle. And there was the Saturday ritual, Zavalita, your day off. They would get up late, have lunch at home, go to the matinee at a local movie, take a walk along the Malecón or through Necochea Park or on the Avenida Pardo (what did we talk about? he thinks, what did we say?), always in places that were visibly empty so as not to run into Sparky or his folks or Teté, at nightfall they would eat in some cheap restaurant (the Colinita, he thinks, at the end of the month in the Gambrinus), at night they would plunge into a movie theater again, a first run if they could manage it. At first they chose their movies with some sort of balance, a Mexican movie in the afternoon, a detective film or western at night. Now almost all Mexican, he thinks. Had you started to give in to keep things running smoothly with Ana or because it didn't matter to you either, Zavalita? On an occasional Saturday they would travel to Ica to spend the day with Ana's parents. They visited no one and had no visitors themselves, they didn't have any friends.

You hadn't gone back to the Negro-Negro with Carlitos, Zavalita, you hadn't gone back to scrounge a free show at nightclubs or brothels. They didn't ask him, they didn't insist, and one day they began to tease him: you've gotten to be a solid citizen, Zavalita, you've become a good bourgeois. Had Ana been happy, was she, are you, Anita? Her voice there in the darkness on one of those nights when they made love: you don't drink, you don't chase women, of course I'm happy, love. Once Carlitos had come to the office drunker than usual; he came over and sat on Santiago's desk and was looking at him in silence, with an angry face: now they only saw each other and talked in this tomb, Zavalita. A few days later, Santiago invited him to lunch at the elf house. Bring China too, Carlitos, thinking what will she say, what will Ana do: no, China and he were on the outs. He came alone and it had been a tense and uncomfortable lunch, larded with lies. Carlitos felt uncomfortable, Ana looked at him with mistrust and the topic of conversation would die as soon as it was born. Since then Carlitos hadn't gone back to their place. He thinks: I swear I'll come see you.

The world was small, but Lima was large and Miraflores infinite, Zavalita: six, eight months living in the same district without running into his folks or Sparky or Teté. One night at the paper, Santiago was finishing an article when someone touched him on the shoulder: hi, Freckle Face. They went out for coffee on Colmena.

"Teté and I are getting married on Saturday, Skinny," Popeye said. "That's why I came to see you."

"I already knew, I read about it in the paper," Santiago said. "Congratulations, Freckle Face."

"Teté wants you to be her witness at the civil ceremony," Popeye said. "You're going to say yes, aren't you? And Ana and you have to come to the wedding."

"You remember that little scene at the house," Santiago said. "I suppose you know that I haven't seen the family since then."

"Everything's all been patched up, we finally convinced your old lady." Popeye's ruddy face lighted up with an optimistic and fraternal smile. "She wants you to come too. And your old man, I don't have to tell you that. They all want to see you both and make up once and for all. They'll treat Ana with the greatest love, you'll see."

They'd pardoned her, Zavalita. The old man must have lamented every day of those months over why Skinny hadn't come, over how annoyed and resentful you must have been, and he'd probably scolded and blamed mama a hundred times, and on some nights he must have come and stood watch in his car on the Avenida Tacna to see you come out of *La Crónica*. They must have talked, argued, and mama must have cried until they got used to the idea that you were married and to whom. He thinks: until we, they've forgiven you, Anita. We forgive her for having inveigled and stolen Skinny, we forgive her for being a peasant girl: she could come.

"Do it for Teté's sake and for your old man most of all," Popeye insisted. "You know how much he loves you, Skinny. And even for Sparky, man. Just this afternoon he told me that Superbrain should start acting like a man and come."

"I'd be delighted to be Teté's witness, Freckle Face." Sparky had forgiven you too, Anita: thank you, Sparky. "You have to tell me what I have to sign and where."

"And I hope you both will always come to our house, you will, won't you?" Popeye said. "You've got no reason to be mad at Teté and me, we didn't do anything to you, did we? We think Ana's very nice."

"But we're not going to the wedding, Freckle Face," Santiago said. "I'm not mad at the folks or at Sparky. It's just that I don't want another little scene like the last one."

"Don't be pigheaded, man," Popeye said. "Your old lady has her prejudices like everyone else, but underneath it all she's a very good person. Give Teté that pleasure, Skinny, come to the wedding."

Popeye had already left the firm he had worked for since his graduation, the company he had set up with three colleagues was getting along, Skinny, they already had a few clients. But he'd been very busy, not so much in architecture or even with his fiancée—he'd given you a jovial nudge with his elbow, Zavalita—but in politics: what a waste of time, right, Skinny?

"Politics?" Santiago asked, blinking. "Are you mixed up in politics, Freckle Face?"

"Belaúnde for all." Popeye laughed, showing a button on the lapel of

560

his jacket. "Didn't you know? I'm even on the Departmental Committee of Popular Action. You must read the papers."

"I never read the political news," Santiago said. "I didn't know a thing about it."

"Belaúnde was my professor at the university," Popeye said. "We'll sweep the next elections. He's a great guy, brother."

"And what does your father say?" Santiago smiled. "Is he still an Odríist senator?"

"We're a democratic family." Popeye laughed. "Sometimes we argue with the old man, but on a friendly basis. Aren't you for Belaúnde? You've seen how they've called us left-wingers, just for that reason alone you should be backing the architect. Or are you still a Communist?"

"Not anymore," Santiago said. "I'm not anything and I don't want to hear anything about politics. It bores me."

"Too bad, Skinny," Popeye scolded him cordially. "If everybody thought that way, this country would never change."

That night, at the elf houses, while Santiago told her, Ana had listened very attentively, her eyes sparkling with curiosity: naturally they weren't going to the wedding, Anita. She naturally not, but he should go, love, she was your sister. Besides, they'd probably say Ana wouldn't let him come, they'd hate her all the more, he had to go. The next morning, while Santiago was still in bed, Teté appeared at the elf houses: her hair in curlers, which showed through the white silk kerchief, svelte, wearing slacks and happy. It was as if she'd been seeing you every day, Zavalita: she died laughing watching you light the oven to heat up your breakfast, she examined the two small rooms with a magnifying glass, poked through the books, even pulled on the toilet chain to see how it worked. She liked everything: the whole development looked as if it had been made for dolls, the little red houses all so alike, everything so small, so cute.

"Stop messing things up, your sister-in-law will be mad at me," Santiago said. "Sit down and let's talk a little."

Teté sat on the low bookcase, but she kept looking around voraciously. Was she in love with Popeye? Of course, idiot, did you think she'd marry him if she wasn't? They'd live with Popeye's parents for a little while, until the building where Freckle Face's folks had given them an apartment as a wedding present would be finished. Their honeymoon? First to Mexico and then the United States.

"I hope you'll send me some postcards," Santiago said. "All my life I've dreamed of traveling and up till now I've only got as far as Ica."

"You didn't even call mama on her birthday, you brought on a flood of tears," Teté said. "But I suppose that on Sunday you'll be coming to the house with Ana."

"Be content with the fact that I'll be your witness," Santiago said. "We're not going to the church and we're not going to the house."

"Stop your nonsense, Superbrain," Teté said, laughing. "I'm going to convince Ana and I'm going to give it to you, ha-ha. And I'm going to get Ana to come to my shower and everything, you'll see."

And in fact, Teté did come back that afternoon and Santiago left them, her and Ana, when he went off to *La Crónica*, chatting like two lifelong friends. At night Ana received him all smiles: they'd spent the whole afternoon together and Teté was so nice, she'd even convinced her. Wasn't it better if they made up with your family once and for all?

"No," Santiago said. "It's better we don't. Let's not talk about it anymore."

But for the whole rest of the week they'd argued morning and night about the same thing, did you feel like it yet, love, were they going to go? Ana had promised Teté they'd go, love, and Saturday night they were still fighting when they went to bed. Early Sunday morning, Santiago went to phone from the drugstore on the corner of Porta and San Martín.

"What's keeping you people?" Teté asked. "Ana agreed to come at eight o'clock to help me. Do you want Sparky to pick you up?"

"We're not coming," Santiago said. "I called to give you my best and don't forget the postcards, Teté."

"Do you think I'm going to get down on my knees, idiot?" Teté said. "The trouble with you is that you've got too many complexes. Stop your foolishness right now and get over here or I won't speak to you ever again, Superbrain."

"If you get mad you're going to look ugly and you've got to be pretty for all the pictures," Santiago said. "A thousand kisses and come see us when you get back, Teté."

562

"Don't act like the spoiled little princess who resents everything," Teté still managed to say. "Come on, bring Ana. They've made a shrimp stew for you, idiot."

Before going back to the elves' quarters, he went to a florist on Larco and ordered a bouquet of roses for Teté. A thousand best wishes for you both from your sister and brother Ana and Santiago, he thinks. Ana was resentful and didn't say a word to him until nighttime.

9

"Not for financial reasons?" Queta asked. "Why, then, because you were afraid?"

"Sometimes," Ambrosio said. "Sometimes more because I was sorry. Out of thankfulness, respect. Even friendship, still keeping my distance. I know you don't believe me, but it's true. Word of honor."

"Don't you ever feel ashamed?" Queta asked. "With people, your friends. Or do you tell them the same thing you're telling me?"

She saw him smile with a certain bitterness in the half-darkness; the street window was open but there was no breeze and in the still and reeking atmosphere of the room his naked body began to sweat. Queta moved away a fraction of an inch so that he wouldn't rub against her.

"Friends like I had back home, not a single one here," Ambrosio said. "Just casual friends, like the one who's Don Cayo's chauffeur now, or Hipólito, the other one, who looks after him. They don't know. And even if they did, it wouldn't bother me. It wouldn't seem bad to them, you know. I told you what went on with Hipólito and the prisoners, don't you remember? Why should I be ashamed because of them?"

"Aren't you ever ashamed because of me?" Queta asked.

"Not you either," Ambrosio said. "You're not going to spread those things around."

"Why not?" Queta said. "You're not paying me to keep your secrets."

"Because you don't want them to know that I come here," Ambrosio said. "That's why you're not going to spread them around."

"What if I told the madwoman what you're telling me?" Queta asked. "What would you do if I told everybody?"

He laughed softly and courteously in the darkness. He was on his back smoking, and Queta saw how the little clouds of smoke blended in the

563

air. No voice could be heard, no car passed, sometimes the ticking of the clock on the night table became present and then it would be lost, to reappear a moment later.

"I'd never come back," Ambrosio said. "And you'd lose a good customer."

"I've almost lost him already." Queta laughed. "You used to come every month before, every two months. And now how long has it been? Five months? Longer. What's happened? Is it because of Gold Ball?"

"Being with you for just a little while means two weeks of work for me," Ambrosio explained. "I can't always give myself those pleasures. Besides, you're not around much either. I came three times this month and I didn't find you any one of them."

"What would he do to you if he knew you were coming here?" Queta asked. "Gold Ball."

"He's not what you think he is," Ambrosio said very quickly, with a serious voice. "He's not a mean man, he's not a tyrant. He's a real gentleman, I already told you."

"What would he do?" Queta insisted. "If one day I met him in San Miguel and told him Ambrosio's spending your money on me?"

"You only know one side of him, that's why you're so wrong about him," Ambrosio said. "He's got another side. He's not a tyrant, he's good, he's a gentleman. He makes a person feel respect for him."

Queta laughed even louder and looked at Ambrosio: he was lighting another cigarette and the instantaneous little flame of the match showed her his sated eyes and his serious expression, tranquil, and the gleaming perspiration on his brow.

"He's turned you into one too," she said softly. "It isn't because he pays you well or because you're afraid. You like being with him."

"I like being his chauffeur," Ambrosio said. "I've got my room, I earn more than I did before, and everybody treats me with consideration."

"And when he drops his pants and tells you do your duty." Queta laughed. "Do you like that too?"

"It's not what you think," Ambrosio repeated slowly. "I know what you're imagining. It's not true, it isn't like that."

"What about when it disgusts you?" Queta asked. "Sometimes it does me, but what the hell, I open my legs and it's all the same. What about you?"

"It's something that makes you feel pity," Ambrosio whispered. "It does me, him too. You think it happens every day. No, not even once a month. It's when something's gone wrong for him. I can tell, I see him get into the car and I think something went wrong. He's pale, his eyes are sunken in, his voice is funny. Take me to Ancón, he says. Or let's go to Ancón, or to Ancón. I can tell. The whole trip without saying a word. If you saw his face you'd say someone close to him had died or that somebody had told him you're going to die tonight."

"What happens to you, what do you feel?" Queta asked. "When he tells you take me to Ancón."

"Do you feel disgusted when Don Cayo tells you come to San Miguel tonight?" Ambrosio asked in a very low voice. "When the mistress sends for you?"

"Not anymore." Queta laughed. "The madwoman is my friend, we're chums. We laugh at him instead. Do you think here comes the sacrifice, do you feel that you hate him?"

"I think about what's going to happen when we get to Ancón and I feel bad," Ambrosio complained and Queta saw him touch his stomach. "Bad here, it starts turning. It makes me afraid, makes me feel sorry, makes me mad. I think I hope we only talk today."

"We talk?" Queta laughed. "Does he take you there just to talk sometimes?"

"He goes in with his funeral face, draws the curtains and pours his drink," Ambrosio said with a thick voice. "I know that something's biting him inside, eating at him. He's told me, you know. I've even seen him cry, you know."

"Hurry up, take a bath, put this on?" Queta recited, looking at him. "What does he do, what does he make you do?"

"His face keeps on getting paler and paler and his voice gets tight," Ambrosio murmured. "He sits down, says sit down. He asks me things, talks to me. He has us chat."

"Does he talk to you about women, does he tell you about filth, show you pictures, magazines?" Queta went on. "All I do is open my legs. What about you?"

"I tell him things about myself," Ambrosio whined. "About Chincha, about when I was a kid, about my mother. About Don Cayo, he makes me tell him things, he asks me about everything. He makes me feel like his friend, you know."

"He takes away your fear, he makes you feel comfortable," Queta said. "The cat and the mouse. What about you?"

"He starts to talk about his business and things, about his worries," Ambrosio murmured. "Drinking all the time. Me too. And all the time I can see by his face that something's eating, something's gnawing at him."

"Is that when you use the familiar form with him?" Queta asked. "Do you dare to during those times?"

"I don't use the familiar form with you, even though I've been coming to this bed for two years, right?" Ambrosio grumbled. "He lets out everything that worries him, his business, politics, his children. He talks and talks and I know what's going on inside him. He tells me he's ashamed, he told me, you know."

"What does he start crying about?" Queta asked. "Because you don't . . . ?"

"Sometimes he goes on for hours like that," Ambrosio grumbled. "Him talking and me listening, me talking and him listening. And drinking until I feel I can't hold another drop."

"Because you don't get excited?" Queta asked. "Does it excite you only when you're drinking?"

"It's what he puts in the drink," Ambrosio whispered. His voice got thinner and thinner until it almost disappeared, and Queta looked at him: he'd put his arm over his face like a man on his back sunbathing at the beach. "The first time I caught on he realized I'd seen him. He realized I was surprised. What's that you put in it?"

"Nothing, it's called yohimbine," Don Fermín said. "Look, I've put some in mine too. It's nothing, cheers, drink up."

"Sometimes not the drink, not the yohimbine, not anything," Ambrosio grumbled. "He realizes it, I can see he does. His eyes make you want to cry, his voice. Drinking, drinking. I've seen him burst out crying, you know. He says go on, beat it, and locks himself in his room. I can hear him talking to himself, hollering. He goes crazy with shame, you know."

"Does he get mad at you, does he put on jealous scenes?" Queta asked. "Does he think that . . . ?"

"It's not your fault, it's not your fault," Don Fermín moaned. "It's not my fault either. A man's not supposed to get aroused by another man, I know."

"He gets down on his knees, you know," Ambrosio moaned. "Wailing, sometimes half crying. Let me be what I am, he says, let me be a whore, Ambrosio. You see? He humiliates himself, he suffers. Let me touch you, let me kiss it, on his knees, him to me, you see? Worse than a whore, you see?"

Queta laughed slowly, rolled over on her back and sighed.

"You feel sorry for him because of that," she murmured with a dull fury. "I feel more sorry for you."

"Sometimes not even then, not even then," Ambrosio moaned. "I think he's going to go into a rage, he's going to go crazy, he's going to . . . But no, no. Go on, beat it, you're right, leave me alone, come back in a couple of hours, in an hour."

"What about when you can do him the favor?" Queta asked. "Does he get happy, does he take out his wallet and . . . ?"

"He's ashamed too," Ambrosio moaned. "He goes to the bathroom, locks himself in and doesn't come out. I go to the other bathroom, take a shower, soap myself up. There's hot water and everything. I come back and he isn't out yet. He takes hours getting washed, putting on cologne. He's pale when he comes out, not talking. Go to the car, he says, I'll be right down. Drop me off downtown, he says, I don't want us to arrive home together. He's ashamed, see?"

"What about jealousy?" Queta asked. "Does he think you never go out with women?"

"He never asks me anything about that," Ambrosio said, taking his arm away from his face. "Or what I do on my day off or anything, only what I tell him. But I know what he'd feel if he knew I went out with women. Not jealousy, don't you see? Shame, afraid that they'd find out. He wouldn't do anything to me, he wouldn't get mad. He'd say go on,

567

beat it, that's all. I know what he's like. He's not the kind to insult you, he doesn't know how to treat people bad. He'd say it doesn't matter, you're right, but go on, beat it. He'd suffer and that's all he'd do, you see? He's a gentleman, not what you think he is."

"Gold Ball disgusts me more than Cayo Shithead," Queta said.

That night, going into the eighth month, she'd felt pains in her back and Ambrosio, half asleep and reluctantly, had given her a massage. She'd awakened with a burning feeling and such lethargy that when Amalita Hortensia began to complain, she'd started to cry, distressed at the idea of having to get up. When she'd sat up in bed, she'd seen chocolate-colored stains on the mattress.

"She thought the baby had died in her belly," Ambrosio says. "She was suspicious of something, because she started to cry and made me take her to the hospital. Don't be afraid, what are you afraid of."

They'd stood in line as usual, looking at the buzzards on the roof of the morgue, and the doctor had told Amalia you're coming in right now. What had he found out, doctor? They were going to have to induce the birth, woman, the doctor had explained. What do you mean, induce it, doctor? and he nothing, woman, nothing serious.

"She stayed there," Ambrosio says. "I brought her things to her, I left Amalita Hortensia with Doña Lupe, I went to drive the jalopy. In the evening I went back to see her. Her arm and one cheek of her behind were all purple from so many injections."

They'd put her in the ward: hammocks and cots so close together that visitors had to stand at the foot of the bed because there wasn't room enough to get close to the patient. Amalia had spent the morning looking out a large grilled window at the huts of the new settlement that was springing up behind the morgue. Doña Lupe had come to see her with Amalita Hortensia, but a nurse had told her not to bring the little girl anymore. She'd asked Doña Lupe to stop by the cabin when she got a chance and see if Ambrosio needed anything, and Doña Lupe of course, she'd fix his dinner too.

"A nurse told me it looks as if they're going to have to operate,"

Ambrosio says. "Is it serious? No, it's not. They were tricking me, you see, son?"

The pains had disappeared with the shots and the fever had gone down, but she'd kept on soiling the bed all day with little chocolate-colored spots and the nurse had changed her sanitary napkin three times. It seems they're going to have to operate, Ambrosio had told her. She'd become frightened: no, she didn't want them to. It was for her own good, silly. She'd started to cry and all the patients had looked at her.

"She looked so depressed that I started making up lies," Ambrosio says. "We're going to buy that truck, Panta and me, we decided today. She wasn't even listening to me. Her eyes were big, like this."

She'd been awake all night because of the coughing spells of one of the patients, and frightened by another one who kept moving about in his hammock beside her and cursing some woman in his sleep. She'd beg, she'd cry, and the doctor would listen to her: more shots, more medicine, anything, but don't operate on me, she'd suffered so much the last time, doctor. In the morning they'd brought mugs of coffee to all the patients in the ward except her. The nurse had come and, without saying a word, had given her a shot. She'd started to beg her to call the doctor, she had to talk to him, she was going to convince him, but the nurse hadn't paid any attention to her: did she think they were going to operate on her because they liked to, silly? Then, with another nurse, she'd pulled her cot to the door of the ward and they'd transferred her to a stretcher and when they had started rolling her along she'd sat up, screaming for her husband. The nurses had left, the doctor had come, annoyed: what was all that noise, what's going on. She'd begged him, told him about the Maternity Hospital, what she'd gone through, and the doctor had nodded his head: fine, good, just be calm. Like that until the morning nurse had come in: there was your husband now, that's enough crying.

"She grabbed me," Ambrosio says. "Don't let them operate, I don't want them to. Until the doctor lost his patience. Either we get your permission or you take her out of here. What was I going to do, son?"

They'd been trying to convince her, Ambrosio and an older nurse, older and nicer than the first, one who'd spoken to her lovingly and told her it's for your own good and for the good of the baby. Finally she said

569

all right and that she would behave herself. Then they took her off on the stretcher. Ambrosio had followed her to the door of the other room, telling her something that she'd barely heard.

"She smelled it, son," Ambrosio says. "If not, why was she so desperate, so frightened?"

Ambrosio's face had disappeared and they'd closed a door. She'd seen the doctor putting on an apron and talking to another man dressed in white and wearing a little cap and a mask. The two nurses had taken her off the cart and laid her on a table. She had asked them raise my head, she was suffocating like that, but instead of doing it they'd said to her yes, all right, quiet now, it's all right. The two men in white had kept on talking and the nurses had been walking around her. They'd turned on a light over her face, so strong that she had to close her eyes, and a moment later she'd felt them giving her another shot. Then she'd seen the doctor's face very close to hers and heard him tell her start counting, one, two, three. While she was counting, she'd felt her voice die.

"I had to work on top of it all," Ambrosio says. "They took her into the room and I left the hospital, but I went to Doña Lupe's and she said poor thing, how come you didn't stay until the operation was over. So I went back to the hospital, son."

It had seemed to her that everything was moving softly and she too, as if she were floating on water and beside her she had barely recognized the long faces of Ambrosio and Doña Lupe. She had tried to ask them was the operation over? tell them I don't feel any pain, but she didn't have the strength to speak.

"Not even a place to sit down," Ambrosio says. "Standing there, smoking all the cigarettes I had on me. Then Doña Lupe arrived and she started waiting too and they still hadn't brought her out of the room."

She hadn't moved, it had occurred to her that with the slightest movement a whole lot of needles would start pricking her. She hadn't felt any pain, more like a heavy, sweaty threat of pain and at the same time a languor and she'd been able to hear, as if they were talking in secret or were far, far away, the voices of Ambrosio, of Doña Lupe, and even the voice of Señora Hortensia: had it been born, was it a boy or a girl?

570

"Finally a nurse came pushing out, get out of the way," Ambrosio says. "She left and came back carrying something. What's going on? She gave me another push and in a little while the other one came out. We lost the baby, she said, but there's a chance we can save the mother."

It seemed that Ambrosio was weeping and Doña Lupe was praying, that there were people milling around them and telling them things. Someone had crouched over her, his lips near her face. They think you're going to die, she'd thought, they think that you're dead. She'd felt a great surprise and much grief for everyone.

"That there was a chance to save her meant that there was a chance she'd die too," Ambrosio says. "Doña Lupe began to pray on her knees. I went over and leaned against the wall, son."

She hadn't been able to tell how much time had passed between one thing and another and had still heard them speaking, but long silences too now, which could be heard, which made noise. She had still felt that she was floating, that she was sinking down in the water a bit and that she was rising and sinking and had suddenly seen the face of Amalita Hortensia. She had heard: wipe your feet before you go into the house.

"Then the doctor came out and put his hand on me here," Ambrosio says. "We did everything we could to save your wife, but God didn't will it that way and I don't know how many other things, son."

It had occurred to her that they were going to pull her down, that she was going to drown, and she had thought I'm not going to look, I'm not going to talk, she wasn't going to move and that way she would keep on floating. She'd thought how can you be hearing things that happened in the past, dummy? and she'd become frightened and had felt a lot of pain again.

"We held her wake at the hospital," Ambrosio says. "All the drivers from the Morales and Pucallpa companies came, and even that bastard Don Hilario came to offer his condolences."

She'd felt more and more pain as she sank and she felt that she was going down and spinning as she fell and she knew that the things she was hearing were staying up above and that all she could do while she sank, while she fell, was bear that terrible pain.

"We buried her in one of the coffins from Limbo," Ambrosio says.

571

"We had to pay I don't know how much for the cemetery. I didn't have it. The drivers took up a collection and even that bastard Don Hilario gave something. And the same day I buried her, the hospital sent someone to collect the bill. Dead or not, the bill had to be paid. With what, son?"

7

"WHAT WAS IT LIKE, son?" Ambrosio asks. "Did he suffer much before . . . ?"

It had been some time after Carlitos' first attack of d.t.'s, Zavalita. One night he'd announced in the city room, with a determined air: I'm off booze for a month. No one had believed him, but Carlitos scrupulously followed his voluntary cure of drying out and went four weeks without touching a drop of liquor. Each day he would scratch out a number on his desk calendar and wave it around with a challenge: that makes ten, that makes sixteen. At the end of the month he announced: now for my revenge. He'd started drinking that night when he left work, first with Norwin and Solórzano in downtown dives, then with some sports writers he ran into who were celebrating someone's birthday in a bar, and dawn found him drinking in the Parada market, he said himself afterward, with some strangers who stole his wallet and his watch. That morning they saw him at the offices of *Última Hora* and *La Prensa* trying to borrow some money and at nightfall Arispe found him sitting at a table of the Zela Bar on the Portal, his nose like a tomato and his eyes bleary, drinking by himself. He sat down with him, but he couldn't talk to him. He wasn't drunk, Arispe told them, he was pickled in alcohol. That night he showed up in the city room, walking with extreme caution and looking straight through things. He smelled of a lack of sleep, of indescribable combinations, and on his face there was a quivering uneasiness,

573

an effervescence of the skin over his cheekbones, his temples, his forehead and his chin: everything was throbbing. Without answering the remarks, he floated over to his desk and stood there, looking at his typewriter with anxiety. Suddenly he lifted it up over his head with great effort and, without saying a word, dropped it: the great noise there, Zavalita, the shower of keys and nuts and bolts. When they went to grab him, he started to run, giving out grunts: he flung paper about, kicked over wastebaskets, stumbled into chairs. The next day he'd been put into the hospital for the first time. How many other times since then, Zavalita? He thinks: three.

"It doesn't seem so," Santiago says. "It seems that he died in his sleep."

It had been a month after Sparky and Cary's wedding, Zavalita. Ana and Santiago received an announcement and an invitation, but they didn't attend or call or send flowers. Popeye and Teté hadn't even tried to persuade them. They'd shown up at the elf houses a few weeks after getting back from their honeymoon and there were no hard feelings. They poured out the details of their trip to Mexico and the United States and then they'd gone for a drive in Popeye's car and stopped for milk shakes in Herradura. They'd continued seeing each other that year every so often, at the elf houses and sometimes in San Isidro when Popeye and Teté moved into their apartment. You got all the news from them, Zavalita: Sparky's engagement, the wedding preparations, your parents' pending trip to Europe. Popeye was all taken up in politics. He would accompany Belaúnde on his trips to the provinces and Teté was expecting a baby.

"Sparky got married in February and the old man died in March," Santiago says. "He and mama were about to leave for Europe when it happened."

"Did he die in Ancón, then?" Ambrosio asks.

"In Miraflores," Santiago says. "They hadn't gone to Ancón that summer because of Sparky's wedding. They'd only been going to Ancón on weekends, I think."

It had been a little while after they had adopted Rowdy, Zavalita. One afternoon Ana came back from the Delgado Clinic with a shoebox that was moving; she opened it and Santiago saw something small and white leap out: the gardener had given him to her with so much affection that she hadn't been able to say no, love. At first he was an annoyance, a cause of arguments. He wet in the living room, on the beds, in the bathroom, and when Ana tried to teach him to do his duty outside by slapping him on the behind or rubbing his nose in the pool of poop and pee, Santiago came to his defense and they had a fight, and when he began to chew on some book, Santiago would hit him and Ana would come to his defense and they would have a fight. After a while he learned: he would scratch on the street door when he wanted to piss and he would give an electrified look at the bookshelf. During the first days he slept in the kitchen on some old rags, but at night he would howl and come whimpering to the bedroom door, so they ended up fixing a corner for him beside the shoe rack. Little by little, he was winning the right to climb onto the bed. That morning when he'd got into the clothes hamper and was trying to get out, Zavalita, and you were looking at him. He'd stood up with his front paws on the edge, he was putting all his weight forward and the hamper began to rock and finally fell over. After a few seconds without moving, he wagged his tail and went forward to his freedom, and at that moment the rap on the window and Popeye's face.

"Your father, Skinny," it was muffled, Zavalita, heavy, he must have run all the way from his car. "Sparky just called me."

You were in your pajamas, you couldn't find your shorts, your legs got tangled up in your pants, and while you were writing a note for Ana, your hand began to tremble, Zavalita.

"Hurry up," Popeye was saying, standing in the door. "Hurry up, Skinny."

They got to the American Hospital at the same time as Teté. She hadn't been at home when Popeye got the phone call, she'd been in church, and she had Popeye's message in one hand and a veil and a prayerbook in the other. They wasted several minutes going back and forth through the corridors until, turning a corner, they saw Sparky. Disguised, he thinks: the red and white pajama top, his pants unbuttoned, a jacket of a different color, and he wasn't wearing socks. He was embracing his wife, Cary was crying and there was a doctor who was moving his lips with a mournful look. He shook your hand, Zavalita, and Teté began to weep loudly. He'd died before they got him to the hospital, the doctors said, he was probably already dead that morning when your mother woke up and found him motionless and rigid, his mouth open. It caught him in his sleep, they said, he didn't suffer. But Sparky was certain that when he, Cary and the butler had put him in the car, he was still alive, that he'd felt a pulse. Mama was in the emergency room and when you went in they were giving her a shot for her nerves: she was raving and when you embraced her she howled. She fell asleep a short time later and the loudest howls were Teté's. Then the relatives had begun to arrive, then Ana, and you, Popeye and Sparky had spent the whole afternoon making the arrangements, Zavalita. The hearse, he thinks, the business with the cemetery, the notices in the newspapers. There you made up with your family again, Zavalita, since then you hadn't had another fight. Between one item of business and another, Sparky would give a sob, he thinks, he had some tranquilizers in his pocket and he was swallowing them like candy. They got home at dusk, and the garden, the rooms, the study were already full of people. Mama had got up and was overseeing the preparations for the wake. She wasn't crying, she wasn't wearing any makeup, and she looked terribly ugly. Around her were Teté and Cary and Aunt Eliana and Aunt Rosa and Ana too, Zavalita. He thinks: Ana too. People were still coming in, all night long there were people who came and went, murmurs, smoke, and the first flowers. Uncle Clodomiro had spent the night sitting by the coffin, mute, rigid, with a waxen face, and when you'd finally gone over to look at him, dawn was already breaking. The glass was fogged and you couldn't make out his face, he thinks: only his hands on his chest, his most elegant suit, and his hair had been combed.

"I hadn't seen him for over two years," Santiago says. "Since I got married. What made me most sad wasn't that he'd died. We all have to die someday, right, Ambrosio? It was that he'd died thinking that I'd broken with him."

The burial was the next day, at three in the afternoon. All morning telegrams, notes, mass cards, offerings and wreaths had been arriving, and in the newspapers the item was edged in black. A lot of people had come, yes, Ambrosio, even an aide to the President, and as they entered the cemetery, the coffin had been accompanied for a moment by a Pradist cabinet member, an Odríist senator, a leader of APRA and a Belaúndist.

576

Uncle Clodomiro, Sparky and you had stood at the cemetery gates receiving condolences for more than an hour, Zavalita. The next day Ana and Santiago spent the whole day at the house. Mama stayed in her room, surrounded by relatives, and when she saw them come in, she had embraced and kissed Ana and Ana had embraced and kissed her, and they both had wept. He thinks: that's the way the world was made, Zavalita. He thinks: is that how it was made? Uncle Clodomiro came by at dusk and was sitting in the living room with Popeye and Santiago: his mind seemed to be elsewhere, he was lost in his own thoughts, and when they asked him something, he would reply with almost inaudible monosyllables. On the following day, Aunt Eliana had taken mama to her house in Chosica so that she could avoid the parade of visitors.

"Since he died I haven't had another fight with the family," Santiago says. "I don't see them very often, but even so, even from a distance, we get along."

❾

"No," Ambrosio repeated. "I haven't come to fight."

"That's good, because if you have, I'll call Robertito, he's the one here who knows how to fight," Queta said. "Tell me right out what the fuck has brought you here, or beat it."

They weren't naked, they weren't lying on the bed, the light in the room wasn't out. From down below the same mixed sound of music and voices at the bar and laughter from the little parlor could still be heard. Ambrosio had sat down on the bed and Queta saw him enveloped in the cone of light, quiet and strong in his blue suit and his pointed black shoes and the white collar of his starched shirt. She saw his desperate immobility, the crazed rage embedded in his eyes.

"You know very well, because of her." Ambrosio was looking straight at her without blinking. "You could have done something and you didn't. You're her friend."

"Look, I've got enough to worry about," Queta said. "I don't want to talk about that, I come here to make some money. Go on, beat it, and most of all, don't come back. Not here and not to my apartment."

"You should have done something," Ambrosio's stubborn voice repeated, stiff and clear. "For your own good."

577

"For my own good?" Queta said. She was leaning against the door, her body slightly arched, her hands on her hips.

"For her good, I mean," Ambrosio murmured. "Didn't you tell me that she was your friend, that even though she was crazy you liked her?"

Queta took a few steps, sat down on the only chair in the room, facing him. She crossed her legs, looked at him calmly, and he resisted her look without lowering his eyes, for the first time.

"Gold Ball sent you," Queta said slowly. "Why didn't he send you to the madwoman? I haven't got anything to do with this. Tell Gold Ball not to get me mixed up in his problems. The madwoman is the madwoman and I'm me."

"Nobody sent me, he doesn't even know that I know you," Ambrosio said very slowly, looking at her. "I came so we could talk. Like friends."

"Like friends?" Queta said. "What makes you think you're my friend?"

"Talk to her, make her be reasonable," Ambrosio murmured. "Make her see that she hasn't behaved well. Tell her he hasn't got any money, that his business is in bad shape. Advise her to forget about him completely."

"Is Gold Ball going to have her arrested again?" Queta asked. "What else is that bastard going to do to her?"

"He didn't put her in, he went to get her out of jail," Ambrosio said without raising his voice, without moving. "He helped her, he paid her hospital bills, he gave her money. Without any obligation, just out of pity. He's not going to give her any more. Tell her that she hasn't behaved well, not to threaten him anymore."

"Go on, beat it," Queta said. "Let Gold Ball and the madwoman settle their affairs by themselves. It's no business of mine. Yours either, don't you get involved."

"Give her some advice," Ambrosio's terse, sharp voice repeated. "If she keeps on threatening him, it's going to turn out bad for her."

Queta laughed and heard her own forced and nervous giggle. He was looking at her with calm determination, with that steady, frantic boiling in his eyes. They were silent, looking at each other, their faces a couple of feet apart.

"Are you sure he didn't send you?" Queta finally asked. "Is Gold Ball scared of the poor madwoman? He's seen her, he knows what a state she's in. You know how she is too. You've got your spy there too, haven't you?"

"That too," Ambrosio said in a hoarse voice. Queta watched him put his knees together and hunch over, watched him dig his fingers into his legs. His voice had cracked. "I hadn't done anything to her, it wasn't my business. And Amalia's been helping her, she's stood by her in everything that's happened. She had no reason to tell him that."

"What's happened?" Queta asked. She leaned toward him a little. "Did she tell Gold Ball about you and Amalia?"

"That she's my woman, that we've been seeing each other every Sunday for years, that I got her pregnant." Ambrosio's voice was torn and Queta thought he's going to cry. But he didn't: only his voice was weeping, his eyes were dry and opaque, very wide. "She's not behaved well at all."

"Well," Queta said, sitting up. "So that's why you're here, that's why you're so furious. Now I know why you've come."

"But why?" Ambrosio's voice was still in torture. "Thinking she could convince him that way? Thinking she could get more money out of him that way? Why did she do a bad thing like that?"

"Because the poor madwoman is really crazy," Queta whispered. "Didn't you know that? Because she wants to get out of here, because she has to get away. It wasn't because she's bad. She herself doesn't even know what she's doing."

"Thinking that if I tell him he's going to get the worst of it," Ambrosio said. He nodded, closed his eyes for an instant. He opened them. "It's going to hurt him, it's going to ruin him. Thinking that."

"Because that son of a bitch of a Lucas, the one she fell in love with, the one who's in Mexico," Queta said. "You don't know about it. He writes her telling her to come, to bring some money, we'll get married. She believes him, she's crazy. She doesn't know what to do anymore, it wasn't because she's bad."

"Yes," Ambrosio said. He raised his hands an inch and sank them fiercely into his legs again, his pants wrinkled. "She's hurt him, she's made him suffer."

"Gold Ball has got to understand her," Queta said. "Everybody's

579

acted like such a bastard with her. Cayo Shithead, Lucas, everybody she ever had to her house, all the ones she took care of and . . ."

"Him, him?" Ambrosio roared, and Queta fell silent. She kept her legs ready to leap up and run, but he didn't move. "He acted bad? Would you please tell me what fault it was of his? Does he owe her anything? Was he obliged to help her? Hasn't he been giving her a lot of money? And to the only person who was ever good to her she does something bad like this. But not anymore, it's all over. I want you to tell her."

"I already have," Queta murmured. "Don't you get involved, you'll be the one who comes out the loser. When I found out that Amalia had told her that she was expecting, I warned her. Be careful not to tell the girl that Ambrosio . . . be careful about telling Gold Ball that Amalia . . . Don't start anything, don't get mixed up in it. It just happened, she didn't do it to be mean, she wants to bring some money to that Lucas guy. She's crazy."

"And he never did anything to her, just because he was good and helped her," Ambrosio murmured. "It wouldn't have mattered so much to me for her to have told Amalia about me. But not to do that to him. That was evil, nothing but evil."

"It wouldn't have mattered for her to tell your woman," Queta said, looking at him. "Gold Ball is all that matters, you're only worried about the fairy. You're worse than he is. Get out of here, right now."

"She sent a letter to his wife," Ambrosio moaned, and Queta saw him lower his head, ashamed. "To his wife. Your husband is that way, your husband and his chauffeur, ask him what he feels when the nigger . . . and two pages like that. To his wife. Tell me, why did she do a thing like that?"

"Because she's crazy," Queta said. "Because she wants to go to Mexico and doesn't know what to do so she can get there."

"She phoned him at home," Ambrosio roared and lifted his head and looked at Queta, and she saw the madness floating in his eyes, the silent bubbling. "Your relatives, your friends, your children are going to get the same letter. The same letter as your wife. Your employees. The only person who has acted good, the only one who helped her without having any reason to."

"Because she's desperate," Queta repeated, raising her voice. "She wants that airline ticket so she can leave. Let him give it to her, let . . ."

"He gave it to her yesterday," Ambrosio grunted. "You'll be a laughingstock, I'll ruin you, I'll screw you. He took it to her himself. It isn't just the fare. That crazy woman wants a hundred thousand soles too. See? You talk to her. She shouldn't bother him anymore. Tell her it's the last time."

"I'm not going to say another word to her," Queta murmured. "I don't care, I don't want to hear anything more. She and Gold Ball can kill each other if they want to. I don't want to get mixed up in any trouble. Are you carrying on like this because Gold Ball has fired you? Are you making these threats so that the fairy will forgive you for the Amalia business?"

"Don't pretend you don't understand," Ambrosio said. "I didn't come here to fight, but for us to have a talk. He didn't fire me, he didn't send me here."

"You should have told me that at the start," Don Fermín said. "I have a woman, we're going to have a child, I want to marry her. You should have told me everything, Ambrosio."

"So much the better for you, then," Queta said. "Haven't you been seeing her secretly for so long because you were afraid of Gold Ball? Well, there it is. He knows now and he hasn't fired you. The madwoman didn't do it out of evil. Don't you get mixed up in this anymore and let them settle it by themselves."

"He didn't fire me, he didn't get mad, he didn't bawl me out," Ambrosio said hoarsely. "He was sorry for me, he forgave me. Can't you see that she mustn't do anything bad to a person like him? Can't you see?"

"What a bad time you must have had, Ambrosio, how you must have hated me," Don Fermín said. "Having to hide that business about your woman for so many years. How many, Ambrosio?"

"Making me feel like dirt, making me feel I don't know what," Ambrosio moaned, pounding hard on the bed, and Queta stood up with a leap.

"Did you think I was going to be mad at you, you poor devil?" Don

581

Fermín said. "No, Ambrosio. Get your woman out of that house, have your children. You've got a job here as long as you want. And forget about Ancón and all that, Ambrosio."

"He knows how to manipulate you," Queta murmured, going quickly toward the door. "He knows what you are. I'm not going to say anything to Hortensia. You tell her. And God save you if you set foot in here again or at my place."

"All right, I'm leaving, and don't worry, I don't intend coming back," Ambrosio murmured, getting up. Queta had opened the door and the noise from the bar was coming in and it was loud. "But I'm asking you for the last time. Talk to her, make her be reasonable. Have her leave him alone once and for all, hm?"

🜨

He'd only stayed on as a jitney driver for three weeks more, which was as long as the jalopy lasted. It stopped for good one morning going into Yarinacocha, after smoking and shuddering in rapid death throes of mechanical bucking and belching. They lifted the hood, the motor had dropped out. The poor thing, at least it got this far, said Don Calixto, the owner. And to Ambrosio: as soon as I need a driver, I'll get in touch with you. Two days later, Don Alandro Pozo, the landlord, had appeared at the cabin, all very pleasant: yes, he already knew that you had lost your job, that your wife had died, that you were in bad shape. He was very sorry, Ambrosio, but that wasn't welfare, you've got to leave. Don Alandro agreed to take the bed, the little crib, the table and the Primus stove in payment for the back rent, and Ambrosio had put the rest of the things in some boxes and taken them to Doña Lupe's. When she saw him so down, she made him a cup of coffee: at least you don't have to worry about Amalita Hortensia, she would stay with her in the meantime. Ambrosio went to Pantaleón's shack and he hadn't come back from Tingo. He got back at dusk and found Ambrosio sitting on his doorstep, his feet sunken in the muddy ground. He tried to raise his spirits: of course he could stay with him until he found a job. Would he get one, Panta? Well, to tell the truth, it was hard here, Ambrosio, why didn't he try somewhere else? He advised him to go to Tingo or to Huánuco. But Ambrosio had had a funny feeling about leaving so soon

582

after Amalia's death, son, and besides, how was he going to be able to make it alone in the world with Amalita Hortensia. So he'd made an attempt to stay in Pucallpa. On one day he helped unload launches, on another he cleaned out cobwebs and killed mice at the Wong Warehouses, and he'd even washed down the morgue with disinfectant, but all that was only enough for cigarette money. If it hadn't been for Panta and Doña Lupe, he would have starved to death. So putting his guts where his heart was, one day he'd shown up at Don Hilario's, not for a fight, son, but to beg him. He was all fucked up, sir, could he do something for him.

"I've got all the drivers I need," Don Hilario said with an afflicted smile. "I can't fire one of them in order to take you on."

"Fire the half-wit at Limbo, then, sir," Ambrosio asked him. "Even if it's just making me a watchman."

"I don't pay the half-wit, I just let him sleep there," Don Hilario explained to him. "I'd be crazy to let him go. You'd get a job in a day or so and where would I be able to get another half-wit who doesn't cost me a cent?"

"He let the cat out of the bag, see?" Ambrosio says. "What about those receipts for a hundred a month he showed me, where had all that money ended up?"

But he didn't say anything to him: he listened, nodded, muttered that's too bad. Don Hilario consoled him with a pat on the back and, when he said good-bye, gave him ten soles for a drink, Ambrosio. He went to eat at a lunchroom on the Calle Comercio and bought a pacifier for Amalita Hortensia. At Doña Lupe's he got another piece of bad news: they'd come from the hospital again, Ambrosio. If he didn't go and talk to them at least, they'd report him to the police. He went to the hospital and the lady in the office bawled him out for hiding. She took out the bills and explained to him what they were for.

"It was like a joke," Ambrosio says. "Close to two thousand soles, just imagine. Two thousand for the murder they'd committed."

But he didn't say anything there either: he listened with a serious face, nodding. So? The lady opened her hands. Then he told her about the straits he was in, he made it bigger to get her sympathy. The lady asked him, do you have social security? Ambrosio didn't know. What had he

583

worked at before? A little while as a jitney driver and before that for Morales Transportation.

"So you do," the lady said. "Ask Don Hilario for your social security number. With that you can go to the ministry office to get your card and then come back here. You'll only have to pay part of the bill."

He already knew what was going to happen, but he'd gone to test Don Hilario's wiles a second time: he'd let out a few clucks, had looked at him as if thinking you're even dumber than you look.

"What social security?" Don Hilario asked. "That's for regular employees."

"Wasn't I a regular driver?" Ambrosio asked. "What was I, then, sir?"

"How could you be a regular driver when you haven't got a professional license," Don Hilario explained to him.

"Of course I do," Ambrosio said. "What's this, if it isn't a license?"

"Oh, but you didn't tell me, so it's not my fault," Don Hilario replied. "Besides, I didn't put you down as a favor to you. Collecting by bill and not being on the payroll saved you the deductions."

"But you deducted something from me every month," Ambrosio said. "Wasn't that for social security?"

"That was for retirement," Don Hilario said. "But since you left the firm, you lost your rights. That's the way the law is, terribly complicated."

"It wasn't the lies that burned me up most, it was that he told me such imbecile stories as the one about the license," Ambrosio says. "Where could you hurt him the most? Something to do with money, naturally. That's where I had to get my revenge on him."

It was Tuesday and for everything to come out right, he had to wait till Sunday. He spent the afternoons with Doña Lupe and the nights with Pantaleón. What would become of Amalita Hortensia if something happened to him one day, Doña Lupe, if he died, for example? Nothing, Ambrosio, she'd stay on with her, she was already like a daughter to her, the one she'd always dreamed of having. In the morning he would go to the little beach by the docks or walk around the square, chatting with the drifters. On Saturday afternoon he saw The Jungle Flash enter Pucallpa; groaning, dusty, its boxes and trunks lashed down and bouncing about, the vehicle went down the Calle Comercio raising a cloud of

584

dust and parked in front of the small office of Morales Transportation. The driver got out, the passengers got out, they unloaded the baggage, and kicking pebbles on the corner, Ambrosio waited for the driver to get back into The Jungle Flash and start up: he was taking it to López' garage, yes. He went to Doña Lupe's and stayed until nightfall playing with Amalita Hortensia, who had grown so unaccustomed to him that when he went to pick her up she started to cry. He appeared at the garage at eight o'clock and only López' wife was there: he'd come for the bus, ma'am, Don Hilario needed it. She didn't even think to ask him when did you go back to work for the Morales Company? She pointed to a corner of the lot: there it was. All set, gas, oil, everything, yes.

"I thought of running it off a cliff somewhere," Ambrosio says. "But I realized that would be stupid and I drove it all the way to Tingo. I picked up a couple of passengers along the way and that gave me enough for gas."

When he got into Tingo María the next morning, he hesitated a moment and then drove to Itipaya's garage: what's this, have you gone back to work for Don Hilario, boy?

"I stole it," Ambrosio said. "In return for what he stole from me. I've come to sell it to you."

Itipaya was surprised at first and then he burst out laughing: have you gone crazy, brother?

"Yes," Ambrosio said. "Will you buy it?"

"A stolen vehicle?" Itipaya laughed. "What am I going to do with it? Everybody knows The Jungle Flash, Don Hilario has probably reported it missing already."

"Well," Ambrosio said. "Then I'm going to drive it off a cliff. At least I'll get my revenge."

Itipaya scratched his head: such madness. They'd argued for almost half an hour. If he was going to drive it off a cliff, it would be better if it served a more useful purpose, boy. But he couldn't give him very much: he'd have to dismantle it completely, sell it piece by piece, repaint the body and a thousand other things. How much, Itipaya, right out? And besides, there's the risk, boy. How much, right out?

"Four hundred soles," Ambrosio says. "Less than you can get for a used bicycle. Just enough to get me to Lima, son."

585

8

"I DON'T WANT TO BOTHER YOU or anything," Ambrosio says. "But it's getting awfully late, son."

What else, Zavalita, what else? The conversation with Sparky, he thinks, nothing else. After Don Fermín's death, Ana and Santiago began having lunch with Señora Zoila on Sundays and there they also saw Sparky and Cary, Popeye and Teté, but then, when Señora Zoila decided to take a trip to Europe with Aunt Eliana, who was going to put her oldest daughter in a school in Switzerland and take a two-month tour through Spain, Italy and France, the family lunches stopped and they didn't start up again later on or will they ever start up again, he thinks: what difference did the time make, Ambrosio, cheers, Ambrosio. Señora Zoila came back less downcast, tanned by the European summer, rejuvenated, her arms loaded with gifts and her mouth loaded with stories. Before a year was out she'd recovered completely, Zavalita, she'd picked up her busy social life again, her canasta games, her visits, her soap operas and her teas. Ana and Santiago went to see her at least once a month and she would cut them short in order to eat and their relationship from then on was distant but courteous, more friendly than familiar, Señora Zoila treated Ana with a discreet friendliness now, a resigned and thin affection. She hadn't forgotten her in the distribution of her European souvenirs, Zavalita, she'd gotten hers too: a Spanish mantilla, he thinks, a blue silk blouse from Italy. On birthdays and anniversaries Ana and Santiago would come by early and give a quick embrace before the guests arrived, and on some nights Popeye and Teté would show up at the elf houses to chat or to take them out for a drive. Sparky and Cary never, Zavalita, but during the South American Soccer Championship he'd sent you a midfield ticket as a gift. You needed money and you resold it at half price, he thinks. He thinks: we finally found the formula for getting along. At a distance, Zavalita, with little smiles, with jokes: it made a difference to him, son, excuse me. It was getting late.

The conversation had taken place quite some time after Don Fermín's death, a week after he'd been transferred from local news to the editorial page of *La Crónica*, Zavalita, a few days before Ana had lost her job at the clinic. They'd raised your salary five hundred soles, changed your shift from night to morning, now you would almost never see Carlitos, Zavalita, when you ran into Sparky coming out of Señora Zoila's. They'd spoken for a moment standing on the sidewalk: could they have lunch together tomorrow, Superbrain? Sure, Sparky. That afternoon you'd thought, without curiosity, all of a sudden, what could he have wanted. And the next day Sparky came by to pick up Santiago at the elf houses a little after noon. It was the first time he'd been there and there he was coming in, Zavalita, and there you saw him from the window, hesitating, knocking at the German woman's door, wearing a beige suit and a vest and that canary shirt with a very high collar. And there was the German woman's look devouring Sparky from head to toe while she pointed to your door: that one, letter C. And there was Sparky setting foot for the first and last time in the little elf house, Zavalita. He gave him a pat on the back, hi Superbrain, and took possession of the two small rooms with a smiling ease.

"You've found the ideal den, Skinny." He was looking at the small table, the bookcase, the cloth where Rowdy slept. "Just the right apartment for a pair of bohemians like you and Ana."

They went for lunch at the Restaurant Suizo in Herradura. The waiters and the maître d' knew Sparky by name, exchanged a few pleasantries with him and fluttered about, effusive and diligent, and Sparky insisted that he try that strawberry cocktail, the specialty of the house, Skinny, syrupy and explosive. They sat at a table that looked out over the sea wall: they saw the rough sea, the sky with its winter clouds, and

Sparky suggested the Lima soup as a starter and then the spiced chicken or duck with rice.

"I'll pick the dessert," Sparky said when the waiter went off with their order. "Crêpes with blancmange. It's just the thing after talking business."

"Are we going to talk business?" Santiago asked. "I hope you're not going to ask me to come to work with you. Please don't spoil the taste of my lunch."

"I know that when you hear the word business you break out in hives, bohemian." Sparky laughed. "But this time you can't get out of it, just for a little while. I brought you here to see if some spicy dishes and cold beer would make the pill easier to swallow."

He laughed again, a bit artificially now, and while he was laughing, that uncomfortable glow had appeared in his eyes, Zavalita, those shiny, restless dots: oh, Skinny, you damned bohemian, he said twice, oh, Skinny, you damned bohemian. Not half crazy, traitor to your class, full of complexes, or Communist anymore, he thinks. He thinks: something more affectionate, vaguer, something that could be everything, Skinny, damned bohemian, Zavalita.

"Let me have the pill right off, then," Santiago said. "Before the soup."

"You don't give a damn about anything, bohemian," Sparky said, stopping his laughter, keeping the halo of a smile on his smoothly shaven face; but in the depths of his eyes the uneasiness was still there, growing, and alarm appeared, Zavalita. "All those months after the old man died and you haven't thought to ask about the business he left."

"I have confidence in you," Santiago said. "I know you'll hold up the family name in the business world."

"Well, let's talk seriously." Sparky put his elbows on the table, his chin on his hand, and there was the glow of quicksilver, his continuous blinking, Zavalita.

"Get on with it," Santiago said. "I warn you, when the soup comes, business stops."

"A lot of matters were left pending, as is logical," Sparky said, lowering his voice a little. He looked at the empty tables around, coughed and spoke with pauses, choosing his words with a kind of suspicion. "The will, for example. It's awfully complicated, we had to go through a long process to make it valid. You'll have to go to the notary's to sign a whole ream of papers. In this country everything is one big bureaucratic complication, all sorts of paper work, you know that."

The poor fellow wasn't only confused, uncomfortable, he thinks, he was frightened. Had he prepared that conversation with great care, trying to guess your questions, imagining what you would ask for and demand, foreseeing what you would threaten? Did he have an arsenal of answers and explanations and demonstrations? He thinks: you were so bashful, Sparky. Sometimes he would fall silent and look out the window. It was November and they still hadn't put up the canopies and there weren't any bathers on the beach; a few cars drove along the Malecón and here and there groups of people were walking by the gray and agitated sea. High, noisy waves were breaking in the distance and sweeping the whole beach and white ducks were gliding silently over the foam.

"Well, it's like this," Sparky said. "The old man wanted to have things in good order, he was afraid of a repetition of the first attack. We'd just got started when he died. Only started. The idea was to avoid inheritance taxes, the damned paper work. We were starting to give the thing a legal aspect, putting the companies in my name with fake transfer contracts and so forth. You're intelligent enough to see why. The old man's idea wasn't to leave all the business to me or anything like that. Just to avoid complications. We were going to make all the transfers and at the same time leave your rights and Teté's in good order. And mama's, naturally."

Sparky smiled and Santiago smiled too. They'd just brought the soup, Zavalita, the plates were steaming and the vapor was mingling with that sudden, invisible tension, that punctilious and loaded atmosphere that had come over the table.

"The old man had a good idea," Santiago said. "It was quite logical to put everything in your name in order to avoid complications."

"Not everything," Sparky said very quickly, smiling, raising his hands a little. "Just the lab, the company. Just the business. Not the house or the apartment in Ancón. Besides, you've got to understand that the transfer is only a fiction. Just because the companies are in my name doesn't mean that I'm going to keep it all. Mama's part and Teté's part have already been arranged."

589

"Then everything's fine," Santiago said. "Business is over and now the soup begins. It has a good look to it, Sparky."

There his face, Zavalita, his fluttering, his blinking, his reticent disbelief, his uncomfortable relief, and the liveliness of his hand reaching for the bread, the butter, and filling your glass with beer.

"I know I'm boring you with all this," Sparky said. "But we can't let any more time go by. We've got to straighten out your situation too."

"What's wrong with my situation?" Santiago asked. "Pass me the chili, please."

"The house and the apartment were going to be in mama's name, naturally," Sparky said. "But she doesn't want to have anything to do with the apartment, she says she'll never set foot in Ancón again. It's some kind of quirk. We've come to an agreement with Teté. I've bought the shares of stock that would have been hers in the lab and the other companies. It's as if she were getting her inheritance, see?"

"I see," Santiago said. "That's why I'm so frightfully bored with all this, Sparky."

"That leaves only you." Sparky laughed, not listening to him, and blinked. "You're a candle holder in this burial too, even though it bores you. That's what we've got to talk about. I've thought that we can come to an agreement like the one we made with Teté. We'll figure out what you have coming and, since you detest business, I'll buy out your share."

"Stick my share up your ass and let me finish my soup," Santiago said, laughing, but Sparky was looking at you very seriously, Zavalita, and you had to be serious too. "I made the old man understand that I would never put my nose in his business, so forget about my situation and my share. I disinherited myself on my own when I moved out, Sparky. So no stocks, no sale, and that puts an end to the whole matter for good, O.K.?"

There was his fierce blinking, Zavalita, his aggressive, bestial confusion: he was holding his spoon in the air and a thin stream of reddish soup poured back into the plate and a few drops spattered on the tablecloth. He was looking at you half surprised and half disconsolate, Zavalita.

"Stop your foolishness," he finally said. "You left home, but you were still the old man's son, weren't you? I'm beginning to think you've lost your mind."

590

"I have," Santiago said. "There's no share for me and, if there is, I don't want a single penny of the old man's money, O.K., Sparky?"

"Don't you want any stock?" Sparky asked. "All right, there's another possibility. I've discussed it with Teté and mama and they agree. We'll put the Ancón apartment in your name."

Santiago started to laugh and slapped his hand on the table. A waiter came over to ask what they wanted, oh, I'm sorry. Sparky was serious and seemed in control of himself again, the uneasiness had left his eyes and he was looking at you now with affection and superiority, Zavalita.

"Since you don't want any stock, that's the most sensible thing," Sparky said. "They agree. Mama doesn't want to set foot there, she's got the notion that she hates Ancón. Teté and Popeye are building a house in Santa María. Popeye's doing quite well in business now that Belaúnde's president, you know. And I'm so loaded down with work I could never afford the luxury of a summer vacation. So the apartment . . ."

"Donate it to the poor," Santiago said. "Period, Sparky."

"You don't have to use it if Ancón gets you fucked up," Sparky said. "Sell it and buy one in Lima and you can live better that way."

"I don't want to live any better," Santiago said. "If you don't stop, we're going to get into a fight."

"Stop acting like a child," Sparky went on, with sincerity, he thinks. "You're a grown man now, you're married, you've got responsibilities. Stop putting yourself on that ridiculous level."

Now he felt calm and secure, Zavalita, the bad moment was over now, the shock, now he could give you advice and help you and sleep peacefully. Santiago smiled at him and patted him on the arm: period, Sparky. The maître d' came over all eager and worried to ask if anything was wrong with the soup: nothing, it was delicious, and they'd taken a few spoonfuls to convince him they were telling the truth.

"Let's not argue anymore," Santiago said. "We've spent our whole life fighting and now we get along, isn't that true, Sparky? Well, let's keep it that way. But don't ever bring this matter up with me again, O.K.?"

His annoyed, disconcerted, regretful face had smiled weakly, Zavalita, and he'd shrugged his shoulders, made a grimace of stupor or final commiseration and remained silent for a while. They only tasted the duck and rice and Sparky forgot about the crêpes with blancmange. They brought the check, Sparky paid, and before getting into the car they filled their lungs with the damp and salty air, exchanging banal remarks about the waves and some passing girls and a sports car that roared down the street. On the way to Miraflores, they didn't say a single word. When they got to the elf houses, when Santiago already had one leg out of the car, Sparky took his arm.

"I'll never understand you, Superbrain," and for the first time that day his voice was so sincere, he thinks, so feeling. "What the devil do you want out of life? Why do you do everything you can to fuck yourself up all by yourself?"

"Because I'm a masochist." Santiago smiled at him. "So long, Sparky, give my best to the old lady and to Cary."

"Go ahead, stay with your nuttiness," Sparky said, also smiling. "I just want you to know that if you ever need anything . . ."

"I know, I know," Santiago said. "Now be on your way so I can take a little nap. So long, Sparky."

If you hadn't told Ana you probably would have avoided a lot of fights, he thinks. A hundred, Zavalita, two hundred. Had pride fucked you up? he thinks. He thinks: see how proud your husband is, love, he refused everything from them, love, he told them to go to hell with their stocks and their houses, love. Did you think she was going to admire you, Zavalita, did you want her to? She was going to throw it up to you, he thinks, she was going to reproach you every time they went through your salary before the end of the month, every time they had to ask the Chinaman for credit or borrow from the German woman. Poor Anita, he thinks. He thinks: poor Zavalita.

"It's getting awfully late, son," Ambrosio insisted again.

⑨

"A little farther, we're getting there," Queta said, and thought: so many workers. Was it quitting time at the factories? Yes, she'd picked the worst hour. The whistles were blowing and a tumultuous human wave rolled down the avenue. The taxi moved along slowly, dodging figures, several faces came close to the window and looked at her. They whistled at her, said delicious, oh mama, made obscene faces. The factories were followed by alleys and the alleys by factories, and over the heads Queta saw

592

the stone fronts, the tin roofs, the columns of smoke from the chimneys. Sometimes in the distance the trees of orchards as the avenue cut through them: this is it. The taxi stopped and she got out. The driver looked into her eyes with a sarcastic smile on his lips.

"Why all the smiles?" Queta asked. "Have I got two heads?"

"Don't get offended," the driver said. "For you it's only ten soles."

Queta paid the money and turned her back on him. When she was pushing open the small door set in the faded pink wall, she heard the motor of the taxi as it drove away. There wasn't anybody in the garden. In the leather easy chair in the hall she found Robertito, polishing his nails. He looked at her with his black eyes.

"Why, hello, Quetita," he said with a slightly mocking tone. "I knew you were coming today. Madame is waiting for you."

Not even how are you or are you better now, Queta thought, not even a handshake. She went into the bar and before her face saw Señora Ivonne's sharp silver nails, the ring that exhaled brilliance and the ball-point pen with which she was addressing an envelope.

"Good afternoon," Queta said. "How nice to see you again."

Señora Ivonne smiled at her without warmth, while she examined her from head to toe in silence.

"Well, here you are back again," she finally said. "I can just imagine what you've been through."

"It was pretty bad," Queta said and was silent and could feel the prick of the injections in her arms, the coldness of the probe between her legs, could hear the sordid arguments of the women around her and could see the orderly with stiff bristly hair crouching down to pick up the basin.

"Did you see Dr. Zegarra?" Señora Ivonne asked. "Did he give you your certificate?"

Queta nodded. She took a folded piece of paper from her purse and handed it to her. You've gone to ruin in one month, she thought, you use three times as much makeup and you can't even see anymore. Señora Ivonne was reading the paper attentively and with a great deal of effort, holding it almost on top of her squinting eyes.

"Fine, you're healthy now." Señora Ivonne examined her again up and down and made a disappointed gesture. "But skinny as a rail. You've got to put some weight on again, we'll have to get some color back in your

593

cheeks. In the meantime, take off those clothes you've got on. Give them a good soaking. Didn't you bring anything to change into? Have Malvina lend you something. Right away, you're not going to stand around full of germs. Hospitals are full of germs."

"Will I have the same room as before, ma'am?" Queta asked and thought I'm not going to get mad, I'm not going to give you that pleasure.

"No, the one in back," Señora Ivonne said. "And take a hot bath. With lots of soap, just in case."

Queta nodded. She went up to the second floor, clenching her teeth, looking at the same garnet-colored carpet with the same stains and the same burns from cigarettes and matches without seeing it. On the landing she saw Malvina, who opened her arms: Quetita! They embraced, kissed each other on the cheek.

"How wonderful that you're all better, Quetita," Malvina said. "I wanted to go visit you but the old woman scared me. I called you a whole lot of times but they told me only people who paid for them had telephones. Did you get my packages?"

"Thank you so much, Malvina," Queta said. "What I thank you for most is the food. The meals there were awful."

"I'm so glad you're back," Malvina repeated, smiling at her. "I got so mad when you caught that dirty thing, Quetita. The world's so full of bastards. It's been so long since we've seen each other, Quetita."

"A month," Queta sighed. "It seemed like ten to me, Malvina."

She got undressed in Malvina's room, went to the bathroom, filled the tub and sank into the water. She was soaping herself when she saw the door open and in peeped the profile, the silhouette of Robertito: could he come in, Quetita?

"No, you can't," Quetita said grumpily. "Go on, get out, beat it."

"Does it bother you for me to see you naked?" Robertito laughed. "Does it bother you?"

"Yes," Queta said. "I didn't give you permission. Close the door."

He laughed, came in and closed the door: then he'd stay, Quetita, he always went against the current. Queta sank down in the tub up to her neck. The water was dark and sudsy.

"My, you were filthy, you turned the water black," Robertito said.

594

"How long has it been since you had a bath?"

Queta laughed: since she went into the hospital, a month! Robertito held his nose and put on a look of disgust: pooh, you little pig. Then he smiled amiably and took a couple of steps over to the tub: was she glad to be back? Queta nodded her head: of course she was. The water became agitated and her bony shoulders emerged.

"Do you want me to tell you a secret?" she said, pointing to the door.

"Tell me, tell me," Robertito said. "I'm mad about gossip."

"I was afraid the old lady would send me away," Queta said. "Because of her mania about germs."

"You would have had to go to a second-rate house, you would have gone down in station," Robertito said. "What would you have done if she'd sent you away?"

"I would have been fried," Queta said. "A second- or third-rate or God knows what kind of house."

"Madame is a good person," Robertito said. "She protects her business against wind and tide and she's right. She's behaved well toward you, you know that she won't take back people who've caught it as bad as you did."

"Because I've helped her earn a lot of good money," Queta said. "Because she owes me a lot too."

She'd sat up and was soaping her breasts. Robertito pointed at them with his finger: hoowee, the way they've drooped, Quetita, you've got so skinny. She nodded: she'd lost thirty pounds in the hospital, Robertito. Then you've got to fatten yourself up, Quetita, if you don't, you won't make any good conquests.

"The old lady said I was skinny as a rail," Queta said. "At the hospital I ate practically nothing, just when one of the packages Malvina sent me came."

"Now you can have your revenge." Robertito laughed. "Eating like a hog."

"My stomach must have shrunk," Queta said, closing her eyes and sinking into the tub. "Oh, this hot water is so delicious."

Robertito came over, dried the edge of the tub with a towel and sat down. He started looking at Queta with a malicious and smiling roguishness.

595

"Do you want me to tell you a secret too?" he said, lowering his voice and opening his eyes, scandalized at his own daring. "Do you want me to?"

"Yes, tell me all the gossip of the house," Queta said. "What's the latest?"

"Last week Madame and I went to pay a call on your ex." Robertito had raised a finger to his lips, his eyelashes were fluttering. "To your ex's ex, I mean. I have to tell you that he behaved like the swine he is."

Queta opened her eyes and sat up in the tub: Robertito was wiping off some drops that had landed on his pants.

"Cayo Shithead?" Queta said. "I don't believe it. Is he here in Lima?"

"He's come back to Peru," Robertito said. "It turns out that he has a house in Chaclacayo with a pool and everything. And two big dogs the size of tigers."

"You're lying," Queta said, but she lowered her voice because Robertito signaled her not to talk so loud. "Has he come back, really?"

"A beautiful house, set smack in the middle of an enormous garden," Robertito said. "I didn't want to go. I told Madame, it's a whim, you're going to be disappointed, and she didn't pay any attention to me. Still thinking about her deal with him. He's got capital, he knows that I treat my partners right, we were friends. But he treated us like a couple of beggars and threw us out. Your ex, Quetita, your ex's ex. What a swine he was."

"Is he going to stay in Peru?" Queta asked. "Has he gotten into politics again?"

"He said he was just passing through." Robertito shrugged his shoulders. "You can imagine how loaded he must be. A house like that, just to stop off in. He's living in the United States. He's exactly the same, I tell you. Old, ugly and nasty."

"Didn't he ask you anything about . . . ?" Queta said. "He must have said something to you, didn't he?"

"About the Muse?" Robertito said. "A swine, I tell you, Quetita. Madame talked to him about her, we felt so awful about what happened to the poor thing, he must have heard. And he didn't bat an eye. I didn't feel so bad, he said, I knew that the madwoman would come to a bad end. And then he asked about you, Quetita. Yes, yes. The poor thing's in the hospital, imagine. And what do you think he said?"

"If he said that about Hortensia, I can imagine what he'd say about me," Queta said. "Come on, don't keep my curiosity waiting."

"Tell her, just in case, that I won't give her a nickel, that I've given her enough already." Robertito laughed. "That if you went to see him to try to extort anything from him, that's why he's got the Great Danes. Those very words, Quetita, ask Madame, you'll see. But don't do that, don't even mention him to her, she came back so distraught, he'd treated her so badly that she doesn't ever want to hear his name again."

"He'll pay for it someday," Queta said. "You can't be such a shit and live so happily."

"He can, that's why he's got money," Robertito said. He started to laugh again and leaned a little closer to Queta. He lowered his voice: "Do you know what he said when Madame proposed a little business deal to him? He laughed in her face. Do you think I'm interested in the business of whores, Ivonne? That all he was interested in now was decent business. And then and there he told us you know the way out, I don't want to see your faces around here again. Those very words, I swear. Are you crazy, what are you laughing about?"

"Nothing," Queta said. "Hand me the towel, it's got cold and I'm freezing."

"I'll dry you too, if you want," Robertito said. "I'm always at your command, Quetita. Especially now that you've got more pleasant. You're not as grouchy as you used to be."

Queta got up, stepped out of the tub and came forward on tiptoes, dripping water on the chipped tiles. She put one towel around her waist and another over her shoulders.

"No belly and your legs are still beautiful." Robertito laughed. "Are you going to look up your ex's ex?"

"No, but if I ever run into him he's going to be sorry," Queta said. "For what he said to you about Hortensia."

"You'll never run into him," Robertito said. "He's way above you now."

"Why did you come and tell me all this?" Queta asked suddenly, stopping her wiping. "Go on, beat it, get out of here."

"Just to see how you'd react." Robertito laughed. "Don't get mad. So

597

you'll see that I'm your friend, I'm going to tell you another secret. Do you know why I came in? Because Madame told me go see if she's really taking a bath."

He'd come from Tingo María in short stages, just in case: in a truck to Huánuco, where he stayed one night, then by bus to Huancayo, from there to Lima by train. When he crossed the Andes the altitude had made him nauseous and given him palpitations, son.

"It was just a little over two years since I'd left Lima when I got back," Ambrosio says. "But what a difference. The last person I could ask for help was Ludovico. He'd sent me to Pucallpa, he'd recommended me to his relative, Don Hilario, see? And if I couldn't go to him, who could I go to, then?"

"My father," Santiago says. "Why didn't you go to him, how come you didn't think of that?"

"Well, it isn't that I didn't think of it," Ambrosio says. "You have to realize, son . . ."

"I can't," Santiago says. "Haven't you said you admired him so much, haven't you said he had such a high regard for you? He would have helped you. Didn't you think of that?"

"I wasn't going to get your papa in any trouble, for the very reason that I respected him so much," Ambrosio says. "Remember who he was and who I was, son. Was I going to tell him I'm on the run, I'm a thief, the police are looking for me because I sold a truck that wasn't mine?"

"You trusted him more than you do me, isn't that right?" Santiago asks.

"A man, no matter how fucked up he is, has his pride," Ambrosio says. "Don Fermín thought well of me. I was trash, garbage, you see?"

"Why do you trust me?" Santiago asks. "Why weren't you ashamed to tell me about the truck?"

"Probably because I haven't got any pride left," Ambrosio says. "But I did have then. Besides, you're not your papa, son."

The four hundred soles from Itipaya had disappeared because of the trip and for the first three days in Lima he hadn't had a bite to eat. He'd wandered about ceaselessly, keeping away from the downtown area, feeling his bones go cold every time he saw a policeman and going over names in his mind and eliminating them: Ludovico, not a thought; Hipólito was probably still in the provinces or had come back to work with Ludovico. Hipólito, not a thought, not a thought for him. He hadn't thought about Amalia or Amalita Hortensia or Pucallpa: only about the police, only about eating, only about smoking.

"Just imagine, I never would have dared beg for something to eat," Ambrosio says. "But I did for a smoke."

When he couldn't stand it anymore, he would stop just anybody on the street and ask him for a cigarette. He'd done everything, as long as it wasn't a steady job and they didn't ask for papers: unloading trucks at Porvenir, burning garbage, catching stray cats and dogs for the wild animals of the Cairoli Circus, cleaning sewers, and he'd even worked for a knife grinder. Sometimes, on the Callao docks, he would take the place of some regular stevedore by the hour, and even though he had to give him a big split, he had enough left over to eat for two or three days. One day someone gave him a tip: the Odriists needed guys to put up posters. He'd gone to the place, had spent a whole night plastering the downtown streets, but they'd only paid them with food and drink. During those months of drifting, ravenous hunger, walking and odd jobs that lasted a day or two, he'd met Pancras. At first he'd been sleeping in the Parada market, under the trucks, in ditches, on sacks in the warehouses, feeling protected, hidden among so many beggars and vagrants who slept there, but one night he'd heard that every so often police patrols came around asking to see papers. So he'd begun to go into the world of the shanty-towns. He'd known them all, slept once in one, another time in another, until he'd found Pancras in the one called La Perla and there he stayed. Pancras lived alone and made room for him in his shack.

"The first person who was good to me in such a long time," Ambrosio says. "Without knowing me or having any reason to. A heart of gold, that nigger has, I tell you."

Pancras had worked at the dog pound for years and when they became friends he'd taken him to the supervisor one day: no, there weren't any vacancies. But a while later they sent for him. Except that he'd asked him for papers: voting card, draft card, birth certificate? He'd had to invent a lie: I lost them. Oh, well, it's out, no work without papers. Bah, don't be foolish, Pancras had told him, who's going to remember that truck, just take him your papers. He'd been afraid, he'd better not, Pancras, and he'd kept on with those little jobs on the sly. Around that time he'd gone back to his hometown, Chincha, son, the last time. What for? Thinking he could get different papers, get baptized again by some priest and with a different name, and even out of curiosity, to see what the town was like now. He'd been sorry he'd gone though. He left La Perla early with Pancras and they'd said good-bye on Dos de Mayo. Ambrosio had walked along Colmena to the Parque Universitario. He went to check on bus fares and he bought a ticket on one leaving at ten, so he had time to get a cup of coffee and walk around a little. He looked in the shop windows on the Avenida Iquitos, trying to decide whether or not to buy a new shirt so that he'd return to Chincha looking more presentable than when he'd left fifteen years before. But he had only a hundred soles left and he thought better of it. He bought a tube of mints and all during the trip he felt that perfumed coolness on his gums, nose and palate. But in his stomach he felt a tickling: what would the people who recognized him say when they saw him like that. They all must have changed a good deal, some must have died, others had probably moved away from town, the city had most likely changed so much that he wouldn't even recognize it. But as soon as the bus stopped on the Plaza de Armas, even though everything had gotten smaller and flatter, he recognized it all: the smell of the air, the color of the benches and the roofs, the triangular tiles on the sidewalk by the church. He'd felt sorrowful, nauseous, ashamed. Time hadn't passed, he hadn't left Chincha, there, around the corner, would be the small office of the Chincha Transportation Co., where he'd started his career as a driver. Sitting on a bench, he'd smoked, looked around. Yes, something had changed: the faces. He was anxiously observing men and women and he'd felt his heart beating hard when he saw a tired, barefoot figure approaching, wearing a straw hat and feeling his way along with a cane: blind Rojas! But it wasn't him, it was a blind albino, still young, who went over to squat under a palm tree. He got up, started walking, and when he got to the shantytown he saw that some of the streets had been paved and they'd built some little houses with gardens that had withered grass in them. In back, where the ditches along the road to Grocio Prado began, there was a sea of huts now. He'd gone back and forth through the dusty alleys of the shantytown without recognizing a single face. Then he'd gone to the cemetery, thinking that the old black woman's grave would probably be next to Perpetuo's. But it wasn't and he hadn't dared ask the guard where she'd been buried. He'd gone back to the center of town at dusk, disappointed, having forgotten about his new baptism and the papers, and hungry. At the café-restaurant called Mi Patria, which was now named Victoria and had two waitresses instead of Don Rómulo, he had a steak and onions, sitting beside the door, looking at the street all the time, trying to recognize some face: all different. He'd remembered something that Trifulcio had told him that night just before he'd left for Lima, while they were walking in the dark: here I am in Chincha and I feel as if I'm not, I recognize everything and I don't recognize anything. Now he understood what he'd been trying to tell him. He'd wandered through still more neighborhoods: the José Pardo School, the San José Hospital, the Municipal Theater, the market had been modernized a little. Everything the same but smaller, everything the same but flatter, only the people different: he'd been sorry he'd come, son, he'd left that night, swearing I'll never come back. He already felt fucked up enough here, son, and on that day back there, besides being fucked up, he'd felt terribly old. And when the rabies scare was over, would your work at the pound be through, Ambrosio? Yes, son. What would he do? What he'd been doing before the supervisor had Pancras bring him in and told him, O.K., give us a hand for a few days even if you haven't got any papers. He would work here and there, maybe after a while there'd be another outbreak of rabies and they'd call him in again, and after that here and there, and then, well, after that he would have died, wasn't that so, son?